SHAKESPEARE 400

Published in Cooperation with

THE SHAKESPEARE ASSOCIATION OF AMERICA

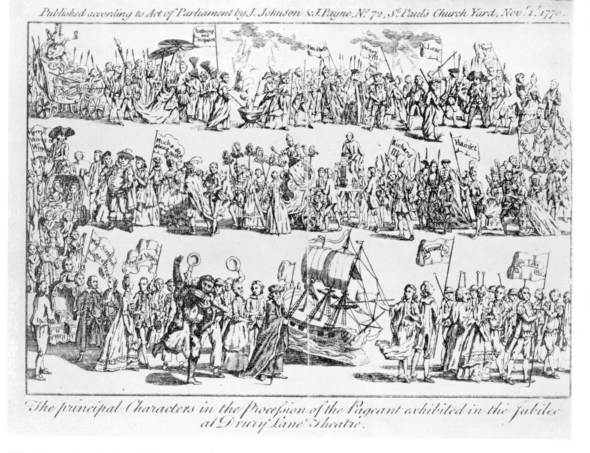

The Procession in Garrick's *Jubilee*, first performed at Drury Lane on 14 October 1769. From the engraving in The Folger Shakespeare Library.

SHAKESPEARE 400

*ESSAYS BY AMERICAN SCHOLARS ON THE
ANNIVERSARY OF THE POET'S BIRTH*——

—— EDITED *BY* JAMES G. McMANAWAY

The Folger Shakespeare Library

HOLT, RINEHART AND WINSTON, INC.

New York · Chicago · San Francisco · Toronto · London

For permission to reprint any essay, in whole or in part, written authorization must be obtained from Holt, Rinehart and Winston, Inc.

Library of Congress Catalog Card Number 64-15945
27823-0614

Printed in the United States of America

Preface

This tribute to William Shakespeare on the four-hundredth anniversary of his birth has been planned for several years. With the knowledge that all the world would be celebrating the event, we decided that the Shakespeare Association of America, whose *Quarterly* customarily carries many contributions from abroad, should honor Shakespeare's anniversary with a special volume comprised wholly of essays by eminent American scholars. Not all the expected names are represented in these pages, partly because of the exclusion of severely technical studies, partly because of prior commitments and of ill fortune. The collection is a sampling of the variety of academic evaluation and literary appreciation. In many it will awaken memories of some of the distinguished American scholars of the past.

What Shakespeare the playwright meant to the United States in earlier days is illustrated by the reproduction of playbills of Shakespearian performances. These cover Colonial Williamsburg and all of the Atlantic Coast and then move westward with the frontier in the Gold Rush decades to California, surging back inland across mountain and desert. In the trading vessels and the covered wagons there was always a Bible and a volume of Shakespeare. With security and prosperity came the actors, and Shakespeare was alive.

In this country, during the subsequent years of growth and progress and anxiety, Shakespeare has continued to hold scholars, actors, and readers. He challenges their minds and delights their hearts. He reveals the hidden things of the moment and the great, timeless universal truths. He deals with the full wheel of human action. Many writers have tried to engage readers' attention to Shakespeare's matchless powers and pay him tribute. And so does this collection of essays.

J. G. M.

Washington, D. C.
February 1964

v

Contents

SHAKESPEARE 400

Shakespeare and the Myth of Perfection

ALFRED HARBAGE

HAKESPEARE'S fourth centenary should be a good time for taking long views and seeing things in perspective. If we cannot all see eye to eye, as perhaps men will at his millenary, at least we can exchange provisional maps sketched from particular points of vantage. One of the things which I seem to see is the protean character of Shakespeare-idolatry as it has emerged in various ages—in forms as varied (and increasingly formidable) as an eighteenth-century textual emendation, a nineteenth-century treatise on the playwright's legal lore, and a twentieth-century volume of "interpretive" criticism.

What might be called, facetiously, the biographical aspect of the subject I am discussing elsewhere. The so-called "authorship controversy" ceases to be bewildering if seen in a context of cultural anthropology. It is illuminated by something which Sigmund Freud (himself a victim of it) has called the "family romance fantasy"—as sublimated into something which Otto Rank (who unfortunately limited his view to primitive and ancient societies) has called the "myth of the birth of the hero". The denial that a certain illustrious man was the son of a Stratford tradesman is a necessary step in a process of deification. Promotion from commoner to lord anticipates further promotion to king or high-priest, demigod or god—in a word to "culture hero". The process, as might be expected, has progressed furthest with the first-nominated of the "true" authors. Francis Bacon's adherents no longer concern themselves with his authorship of the Shakespearian plays and other Renaissance masterpieces, since this is regarded as obvious, but with his claim to the throne of Britain as unacknowledged son of the allegedly virgin Queen. His titanic figure, all-wise, all-creative, and, if right had prevailed, all-powerful, looms as a creature of religious mystery, such as Lord Oxford is destined to become among rival true believers. Ultimately an amalgam may occur, with all sects united in common worship of the nameless one, designated simply as *Author*.

It may seem a far cry from the militant Baconian or Oxfordian to the obscure eighteenth-century don demonstrating Shakespeare's knowledge of Greek, or the mild nineteenth-century naturalist demonstrating his knowledge of botany, but there is a connection both practical and theoretic. The scholar who "proves" that the author was a scholar provides footing for the myth-maker who "proves" that he could not have been a non-university man. This is the practical connection. The theoretic is more interesting. It may be touching to observe the naturalist bestowing upon his revered fellow-countryman, who he stoutly maintains was yeoman born and bred, all his own specialized knowledge of Warwickshire flora and fauna, but what if Shakespeare actually possessed no such knowledge? could even err on occasion about the color of a wildflower or the source of its perfume? Apparently he knew that snakes cast their enameled skins, but it is doubtful if he knew how they injected their venom. He surely knew that toads bore no precious jewels in their heads, but he may have believed them to be poisonous as well as ugly; whether he knew how they "engendered" is a moot point. What the enthusiastic naturalist has done, although it seems cruel to say so, is to indulge in a form of idolatry, by creating a god in his own image.

So with the various musicians, sailors, soldiers, doctors, and others, especially lawyers, who have brought their offerings to the shrine, and have fostered the idea that Shakespeare not only knew and loved music, as he truly did, but could take down and reassemble a spinet (if he did not invent the instrument) as well as navigate a ship, command an army, and perform a frontal lobotomy, while his exhaustive knowledge of the law might have ruptured even the capacious brain of the Lord Chief Justice. Of course none of these things are true, since the plays and poems, in indicating that their author was well-informed—an excellent observer, especially of nature—are also indicating that he possessed specialized knowledge of nothing, except how to write plays and poems. The notion of his prodigious "knowledge" is attributable in part to his skill as an illusionist. Anyone who has written even a routine piece of fiction is aware of the necessity of faking—of using strategically his bits of technical knowledge so that his lawyers will seem like lawyers, his doctors doctors, his priests priests, and so on. The bits expand in the reader's imagination into a comprehensive body of knowledge, undefined in the layman's but specialized in the specialist's, providing the character to whom they are attached is convincing. The naïve response is to identify the presumed knowledge of the characters with the actual knowledge of the author, when often, in such cases, the part of the iceberg of knowledge which shows is the only part which exists. But Shakespeare's more than routine skill in deception fails to account in full for the myth of his omniscience. The myth derives from and contributes to an embracing myth. Had he not already assumed superhuman proportions in their minds, the specialists would have noted his misses as well as hits in their fields of competence, and would not have collaborated in making him still more superhuman by endowing him with specialized knowledge of all the specialities.

My primary concern is with the effect of *mythos* upon current Shakespearian criticism. The approach may seem devious, but myths mature slowly, and the way that ancient editors looked at single words throws light on the way that modern critics look at whole plays. It is common knowledge that some of the eighteenth-century editors blamed every defect in the texts upon the interpolation of actors, the incompetence of scribes and printers, and the villainy of former editors. Positing an original composition "worthy" of Shakespeare, they corrected the grammar, regularized the meter, improved the diction, and straightened out classical, geographical, and other allusions. This is a stale subject, and I do not wish to make capital of the misdemeanors of the "bad" editors. I shall cite the respectable ones, as later I shall refer in general to respectable critics.

Lewis Theobald was one of the best. In preparing his edition of 1733, he was confronted by the following in the Folio text of *Measure for Measure*:

> But this new Gouernor
> Awakes me all the inrolled penalties
> Which haue (like vn-scowr'd Armor) hung by th' wall
> So long, that ninteene Zodiacks haue gone round,
> And none of them beene worne; . . .

Thus Claudio in I. iii. But in the very next scene, less than fifty lines later, the Duke says,

> We haue strict Statutes, and most biting Laws,
> (The needfull bits and curbes to headstrong weedes,)
> Which for this fourteene yeares, we haue let slip, . . .

Whether "weedes" had better be emended to "steeds" or "wills" and "slip" to "sleep" are debatable points with which we need not linger (although editors have properly done so) except to observe that two questionable readings in three lines throw some suspicion upon the accuracy of the Folio at this point. The glaring discrepancy is between the Duke's "fourteene" and Claudio's "ninteene". Says Theobald in reference to it, "For *fourteen* I have made no Scruple to replace *nineteen*. . . . The Author could not so disagree with himself in so narrow a Compass." In the words *could not* (which should have been *probably did not*) we detect just a hint of the myth of perfection. Theobald adds, "The Numbers must have been wrote in Figures, and so mistaken. . . ."[1] When we understand what this acute editor was implying—that if the author's script contained roman numerals, his *xix* might easily have been mistaken by a scribe or compositor for *xiv*—we can appreciate the cogency of his reasoning.

But there is a catch in it. If *xix* might easily have been mistaken for *xiv*, then *xiv* might just as easily have been mistaken for *xix*, so that it may be Claudio's figure which needs correction. Peter Whalley raised the issue in his own way, by saying, with a true-born Englishman's respect for rank, which he assumed that Shakespeare shared, "I am disposed to take the Duke's words". Here there is more than a hint of the myth of perfection, because the grounds are not graphic plausibility but simply "Shakespearian" propriety. Finally Edmond Malone cut the knot by asserting that both the "nineteen" and "fourteen" should stand: "Claudio would naturally represent the period during which the law had not been put in practice greater than it was."[2] Now here, although Malone was neither idolatrous nor an inferior editor, by the standards of his day, we have the myth of perfection full-blown. A blemish has been rationalized into a beauty, a discrepancy into a subtlety, a numerical error into a "touch of nature".

In 1863 the Cambridge editors stated a good general principle by which the "nineteen-fourteen" dilemma might be resolved: "If [a] defect can be made good

---

[1] *The Works of Shakespeare*, 7 vols. (London, 1733), I, 319, 321.

[2] The quoted comments illustrate my point whoever made them, but I hope I am citing the right persons. They are attributed to Whalley and Malone in *The Plays of William Shakespeare*, 15 vols. (London, 1793), IV, 205, and in subsequent "variorum" editions by Isaac Reed, James Boswell, etc., but I do not find the comment by Whalley in his *Enquiry* (London, 1748), while Malone makes a different and more judicious comment in *The Plays and Poems of William Shakespeare*, 10 vols. (London, 1790), II, 19.

in more ways than one equally plausible, or, at least, equally probable, we have
registered but not adopted these improvements, and the reader is intended to
make his own selection out of the notes."[3] In all modern editions the "nineteen-
fourteen" discrepancy is permitted to stand, but usually there is no note, and we
do not know whether it is for Malone's reason, or for the Cambridge editors'
reason—or for a reason elsewhere given by Malone himself (". . . our author is
often incorrect in the computation of time")[4] and endorsed by Dover Wilson
("The discrepancy may well be Shakespeare's").[5] This is one of the thousands
of tiny bones which faintly rattle in the textual closet. In 1905 H. C. Hart reverted to the position of Whalley: ". . . his [the Duke's] word must, of course,
be accepted."[6] About Malone's explanation, that people naturally exaggerate
figures in the direction of their desires, Hart asks plaintively, "Is this convincing?" We must admit that it is not. But (disregarding the possibility that
Shakespeare was cryptically predicting the advent of the First World War) we
may suggest that the Duke, who is still a bachelor and hence relatively young,
only succeeded to the dukedom fourteen years before, at which time the law
had already lain dormant for five years, so that Claudio's "nineteen" and his
"fourteen" are both literally correct. Is this convincing? No.

The trouble with the type of explanation based upon a presumed psychological or factual consistency is that, in laying one ghost, it raises thousands
more. When Romeo sees Juliet across a crowded room and asks a servant who
she is, we get:

> *Servant.*   I know not, sir.
> *Romeo.*   O, she doth teach the torches to burn bright.

One can imagine a reader (more interested in hard facts than in love) being
more moved by the servant's line than by Romeo's: "Why this is preposterous!
A lovely heiress, and the only child of the house, and yet this servant does not
even know who she is!" In which case, following Malone's example, we would
have to suggest that this particular servant must be part-time help, or that
since Juliet is only fourteen years old come Lammas-tide, she has been drilled
not to speak to strangers and the servants not to give out information.

In all the plays of Shakespeare there are discrepancies—real ones, not conventional ones like the convenient ignorance of the Capulet servant. At one
point in *The Merchant of Venice* all the early texts read "Mantua" where
clearly the right place is "Padua". A kind of territorial restitution is made
in *The Taming of the Shrew* where the Folio reads "Padua" when clearly the
right place is "Mantua" (or "Pisa"). In the first scene of *The Merry Wives of
Windsor* the first name of Master Page is "Thomas", but thereafter it becomes
"George". Names can change in whole as well as in part. In *Measure for
Measure* the character designated simply as "Clown" in the speech-prefixes is
first addressed as "Thomas Tapster", but when his name is formally demanded
of him, it proves to be "Pompey Bum". (In *King John* it is a monarch's name
which fluctuates, not just a lowly pimp's.) Characters can change their physical

---

[3] *The Works of Shakespeare,* ed. W. G. Clark, J. Glover, & W. A. Wright, 9 vols. (Cambridge
& London, 1863-66), I, xii.

[4] See note 2, above.

[5] *Measure for Measure* (Cambridge, 1922), p. 122.

[6] *Measure for Measure* (Arden edition, London, 1905, revised 1925), p. 16.

characteristics. In *As You Like It* Celia is "taller" than Rosalind until it is time for them to assume disguises, whereupon Rosalind becomes taller than Celia. Characters can evaporate completely—or never really materialize. Several are mentioned in the original stage directions of *2 Henry IV* who are given nothing to do or say. The most remarkable instance of this kind is the strange case of Hero's mother. Let me quote the delightful comment of Sir Edmund Chambers: "Leonato is accompanied by 'Innogen his wife' at the beginning of *Much Ado About Nothing*. She recurs in one later scene, but has not a word throughout the play. A Lady, whose daughter is successively betrothed, defamed, repudiated before the altar, taken for dead, and restored to life, ought not to be a mute. It is not motherly."[7]

The editor of the fine "New Variorum" text of *2 Henry IV* speaks of the silent and superfluous characters whom Shakespeare "forgot to write a part for."[8] In reference to Innogen in *Much Ado About Nothing* Chambers speaks of the possibility of abridgement, and then asks, "But did Shakespeare sometimes write initial entries before he had thought out the dialogue, and omit through carelessness to correct them by eliminating characters for whom he had found nothing to say, and ought to have found something to say, if they were to be on the stage at all?"[9] Professor Shaaber's word "forgot" and Sir Edmund's word "carelessness" would have offended the piety of some of their predecessors. Modern editors are aware that Shakespeare cannot be wholly exonerated of responsibility for the many imperfections which appear in the texts, even though they may alter "Mantua" to "Padua" (or "Padua" to "Mantua"), "Thomas" to "George", and ruthlessly delete "Innogen". If they diminish a "taller" Celia to a "smaller" Celia, at least they do not argue that Rosalind grew in stature when she fell in love. I have given only a meager sampling of the many discrepancies that cannot be attributed to any deep and dark design. Since the eighteenth century, the myth of perfection has steadily waned among textual scholars, but this does not mean that the myth has been on the wane.

At the beginning of *A Midsummer Night's Dream* Theseus and Hippolyta reiterate the fact that *four* days must intervene before their nuptials, but that happy event ensues in two. In 1879 F. Gard Fleay tackled this problem[10] after his contemporaries had wrestled with the wayward behavior of time in the other plays and had devised schedules to their satisfaction. He gained one day by coolly asserting the existence of a twenty-four-hour interval in the first scene, and a second day by suggesting that the sleep of the lovers in the wood endured for twenty-four hours. Their peculiar torpor he explained as follows: the nuptials take place on a May-Day, the play was performed in 1592, and in 1592 the day before May-Day was a Sunday. The reasoning is not wholly perspicuous; presumably we must deduce that on Sundays even bivouacking lovers sleep late, or that since Sunday marriages were interdicted, sleeping out the day was the only thing Shakespeare could find for them to do.

---

[7] *William Shakespeare* (Oxford, 1930), I, 231.

[8] *2 Henry IV*, ed. M. A. Shaaber (Philadelphia, 1940), p. 132.

[9] *Loc. cit.*

[10] Fleay's comment is quoted from *Robinson's Epitomy of Literature*, 1 April, 1879, by H. H. Furness in the "New Variorum" edition of *A Midsummer Night's Dream* (Philadelphia, 1895), p. 298.

Fleay's effort is an extreme example of nineteenth-century rationalizations. The eighteenth-century sophisticators of the text were scolded by the nineteenth-century explicators, at the same time that the latter were imitating them. Idolatry was not falling into decay; it was rebuilding on higher ground. Malone's comment on Claudio's "nineteen" really links him with the romantic critics rather than with the "bad" editors like Pope, Warburton, and Hanmer. These critics, from Morgann to Bradley, have been sufficiently reproved for their "character-mongering" and "psychologizing" to spare me the task of illustrating their tactics. Of course the discussion of characters and psychology is not in itself inappropriate in commentary on dramatic works, and the charge against the "romantics", so far as it is valid, means only that they carried this kind of commentary beyond the point where it is either valid or relevant. The assumption of perfection, of a "true-to-life" consistency, led to hypothetical constructions, perhaps consistent with themselves, but only coincidentally related to Shakespeare's plays. Reference was made to the childhood of the characters, their behavior offstage, and their private domestic arrangements, for instance the present whereabouts of the child whom Lady Macbeth has borne and suckled. As with the earlier editors, so with these later explicators, the scent of incense is strongest in the vicinity of the least able.

In the twentieth century the explicators have been succeeded by the exegetes, who again imitate as they scold; but no longer can we say that the scent of incense is strongest in the vicinity of the least able. A really ominous progression has occurred. It is now the major Shakespearian critics who serve the myth of perfection. Let me pause for a definition. The mark of idolatry is not excessive enthusiasm, a rapturous tone, the use of superlatives, the invention of new terms of praise in ecstatic prose or verse. Were such the case, Ben Jonson would qualify as a Shakespeare-idolator; he is one of the few, after all, who have equated the poet with actual gods—"like Apollo . . . like a Mercury". The mark of idolatry is the assumption that because the plays are excellent, they are excellent in every way—in a word that they are *perfect*—with the perfection which is finally assumed so distinctly in the beholder's way, so exclusively *his* conception of perfection, that for the excellence they truly possess is substituted an excellence (if we may call it such) which they do not possess, and which might not even be proper to works of art as distinct from academic manuals, case histories, or social and ethical tractates. If this definition is tenable, as it seems to be in respect to the faulty past, we are in a parlous state because no longer, as in that past, are the major critics free.

Samuel Johnson was the major Shakespearian critic of the eighteenth century, and his freedom from idolatry need not be argued but taken as read. Samuel Coleridge was the major Shakespearian critic of the nineteenth century, and his *relative* freedom from idolatry, although it cannot be adequately argued in a paragraph, can be reasonably maintained if we admit the crucial distinction between extravagant praise and transmutation of the thing praised. I can only point out that Coleridge's *Hamlet* criticism, which is his most idolatrous, is not his total Shakespearian criticism, and that his statement (or, rather, the statement approximately his) that "Assuredly, that criticism of Shakespeare will alone be genial which is reverential"[11] is by no means a religious manifesto.

[11] The familiar wording is from the *Literary Remains* edited by H. N. Coleridge in 1836.

Quite often those very turns of phrase most suggestive of idolatry to modern ears are evidence of the reverse. They are most apt to occur when Coleridge is having honest doubts: "It is too venturesome to charge a speech in Shakespeare with want of truth to nature. And yet. . . ." (I, 104); whereupon he explains why a speech in *As You Like It* gives him pause. He comments unhappily upon a speech in *Coriolanus* and concludes, "I cherish the hope that I am mistaken, and, becoming wiser, shall discover some profound excellence in what I now appear to myself to detect an imperfection" (I, 91). This sounds pious, indeed mealy-mouthed, but the great point is that he had *not* discovered, had not *forced* himself to discover, a "profound excellence" in what looked like an "imperfection". And when he disliked a play he could say so in round terms— to him *Measure for Measure* seemed a "hateful" work.

By major critics I mean those most widely read and influential. It is hard to imagine the major Shakespearian critics of the twentieth century being given pause by anything, or failing to discover any excellence which they hope to find, or—and this especially—viewing *Measure for Measure* as a "hateful" work or, indeed, marred by a single flaw. The recent critical history of this play illustrates perfectly the increasing pervasiveness of the myth of perfection.

Let me return for a moment to the matter of the state of Shakespeare's texts. Those who read the plays only in modern editions are spared many annoyances but they are denied many small revelations. The cumulative impact of the latter can be considerable. After meeting in every play such instances as the "Mantua" which should be "Padua", the "Thomas" who should be "George", and the ghost like "Innogen" who should not be there at all, one draws new conclusions about the kind of material with which one is dealing. Granted that the great majority of the discrepancies are owing to scribal and printing errors (themselves eloquent of the disturbing fact that Shakespeare never found it worthwhile to oversee the printing and proof-reading of a single play, including the "good" quarto of *Hamlet*), a residue still remain for which his habits of composition must be held accountable. It becomes evident to the secular-minded that he was capable of offhand improvisation, that he sometimes began a play without knowing how it was going to end, that he often failed to name characters until he was far along in the script, and that he just as often failed to clear away chips as he hewed to an emerging line. Celia's initial tallness may be a minor case in point. It would have been natural for him to visualize Rosalind as a pert little brunette like Hermia, Celia a willowy blonde like Helena, until he came to the point of disguising them as brother and sister, and absent-mindedly canceled the conception. This may not be what happened, but parallel discrepancies leave no doubt that it *could* have happened.

Shakespeare could even get hopelessly bogged down in his syntax, and yet let the snarled passage stand. Even in texts as good as that of *The Tempest*, or in dual texts with independent authority like those of *Hamlet*, where identical recurrence of certain passages performs an authenticating function, there are lines which should have been revised or "blotted". Notorious passages appear both in early plays like *The Comedy of Errors* and in late ones like *Cymbeline*,

---

Samuel Coleridge seems actually to have said, "The task [of criticizing Shakespeare] will be genial in proportion as the criticism is reverential." Cf. *Coleridge's Shakespearean Criticism*, ed. T. M. Raysor, 2 vols. (Cambridge, Mass., 1930), I, 126.

where no reasonable emendation can cure the incoherence or obscurity. Commentators must suggest a "missing line", or maintain a gloomy silence. The reader may wish to exercise himself by trying to parse (with the aid of Abbott) the following from the last scene in *Cymbeline:*

> The peece of tender Ayre, thy vertuous Daughter
> Which we call *Mollis Aer,* and *Mollis Aer*
> We terme it *Mulier;* which *Mulier* I diuine
> Is that most constant Wife, who euen now
> Answering the Letter of the Oracle,
> Vnknowne to you, vnsought, were clipt about
> With this most tender Aire.

Here the meaning is clear enough, but in similar cases it can only be guessed.

My intention, of course, is not to "debunk" Shakespeare. Surely we can tolerate the bad passages in view of others where an almost equally cavalier disregard for syntax accompanies magnificent effects. And there are indeed apparent discrepancies which are in fact subtleties, or at least the product of conscious artistic calculation. And plays retaining the debris of false starts, like *Much Ado About Nothing,* can turn out fine in the end. Nevertheless we must recognize that the merit in Shakespeare's plays does not extend to merit in every detail in them; and whether particular defects, in minor or major features, are attributable to Shakespeare himself or to accidents of transmission, the fact remains that they are there. Reliable conclusions cannot be drawn from unreliable or incomplete data. Disquisitions upon dramatic structure are worthless if based upon act-divisions carelessly dubbed in by the publishers of the Folio; and ecstacies over the inspired placing of a colon are unrewarding if the colon represents not Shakespeare's "dramatic punctuation" but the bright idea of a printer's apprentice. If there are inconsistencies in things so consipicuous as the naming of persons and places, there can be inconsistencies in the choice of images, so that the plays cannot be treated as if they were machine-tooled mechanisms, with each word, image, or symbol meshing perfectly with all other words, images, and symbols, as in a series of well-lubricated cogs. This is so even if the forward thrust of the cogs is not made to eject, as it often is, the "message" the critic was predisposed to find. Evidence of blindness to defects or inconsistencies casts suspicion upon testimony about merits or consistencies. The most subtle and convincing verbal analysis of a fine passage loses authority when the critic finds identical virtues in a passage far from fine. The truth ceases to be true if it would be uttered whether it was true or not. What shall we think of praises of *Hamlet* by one who has raved over *Titus Andronicus?* For the idolator, all the works of the idol are equally or almost equally perfect.

Measure for Measure is a play with great merits and great defects. The defects are of kinds sometimes attributable to the author, sometimes to accidents of transmission, sometimes to either, we cannot tell which. They are often petty, like the discrepancy between "nineteen" and "fourteen", or between "Thomas Tapster" and "Pompey Bum". They are often less petty, like the rough structural joints (at several spots characters fall quite outside the class of the Capulet servant, by knowing a fact at one moment and proving ignorant of it the next), or like the incoherence of

> Then no more remaines
> But that, to your sufficiency, as your worth is able,
> And let them work:

and the thumping redundance of,

> Noueltie is onely in request, and as it is as dangerous to be aged in any
> kinde of course, as it is vertuous to be constant in any undertaking.

And, finally, they are in the aggregate the reverse of petty since they distort the entire conception. We seem to have, not one kind of play, but two, very imperfectly soldered together. We can even pinpoint the line where the fracture is so obvious that it cannot be ignored. After Claudio's, "O hear me, Isabella" (III. i. 151) all the major characters lose their capacity for emotional response, and can hear of black treachery, their own impending deaths, or the supposed death of loved ones, with relative aplomb. Intrigue takes over, and Duke Vincentio ceases to resemble Haroun al Raschid so much as he resembles Brainworm. There have been earlier signs that the playwright was heading for trouble.

The fact that the play contains some of the greatest scenes in Shakespeare, and some of the most marvelous poetry, does not alter the fact that it is not a success in the same sense in which *King Lear* is a success, or even *The Comedy of Errors* is a success. Of course we value it more than the latter, but we do so because of its parts. It had not, when it assumed its present form, crystalized into a satisfying artistic whole; and it is doubtful, in view of its materials, if it could ever have done so. The romantic and postromantic invectives against Isabella have been properly reproved by such historical critics as W. W. Lawrence and R. W. Chambers, but these knew when to stop in their work of rehabilitation. The merits and defects of the piece have been capably outlined by E. M. W. Tillyard[12] in the kind of essay usually patronized for its "common sense" (because it is uncommonly sensible), but the voice of moderation is not the voice which prevails.

The prevailing voices in Shakespearian criticism demonstrate pretty clearly that Lascelles Abercrombie's plea for "liberty of interpreting" has been followed by liberty of prophesying, and that the question we must now ask is not "How many children had Lady Macbeth?" but "How much sanctity had Duke Vincentio?" The impulse of the anti-Stratfordians to deify Shakespeare is being matched by the critical impulse to treat his works as holy writ. The commentary, whether it is accretive and rabbinical in character, or "analytical" and scholastic, or apocalyptic and inspired, is uniformly solemn. One would not guess that there are *laughs* in the play (or anywhere else in Shakespeare)—Pompey and Lucio, if they are mentioned at all, are always strangely etherealized. When such criticism is written from the viewpoint of the orthodox Catholic or Protestant, or the spokesman for "Christian Humanism", it is relatively unembarrassing because there is at least an external point of reference and we can accept or reject the argument. But usually there is no stated body of belief to which we can refer. Shakespeare is Allah, and the Critic is his prophet. The only point of reference is the various notions which simmer about in the critic's mind. Not only does each detail in the play prove to articulate with all other details, but

---

[12] "Measure for Measure", *Shakespeare's Problem Plays* (London, 1950) pp. 118-138.

the whole expresses an "idea", unmistakable and yet hitherto mistaken, perfectly expressed, yet in need of "interpretation". Duke Vincentio emerges as a Christ-figure, but a very peculiar Christ-figure, and one sometimes sharing his ministry with Lucio—not the Lucio we thought we knew, but one prefiguring the divine spirit later made incarnate in D. H. Lawrence.

The interpretations of *Measure for Measure* offer only an extreme example. The other plays, especially the tragedies and romances, are receiving the same treatment. This kind of writing is less criticism than a misty form of apologetics, with its religiosity unrelated to any religion except incidentally—as in the reestablishment of a hell, whither Shakespeare's tragic heroes may be sent along with any critic who has (sentimentally) ever put in a good word for them. My intention, I repeat, is not (on this four hundredth anniversary) to attack *Measure for Measure* or to imply that it is unworthy of thoughtful discussion. It is one of my favorite plays. My fear is that the idolatrous transformation of it into something it is *not* will rob us of the wonderful thing which, in parts, it really *is*. And that is the danger in general—that we shall trade our birthright of great artistry for a mess of third-rate philosophy.

I have refrained from mentioning particular names less because it would be ungracious than because it would be unjust. The names which come to mind are not those of the uniquely idolatrous, but those of the most successfully so. I once heard a lecture by a former Paulist father who had become a Unitarian minister. It was called "From the Apostles to the Creeds". All that I now remember of it is that the speaker approved of the apostles but disapproved of the creeds—that, and the fact that he placed the time interval between the two at four hundred years. Perhaps the second circumstance is why I recall the lecture in the year of Shakespeare's fourth centenary. And perhaps what I am really saying is that I am devoted to primitive Shakespearianity. None of us can claim total immunity from the effects of the myth of perfection.

And yet we should combat it, in others and ourselves. It may well be that Shakespeare-idolatry is drawing strength from something other than its roots in the past. Having lost their anchorage in the faith of their fathers, many are seeking a substitute in secular literature, and perhaps, in a materialistic age, any form of idealism has something to be said for it. But for some forms very little can be said—specifically, any that cannot be judged on their own merits, and cannot stand on their own feet, rather than on Shakespeare's. Besides, faith should begin where we reach the limits of knowledge.

We must still take into account who Shakespeare actually was and what he actually wrote. There remains a mission for the sons of Martha—the biographer studying documents rather than cryptograms, the textual student, the literary historian, even the rational critic. These have no large congregation—only a small audience—but I believe that they love Shakespeare and do honor his memory, on this side idolatry, as much as any.

Harvard University

Man Successful

HARDIN CRAIG

OME remarkable things have in recent years become matters of common knowledge with reference to the scope of the human brain. It is said, for example, that the brain has, as a neural instrument, nine billion possibilities of ideation, and some pessimistic persons add that the ordinary and normal achievements amount to seven-tenths of one per cent of the mathematical total. Since this, unless my arithmetic is wrong, amounts to the quite respectable total of six million three hundred thousand, something might be said about the bases of such beliefs; but this is no treatise about brain mechanisms and human thought. I shall be contented if it is admitted, as of course it will be, that there are obvious though incalculable differences among human beings with reference to achievement, quality, and scope of mind.

It is with increasing wonder, after years of acquaintance, that I observe new ranges and instances of intellectual power continuing to present themselves in Shakespeare, and convincingly. Did Shakespeare have a brain like that of John Doe and Richard Roe, or rather do these worthies have brains like Shakespeare's? Except in vitality and effectiveness it is not enough to answer no to either question. The old way was to import mystically a condition called "genius", but that is no longer acceptable to neurologists, to students of the evolution of the cerebral cortex, or to other scientists who wish to know the truth. To some of us it seems not only more divine but also more respectable for the Creator to put into every human head a means of success and salvation rather than to indulge in wand-waving and wilful favoritism.

This superiority is no mere affair of Shakespeare, since human history is full of it. There are Plato, Aristotle, Bacon, Newton, and Einstein, on the one side, Homer (if one rejects multiple authorship), Sophocles, Dante, Milton, and Goethe, on the other. There is moreover from these heights a road full of travelers one behind another, innumerable but discriminable. Historical time cuts a small figure, since, in the slow process of evolution, the time between Hector and Hornblower is not so much as a watch in the night.

Let us suppose that William Shakespeare was a human being with a human brain of the better sort consisting of a lower neural organization devoted to sense perception and shared in varying degrees with the rest of the animal kingdom, and an upper brain, the cerebral cortex, largely special to man and devoted to cognition or thought. This much we ask may be granted on this occasion. Let us try to find out something about Shakespeare's mind. We shall proceed as simply as possible and make use, in the first instance, of Locke's great discovery that the brain operates on two levels, that of sense perception and that of something added to it that he called "reflection".[1] We shall add to this a modern amplification and analysis of Locke's concept of reflection best and most clearly presented by the late Alfred North Whitehead, who applied to the total process the term "concrescence".[2] Let us, however, narrow the field by taking it for granted that Shakespeare was a master of the concrete and must have had a power of sense perception of the highest order.[3] We shall follow in slightly simplified form Whitehead's analysis of concrescence, which he apparently regards as a process of the upper brain. His summary of elements is given in *Adventures of Ideas,* chapter iv, section 16, and for the convenience of the reader we repeat in a note a crucial paragraph.[4]

When we look into Shakespeare to see if associational and reflective thought is habitual with him, we find an abundance of riches. Broad and perfect concrescence is in almost every scene and may be chosen almost at random. Let us take the Queen's description of the death of Ophelia in *Hamlet.*[5]

> There is a willow grows aslant a brook,
> That shows his hoar leaves in the glassy stream;
> There with fantastic garlands did she make
> Of crow-flowers, nettles, daisies, and long purples
> That liberal shepherds give a grosser name,
> But our cold maids do dead men's fingers call them:
> There, on the pendent boughs her coronet weeds
> Clambering to hang, an envious sliver broke;
> When down her weedy trophies and herself
> Fell in the weeping brook. Her clothes spread wide;
> And, mermaid-like, a while they bore her up:
> Which time she chanted snatches of old tunes;
> As one incapable of her own distress,
> Or like a creature native and indued
> Unto that element: but long it could not be
> Till that her garments, heavy with their drink,
> Pull'd the poor wretch from her melodious lay
> To muddy death.

Some parts of this are cool, clear observations of nature. The word "aslant" itself is characteristic of willows that grow beside brooks, since their roots lack

---

[1] *An Essay Concerning Human Understanding* (1690), particularly Part II.

[2] Whitehead's most ample treatment is to be found *passim* in *Process and Reality* (1928), although the briefer treatment in *Adventures of Ideas* (1933) should not be neglected. Treatments of the idea with differing terminology will be found in the philosophical works of Samuel Alexander (1859-1938), Lord Russell, and other writers on epistemology. We shall on this occasion follow Whitehead.

[3] If highly specialized scholars with the noncommittal attitude of experimental scientists reject this, we shall have to stop here, for Shakespeare died 346 years ago; but we shall resort to perhaps the oldest and most reliable of all epistemological practices, namely, the argument from effect to cause. There are many books devoted to Shakespeare's knowledge of the actual. I began, as I remember, with a charming book by D. H. Madden, *Diary of Master William Silence* (London, 1897).

[4] Whitehead's paragraph:
> Thus to arrive at the philosophic generalization which is the notion of a final actuality conceived in the guise of a generalization of an act of experience, an apparent redundancy of terms is required. The words correct each other. We require 'together', 'creativity', 'concrescence', 'prehension', 'feeling', 'subjective form', 'data', 'actuality', 'becoming', 'process'.

[5] IV. vii. 167-184.

support on the water-side. A common variety of willows has leaves that are white on the bottoms and therefore look "hoar" in the glassy stream, and, as for that "envious sliver", most of us know from boyhood how treacherously brittle the branches of willows are. Other parts have appropriate associations with Ophelia and her condition. Over the whole there is an atmosphere of suitability, so that the whole is an example of perfect concrescence—consummation of elements, novelty, feeling, fitness, fact, actuality, and process. There is even an element of what Whitehead calls "subjective form", for Shakespeare does not often explain or generalize, but makes his readers and hearers perform those operations.[6]

When, however, Shakespeare passes into an area of ancient rhetoric where argument or persuasion is the object, he shows a perfect consciousness of the power of the concrete in securing conviction, and he abstracts freely and clearly. Such passages are Cassius' attack on Brutus in *Julius Caesar* and the argument of Ulysses addressed to Achilles in *Troilus and Cressida*.[7]

Shakespeare apparently did not, like Plato, examine the world for the purpose of discovering and announcing eternal principles. That their principles were very different one cannot say. In fact, they seem about equally interested in temperance, justice, courage, and wisdom. Plato established and explained these virtues; Shakespeare did not. Perhaps Plato was an avowed and consecrated teacher, and Shakespeare was a dramatist, this difference being, in Whitehead's phrase, a difference in "subjective form".

This brings up a question of some difficulty. If Shakespeare frequently refrains, as he seems to do, from the statement of general principles in general terms, does this mean that he never rises to the highest and broadest abstractions? It certainly does not, although Shakespeare maintains his reticence and usually makes us find the general ideas and utter them for ourselves. They are usually recognizable, patent in fact, and there are considerable numbers of them that may be regarded as actual—his stress in later plays on forgiveness, for example. Two of them seem to be of special importance, but in both of them there is the temptation to say that Shakespeare's highest abstractions take the form of personality and personal conduct. It seems unnecessary to invent agencies, as is sometimes done, to attend to abstractions on the highest levels, since it might be better to make use of more of the nine billion possibilities of ideation in the cerebral cortex and thus avoid superstition.

In the figure of Brutus in *Julius Caesar* there appears as background a stoical principle, the idea of bearing the ills of life to death itself with fortitude. This is the very key to Hamlet, who is not an Aristotelian hero, was never proud or successful, and did not meet his end at the hands of fate. Hamlet's success was as ultimate as his death, and his success and his death come together. The same fortitude comes to the rescue of Cleopatra, who goes forward to her death "after the high Roman fashion".[8] What is to me the final example of stoical tragedy is afforded by Queen Katharine in *Henry VIII*. This principle affects

---

[6] The late Professor Una Ellis-Fermor in her posthumous book *Shakespeare the Dramatist* (London, 1961) observed this quality, saw it had the quality of arousing interest, and spoke of it as "evocative". See pp. 11, 28, 37, *et passim*.

[7] See *Julius Caesar* I. ii. 25-177, and *Troilus and Cressida* III. iii. 112-215.

[8] See *Antony and Cleopatra* IV. xv. 73-91.

the nature of tragedy itself, and I would hazard the conjecture that it appeared first in Humphrey Duke of Gloucester in *2 Henry VI*.[9]

There is another great formative idea in Shakespeare that seems also to grow in importance. If it is actual, and I submit the evidence, it is not only of great interest but also of great importance in the interpretation of Shakespeare. One might suggest the theme by asking a question: Is man monarch of all he surveys, and, if he is not, how might he become so?

Shakespeare was not oblivious of masterful men. Biron was not without independence and forceful self-assertion, there is a practical streak in Romeo, and even Petruchio, in the difficult task of taming Kate, is not without ingenuity and efficiency. There is a high quality of general mastery in the Duke in *Measure for Measure*. But everyone will see that Shakespeare's outstanding achievement in the depiction of triumphant man of the here and now is King Henry V. He may have had in mind, for all we know, a contrast in kings between the beautiful, sentimental, and impractical Richard II in the first play of the Lancastrian tetralogy[10] and the hero of the last. Henry V could not fail. The treachery of Cambridge, Scroop, and Grey at Southampton, the fortifications of Harfleur, and the dangers and difficulties of Agincourt collapse before his genius for success. Whatever one may think of his wooing of the French princess, which is crude and makes one think he is selling a horse, one must admit that it is eminently successful.

But these men all have their feet on the ground. Is there a road to mastery not of that kind? Bacon thought there was, thought it was to be found in knowledge, especially perhaps in knowledge of the physical environment. The Elizabethan age thought so and tried to find it.[11] The pathway to unqualified success seemed always to rely on learning and failure to the lack of it—on knowledge, philosophy, and magic. Did Shakespeare anywhere reveal this distant and difficult hope for triumphant man? I think he did, and I offer it for the consideration of Shakespeare scholars and readers. It will be seen at once that I have in mind Prospero in *The Tempest*. I think it possible that that play has in it something more than a mere imitation of the magical hocus-pocus of earlier Elizabethan plays.

In so familiar a play as *The Tempest* it is unnecessary to go into great detail. The plot was a success story from the start,[12] and bookish. Prospero devotes too much time to study, a thing reprehensible in modern eyes, and his deputy for state affairs, his own brother, seizes, with the connivance of the king of Naples and with the loss of independence, the dukedom of Milan. There is no doubt that Antonio, the brother, was a bad man, so that his forgiveness was a difficult undertaking. He placed Prospero and his little daughter in a leaky boat and set them adrift. They would have perished but for the good Gonzalo, who gave them necessities of life and, moreover, gave Prospero his book. One

---

[9] See my article, "The Shackling of Accidents: A Study of Elizabethan Tragedy", *PQ*, XIX (1940), 1-19.

[10] My reason for calling Richard II "beautiful" is my recollection of a miniature portrait of him, thought to be of Italian origin, in the South Kensington Museum many years ago.

[11] See my *The Enchanted Glass* (1935, reprinted by Blackwell in Oxford 1950), chapter ii, *et passim*.

[12] See Henri Grégoire, "The Bulgarian Origins of Shakespeare's *The Tempest*", *SP*, XXXVII (1940), 236-256.

thinks of it as a big black book. On the island Prospero has time for study and thought, so that he masters his art, and the island blossoms like a rose. Prospero had no radar or even a telephone, knew nothing of nuclear physics, but he did the best he could and from our point of view not too well. He apparently hit upon an early and imperfect form of Rosicrucianism. Christian Rosenkreutz was possibly at work on the spirits of fire and air, earth and water when Shakespeare wrote his play. J. V. Andrea published his description in 1614. Maybe Shakespeare had heard of Rosenkreutz's system of natural magic. In any case Prospero was successful, and what a success! It was, in fact, a model of true success, full of competency, justice, and human charity. No wonder he can break his staff and drown his book, for Prospero has arrived, and the plain inference is that the next fellow who wishes to rule the world will have to get a copy of that book and read it for himself. Prospero foresees his own death and remembers that such a book is for the sole use of the select few.

How does one suppose that Shakespeare, and Bacon too for that matter, got the idea of the mastery of the world through learning? Historically it is a long story of ignorant veneration of learned pretense. In the realm of the tantalizing issue between possibility and actuality the answer is in the early paragraphs of this essay. Shakespeare must have had a brain like ours only better, capable of almost illimitable cerebration, a brain that would defy chronology and make ludicrous the stodgy positivistic belief that the function of scholars and men of learning is to build a temple of inclusive truth by the addition of one little brick after another.

Houston, Texas

By PERMISSION of the Honble *ROBERT DINWIDDIE*, Efq; His Majefty's Lieutenant-Governor, and Commander in Chief of the Colony and Dominion of *Virginia*.

By a Company of COMEDIANS, *from* LONDON, *At the* THEATRE *in* WILLIAMSBURG, On *Friday* next, being the 15th of *September*, will be prefented, A PLAY, Call'd,

THE
MERCHANT of *VENICE*.

(Written by *Shakefpear*.)

The Part of *ANTONIO* (the MERCHANT) to be perform'd by

Mr. CLARKSON.

GRATIANO, by Mr. SINGLETON,

Lorenzo, (with Songs in Character) by Mr. ADCOCK.

The Part of *BASSANIO* to be perform'd by

Mr. RIGBY.

Duke, by Mr. Wynell.

Salanio, by Mr. Herbert.

The Part of *LAUNCELOT*, by Mr. HALLAM.

And the Part of *SHYLOCK*, (the JEW) to be perform'd by

Mr. MALONE.

The Part of *NERISSA*, by Mrs. ADCOCK,

Jeffica, by Mrs. Rigby.

And the Part of *PORTIA*, to be perform'd by

Mrs. HALLAM.

With a new occafional PROLOGUE.

To which will be added, a FARCE, call'd,

The ANATOMIST:
OR,
SHAM DOCTOR.

The Part of *Monfieur le Medecin*, by

Mr. RIGBY.

And the Part of *BEATRICE*, by Mrs. ADCOCK.

** No Perfon, whatfoever, to be admitted behind the Scenes.

BOXES, 7s. 6d. PIT and BALCONIES, 5s. 9d. GALLERY, 3s. 9d.

To begin at Six o'Clock.

Vivat Rex.

The Devil Can Cite Scripture

ERNEST A. STRATHMANN

NTONIO, the merchant of Venice, scornfully rejects Shylock's attempt to find in the story of Jacob and the pied lambs justification for usury.

> Mark you this, Bassanio,
> The devil can cite Scripture for his purpose.
> An evil soul producing holy witness
> Is like a villain with a smiling cheek,
> A goodly apple rotten at the heart.
> O, what a goodly outside falsehood hath! (I. iii. 98-103)

The admonition to Bassanio has its origin in Scripture, its analogues in the ethical philosophy of the Renaissance, and its illustration in other characters than Shylock.

The devil does cite scripture in tempting Jesus to cast himself down from the temple: "For it is written, He shall give his angels charge over thee, to keep thee";[1] and Jesus exposes the fallacy in the invitation to wilful test of his divinity. In Shakespeare's plays, as in the poems of Spenser and Milton, falsehood has a goodly outside which is not so readily penetrated by frail mortals. In broad terms, the deception is at the heart of the bitter contrast between the appearance and the reality which shocks and ultimately destroys the great tragic heroes. Hamlet's first extended speech is an outraged rejection of "seeming", and his first soliloquy expresses the anguish of disillusionment; Othello is deceived by "honest" Iago; Lear is driven to madness by the cruelty of the daughters who flattered him; Macbeth discovers, too late, the equivocation in fair promises. In the narrower terms by which this essay is limited, Antonio's principle is illustrated in the speeches of villains who give good advice and pronounce sound doctrine. I propose to examine, in their dramatic context, a few speeches of which it may be said "tropically" that the devil can cite scripture.

I

Iago's advice to the disconsolate Roderigo is a simple and clear illustration of the corrupt application of sound doctrine. Roderigo, having lost Desdemona, threatens to drown himself, and Iago professes himself appalled at such a deficiency in self-love.

> *Rod.* What should I do? I confess it is my shame to be so fond, but it is not in my virtue to amend it.
>
> *Iago.* Virtue! a fig! 'tis in ourselves that we are thus or thus. Our bodies

---

[1] Psalms XCI: 11-12; Luke IV: 10-11. Quotations from Shakespeare are from *The Complete Plays and Poems*, ed. by W. A. Neilson and C. J. Hill (Cambridge, Mass., 1942).

are our gardens, to the which our wills are gardeners; so that if we will
plant nettles or sow lettuce, set hyssop and weed up thyme, supply it with
one gender of herbs or distract it with many, either to have it sterile with
idleness or manured with industry, why, the power and corrigible authority
of this lies in our wills. If the balance of our lives had not one scale of
reason to poise another of sensuality, the blood and baseness of our natures
would conduct us to most preposterous conclusions; but we have reason to
cool our raging motions, our carnal stings, our unbitted lusts, . . . (I. iii.
319-336)

Had Iago stopped here, his speech could stand as a brief treatise on the belief
that man—made a little lower than the angels—is man by virtue of the exercise
of the distinctive gift of reason. Shakespeare accepts without question and uses
freely the prevalent idea that reason sets man apart from the lower animals.
Hamlet tells us that "a beast, that wants discourse of reason", would have
mourned his father's death longer than his mother did. Lady Macbeth can
distort the principle into a reproach of her husband's hesitation to murder
Duncan.

> *Macbeth.*   Prithee, peace!
> I dare do all that may become a man;
> Who dares do more is none.
>   *Lady Macbeth.*   What beast was 't, then,
> That made you break this enterprise to me?
> When you durst do it, then you were a man;
> And, to be more than what you were, you would
> Be so much more the man. (I. vii. 45-51)

But Iago is not speaking out of character in a moral lecture on the rational
soul. His speech concludes,

> . . . our unbitted lusts, whereof I take this that
> you call love to be a sect or scion.

Love is simply an offshoot of lust. As a man you should control this love (lust)
for your own self-interest. Iago manages in the few words of his conclusion
not only to pervert the application of his moral lesson but to confuse love with
sensuality. His cynical degradation of love evokes comparison with another
pronouncement on the subject:

> Call it not love, for Love to heaven is fled,
> Since sweating Lust on earth usurp'd his name;
> Under whose simple semblance he hath fed
> Upon fresh beauty, blotting it with blame;
>   Which the hot tyrant stains and soon bereaves,
>   As caterpillars do the tender leaves.
>
> Love comforteth like sunshine after rain,
> But Lust's effect is tempest after sun;
> Love's gentle spring doth always fresh remain,
> Lust's winter comes ere summer half be done;
>   Love surfeits not, Lust like a glutton dies;
>   Love is all truth, Lust full of forged lies. (*Venus*, ll. 793-804)

Or with the more sophisticated sonnet 129:

> Th' expense of spirit in a waste of shame
> Is lust in action; . . .

The irony of Iago's advice is that he convinces not only the gull Roderigo; he has convinced himself. More than one commentator on *Othello* has observed that Iago's failure to understand love leads to his undoing.

II

In his derisive rejection of judicial astrology Edmund is citing the church fathers, if not scripture. Some commentators have not recognized that the seemingly bold skepticism of his soliloquy is in harmony with Christian doctrine. As in Iago's moral lecture, though less apparently today, it is not the philosophy that is wrong, but its application.

The Earl of Gloucester has exclaimed upon the controversial incidents portended by the late eclipses. After his father leaves, Edmund remarks contemptuously upon his credulity.

> This is the excellent foppery of the world, that, when we are sick in fortune,—often the surfeits of our own behaviour,—we make guilty of our disasters the sun, the moon, and stars, as if we were villains on necessity, fools by heavenly compulsion, knaves, thieves, and treachers by spherical predominance, drunkards, liars, and adulterers by an enforc'd obedience of planetary influence, and all that we are evil in, by a divine thrusting on. An admirable evasion of whore-master man, to lay his goatish disposition on the charge of a star! My father compounded with my mother under the dragon's tail, and my nativity was under *Ursa major;* so that it follows, I am rough and lecherous. Fut, I should have been that I am, had the maidenliest star in the firmament twinkled on my bastardizing. (I. ii. 128-145)

Edmund is in good company in rejecting the influence of the stars on the will of man. One of the ethical arguments against the practice of judicial astrology —that branch of astrology concerned with foretelling the future—was that evildoers tend to blame the stars for their wrongdoing. On religious grounds judicial astrology was rejected as implying a limitation upon God's omnipotence. An apologist for judicial astrology, Christopher Heydon, does not allow the stars an influence upon the *will* of man. An infinite number of scholars, he writes,

> . . . all with one consent teach no further, than our schoolmen and divines do second them, namely that the heavens do incline, but not enforce, because they have no direct power over the will of man from whence all human actions, as from their original, do naturally flow.[2]

Robert Gray, a clergyman, is in essential agreement with Heydon:

> The stars do sometimes foreshow such things as happen, but they are not the enforcing causes of such things as happen. Most impious and

---

[2] *A Defence of Judicial Astrology* (Cambridge, 1603), pp. 3, 20-21. For a brief account of Elizabethan opinions on astrology, see E. A. Strathmann, *Sir Walter Ralegh: A Study in Elizabethan Skepticism* (New York, 1951), pp. 192-197, and the references there cited, especially p. 192, n. 42.

blasphemous it is, to ascribe these things to the influence and operation of
the stars: for it is to rob God of his honor, to derogate from his power, to
overthrow his providence, and to tie God to secondary and subordinate
causes, and in respect of ourselves, it extinguisheth the fear of God in us,
it hinders our repentance and conversion unto God, it draws us to atheism,
and to a flat contempt both of God and his judgments.[3]

Sir Walter Ralegh denies the direct influence of the stars upon the will of man,
but argues for an indirect influence "by mediation of the sensitive appetite".
He quotes the opinion of St. Augustine in language not unlike Edmund's
strictures.

But in this question of fate, the middle course is to be followed, that
as with the heathen we do not bind God to his creatures, in this supposed
necessity of destiny, so on the contrary we do not rob those beautiful creatures of their powers and offices. For had any of these second causes de-
spoiled God of his prerogative, or had God himself constrained the mind
and will of man to impious acts by any celestial enforcements, then sure
the impious excuse of some were justifiable; of whom St. Augustine . . .
"Where we reprehend them of evil deeds, they again with wicked perverseness urge that rather the Author and Creator of the stars, than the doer
of the evil is to be accused."
But that the stars and other celestial bodies incline the will by mediation
of the sensitive appetite, which is also stirred by the constitution and com-
plexion, it cannot be doubted.[4]

In brief, Edmund's derisive attack on judicial astrology has reputable support, both ethical and religious; but, as in Iago's advice to Roderigo, the lesson
is misapplied. Edmund does not conclude that man must discipline his will
and fear God. Both critics of judicial astrology and its apologists agreed that
sound education and religious nurture could counteract the limited and indirect
influence of the stars. But Edmund has rejected moral responsibility and religious duty along with judicial astrology. In his first speech in scene ii he
invokes nature as his goddess, and in denying the influence of the stars he has
simultaneously declared his freedom from the laws of man and God. The
speech on astrology is preceded by Edmund's seemingly reluctant insinuations
against Edgar. The speech ends, when Edgar enters, with Edmund pretending
a belief in the astrology which he has just denounced.

III

Unlike Iago and Edmund, Claudius does not disclose his villainy at the
beginning of the play. Not until the beginning of Act III of *Hamlet* do we
hear from Claudius himself an acknowledgment of wrongdoing. Polonius,
having ordered Ophelia to "read on this book" as a pretended occupation while
she awaits Hamlet, comments:

We are oft to blame in this,—
'Tis too much prov'd—that with devotion's visage
And pious action we do sugar o'er
The devil himself. (III. i. 46-49)

[3] *An Alarum to England* (1609), sigs. C 1ᵛ-C 2ʳ.
[4] *History of the World* (1614), bk. 1, ch. 1, sec. xi, p. 15.

The words catch the conscience of the King, who confesses in an aside:

> O, 'tis true!
> [*Aside.*] How smart a lash that speech doth give my conscience!
> The harlot's cheek, beautied with plast'ring art,
> Is not more ugly to the thing that helps it
> Than is my deed to my most painted word.
> O heavy burden! (III. i. 49-54)

In Act I we know nothing of this. As the second scene of *Hamlet* opens we are aware of something amiss, since a ghost in the semblance of King Hamlet has appeared; but we have not yet been told emphatically that "Something is rotten in the state of Denmark", and we are yet to hear Hamlet's soliloquy on the deep-seated causes of his grief and melancholy. The good advice that Claudius gives Hamlet concerning grief, therefore, presents a contrast between words and motives that is less sharply apparent, at the time, than in the speeches of Iago and Edmund.

If we can encompass the feat of watching scene ii unfold as if for the first time, we find ourselves witnessing a formal court scene in which a mild-spoken king seems to be in judicious control of events. True, we are shocked to learn that this king, in succeeding his brother, has promptly married his brother's widow; but the court has acquiesced and the only discordant element is the silent Prince Hamlet, clad in black. The king is alert in countering the threat from Norway, gracious in granting Laertes leave to depart for France, and kindly—uneasy perhaps?—in addressing Hamlet, Gertrude's solicitous entreaty to Hamlet has culminated in an unhappy phrase. If death is common, "Why seems it so particular with thee?" In Hamlet's view, there has been too much of seeming, and his retort is passionate:

> Seems, madam! Nay, it is; I know not "seems."
> 'Tis not alone my inky cloak, good mother,
> Nor customary suits of solemn black,
> Nor windy suspiration of forc'd breath,
> No, nor the fruitful river in the eye,
> Nor the dejected haviour of the visage,
> Together with all forms, moods, shows of grief,
> That can denote me truly. These indeed seem,
> For they are actions that a man might play;
> But I have that within which passeth show,
> These but the trappings and the suits of woe. (I. ii. 76-86)

It is in reply to this outburst that Claudius gives the Prince advice of which no Christian moralist would disapprove.

> 'Tis sweet and commendable in your nature, Hamlet,
> To give these mourning duties to your father.
> But, you must know, your father lost a father;
> That father lost, lost his; and the survivor bound
> In filial obligation for some term
> To do obsequious sorrow. But to persever
> In obstinate condolement is a course
> Of impious stubbornness; 'tis unmanly grief;

It shows a will most incorrect to heaven,
A heart unfortified, a mind impatient,
An understanding simple and unschool'd;
For what we know must be, and is as common
As any the most vulgar thing to sense,
Why should we in our peevish opposition
Take it to heart? Fie! 'tis a fault to heaven,
A fault against the dead, a fault to nature,
To reason most absurd, whose common theme
Is death of fathers, and who still hath cried,
From the first corse till he that died today,
"This must be so." (I. ii. 87-106)

Intemperance in grief is an affront to heaven; even apart from Christian duty the intemperance is a moral fault. The first encounter of Sir Guyon with intemperance may serve as an analogue. In Book Two of *The Faerie Queene,* a brief and righteous display of anger, induced by Archimago's slander of the Red Crosse Knight, is dispelled by mutual recognition. Then Guyon and the Palmer, in their first adventure, meet Amavia, who, in the intemperance of grief over the death of her husband, has given herself a mortal wound. First Guyon and then the Palmer moralize upon the scene.

Then turning to his Palmer said, Old syre
  Behold the image of mortalitie,
  And feeble nature cloth'd with fleshly tyre,
  When raging passion with fierce tyrannie
  Robs reason of her due regalitie,
  And makes it seruant to her basest part:
  The strong it weakens with infirmitie,
  And with bold furie armes the weakest hart;
The strong through pleasure soonest falles, the weake through smart.

But temperance (said he) with golden squire
  Betwixt them both can measure out a meane,
  Neither to melt in pleasures whot desire,
  Nor fry in hartlesse griefe and dolefull teene.
  Thrise happie man, who fares them both atweene: . . .[5]

The brief sermon by Claudius on the sin of immoderate grief deserves the approbation of the learned and godly. The speech concludes with an invitation to Hamlet to regard the king as his father, with the pronouncement that Hamlet is next in line of succession—and with a refusal of permission to return to Wittenberg, the kind of permission just granted to Laertes. If a ghostly visitor and an uncanonical marriage have put us on the alert, we just possibly may be suspicious of this refusal of permission to travel. Although the passage does not present an immediately apparent contrast between "fair terms and a villain's mind" (in Bassanio's apt phrase), we hear in a soliloquy that begins only a dozen lines later Hamlet's condemnation of the moralizing king. And that night Hamlet is impelled to set down in his tables "That one may smile, and smile, and be a villain!"

    [5] *F. Q.,* II. i. 57-58. For some other counsels on temperance in grief, see L. B. Campbell, *Shakespeare's Tragic Heroes* (Cambridge, 1930), pp. 114-117.

IV

From the deceptions practiced by Spenser's Archimago and Duessa to the temptation of Eve by Milton's Satan, evil presented as a "fair appearing good" is a recurrent theme of Elizabethan poets, dramatists, and tellers of tales. When even an angel cannot penetrate false-seeming, as Uriel at first fails to recognize the disguised Satan, small wonder that a wise man is ensnared.

> For neither man nor Angel can discern
> Hypocrisy, the only evil that walks
> Invisible, except to God alone. (*P.L.*, III. 682-684)

The three speeches upon which I have concentrated my attention merely epitomize a problem within which Shakespeare framed his major dramatic conflicts. Two of the speeches, those by Iago and Edmund, have sometimes been misunderstood, to the extent that Iago's speech has been considered totally immoral and Edmund's totally irreligious. In fact, all three speeches serve to isolate the disparity between words and deeds, between pretense and reality. In an age which gave primacy to the didactic function of literature, good words meant little unless they produced good deeds. Portia, half mockingly, tells her maid:

> If to do were as easy as to know what were good to do, chapels had been churches and poor men's cottages princes' palaces. It is a good divine that follows his own instructions; I can easier teach twenty what were good to be done, than to be one of the twenty to follow mine own teaching. (I. ii. 13-18)

In a more somber vein, and in language closer to our text, Sir Walter Ralegh laments that the intellectual grasp of the principle does not assure the practice of the virtue, that the devils are more learned in divinity than men.

> For although religion and the truth thereof be in every man's mouth . . . what is it other than an universal dissimulation? We profess that we know God, but by works we deny him. For beatitude doth not consist in the knowledge of divine things, but in a divine life; for the devils know them better than men. . . . We are all (in effect) become comedians in religion: and while we act in gesture and voice divine virtues, in all the course of our lives we renounce our persons and the parts we play.[6]

In brief, the devil can cite Scripture for his purpose. Antonio's rebuke of Shylock has a larger context than the story of the bond, larger even than the conflicts of the great tragedies.

Pomona College

---

[6] *History of the World* (1614), Preface, sig. C 2ᵛ.

By Authority.

By the AMERICAN COMPANY,
At the *NEW THEATRE* in SOUTHWARK; On *TUESDAY*,
The *Seventh* of *April*, will be presented, *BY PARTICULAR DESIRE*,
A *TRAGEDY* called

ROMEO AND JULIET,

Romeo by Mr. HALLAM,
Mercutio by Mr. DOUGLASS,
Capulet by Mr. MORRIS,
Fryar Lawrence by Mr. ALLYN,
Mountague by Mr. TOMLINSON,
Escalus by Mr. BROADBELT,
Tibalt by Mr WALL,
Paris by Mr. WOOLLS,---*Benvolio* by Mr. GODWIN,
Balthazer by Mr. GREVILLE,---*Fryar John* by Mr. PLATT,
Lady *Capulet* by Mrs. DOUGLASS,
Nurse by Mrs. HARMAN,
Juliet by Miss CHEER.

With the Funeral Procession of *Juliet*,

To the Monument of the *Capulets*;

And a SOLEMN DIRGE:
The *VOCAL PARTS* by Mr. WOOLLS, Mr. WALL, Miss WAINWRIGHT,
Miss HALLAM, Mrs. HARMAN, Mrs. MORRIS, &c.
With DANCES incident to the *PLAY, Viz.*
A *COMIC DANCE* by Mr. GODWIN;
A *MASQUERADE DANCE*;
And a *MINUET* by Mr. HALLAM and Miss CHEER.
To which will be added, A *DRAMATIC SATIRE* called

LETHE, or *Æsop in the Shades.*

Drunken-Man by Mr. HALLAM,
Frenchman by Mr. ALLYN,
Old Man by Mr. MORRIS, .
Mercury (with Songs) by Mr. WOOLLS,
Fine Gentleman by Mr. WALL,---*Charon* by Mr. TOMLINSON,
Æsop by Mr. DOUGLASS,
Mrs. *Tattoo* by Miss HALLAM,
Mrs. *Riot* (with a Song in Character) by Miss WAINWRIGHT.
To begin exactly at Half an Hour after SIX *o'Clock.*----Vivant Rex & Regina.
No Persons can, on any Pretence whatsoever, be admitted behind the Scenes.
TICKETS are sold at the *London Coffee-House*, at Mr. *Hawkins's* in *Walnut-Street*, and at
Mrs. *Scott's* in *Lombard-Street*; at which last *Office*, PLACES in the BOXES are to be had.
BOXES *Seven Shillings and Sixpence.* PIT *Five Shillings.* GALLERY *Three Shillings.*

Playbill of The American Company for a performance of *Romeo and Juliet* at
the New Theatre in Southwark, Philadelphia, on 7 April 1767. 7¾" x 10½".
Reproduced by permission of The New York Public Library.

The blind tooled calf binding of Surrey's *Songes and Sonettes* (1557) once owned
by Shakespeare.

Title-page of the copy of Surrey's *Songes and Sonettes* given by Shakespeare to
Alexander (?) Brome and by his descendant to David Garrick.

A Book from Shakespeare's Library Discovered by William Van Lennep

JOHN F. FLEMING

XACTLY thirty years ago, William Van Lennep,[1] the then recently appointed assistant curator of Harvard's Theatre Collection, was helping D. M. Little to prepare the letters[2] of David Garrick for publication. In one of the letters to George Steevens[3] he came upon the following postscript:

> The Letter sign'd Brome comes from a descendant of ye famous Author Brome—Shakespeare gave ye first Ed: of Surry's Poems to one of his Ancestors living in Warwickshire—Brome sent [it] to me & I lent it to D^r. Percy.[4]

This immediately led Van Lennep to H. E. Rollins' edition of *Tottel's Miscellany*, where, in the register of known copies, he noticed one upon whose title-page was written: "Robt. Brome Lichfield". I cannot imagine young Van Lennep accepting with equanimity his momentous bibliophilic discovery except that the following letter to Dr. A. S. W. Rosenbach, then owner of the volume, shows a restraint worthy of the most seasoned veteran:

241 Brattle St
Cambridge, Mass.
Sept. 28, 1934

My dear Dr. Rosenbach,

I am sending you this in care of Mr. Lawler. I think it will interest you both.

According to Professor H. E. Rollins of Harvard, the Rosenbach Co. has in its possession a copy of the *Songes and Sonettes written by the Earle of Surrey and other* (1557), Rollins' "C" edition. On its title page is enscribed "Robt. Brome Lichfield" (*Tottel's Miscellany*, 1929, II, 12). From information which I have recently discovered, I am able to furnish you with the provenance of your copy. I have been working with Mr. D. M. Little on the letters of David Garrick, preparing them for publication. In an unpublished letter from Garrick to George Steevens, dated by external evidence Jan. 4, 1774 (in the Folger Shakespeare Library), there occurs this curious passage: "The Letter signed Brome comes from a descendant of the famous Author Brome. Shakespeare gave the first edition of Surrey's Poems to one

---

[1] His untimely death occurred in the summer of 1962.

[2] After the death of D. M. Little, Professor George M. Kahrl continued the work, and the edition is now about to appear with the imprint of the Harvard University Press.

[3] George Steevens (1736-1800), celebrated editor of Shakespeare and commentator.

[4] Folger Shakespeare Library, MS. W. a. 180.

of his Ancestors living in Warwickshire. Brome sent [it] to me and I lent it
to Dr. Percy."

"The letter signed Brome" is probably not extant but its writer was
undoubtedly Robert Brome, proctor in the Lichfield Consistory Court and
one of Garrick's many Lichfield acquaintances (S. Shaw, *Hist. of Stafford-
shire,* 1798, I, 373). The "famous Author Brome" was presumably Alexander
Brome (1620-66), dramatist and Royalist poet, a man of gentle blood, rather
than Richard Brome (d. 1652), dramatist, servant and follower of Jonson, a
writer of humble origin (see J. L. Brooks, *The Life and Works of Alexander
Brome,* an unpublished thesis in the Harvard College Library). Garrick
owned a copy of Alexander Brome's *Songs and other Poems* (1661).[5]

The ancestor living in Warwickshire to whom Shakespeare gave your
copy of the *Songes and Sonettes* (if we may believe this statement of Garrick's), was perhaps Reginald Brome, a descendant of the Bromes of
Baddesley Clinton, Warwickshire, husband of Elizabeth, daughter and
co-heir of Thomas Skeffington (W. Dugdale, *Antiquities of Warwickshire,*
1656, p. 710, C. Stopes, *Shakespeare's Family,* 1901, p. 11). Great great
grandfather of Robert Brome of Lichfield, he was living at Woodlow, Warwickshire, in 1578 (Shaw, *loc. cit.;* J. Nichols, *Collectanea Topographica . . .,*
1843, VIII, 301). If Shakespeare did give the copy of the *Songes and
Sonettes* in your possession to Reginald Brome of Woodlow (or his wife) it
was undoubtedly passed down from father to son until it became the property of Robert Brome of Lichfield in the latter part of the 18th century. The
pedigree of the Brome family down to Robert and his brother Thomas, of
Burton-upon-Trent, is given partly under the pedigree of the Bromes of
Baddesley Clinton (see Dugdale, *loc. cit.*) This discloses that Robert Brome's
family dates back to the 14th century.

Garrick lent the Brome copy of the *Songes and Sonettes* to Bishop Percy
because the latter was at that time engaged upon the edition of Surrey's
poetry.[6] It is not listed in the catalogue of Percy's or Garrick's library. Therefore, we may assume that the book was returned to Robert Brome.

Shakespeare was no doubt well acquainted with *"Tottell's Miscellany",*
for he mentions it in *The Merry Wives of Windsor:*

> Slender: I had rather than forty shillings I had my Book of Songs
> and Sonnets here.

Very truly yours,

[signed] William Van Lennep

Percy never returned the book to Garrick. He left England in 1782, taking
his library with him, to become Bishop of Dromore in Ireland.

Soon after Percy's death in 1811, the Second Earl of Caledon purchased his
library en bloc. Sir Shane Leslie in a letter from Castle Leslie, Glaslough,
County Monaghan, Eire, dated May 17, 1963, writes:

> In late 18 c[entury] the Alexanders of Derry produced what was called
> a *Nabob* or adventurer-trader-speculator in India. With this wealth they
> bought Kennard (2 miles from here) renamed the estate Caledon and ob-
> tained a Peerage. The 2nd Lord Caledon succeeded in 1802. They built a
> fine Georgian house and filled it with Oriental paper and china. When in

---

[5] Sold at auction by Saunders in London on April 24, 1823, lot 311, for 10 shillings, 6 pence,
to Burn.

[6] Published in 1763.

need of a 'gentleman's library' they heard that the local Bishop Thomas Percy (of Reliques) had died in 1811 and that his library (collected in England) had accompanied him to Ireland and was for sale at Dromore, the name of his Episcopal See in County Down. . . . Bishop Percy collected every possible rare book illustrating the language, also every single pamphlet of 18th century [sic]. These Lord Caledon 2nd bought whole and the tradition is they were brought in carts, wrapped in straw, to Caledon to fill the shelf spaces, where, needless to say, they were never read. A chaplain or secretary made a rough catalogue about 1870. I never found out the price paid. . . .

On April 28, 1928, the same Sir Shane Leslie escorted Dr. Rosenbach to Caledon, where he purchased from the fifth Earl, among other great books, the Percy copy of Surrey's *Songes and Sonettes*.[7] On the death of Rosenbach on July 1, 1952, the volume was in his private collection, part of which was sold in 1954 to John F. Fleming, Inc. On February 1, 1956, the Shakespeare-Brome-Garrick-Percy-Caledon copy of Surrey's *Songes and Sonettes* was sold by Fleming to William A. Jackson as agent for Arthur A. Houghton, Jr., in whose collection it now rests.

New York

[7] See *Rosenbach, a Biography*, by Edwin Wolf 2nd with John F. Fleming (Cleveland and New York, 1960), Pp. 293-294.

Boston Theatre.

Mr. S. POWELL's Benefit.

Wednesday Evening, June 4,

Will be performed a Tragedy, Called,

ROMEO AND JULIET.

Romeo,	Mr. S. POWELL,
Mercutio,	Mr. POWELL.
Capulet,	Mr. BAKER.
Montague,	Mr. KENNY.
Tibalt,	Mr. COLLINS.
Benvolio,	Mr. NELSON.
Paris,	Mr. BARTLETT.
Friar Lawrence,	Mr. JONES.
Juliet,	Miss HARRISON.
Lady Capulet,	Mrs. BAKER.
Nurse,	Mrs. POWELL.
Virgins,	Miss BAKER, Mrs. COLLINS, Mrs. ABBOT.

In Act I. for the Masquerade, will be displayed an elegant new PALACE, executed by Mr. GULAGER.

To which will be added, a Musical Entertainment, Called,

NO SONG, NO SUPPER,

Robin,	Mr. JONES.
Frederick,	Mr. BARTLETT.
Endless,	Mr. BAKER.
William,	Mr. COLLINS:
Thomas,	Mr. KENNY.
Crop,	Mr. NELSON.
Dorothy,	Mrs. BAKER.
Louisa,	Miss BAKER.
Nelly,	Mrs. COLLINS.
Margaretta,	Mrs. ABBOT.

☞ The Curtain will be drawn up precisely at Seven o'clock; and no persons can be admitted behind the Scenes, but such as are under the immediate direction of the Manager.

Playbill for Mr. S. Powell's benefit on 4 June 1794, a performance of *Romeo and Juliet* in Boston. 8⅛″ x 10″. Reproduced by permission of The Folger Shakespeare Library.

On WEDNESDAY,

The TWENTY-FIFTH Day of MARCH, 1778,

At the Theatre in Southwark,

For the Benefit of a PUBLIC CHARITY,

Will be represented,

The First PART of

King Henry IV.

TO WHICH WILL BE ADDED, THE

Mock Doctor.

The CHARACTERS by the OFFICERS of the Army and Navy.

TICKETS to be had at the Printer's; at the Coffee-house in Market-street; and at the Pennsylvania Farmer, near the New-Market, and no where else.

BOXES and PIT, ONE DOLLAR.—GALLERY, HALF A DOLLAR.

Doors to open at Five o'Clock, and begin precisely at Seven.

No Money will, on any Account, be taken at the Door.

N. B. Places for the Boxes to be taken at the Office of the Theatre in Front-street, between the Hours of Nine and Two o'clock: After which Time, the Box-keeper will not attend. Ladies or Gentlemen, who would have Places kept for them, are desired to send their Servants to the Theatre at Four o'clock, otherwise their Places will be given up.

****
PHILADELPHIA: Printed by JAMES HUMPHREYS, JUN.

Playbill of a benefit performance of *1 Henry IV* on 25 March 1778 in The Southwark Theatre, Philadelphia. 8″ x 12 9/16″. This was during the British occupancy of the city, and the members of the cast were officers in the British army and navy. Reproduced by permission of The Library Company of Philadelphia.

The Origins
of the Shakespearian Playhouse

RICHARD HOSLEY

N a sense there are almost as many "origins" of the Elizabethan public and private playhouses—what I have called in my title the Shakespearian playhouse—as there were situations in which spectacular entertainment was presented before establishment of the first "regular" theaters in 1575-1577. Springs or fountains of varying importance include the Place or *platea* with scaffolds sited round its perimeter, pageant wagons, the tiltyard, the inn-yard, the courtyard of a castle or palace or great house, chapel- or altar-screens in churches, gateways or triumphal arches—and the list might be extended. But four origins of the Shakespearian playhouse are major tributary streams: the bull- or bearbaiting house, the hall, the hall screen, and the booth stage. These—as distinguished from the others mentioned—are "immediate" origins in the special sense that they were used for the performance of plays immediately before establishment of the regular playhouses, that they were so used after that development, and that each physically resembles a major component of those playhouses more closely than any other proposed origin. Investigators who have especially emphasized various of these four origins include W. J. Lawrence,[1] William Poel,[2] Sir Edmund Chambers,[3] Richard Southern,[4] C. Walter Hodges,[5] and Glynne Wickham.[6] In the present essay I should like to examine the animal-baiting houses and the hall screen in more detail than has hitherto been done, and to suggest a theory of origins that will account for the major components of the Shakespearian playhouse.

I

A hitherto unreproduced pictorial source for the Bankside baiting-houses provides us with new information about those buildings and makes possible a more precise theory of their influence upon the public playhouses. The source, a panoramic view of London from the south, is an engraving preserved in the

[1] "The Evolution and Influence of the Elizabethan Playhouse", in *The Elizabethan Playhouse* (1912), pp. 2, 6.

[2] "Some Notes on Shakespeare's Stage and Plays", *Bulletin of the John Rylands Library*, III (1916), 219, 220.

[3] *The Elizabethan Stage* (1923), II, 355.

[4] *The Open Stage* (1953), pp. 15-22; "On Reconstructing a Practicable Elizabethan Public Playhouse", *Shakespeare Survey 12* (1959), pp. 31-34; "The Contribution of the Interludes to Elizabethan Staging", in *Essays on Shakespeare and Elizabethan Drama in Honor of Hardin Craig* (1962), p. 14.

[5] *The Globe Restored* (1953), pp. 37, 171; 40-42.

[6] *Early English Stages*, vol. II, pt. 1 (1963).

print collection of the Folger Library.[7] (Plates 1, 2a.) It is entitled "A View of London about the Year 1560" and may be tentatively dated early in the 18th century.[7a] The view shows a bullbaiting house and the first Beargarden, both supposed to have been built around the middle of the 16th century.[8] (The Beargarden collapsed in 1583, and the bullbaiting house had apparently disappeared by 1593, for it is not shown in the first Norden Map.) In the "1560" View the two baiting-houses are similar. Each has a "round" frame two storeys high and is constructed in some sixteen or more bays. Each has a peaked roof from which four flags are flying. Spectators are depicted in the lower gallery of each baiting-house, and there appears to be a single spectator in the upper gallery of the Beargarden. Neither building has a hut or any visible stairs.

The 1560 View of London throws into sharp relief the two pictorial sources hitherto relied on for information about the Bankside baiting-houses—the Agas Map (1569-1590, printed 1631) and the Braun and Hohenberg (or Höfnagel) Map (1554-1558, printed in *Civitates orbis terrarum,* 1572). (Plate 2b, c.) These also show two baiting-houses, in approximately the same location as those depicted in the 1560 View. Since the Agas Map and the Braun and Hohenberg Map agree in numerous particularities, it is clear that they represent a single tradition. Significant concurrences of the two sources are the depiction of animals in the pits of the two baiting-houses, the four kennels to which dogs are chained, the three pools between the baiting-houses, the rectangular area immediately to the south of each baiting-house, and the two pairs of Bankside houses with ridges running at right angles to the river.

Of the two sources, it has usually been assumed[9] that the Agas Map is the "derived" document, Braun and Hohenberg the "substantive" one.[10] The inference follows easily from the earlier date of Braun and Hohenberg and

[7] I am indebted to Miss Dorothy Mason for invaluable assistance in my researches among the holdings of the Folger Library.

[7a] Mr. R. A. Skelton, Superintendent of the Map Room, British Museum, has kindly furnished more precise information about the 1560 View of London. "The print is an engraving made in 1738 for Maitland's *History of London.* It resembles the 1560 view attributed to Agas but with certain differences from the three surviving examples of the latter; for instance the 1738 print does not show the Royal Exchange (built in 1566). The extant impressions of the 'Agas' view are of course late, of the 17th century, and have had certain corrections made to them (e.g. the insertion of the Royal Exchange). The 1738 view has an imprint (apparently cropped from the Folger copy) reading 'Reduced to this Size from a Large Print in the Collection of S^r. Hans Sloane Bar^t. anno 1738'. The original in Sloane's collection has never been found and seems to have disappeared; it may have been an impression of the 'Agas' blocks in their original state.—The relationship of the various versions of this view (including the one engraved on pewter plates belonging to Vertue) is somewhat confused and difficult to reconstruct. The recent discovery of two plates of a large plan engraved (on fifteen or twenty copper plates), apparently about 1560, has however put the matter into a somewhat new light. One of these plates is now in the London Museum, and a pull from the other in the British Museum. Some information on this may be found in M. R. Holmes, *Moorfields in 1559: an engraved copper plate from the earliest known map of London* (London, H.M.S.O. for London Museum, 1963).—The most likely explanation of the differences in the various surviving versions is that not all of them derive from the 'Agas' map but that some go back directly to the copper-plate original. It is accordngly permissible to cite some of the later versions, where they differ from Agas, as independent testimony to the topography about 1560."

[8] Joseph Quincy Adams, *Shakespearean Playhouses* (1917), p. 124.

[9] For example, by I. A. Shapiro, "The Bankside Theatres: Early Engravings", *Shakespeare Survey 1* (1948), p. 26.

[10] The terms are used in the senses established by R. B. McKerrow, *Prolegomena for the Oxford Shakespeare* (1939), p. 8.

Plate 1. A View of London about the Year 1560 (courtesy of The Folger Shakespeare Library).

Plate 2. Three Representations of the Bankside Baiting-houses
(a) The "1560" View (courtesy of the Folger Library)
(b) The Agas Map (courtesy of the Guildhall Library, London)
(c) The Braun and Hohenberg Map (courtesy of the Folger Library)

Plate 3. The Great Hall Screen of Hampton Court Palace (by gracious permission of Her Majesty the Queen)

Plate 4. The Hall Screen of the Middle Temple (courtesy of The Honourable Society of the Middle Temple)

from its general artistic superiority. Nevertheless, the greater detail and presumably higher accuracy of the Agas Map as regards the baiting-houses incline me to the view that Agas is the more "original" source—or, to be more exact, that it is a source which (in the matter of the baiting-houses and their immediate environs) is closer to a presumed lost original than Braun and Hohenberg. In Agas each baiting-house has a peaked roof drawn with considerable sophistication. Significant details are the rounding of the ridge as it reverses direction, the angle of the roofs, and the shading on convex and concave surfaces of the roofs. These careful touches are absent from Braun and Hohenberg, where the roofs of the baiting-houses are depicted only by two concentric rings. Again, in the Agas Map the baiting-houses are represented as two-storey buildings, an interpretation made momentarily doubtful by the omission of posts from the inner face of each upper gallery but soon confirmed by the row of bressumers shown at mid-height in the outer face of each frame and by the depiction of a spectator in the upper gallery of the Beargarden. In Braun and Hohenberg the baiting-houses appear to be only one storey high. (The supposed error of telescoping two storeys into one may have resulted from the absence of posts from the upper gallery in the source—as in Agas—and from the Braun-and-Hohenberg artist's literal interpretation of the size of the human figures outside the baiting-houses. That the size of these figures in Agas, like that of the various animals, is conventionally exaggerated is suggested by the waist high height of the open door of the bullbaiting house, this being the same as the height of doors in nearby private houses.) Again, in Agas a door is shown leading into the bullbaiting house. This door is not represented in Braun and Hohenberg. (The supposed omission of a door is consistent with the impression that the persons standing outside each baiting-house in Braun and Hohenberg are not, as apparently in Agas, in process of entering or leaving the house, but are engaged rather in looking *through* the structure at the spectacle within—a mode of viewing that would lead us to suppose that we were concerned not with a roofed gallery but with a sort of circular corral with a single row of posts supporting a cornice or cap and thus defining breast-high openings in the barrier.)

Comparison shows that the 1560 View belongs to a tradition which is independent of that of the Agas Map. (It is possible that the Agas tradition may have slightly influenced the 1560 View, as for example in the text of the labels designating the two baiting-houses, or in the depiction of a single spectator only in the upper gallery of the Beargarden.) Significant variations in the 1560 View are baiting-house frames constructed in about sixteen bays (as opposed to about twenty in Agas), flags flying from the roofs of the baiting-houses, the absence of animals from the pits of the houses, the absence of human figures standing outside the houses, the absence of kennels and chained dogs, a single pool between the baiting-houses (as opposed to three in Agas), the absence of a rectangular space immediately to the south of each baiting-house, and the depiction (to the north of the bullbaiting house) of four (rather than two) Bankside houses with ridges running at right angles to the river. It seems unlikely that the 1560 View is the original document of its tradition, especially in view of its supposed late date, but the only other source I have seen which belongs to the 1560 tradition, the Wilkinson Map (in the Huntington Library), is of later date than, and in part derived from, the 1560 View. It therefore seems clear that the 1560 View of London provides us with a second substantive source (in addition to the Agas Map) for the Bankside baiting-houses.[11]

Considering the two substantive sources together, we may draw the following conclusions about the baiting-houses. They were "round" buildings with a pit open to the sky—what may be referred to in the strict sense of the word as *amphitheaters* (*OED*, 1, 2). They were apparently constructed in a large number of bays—perhaps about sixteen (1560 View), perhaps about twenty (Agas Map). They were of two storeys. Flags were sometimes flown from the roofs of the houses (1560 View). Apparently neither house had a hut or any other superstructure, nor is there any evidence for the stairs which in each house presumably gave access to the upper gallery. Finally, we may suppose that the pits of the baiting-houses were unpaved, for the better accommodation of the animals.

II

A hall screen runs the width of the lower end of the hall (opposite the dais), thus forming a passageway leading into the hall from the room or courtyard on either side of the end of the hall and from the "offices" (pantry, kitchen, buttery) situated beyond the end of the hall.[12] Hence the screen may conceal as many as five doors: one in each of the side walls of the hall, three (or sometimes fewer) in the end wall (see Fig. 4 below). The width of the passageway varies (not always in proportion with the size of the hall), being sometimes as narrow as 5 or 6 feet, sometimes as wide as 10 or 12. The screen itself usually has two doorways, but sometimes one and sometimes (though very rarely) three. In the Tudor period the doorways were usually without doors, though doors were generally placed in the doorways at a later period. Presumably hangings were often fitted up in, or in front of, the doorways, much as they occasionally are today (even in the case of doorways now fitted with doors). Since hall screens vary in length directly as the width of the containing halls, the largest screens are a bit over 40 feet long.

Originally the hall screen was only one storey high, but around the middle of the 16th century an important modification was effected in many examples, both new-built and reconstructed. The passageway was roofed over, so that the screen formed (so to speak) a long narrow box at the lower end of the hall. The top of the box constituted a floor, and this was frequently made into a gallery in one of two ways. In many examples the height of the screen was increased by a barrier about 3 feet high, the resulting gallery thus being "open". An illustration is the Great Hall screen of Hampton Court Palace (1531-1536). (Plate 3.) In other examples, however, the height of the screen was increased by a full second storey, the resulting gallery thus being "enclosed" and having (usually) a row of windows running along its length. An illustration is the hall

[11] Presumably the color drawing by William Smith (Adams, *Shakespearean Playhouses*, facing p. 120) is derived from the Agas tradition.

[12] My view of the hall screen is based on examination of surviving Tudor and Jacobean examples in London, Oxford, Cambridge, and elsewhere; and on the following printed sources: Thomas Garner and Arthur Stratton, *Domestic Architecture of England during the Tudor Period* (2nd ed., 1929), H. Avray Tipping, *English Homes* (1937), and the various surveys of the Royal Commission on Historical Monuments.

screen (1574) of the Middle Temple. (Plate 4.) (The doorways of the Middle Temple hall screen were originally without doors, the present doors having been added in 1671.) Thus we may distinguish two main classes of hall screen with gallery, the point of distinction being the treatment of the gallery as open or enclosed.

The Tudor hall screen is remarkably similar to the tiring-house façade of the Swan Playhouse as recorded in the De Witt drawing (c. 1596), and the similarity is especially pronounced if comparison of the tiring-house façade is made with a screen having an enclosed gallery. The two doors and windowed gallery of the tiring-house correspond closely to the two doorways and windowed gallery of the hall screen; and each of the two façades stands at the rear of an area used for acting: the playhouse stage in the one case, the floor of the hall or a stage set up against the hall screen in the other.

But the similarity is not only general. It extends also to various specific dimensions, as can be seen from a detailed comparison of the Swan tiring-house façade with the hall screens at Hampton Court Palace and the Middle Temple. To assist the comparison, let us imagine a large stage placed in front of each hall screen. Stages set up against hall screens are recorded in the *Wits* frontispiece (1662) and in two drawings by Inigo Jones preserved in Lansdowne Manuscript 1171 in the British Museum, both relating to a production with scenes of the lost pastoral play *Florimène* (1635).[13] The stage depicted by Jones is 40 feet wide (the width of the containing hall, the Great Hall at Whitehall) and raked from a height of 4 feet, 6 inches, at the front to a height of 5 feet, 6 inches, near the back. Again, a stage 40 feet square and 4 feet high ("wth wheeles to goe on") was provided for the performance of Jonson's *Masque of Blackness* in the "old" Banqueting House at Whitehall in 1605, and a stage 4 feet high on trestles was set up for the performance of the same writer's *Masque of Queens* in the "new" Whitehall Banqueting House in 1609.[14] Figs. 1 and 2 are generalized elevations of the hall screens at Hampton Court Palace and the Middle Temple, each with a stage 4 feet high placed in front of it and running the full length of the screen (in each case 40 feet long).[15] These diagrams may be compared with a generalized elevation of the Swan tiring-house façade (Fig. 3), as reconstructed by the present writer.[16] The several significant dimensions (in some cases approximate) are set forth in the following table.

HALL SCREEN AND TIRING-HOUSE FAÇADE: A TABLE OF CORRESPONDING DIMENSIONS

	Hampton Court	Middle Temple	Swan
Width of stage	40′0″	40′0″	43′0″
Height of stage	4′0″	4′0″	5′6″
Length of screen (façade)	40′0″	40′0″	41′0″

[13] The drawings are reproduced by Richard Southern, *Changeable Scenery: Its Origin and Development in the British Theatre* (1952), Plates 4, 5. The ground plan is reproduced also by Allardyce Nicoll, *Stuart Masques and the Renaissance Stage* (1938), Fig. 4. In a later publication I shall argue the proposition that both drawings relate to the stage of *Florimène* in the Great Hall at Whitehall.

[14] *Ben Jonson*, ed. C. H. Herford and Percy Simpson, X (1950), 445, 494.

[15] I am extremely grateful to my friend Richard Southern for making the drawings which illustrate this paper.

[16] "Reconstitution du théâtre du Swan", in *Le lieu théâtral à la Renaissance*, ed. Jean Jacquot (1964).

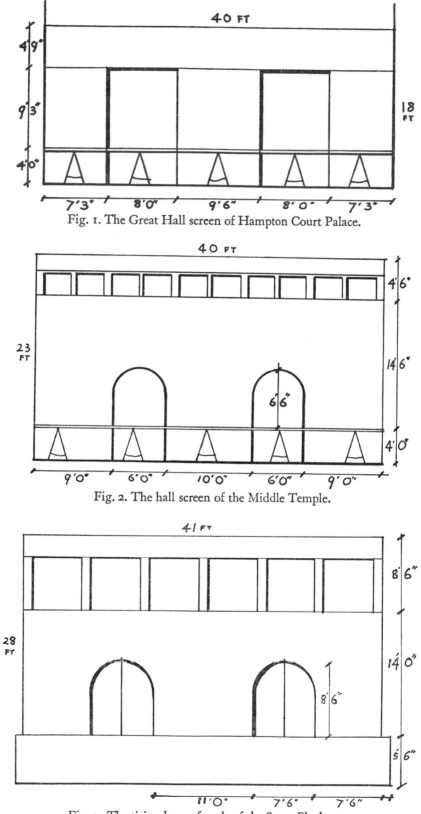

Fig. 1. The Great Hall screen of Hampton Court Palace.

Fig. 2. The hall screen of the Middle Temple.

Fig. 3. The tiring-house façade of the Swan Playhouse.

HALL SCREEN AND TIRING-HOUSE FAÇADE: A TABLE OF CORRESPONDING DIMENSIONS

	Hampton Court	Middle Temple	Swan
Height of screen (façade) above floor (yard)	18′0″	23′0″	28′0″
Height of gallery barrier above stage	14′0″	14′6″	14′0″
Height of doorways above floor	13′3″	10′6″	——
Height of doorways above stage	9′3″	6′6″	8′6″
Width of doorways	8′0″	6′0″	7′6″
Space between doorways	9′6″	10′0″	11′0″
Space outside each doorway	7′3″	9′0″	7′6″

Correspondence of form and dimension between the Swan tiring-house façade and the Tudor hall screen is reflected in the timber framing of the two façades. Structurally, a hall screen is a partition framed of six principal posts placed so as to define five divisions of approximately equal width (see Fig. 4). The first, third, and fifth divisions are usually boarded in to become solid panels, whereas the second and fourth divisions are left open to serve as door-ways. (In a three-doorway screen the third division is also left open.) The fivefold nature of the hall screen is sometimes emphasized (as at the Middle Temple) by the use of six decorative columns in front of the principal posts; and it also tends to be emphasized in a screen with an enclosed gallery, for in such a screen the supports of the gallery roof usually define five openings of approximately equal width—though the basic pentadic pattern is sometimes obscured, as at the Middle Temple for example, by additional supports which subdivide each of the five basic openings in two, thus producing a gallery with ten openings. In the first storey of the Swan tiring-house façade there must have been a similar division of the frame into five sections through the use of six principal posts—two flanking each door and one at each end of the frame (see Fig. 5). In the second storey, seven rather than six supports were used, with the result that the gallery face of the Swan tiring-house consisted of six divisions instead of the usual five of a hall screen with enclosed gallery.

III

On the basis of the resemblance between the tiring-house façade of the Swan Playhouse and a hall screen with an enclosed gallery like that of the Middle Temple (1574), I would suggest that the Swan tiring-house originated in the hall screen; or, more precisely, since the Swan (built in 1595) presumably fol-lowed the architectural tradition of the earlier public playhouses the Rose (c. 1587), the Curtain (1577), and the Theater (1576),[17] that the tiring-house of the Elizabethan public playhouse originated in the Tudor hall screen. Thus we may suppose that James Burbage, when he came to build the Theater in 1576, took a hall screen with an enclosed gallery as the model for his tiring-house, simply setting doors in the doorways of the received form as a necessary pro-tection of the tiring-house interior against the weather; and that the form re-mained essentially the same in the Curtain and the Rose, passing unchanged

[17] The playhouse at Newington Butts (c. 1586) has been left out of consideration as an almost entirely unknown quantity.

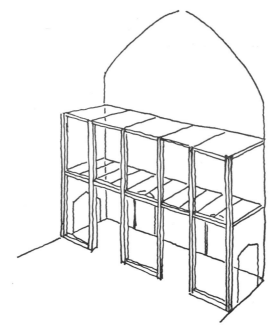

Fig. 4. The timber framing of a hall screen
with an enclosed gallery.

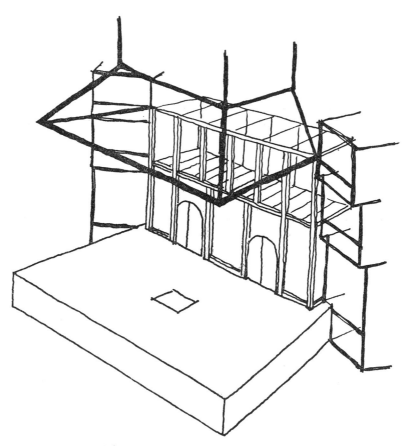

Fig. 5. The timber framing of the Swan tiring-house.

from those playhouses and the Theater to the Swan in 1595. Furthermore, since the plays assignable to later public playhouses have, in general, the same staging needs as those assignable to the earlier ones, we may suppose also that the tiring-houses of later public playhouses—the Globe (1599), the Fortune (1600), the Red Bull (c. 1605), the Hope (1613-1614), the Second Globe (1614), and the Second Fortune (1623)—were essentially similar to that of the Swan, the only difference being that one or two of the later public playhouses (like one or two of the earlier ones) may have had a three-door instead of a two-door tiring-house.

We have no record of the use of a baiting-house as a theater. Nevertheless, if the Hope was later used for the baiting of bears, there seems no reason why the Beargarden should not earlier have been used for the performance of plays. Hence it seems reasonable to suppose that, during the period immediately preceding construction of the first public playhouses, the players occasionally set up a booth stage within a baiting-house, much as suggested by Hodges in one of his drawings in *The Globe Restored* (p. 171). The advantages of such an arrangement would have been obvious, and hence we may suppose further that the essence of Burbage's action, when he built the Theater in 1576, was to adopt the form of a baiting-house and convert it into a playhouse. In order to do so he made, presumably, five major innovations in the received form. First (though not necessarily immediately), he paved the ring, thus transforming what had been a pit into a yard. (That the playhouse yards were paved is a speculation, there being no clear evidence on the question, presumably the Hope—called by Jonson in 1614, soon after its opening, "as dirty as Smithfield, and as stinking ever whit" in the induction to *Bartholomew Fair*—resembled the baiting-houses in not being paved.) Here Burbage's model may well have been the pavement of an inn-yard. Second, he erected a stage in the yard. Here his model was the booth stage of the market theater, built rather larger than any recorded example and also as a permanent rather than a temporary structure. Third, he erected a permanent tiring-house in place of the booth presumably fitted up in front of a few bays of the frame in the earlier temporary arrangement in a baiting-house. Here, as I have suggested, his model was the screen of a Tudor hall with an enclosed gallery, modified to withstand the weather by the addition of doors and occasionally furnished with hangings in, or in front of, the (open) doors so as to reproduce an essential characteristic of the curtained booth. Fourth, he added a third gallery to the frame, for the Bankside baiting-houses were apparently two-storey buildings. Here he may have been influenced by contemporary inns having three storeys or by a three-storey tiltyard scaffold. And fifth, he built a cover partly over the stage, supported by posts rising from the yard and surmounted by a hut. The precise origin of such a "stage superstructure" is difficult to identify, but it must have been designed chiefly to house suspension-gear for flying effects, and such gear, as Wickham points out,[18] had been used in the English street theater as early as the end of the 14th century. Possibly exterior stair-towers, as we know them from Hollar's Long View of London (1647) or perhaps in more elementary form (open, for example, instead of roofed and enclosed), already existed in the baiting-houses (though unrecorded in the pictorial sources) and were taken

[18] *Early English Stages,* I (1959), 94.

over from them by Burbage along with the "round" frame. One additional consideration strengthens the theory that the frame of the Elizabethan public playhouse originated in the frame of the baiting-house.[19] This is the probability that the well-known custom of flying a flag from the playhouse huts had its origin in a custom, recorded in the "1560" View of London, of flying flags from the baiting-house roofs.

It has seemed desirable to discuss the public playhouse before the private, for the reason that we have a pictorial source for the interior of a public play-house (the De Witt drawing), not to mention numerous pictorial sources for the exteriors of public playhouses, whereas we have no (known) pictorial source of either kind for a private playhouse. Sound method would seem to require that we work from the area for which there is pictorial evidence, however difficult of interpretation, toward the area for which there is none. But the private play-house may well be the anterior form. It is generally accepted that the form of the private playhouse originated in the Tudor hall—a reasonable supposition in view of the fact that the Second Blackfriars and the Whitefriars were created by restoring or converting existing halls, and in view also of the fact that the hall seems to have been the lowest common denominator of indoor theatrical production before establishment of the regular playhouses: we find, or may suppose, performances of plays in private houses both great and small, castles, schools, University Colleges, Inns of Court, royal palaces, ecclesiastical buildings —all (as a rule) equipped with halls. It is perhaps an unanswerable question whether the tiring-house of the public playhouse (as recorded in the De Witt drawing) was developed directly from the hall screen or from the tiring-house of a private playhouse which was itself an adaptation of the hall screen—but at least the question must be asked. Certainly we must allow for the second pos-sibility, especially since, as William A. Armstrong points out,[20] a private play-house, the theater of the Paul's Boys, was apparently established as early as 1575, a year before the first public playhouse, the Theater.

However that may be, we may suppose that the creators of the earlier private playhouses—the Paul's Playhouse (1575), the First Blackfriars (1576), the Sec-ond Blackfriars (1600), and the Whitefriars (c. 1606)—either adapted an existing hall screen as a tiring-house or, if the room or hall converted into a playhouse was without a screen, built a tiring-house on the model of a hall screen, much as the builders of the first public playhouses did. (As in the case of the public play-houses, the hangings and the essential function of the private-theater tiring-house were presumably derived from the booth stage.) The supposition explains why the staging needs of private-theater plays are, in general, the same as those of public-theater plays, and it is confirmed by two considerations: the use of a music-room over the stage in the private playhouses,[21] this apparently being a development of the custom of locating musicians in the gallery of a hall screen;

---

[19] The theory applies to the "round" playhouses and not, of course, to the square Fortune, the shape of which may have been influenced by the tiltyard, the courtyard of a great house or palace, or the inn-yard.

[20] *The Elizabethan Private Theatres* (1958), p. 3.

[21] A music-room over the stage was apparently peculiar to the private playhouses down to about 1608, after which date there is evidence for music-rooms also in the public playhouses. The subject is discussed in my article, "Was There a Music-Room in Shakespeare's Globe?", *Shake-speare Survey 13* (1960), pp. 113-123.

and by the fact that the *Wits* frontispiece (1662) records a one-doorway hall screen with an enclosed gallery which has been converted into a tiring-house by the addition of hangings above and below. Presumably (on evidence of the essentially unchanging staging requirements of private-theater plays) the later, new-built private playhouses—Porter's Hall (1615), the Cockpit or Phoenix (1617), and Salisbury Court (1629)—had tiring-houses generally similar to those of the earlier private playhouses. One or more of the private-theater tiring-houses may have been equipped with three doors, either through adaptation of a three-doorway hall screen or through construction of a tiring-house on the analogy of such a screen.[22]

University of Arizona

[22] I am indebted to the Director and Trustees of the Folger Library for a fellowship grant which made possible the research underlying this essay.

(BY PERMISSION.)

—————✳—————

At the Theatre in Baltimore,

On TUESDAY EVENING, the 4th of *March*, 1783,

Will be prefented, the TRAGEDY of

ROMEO AND JULIET.

Romeo,   Mr.   W   A   L   L ;

Benvolio,   Mr.   H   E   A   R   D ;

Tibalt,   Mr.   T   I   L   Y   A   R   D ;

Paris,   Mr.   S   M   I   T   H ;

Capulet,   Mr.   L   E   W   I   S ;

Friar Lawrence,   Mr.   D   A   V   I   D   S ;

Prince, Mr. Browne ; *Montague,* Mr. Church ; *Peter,* Mr. Atherton ;

Mercutio,   Mr.   R   Y   A   N.

Lady Capulet,   Mrs.   F   O   S   T   E   R ;

Nurfe,   Mrs.   P   A   R   S   O   N   S ;

And *Juliet,*   Mrs.   R   Y   A   N.

In Act I. a MASQUERADE.

End of Act IV. a FUNERAL PROCESSION
and SOLEMN DIRGE.

To which will be added, a PANTOMIME ENTERTAINMENT, called

THE WITCHES;

Or, *Birth, Vagaries,* and *Death* of

HARLEQUIN.

Harlequin,   Mr.   A   T   H   E   R   T   O   N ;

Pantaloon,   Mr.   H   E   A   R   D ;

Maccaroni,   Mr.   D   A   V   I   D   S ;

Clown,   Monf.   R   O   U   S   S   E   L ;

Hecate,   Mr.   W   A   L   L ;

Witches, Meffrs. Lewis and Smith ; Mrs. Fofter, Mifs Wall, &c. &c.

Watchman, Mr. Tilyard ;

Columbine,   Mrs.   P   O   T   T   E   R.

TICKETS to be had at Mr. *James Young's,* near the Poft-Office
---at the *Exchange Coffee-Houfe,* Fell's-Point---and at the *Office*
of the *Theatre,* where Places for the Boxes may be taken, from
Ten to Twelve o'Clock every Day.

〰〰〰〰〰〰〰〰〰〰〰〰〰〰

BALTIMORE: Printed by M. K. GODDARD

Playbill of a performance of *Romeo and Juliet* in Baltimore on 4 March 1783.
7⅛" x 13⅛". Reproduced by permission of The Folger Shakespeare Library.

Marlowe and Shakespeare

IRVING RIBNER

N the widespread celebration of the four hundredth anniversary of Shakespeare's birth, the birth some two months earlier of Christopher Marlowe seems almost to have been forgotten. This is regrettable because in any estimate of the achievement of English Renaissance drama these two titans deserve to be considered together. I do not believe that this is so because, as is commonly stated, Marlowe laid the foundations for Shakespeare's dramatic artistry, but rather because these two men represent diametrically opposed reactions to the complex of Elizabethan life, each in his own way forging a poetically valid vision of reality beyond the comprehension of the other. Born in the same year, both were of humble origins, springing from the merchant classes just beginning to emerge as an important element in English life, one the son of a master shoemaker of Canterbury, the other of a Warwickshire farmer and petty merchant. Both made their mark upon the public stage, the one coming with an M.A. from Cambridge and the other from what still remains the source of controversy among scholars, but which may well have been a stint of teaching in the provinces.[1] Both confronted, as no dramatist ever had before them, the crucial issues of man's position in the universe at a time in history when old conceptions of universal harmony, order, and degree were breaking down under the pressure of an awakening and expanding world. It was a time of new social mobility reflected in the very rise from obscurity of these poets themselves. Faced with cosmic problems in an age of flux and uncertainty, Marlowe and Shakespeare developed in contrary directions, so that the plays of each man seem to mirror to a consummate degree an opposing reaction to the Renaissance world in which both lived.

Marlowe begins his career upon the public stage with the most optimistic of Elizabethan plays, the first part of *Tamburlaine,* with its triumphant glorification of human potential, singing the thirst for power as the highest attribute of man:

> The thirst of reign and sweetness of a crown,
> That caused the eldest son of heavenly Ops
> To thrust his doting father from his chair,
> And place himself in the imperial heaven,
> Moved me to manage arms against thy state.
> What better precedent than mighty Jove?
> Nature, that framed us of four elements
> Warring within our breasts for regiment,
> Doth teach us all to have aspiring minds.

[1] Cf. J. S. Smart, *Shakespeare, Truth and Tradition* (London, 1928), pp. 86-87.

Our souls, whose faculties can comprehend
The wondrous architecture of the world
And measure every wandering planet's course,
Still climbing after knowledge infinite,
And always moving as the restless spheres,
Wills us to wear ourselves and never rest,
Until we reach the ripest fruit of all,
That perfect bliss and sole felicity,
The sweet fruition of an earthly crown.

(II. vii. 12-28)[2]

Marlowe dwells with sensuous delight upon the joys of kingship, rendering it even greater than the power of the gods themselves:

A god is not so glorious as a king.
I think the pleasure they enjoy in heaven
Can not compare with kingly joys in earth:
To wear a crown enchased with pearl and gold,
Whose virtues carry with it life and death;
To ask, and have, command and be obeyed;
When looks breed love, with looks to gain the prize,
Such power attractive shines in princes' eyes.

(II. v. 57-64)

In *Henry VI, Part Two,* if not the earliest of Shakespeare's plays, as many continue to believe, certainly among the very first, and written in any case not more than a year later than *Tamburlaine,*[3] we find the young Richard of Gloucester uttering lines which at once recall Marlowe's play:

How sweet a thing it is to wear a crown,
Within whose circuit is Elysium,
And all that poets feign of bliss and joy.

(I. ii. 29-31)

Marlowe's play closes with his conqueror the master of the world, enjoying the human felicity he had envisaged, and in the sequel play it is only death which is able at last to defeat him, and then only at the very height of his triumph. The first part of *Tamburlaine* is a dramatic affirmation of the hero's visionary aspirations, but in the play in which Richard speaks there is no such affirmation. The three parts of *Henry VI* offer one long bloody pageant of the futility of the quest for earthly power, the feeling of the trilogy being perhaps best expressed in the words of the sad king Henry VI as he sits upon his molehill, recording not the joys of kingship but their sorrows:

Gives not the hawthorn bush a sweeter shade
To shepherds, looking on their silly sheep,
Than doth a rich embroider'd canopy
To kings, that fear their subjects' treachery?
O yes! it doth; a thousand-fold it doth.

---

2 All Marlowe references are to *The Complete Plays of Christopher Marlowe,* ed. Irving Ribner (New York, 1963). Shakespeare references are to the Oxford edition by W. J. Craig.

3 A. S. Cairncross, *The Second Part of King Henry VI* (London, 1957), dates the play most reasonably in 1590, the same year in which *Tamburlaine* was printed for the first time.

And to conclude, the shepherd's homely curds,
His cold thin drink out of his leather bottle,
His wonted sleep under a fresh tree's shade,
All which secure and sweetly he enjoys,
Is far beyond a prince's delicates,
His viands sparkling in a golden cup,
His body couched in a curious bed,
When care, mistrust, and treason wait on him.
(II. v. 42-54)

And in the death of the aspiring Duke of York, and that of his son King Richard III in the succeeding play, are graphic illustrations of what King Henry here laments. Instead of Marlowe's celebration of victory in self-sufficient human power, bound by no higher law, in the early Shakespeare there is an awareness of human limitation and frailty, the knowledge that kingship imposes upon weak humanity an awesome burden and responsibility, and that dwelling upon order and degree which runs through all of the plays of his canon.

Thus both poets begin, close in time, but with utterly different conceptions of the human condition, and each poet continues to move in his own direction. The lustful exuberance of the first part of *Tamburlaine* is succeeded by a second part with a new awareness of the limitation imposed upon humanity by death, and with a glimpse of the human price of power in the deaths of Calyphas and Olympia. When Marlowe comes to write *The Massacre at Paris*, we have not the victory of the aspiring superman but his ignominious defeat, cuckolded by his wife, trapped, and treacherously slain, with the virtuous Henry of Navarre winning whatever final victory the play entails. Near the end of his career, in *Edward II*, Marlowe casts the double tragedy of a king who is destroyed by his inability to wield absolute power and of a Mortimer destroyed by his very exercise of it. Marlowe comes at last to a point of negation in which the youthful values of *1 Tamburlaine* are revealed as merely vain illusion, and he can offer no new meaningful values in their stead.

Shakespeare's exploration of kingship and power leads him instead to the glorious victory of his "mirror of all Christian kings", Henry V. He continues always to dwell upon the heavy burden of rule which had occupied him in his earliest plays; there is probably no more perfect statement of the human cost of power than that in *2 Henry IV*, when a sick and weary King Henry repeats the motifs Shakespeare had expressed years before:

Canst thou, O partial sleep! give thy repose
To the wet sea-boy in an hour so rude,
And in the calmest and most stillest night,
With all appliances and means to boot,
Deny it to a king? Then, happy low, lie down!
Uneasy lies the head that wears a crown.
(III. i. 26-31)

But at the same time we have as the theme of Shakespeare's second tetralogy the education of the king to bear his burden and responsibility, his learning to separate the public from the private man when rule demands it, but to keep his public virtues grounded always in the private, so that Henry V, while he can condemn the Earl of Cambridge for treason, may still be a brother to his men and cheer them with "a little touch of Harry in the night".

Shakespeare's kings must learn to exercise their power in a world of degree and order in which the divine presence is always felt. Marlowe's exercise theirs in an intrinsically hostile world upon which order can be imposed only by the power of the ruler himself. The absolute authority of the king, without responsibility to god or subject, appears even in *Dido Queen of Carthage:*

> Those that dislike what Dido gives in charge,
> Command my guard to slay for their offence.
> Shall vulgar peasants storm at what I do?
> The ground is mine that gives them sustenance,
> The air wherein they breathe, the water, fire,
> All that they have, their lands, their goods, their lives;
> And I, the goddess of all these, command
> Æneas ride as Carthaginian king.
>
> (IV. iv. 71-78)

In this very preoccupation with power in the absolute, we find an alienation of the poet himself from the basic concerns of humanity. Marlowe's striving supermen must negate all human ties, as Tamburlaine does in ordering the deaths of the virgins of Damascus, and in their defiance of common morality—to which, owing no allegiance to the God who is its source, they can never be subject— they often become, like the Guise in *The Massacre at Paris,* monstrous in their inhumanity. Shakespeare's *Richard III* is close to *The Massacre at Paris* in dramatic structure as well as time of composition.[4] Both heroes are virtual prototypes of the aspiring "Machiavel", but Shakespeare's Richard is capable in his final moments of a terror and even a remorse which relate him to ordinary humanity as the Guise is never related.

This alienation from common human concerns is apparent in the treatment of love in Marlowe's *Dido, Queen of Carthage,*[5] which we need only compare with *Romeo and Juliet.* For Marlowe love is the weakness which momentarily stays the superman Æneas from his heroic destiny, and Dido's death, the price of that weakness, is of small consequence in the great scheme of things manipulated by the gods whose end is the founding of Rome. In *Romeo and Juliet,* the love of man and woman is an all-embracing commitment which causes youth to grow in maturity and wisdom and which, while it may lead to death, is the force which heals the ancient hatreds of society, restoring harmony and order.[6]

Shakespeare and Marlowe are the only two dramatists of their age whose works include a play in which a principal character is a Jew. It is not true, as is sometimes supposed, that Elizabethan stage convention made of the Jew a stereotyped caricature of the devil. No matter what contemporary attitudes towards Jews may have been—and they were never simple[7]—there just are not

---

[4] It is impossible to date *The Massacre* with any certainty, but it must have been written sometime between 1590 and Marlowe's death in 1593. *Richard III* was probably written between June 28, 1592, and the end of 1593. Cf. J. D. Wilson, ed., *Richard III* (Cambridge, 1954), pp. ix-x.

[5] The share of Thomas Nashe in this play, which was printed in 1594 with both names upon the title-page, cannot have been a very large one, if any sign of their possible collaboration remains at all in the text which has come down to us.

[6] I have developed this theme in *Patterns in Shakespearian Tragedy* (London, 1960), pp. 25-35.

[7] For those who still believe that either Marlowe or Shakespeare based their Jews upon their

enough Jews in the extant Elizabethan drama to support such a supposition. Indeed, the one notable portrait of a Jew earlier than Marlowe, Gerontus, the Jew of Robert Wilson's *The Three Ladies of London* (1584), although a simple morality play symbol of usury, is not treated unsympathetically.[8]

When *The Merchant of Venice* and *The Jew of Malta* are compared—and it is perhaps inevitable that they should be—it is usually with the assumption that Shakespeare imitated Marlowe, although critics have found it difficult to agree on just what form this supposed imitation took. To some we have Shakespare palliating the antisemitism of Marlowe with a more sympathetic portrait of a Jew; to others we have Shakespeare striving to outdo Marlowe in antisemitism by presenting a more sympathetic view of the Christian world than Marlowe's so that the blackness of his Jewish stereotype may stand out in sharper contrast.[9]

That *The Jew of Malta* exerted much influence upon *The Merchant of Venice* is a questionable proposition which can be positively neither denied nor affirmed. The elopement of Jessica, supposed commonly to have been inspired by Abigail of Marlowe's play, has its probable origins, as Geoffrey Bullough points out,[10] in the *Novellino* of Masuccio of Salerno. It is, at any rate, not so close to Marlowe's play that it could not have appeared in Shakespeare's whether or not *The Jew of Malta* ever had been written.[11]

That Shylock owes much to Barabas, or that Shakespeare is indebted to Marlowe for "much of the atmosphere of his Jewish theme" as Bullough holds (p. 456), are dubious propositions at best. The differences between Shylock and Barabas are far greater than any similarity. Each, of course, is influenced by common Elizabethan stereotyped notions about Jews, but more than that, each is shaped by his position in a play which in its essential elements, theme, structure, and general conception of reality is entirely alien to the other. If these two plays are to be compared, it must not be for what we may learn about the influence of one dramatist upon the other, but for the insight such comparison may afford into the vast gulf which divides the two major Elizabethan dramatists.

---

own contemporary observations of Jewish life, the result of C. J. Sisson's investigations may be pertinent: "Full toleration certainly was not yet achieved. But the Jews in London had the immense comfort of communal life, undisturbed, with full freedom to carry on their trades and professions, and even the further solace of the regular practice of religious rites in the home, even if in secret. The Jewish problem was, in truth, no problem in the reign of Elizabeth. The Jews that London knew, and that Shakespeare might have met, were not Shylocks." Cf. "A Colony of Jews in Shakespeare's England", *Essays and Studies*, XXIII (1938), 38-51.

8 M. J. Landa, *The Jew in Drama* (London, 1926), pp. 53-54, finds this play a notable exception to the general tradition of Jewish vilification in pre-Shakespearian drama, but he can find little evidence of this tradition other than the Jews in the medieval plays of the crucifixion, the Croxton *Play of the Sacrament*, and Stephen Gosson's elliptical reference to *The Jew*, a play about which, unfortunately, we know nothing.

9 Cf. H. B. Charlton, *Shakespearian Comedy* (London, 1949), p. 127: "About 1594, public sentiment in England was roused to an outbreak of traditional Jew-baiting; and for good and evil, Shakespeare the man was like his fellows. He planned a *Merchant of Venice* to let the Jew dog have it, and thereby to gratify his own patriotic pride of race."

10 *Narrative and Dramatic Sources of Shakespeare* (London, 1957), I, 456-457.

11 The old notion that Shakespeare's play was written to capitalize upon a wave of antisemitism following the Lopez affair, and marked by revival of *The Jew of Malta* which had fifteen performances in 1594, the year of Lopez's execution, rests upon the supposed allusion to Lopez at IV. i. 133-138. That this allusion is questionable indeed has been well shown by J. R. Brown, ed., *The Merchant of Venice* (London, 1955), pp. xxiii-xxiv.

The Merchant of Venice is a comedy of affirmation whose subject is love, while *The Jew of Malta* is a tragedy of defeat and negation whose subject is hatred. If Shylock is to be compared with Barabas and Jessica with Abigail, it must always be within this context. That there is, in spite of the crude buffoonery of the final acts of *The Jew of Malta,* a tragic conception which comes through the imperfect version of Marlowe's play that has come down to us, I have elsewhere suggested.[12] We have in Barabas the defiant heathen wronged by Christian "policy" who, seeking revenge upon his wrongers, adopts the same "policy" they have used against him, and by its corrupting force is himself destroyed. This is a tragic progression, but unlike the tragedies of Shakespeare, it is one without victory or affirmation of any kind, for those who survive at the end of the play are as evil as Barabas; they have triumphed merely by an exercise of "policy" more skillful than his, and the final element in the collapse of Barabas' own "policy", as Harry Levin has suggested,[13] has been his need for love which has caused him to trust those whom the true man of "policy" would have known never could be trusted. Rather than the Shakespearian promise of rebirth, such as comes at the end of *Hamlet, Lear,* or *Macbeth,* we have only the continuance of a vitiated moral system whose Christianity is a hypocritical and hollow pretense.

In this vision of human futility, Abigail serves as the innocent victim. One recent critic[14] has seen her as a saint-like figure and argued that in her supposed salvation is Marlowe's affirmation of an orthodox Christian position. But there is no salvation for Abigail. That she is the symbol of the sacrifice demanded by the corrupt world of the play is made clear in the first lines in which she is mentioned:

> I have no charge, nor many children,
> But one sole daughter, whom I hold as dear
> As Agamemnon did his Iphigen;
> And all I have is hers.   (I. i. 134-137)

But this Iphigen must be sacrificed for no noble cause. As the instrument of her father's villainous revenge, she must, in spite of herself, participate in the murder of the man she truly loves. When she has been poisoned, she professes Christianity and dies with the hope of salvation:

> Ah gentle friar,
> Convert my father that he may be saved,
> And witness that I die a Christian. (III. v. 36-40)

But the bitter irony of her dying hopes is made clear not only by our immediate knowledge that the conversion of Barabas is impossible, but in the coarse sexual terms which her death is greeted:

> Ay, and a virgin too; that grieves me most.
> But I must to the Jew, and exclaim on him,
> And make him stand in fear of me. (41-43)

---

[12] "Marlowe's 'Tragicke Glasse' ", in *Essays on Shakespeare and Elizabethan Drama in Honor of Hardin Craig* (Columbia, Mo., 1962), pp. 101-104.

[13] *The Overreacher* (Cambridge, Mass., 1952), pp. 78-79.

[14] Douglas Cole, *Suffering and Evil in the Plays of Christopher Marlowe* (Princeton, 1962), pp. 129-131.

Not only does the friar lament above all else the death of a seducible virgin, but rather than seek the conversion of Barabas, he will use this death confession as an instrument of "policy" himself. He will attempt to win gold in the same immoral game played by Barabas, Ferneze, and Calymath. The "conversion" they do attempt to effect is revealed as the most patent and gross hypocrisy, and the final issue of Abigail's acceptance of the "true faith" is the self-destruction of the two friars as they vie with one another for the gold of Barabas.

Gold is a dominant poetic motif in *The Jew of Malta* as it is in Shakespeare's *Merchant of Venice*. In both plays it is revealed finally as the worthless negation of love, but in Shakespeare's play we are offered a meaningful contrary value, whereas in Marlowe's we are offered none. *The Merchant of Venice* is rich in biblical allusion and analogy,[15] and even if we are reluctant to accept the notion of Antonio as a consistent symbol of Christ[16] we must see the play as an affirmation of ethical values basic to Christian belief. In the opposition between Shylock and Antonio, we have, as has often been pointed out,[17] the conflict between justice and mercy. As mercy is a reflection of the love of God for man, this theme is woven into the stories of the wooing of Portia and the elopement of Jessica. The highest reflection in terms of human love of God's divine love for man is the kind of love reflected in Antonio's sacrifice for his friend, of Bassanio's willingness to choose blindly and hazard all, and of Jessica's readiness to leave her father and his gold for Christian salvation. These are reflections of the supreme love of God for man which Portia evokes in her plea that Shylock spare the life of Antonio, in spite of the justice of his cause:

> Therefore, Jew,
> Though justice be thy plea, consider this,
> That in the course of justice none of us
> Should see salvation: we do pray for mercy,
> And that same prayer doth teach us all to render
> The deeds of mercy. (IV.i. 197-202)

Shakespeare's play involves a conflict between gold, the evanescent, meaningless value of this world, and love, the permanent value of heaven, and in this conflict it is love that triumphs, whereas in Marlowe's play love—in the fidelity of Abigail, and in Barabas' need for companionship—breeds only greater destruction. This difference between Marlowe's play and Shakespeare's shapes entirely disparate roles for their Jewish characters. While Barabas and Abigail are destroyed by a world of "policy" in which Christianity is a pretense and love has no place, Shylock and Jessica are saved by the reality of love, and they both come at the end to a recognition of the position to which Shylock had at first stood opposed.

It is fitting that Jessica and Lorenzo should open the final act at Belmont and experience the harmony of creation which the total play affirms:

> How sweet the moonlight sleeps upon this bank!
> Here will we sit, and let the sounds of music

[15] See Barbara K. Lewalski, "Biblical Allusion and Allegory in *The Merchant of Venice*", *SQ*, XIII (1962), 327-343.

[16] See J. A. Bryant, Jr., *Hyppolyta's View* (Lexington, Ky., 1961), pp. 33-51.

[17] Cf. for instance, Nevill Coghill, "The Basis of Shakespearean Comedy", *Essays and Studies*, III (1950), 1-28.

> Creep in our ears: soft stillness and the night
> Become the touches of sweet harmony.
> Sit, Jessica: look, how the floor of heaven
> Is thick inlaid with patines of bright gold:
> There's not the smallest orb which thou behold'st
> But in his motion like an angel sings,
> Still quiring to the young-eyed cherubins. (V. i. 54-63)

The conversion of Jessica is an obvious and crucial element in the play. The long stage tradition, stemming perhaps from Edmund Kean, which would see Shylock as the eternally defiant, demonic figure, deeply wronged, has tended to obscure the fact that Shylock is converted as well, and that this is just as real an element in the play. The conversion of the Jews was an essential element in medieval antisemitic legend, and it is the culminating feature of the crude Croxton *Play of the Sacrament,* dated usually in the latter half of the fifteenth century, where Jonathas' experiences lead him at last to embrace Christianity. The punishment which Shylock at the end receives is his reception into the Christian community in which he will assume the normal obligations of that community, providing his daughter with a dowry and leaving his wealth upon his death to the son-in-law who is his only heir:

> So please my lord the duke, and all the court,
> To quit the fine for one half of his goods,
> I am content; so he will let me have
> The other half in use, to render it,
> Upon his death, unto the gentleman
> That lately stole his daughter:
> Two things provided more, that, for this favour,
> He presently become a Christian;
> The other, that he do record a gift,
> Here in the court, of all he dies possess'd,
> Unto his son Lorenzo, and his daughter. (IV. i. 381-391)

Shylock's final lines:

> I pray you give me leave to go from hence;
> I am not well. Send the deed after me,
> And I will sign it. (396-398)

are perhaps deliberately ambiguous in their intent, and they have furnished much room for critical speculation. Shakespeare captures the essence of the proud man defeated and broken, but certainly there is in the lines the suggestion that what Shylock has stood for has been defeated and is no more. If this is so, he will be a better and a happier man, and this is one reason that an audience has no difficulty in accepting the view of Jessica's carefree happiness at the beginning of the succeeding act, which might otherwise seem grossly cruel and unnatural. Shakespeare's Jew comes at last to generate love in spite of himself and in this is some victory, whereas Marlowe's Jew generates only hatred in a gruesome, almost ludicrous death which is the result of his own machinations. Jessica is an agent of her father's redemption, while Abigail is the sacrificial victim of her father's villainous perdition. In these differences—

far greater than anything the two plays may have in common—is a measure of the difference between the two poets.

Marlowe and Shakespeare are also the authors of two great tragedies of apostasy. *Doctor Faustus* and *Macbeth* are both plays in which an attractive and heroic figure deliberately accepts damnation in specifically Christian terms, suffers the inevitable consequences of his choice, and comes at the last to recognize the futility of what he has chosen as a higher good than the salvation of his soul.[18] These plays are virtually unique in their age for the fine delineation of the Christian scheme in terms of which the erring hero's fate is presented. Only Cyril Tourneur's *Atheist's Tragedy* (1611) among contemporary plays seems to be constructed upon a similar dramatic conception, and Tourneur's text makes it apparent that he learned much from the examples of both Marlowe and Shakespeare, in spite of his inability to catch the fire of their genius.[19] Marlowe brought to *Faustus* all of the theological learning he had acquired at Cambridge,[20] while Shakespeare seems to have brought to *Macbeth* little more than the ordinary Christian assumptions which were the property of most intelligent and literate Elizabethans. Yet Shakespeare's drama of human damnation is a play of final affirmation and hope, whereas Marlowe's is essentially non-Christian in the sense of negation and despair with which it closes.

Macbeth and Faustus both begin with a full awareness of the Christian promise of salvation and the threat of damnation for those who will not accept it. This promise Faustus rejects with a facile syllogism which ignores the possibility of divine grace:

> If we say we have no sin,
> We deceive ourselves, and there's no truth in us.
> Why then belike we must sin,
> And so consequently die.
> Ay, we must die an everlasting death. (I. i. 43-47)

And he vaunts his defiance of the threat of hell:

> This word 'damnation' terrifies not me,
> For I confound hell in Elysium.
> My ghost be with the old philosophers! (I. iii. 59-61)

Macbeth, too, knows that in his decision to murder Duncan he has elected damnation, that he has "mine eternal jewel / Given to the common enemy of man" (III. i. 68-69), and in his perseverance in crime, knowing full well that he cannot "jump the life to come" (I. vii. 7), there is a defiance of the threat of hell not unlike that of Faustus. Driven by his "vaulting ambition", Macbeth will face the terrors of hell for what in his delusion he sees as a greater good than salvation, the "sweet fruition of an earthly crown" which had so enthralled Tamburlaine.

In both plays we behold the futility of the tragic choice. All that Faustus receives for his soul is revealed as worthless; he can find no answers to the

---

[18] Cf. Helen Gardner, "Milton's 'Satan' and the Theme of Damnation in Elizabethan Tragedy", *English Studies*, I (London, 1948), 46-66.

[19] Tourneur's indebtedness is discussed more fully in my forthcoming edition of *The Atheist's Tragedy* in the "Revels Plays" series.

[20] See Cole, pp. 191-243.

cosmic questions he had sought to resolve, and all his power can effect little more than petty trickery. In *Macbeth* the sinful choice issues in corruption upon every level of creation, destruction of the state to which as a valiant soldier Macbeth had devoted himself, of the family relation which before the crime Shakespeare reveals as among the closest in all literature. Macbeth must even see the universe itself undergo corruption, with horses turning against their rightful masters and devouring one another, and the sun blotted out over Scotland. He must die at last, friendless and alone, the valiant hero of the opening scenes reduced to a "bloody butcher" whose head must be held aloft in triumph.

Macbeth dies fully aware of his tragic error:

> And be these juggling fiends no more believ'd,
> That palter with us in a double sense;
> That keep the word of promise to our ear,
> And break it to our hope. (V. vii. 48-51)

This final recognition may well be compared with the sorrow and remorse of Faustus' farewell to his fellow scholars:

> But Faustus' offence can ne'er be pardoned. The serpent that tempted Eve may be saved, but not Faustus. Ah gentlemen, hear me with patience and tremble not at my speeches. Though my heart pants and quivers to remember that I have been a student here these thirty years, O, would I had never seen Wittenberg, never read book. And what wonders I have done, all Germany can witness—yea, all the world—for which Faustus hath lost both Germany and the world, yea heaven itself, heaven the seat of God, the throne of the blessed, the kingdom of joy, and must remain in hell for ever. Hell, ah hell for ever! Sweet friends, what shall become of Faustus, being in hell forever? (V. ii. 41-51)

In these respects the plays are remarkably similar. The crucial difference which separates Shakespeare from Marlowe, however, is that in *Doctor Faustus* there is no real alternative to the damnation Faustus must suffer. For him to have accepted the offer of mercy which is constantly extended to him by the Good Angel and urged by the Old Man, and against the temptation of which he struggles throughout the play, would have been to deny those very aspirations to rise beyond the state of ignorant and impotent man which had led him to pledge his soul to Lucifer, and which have lent him the heroic stature which renders him a tragic figure. It is, after all, the Promethean Faustus who will not accept the limitations of humanity who captures our imagination and prevents us from seeing this play, as some recent critics have seen it,[21] as a simple Christian morality play teaching the fate of the unrepentant sinner. We are shown at the end the terrible spectacle of this once heroic figure reduced to a cringing wretch, calling in vain for the solace of Christ's blood which a cruel and impersonal universe will not grant him, his body finally to be torn apart by the fiends who are a part of this universe. In Marlowe's greatest and almost certainly final tragedy there is only despair and frustration, and little hope for humanity.

Macbeth also ends with a gruesome spectacle as the severed head of the once

---

[21] Cole; Leo Kirschbaum, "Marlowe's *Faustus*: A Reconsideration", *RES*, XIX (1943), 225-241.

heroic figure is held aloft, but in his own death Macbeth, unlike Faustus, is able to retain something of his heroic stature as he fights with Macduff. But what is most important is that *Macbeth* is framed so that out of the very corruption of the total cosmos which Macbeth's crime has entailed are born the forces which must restore order, and we have at the end Macduff, Malcolm, and the saintly King Edward of England. There is a constant dwelling in the play upon the power of evil to work itself out in a universe in which evil is unnatural, and we end with the promise of rebirth, the end of disorder and tyranny with the reign of Malcolm, who has been carefully delineated for us as a king who will rule with all of those virtues alien to the dead tyrant.[22]

Marlowe's tragedy, in short, can only offer a view of death and damnation as the fate of those who would seek to escape the limitations of the human condition, whereas Shakespeare can offer a compensating view of order emerging to expel evil from an essentially harmonious universe. In Marlowe's play evil is natural and heroic, an expression of the nature of mankind to aspire; in Shakespeare's it is unnatural and doomed to extinction. It may be because of this crucial difference that Tourneur in writing *The Atheist's Tragedy* felt obliged to offer in juxtaposition to the view of D'Amville's damnation the rather prosaic vision of the triumph through virtue of Charlemont and Casta-bella. Tourneur, of course, was not the artist that Shakespeare was, and if his view of the alternative to apostacy is not so convincing as Shakespeare's, this is not to deny its crucial importance in the total dramatic structure he envisaged.

What then did Shakespeare learn from Marlowe? That he taught Shakespeare much about the handling of dramatic blank verse is likely, but there is a great difference between Marlowe's verse and that even of the early Shakespeare, as F. P. Wilson has pointed out.[23] Shakespeare from the very beginning thought in terms of images, whereas Marlowe never did. Marlowe's lines are rhythmic and sensuous, but they never derive their force from the succession of clear, simple, visual impressions which is so characteristic of Shakespeare. Marlowe's plays are far richer than Shakespeare's in classical allusion, but these are often mere ornamentation. They are never worked into the thematic texture of a speech as are those of Shakespeare. We may consider Portia's speech to Bassanio, as she invites him to choose the proper casket:

> Now he goes,
> With no less presence, but with much more love,
> Than young Alcides, when he did redeem
> The virgin tribute paid by howling Troy
> To the sea-monster: I stand for sacrifice;
> The rest aloof are the Dardanian wives,
> With bleared visages, come forth to view
> The issue of the exploit. Go, Hercules!
> Live thou, I live; with much, much more dismay
> I view the fight than thou that mak'st the fray. (III. ii. 53-62)

Here the notions of love as hazardous self-giving and sacrifice, which are so crucial to the play, are evoked by allusion to the rescue of Hesione by Hercules,

---

[22] I have argued these points in detail in *Patterns in Shakespearian Tragedy*, pp. 153-167.
[23] *Marlowe and the Early Shakespeare* (Oxford, 1953), pp. 122-123.

and we feel that what Bassanio is daring is no less noble than the quest of "young Alcides".

We may turn by way of contrast to one of the richest of Marlowe's many evocations of classical story:

> Content, but we will leave this paltry land
> And sail from hence to Greece, to lovely Greece.
> I'll be thy Jason, thou my golden fleece.
> Where painted carpets o'er the meads are hurled,
> And Bacchus' vineyards overspread the world,
> Where woods and forests go in goodly green,
> I'll be Adonis, thou shalt be Love's queen.
>
> (*Jew of Malta* IV. iv. 84-90)

But these are the lines addressed by the ignorant slave Ithamore to the courtesan, Bellamira, and as such the richness of the classical allusion seems almost ludicrous by its contrast with the sordid situation in which it appears. This is pure decoration, unrelated in any way to the substance of the scene in which it occurs, and if anything, capable only of distraction from it.

Or we may turn to *1 Tamburlaine* as Mycetes charges Theridamas to go forth to conquer Tamburlaine:

> Go frowning forth, but come thou smiling home
> As did Sir Paris with the Grecian dame.   (I. i. 65-66)

There certainly is no meaningful analogy to be made between the journey of Paris and the battle foray of Theridamas, particularly if we recall that Paris stole Helen by a display of anything but the martial valor Mycetes is calling for. Even if we try to explore the farthest implications of the comparison in the context of Marlowe's play, we find that the journey of Paris was to result in the most terrible of wars; that of Theridamas, in peaceful collusion with the enemy. Examples of such embellishment by classical allusion can be found throughout Marlowe's plays, but seldom in Shakespeare's. Even the extravagant rhetorical figures of Shakespeare's earliest plays are rarely unrelated to the dramatic contexts in which they appear.

That the echoes of Marlowe's language are very numerous in Shakespeare's early plays has often been pointed out and can scarcely be doubted. Perhaps the most striking is Richard II's

> Was this the face
> That every day under his household roof
> Did keep ten thousand men? Was this the face
> That like the sun did make beholders wink?
> Was this the face that fac'd so many follies,
> And was at last out-fac'd by Bolingbroke?   (IV. i. 281-286)

This, of course, recalls Faustus'

> Was this the face that launched a thousand ships
> And burnt the topless towers of Ilium?   (V. i. 99-100)

But it must be noticed that Shakespeare extends and amplifies Marlowe's striking image, playing with it, and turning it at last into a triple pun. This is the kind of verbal dexterity in which Marlowe never indulges. It is difficult to say with certainty that there are in Shakespeare's plays a great many conscious imitations of Marlowe's language, although it is clear that there are some. Shakespeare drew upon a body of poetic diction which was the general property of his age, but which we can say that Marlowe did more than any other of Shakespeare's predecessors to establish.

So far as dramatic craftsmanship is concerned, it cannot really be said that Shakespeare's debt to Marlowe was extraordinary. Although *Tamburlaine* was probably the most widely imitated play of its age, being aped by Greene in *Alphonsus,* Peele in *The Battle of Alcazar,* and Lodge in *The Wounds of Civil War,* it seems to have made little impression upon Shakespeare. The closest he came to this form of heroic drama is in *Henry V,* some ten years later, and this is a play of a different sort which cannot be considered apart from the three historical plays which preceded it.

The supposed influence of *The Jew of Malta* on *The Merchant of Venice,* as I have suggested, has been grossly overestimated. The one area in which Shakespeare seems to have learned much from Marlowe is that of the historical drama. In *Edward II* Shakespeare found the dramatic pattern he was to develop in *Richard II,* with two parallel movements, a weak king falling because of his inability to wield power, while a powerful adversary declines in human quality even as, because of his superior abilities, he rises in the fallen king's place. Since *Richard II* represents a crucial stage in Shakespeare's own development as a writer of tragedy we must conclude that the lessons Shakespeare learned from *Edward II* were to influence the greatest achievements of his later career. But this indebtedness is not a one-sided matter, for it has been shown by A. P. Rossiter[24] that *Edward II* must be later in date than Shakespeare's *Henry VI* plays, and that much of what made Marlowe's play the great achievement that it is he had learned in turn from Shakespeare's example.

If we are to assess the relation of Marlowe to Shakespeare we cannot do so in terms of any master-disciple relationship. Both men came upon the scene at the same moment, when some thirty years of dramatic activity had already begun to give signs of the burgeoning of a new splendor. Each forwarded this new growth in his own independent way, Shakespeare with an essentially optimistic view of life which sought always for order and meaning in the universe, Marlowe with a restless skepticism which moved from an early visionary hope of human achievement to a final frustration and despair. If Marlowe had disciples in his age, Shakespeare was not one of them; they were, as Una Ellis-Fermor has pointed out,[25] the Jacobean dramatists who were Shakespeare's later contemporaries.

Tulane University

24 *Woodstock, A Moral History* (London, 1946), pp. 69-71.
25 *The Jacobean Drama* (London, 1936), pp. 6-8.

Mr. *KING*'s BENEFIT.

On FRIDAY EVENING, the 29th of *April,* will be prefented,

A COMEDY, *(never acted here)* called,

AS YOU LIKE IT.

WRITTEN BY *SHAKESPEARE.*

Touchftone,		Mr. HALLAM,
Orlando,		Mr. CLEVELAND,
Oliver,		Mr. PRIGMORE,
Banifh'd Duke,		Mr. KING,
Amiens,	*(with Songs)*	Mr. TYLER,
Adam,		Mr. JOHNSON,
Corin,		Mr. ROBERTS,
Ufurping Duke,		Mr. Des MOULINS,
Le Beau and William,		Mr. JEFFERSON,
Sylvius,		Mr. MUNTO,
Jaquez de Bois,		Mr. M'KENZIE,
Charles,		Mr. LEE,
And, Jaquez,		Mr. HODGKINSON.
Celia,	*(with the Cuckoo Song)*	Mifs BROADHURST,
Audrey,		Mrs. BRETT,
Phœbe,		Mrs. MUNTO,
And, Rofalind,		Mrs. JOHNSON.

IN ACT 5th,

A DANCE, by Mr. *Francifquy,* Mr. *Durang,* and Mde. *Gardie.*

After the *Play,* a *Pantomimic Interlude,* called,

POOR JACK; or, *The Sailor's Landlady*

Poor Jack,	*(with a Hornpipe)*	Mr. DURANG,
Ben Bobftay,	with a Song, called, *America, Commerce and Freedom*	Mr. MUNTO,
Joe Tackle,		Mr. TOMPKINS,
Will Forecaftle,		Mr. WOOLLS,
Sam Stern,		Mr. LEONARD,
And, Ned Haulyard,		Mr. M'KNIGHT.
Landlady,		Mr. LEE,
Laffes,		Mrs. *Tompkins,* Mrs. *Durang, &c.*
And, Orange Girl,		Mde. GARDIE.

To which will be added, a COMIC OPERA, called, The

POOR SOLDIER.

Patrick,		Mr. TYLER,
Captain Fitzroy,		Mr. MUNTO,
Dermot,		Mr. PRIGMORE,
Father Luke,		Mr. KING,
Bagatelle,	*(for that Night)*	Mrs. CLEVELAND,
And, Darby,		Mr. HALLAM.
Norah,		Mifs BRETT,
And, Kathleen,		Mifs BROADHURST.

PLACES in the BOXES may be taken of Mr. *Faulkner* at the Box-Office, from *Ten* to *Twelve,* A. M. and on the Days of Performance, from *Three* to *Five,* P. M. where alfo Tickets may be had, and at Mr. *Gaine's* the Bible, in *Pearl-Street.*

Playbill of the benefit performance of *As You Like It* on 27 April 1796 in New York. 9″ x 15½″. Reproduced by permission of The Folger Shakespeare Library.

The Range of Shakespeare's Comedy

EDWARD HUBLER

HE man who talks about the nature of comedy does a danger-ous thing, and he knows it, for his reading in the criticism of many times and places suggests to him that he has a very slim chance of making sense. Still, it seems best to begin with the general and to say that the difference between tragedy and comedy has nothing, absolutely nothing, to do with subject matter. Tragedy and comedy are different ways of looking at life, and Shake-speare used both tragedy and comedy in his attempt to look at the whole of it. There is no other dramatist of whom this is true to a comparable degree, and I know of no theory of comedy which begins to comprehend his comic achieve-ment. What is comedy? Well, to the man in the street a comedy is a play which is to some considerable extent funny; and he is, of course, right. That is what comedy is, and everybody, or almost everybody, knows it. But this is a view which marks off the common man from the tradition of learned commentators on comedy, especially from the vast majority of those of Shakespeare's day.

Sir Philip Sidney, whose affinity with comedy was negligible, remarks that "our comedians think there is no delight without laughter, which is very wrong...." And he goes on to say that "laughter hath only a scornful tickling". To him laughter was an unsympathetic enjoyment; that is, we laugh only at things for which we feel some scorn. Yet he would not deny that laughter and delight "may go well together". Ben Jonson tells us in *Timber* that "as Aristotle rightly says, the moving of laughter is a fault in comedy". This is the learned Jonson speaking, and it stands for the kind of nonsense which learned men in general commit themselves to when writing on comedy. The complete Jonson, the man who wrote the plays, knew better; but in *Timber* he is being a critic, and he writes as half a man. This is the besetting weakness of much criticism. It tends to select those aspects of a subject it feels capable of criticizing, while pretending that the other aspects do not exist. Jonson goes so far as to say, "Philosophers ever think laughter unfitting in a wise man". There is a good deal of good writing on individual comedies, but almost always when a man sits down to write seriously on the nature of comedy, he writes with a desperate resolve, saying the things which no sensible man, all his faculties in control, has ever thought, though they have often been well expressed. Plato has Socrates say that important people in public life should laugh as little as possible, but he is not speaking for himself. This is advisory. He knew how readily the public man's constituents confuse gravity with wisdom. In *Cratylus* Socrates remarks in passing that the gods, too, love a joke; but these are pagan gods, and no one, as far as I know, has spoken for our own. Although in his *Laws* Plato commits himself to the belief that comedy is either satirical or farcical (he was, of course, speaking truthfully of the only comedy he knew), he seems to have been the one philosopher who might have given us a comprehensive study of comedy had he put his mind to it. At the end of Plato's *Symposium* Socrates is arguing that the genius of comedy is the same as the genius of tragedy, and this might have led to something but everyone was too drunk to listen; so Socrates put Aristophanes, who needed to hear the argument, to bed and went away. This is Plato's neatest finesse. Had he done his job, the discussion of comedy through the ages would have been different. Three weighty volumes attest to Professor Marvin Herrick's monumental knowledge of the criticism of comedy. At the close of one of them he remarks:

> Comic practise has always been more important than theory, of course, and doubtless always will be more important. . . . The sixteenth century theory of comedy was the work of learned men addressed to learned men; it was an intellectual theory emphasizing a strict decorum of plot, character, sentiment, and diction and emphasizing the philosophical lessons in human conduct to be gained from literary comedy. Consequently it is a relatively narrow theory, which fails to take into account the broader practices of the comedians. But our modern theory of literary comedy is still intellectual.

This statement is distinguished both by its truth and its moderation.

A purely intellectual theory of comedy will not do. The belly-laugh and lots of other nonintellectual elements of comedy are here to stay. The thing is, of course, to find some notions of comedy which will be consonant with our experience of comedies, and that cannot be done solely in terms of the mind. And this presents some difficulties, for if there is anything more difficult than knowing what we think, it is knowing what we feel. Now, since the laughable is perceived only in part by the intellect, we cannot encompass it solely in terms of the mind; and this leads to still further difficulties, because nowadays we tend to distrust what we cannot explain. In our explanations we tend to divide our natures into intellect, will, emotion, passion, and so on, as though each were naturally separate from the other; then, having abstracted these faculties into entities, we tend to arrange them in an order of precedence in which the more impulsive ones take the lower ranks; and since laughter cannot be separated from the impulsive and is by nature irreverent, comedy is not only isolated, it is downgraded. Even the jester knows that his place is at the end of the procession, and the upright in heart naturally feel, and take their feeling for granted, that there is something potentially base about laughter. Witness Sir Walter Scott:

> Where lives the man who has not tried
> How mirth can into folly glide,
> And folly into sin.

But before we assume that this condescension to laughter is a part of our own provincialism, let us remember that Aristotle tells us why he has nothing to say of the earlier stages of comedy: "It has no history because it was not at first treated seriously."

There is, of course, some motivation to this refusal to look comedy squarely in the face. Baudelaire found that comedy was satanic, but however this may be, it is clear that comedy cannot live with perfection. Golden ages, past and to

come, Christian, Hebraic, pagan, and Marxist, are not noted for their concern
with comedy. It may well be that comedy came into the world with the fall of
man and will depart this world when we move into whatever Utopia is in store
for our descendants and happily not for us. Milton tells us that for Adam and
Eve

> the unwieldy elephant
> To make them mirth us'd all his might, and wreath'd
> His lithe proboscis,

but he does not say that they laughed. However, when Eve was "satiate at
length" with the forbidden fruit, she became "jocund and boon". She told the
story of her fall to Adam with "countenance blithe", and together, after Adam
had eaten, they "swam in mirth". "Lord, what fools these mortals be", cries Puck
in *A Midsummer Night's Dream,* and it is the basic theme of the play, though
it is qualified, transformed even, by the mood in which the play is conceived.
Shakespeare, too, had been a fool in love, if we may believe the sonnets. And
so although the young lovers of the play and Bottom are fools, they are not cut
off from the rest of us. "It is important not to be a fool", said Santayana,
"though it is very hard." But we need not worry about this as much as we
sometimes do. In *A Midsummer Night's Dream* all the people in love find the
going too hard, and fools they are, all, that is, except Theseus and Hippolyta
who, untouched by the midsummer madness, retain their good sense, though
Theseus is, at times, less lovable than he should be. On the other hand, no man in
his right mind ever wished Bottom to be more sensible than he is, and we shall
do Shakespeare no discredit to acknowledge that that is how he wanted it to be.
Folly may lead us not only into sin but into a state of profound well-being. The
authority for this is no less respectable than Erasmus:

> To go on contriving at your friends' vices, passing over them, being blind
> to them and deceived by them, even loving your friends' egregious faults
> as if they were virtues—does not this seem pretty close to folly? Think a
> moment of the fellow who kisses a mole on his mistress's neck, or of the one
> who is delighted by the growth on his little lady's nose, or of the father who
> says of his cross-eyed son that his eyes twinkle. What is all this, I ask you,
> but sheer folly? Ay, you all vote—triple and quadruple foolishness! Yet
> this same foolishness both joins friends, and after joining them, keeps their
> friendship alive.

It is, of course, Folly herself speaking, but she scores a hit. It is an orthodox
Christian doctrine that nothing is entirely evil, not evil itself, for good may
grow out of it: so may we not have a little more regard for folly?

It is true that the opposition of folly and good sense is often the heart of
comedy. It is, indeed, the center of what we most often mean by comedy, but
comedy is not confined to it, as every reader of *Don Quixote* knows. We laugh
as Quixote's follies are exposed, but we rejoice, too, at the inability of the world
to break his spirit. Our good sense makes us aware of his follies—and a good
thing, too—but it is equally good that we have felt wisdom to make us rejoice,
that our hearts go out to Quixote and Parson Adams and other members of
"the poor damned human race". We call ourselves *homo sapiens,* and we repeat

endlessly that man is the only animal with the power of reason, even though the assertion does not always square with our observation of animals or of men. We might better call ourselves *homo ridens,* for man *is* the only laughing animal. It may be that the other animals have not yet fallen from grace. Laughter is basic to our humanity, to our flawed humanity, if you will, and it resists all attempts to reduce it to other terms.

Congreve took humor "either to be born with us, and so of a natural growth, or else to be grafted into us by some accidental change in the constitution, or revolution of the internal habit of the body, by which it becomes, if I may call it so, naturaliz'd. Humor is from nature, habit from custom, and affectation from industry. Humor shows us as we *are.*" Humor sees through our affectations, pretensions, and idiocies and permits us a glimpse of ourselves, poor, bare, forked creatures as we are, in all our endless variety. And this is why there is so little agreement on the nature of the comic. The comic muse looks everywhere; the whole world is her province. She will laugh at anything, and by anything I mean anything. On the other hand the tragic muse has a more restricted view. She looks at the pathetic, the horrible, the heroic, the terrifying, and the world is pretty well agreed on what these things are. But the comic is little less inclusive than life itself, and it is as confusing. It is not surprising, then, that even the most informed studies of comedy restrict their subject matter; they whittle it down to size, which is to say to the size of the whittler. Let us take an example.

It is remarkable how far-reaching Bergson's theory of comedy can be, but extend it as we will, it does not begin to cover its subject. Writing from the point of view of one to whom life is in a state of becoming, he regards the comic as "something mechanical encrusted on the living", as man's ludicrous "substitution of rigidity for the pliancy of the living organism", and to this he traces every variety of laughter he sees fit to consider. He has four main principles. First, he says that the comic does not exist outside the pale of what is strictly human. "A landscape may be beautiful, charming and sublime, or insignificant and ugly; it will never be laughable." Second, he says that laughter is an unsympathetic enjoyment incompatible with pity: ". . . the comic demands something like a momentary anesthesia of the heart. Its appeal is to the intelligence pure and simple." Third, he says that laughter is a social phenomenon belonging to men in groups: "You would hardly appreciate the comic if you felt yourself isolated from others. Laughter appears to stand in need of an echo." In order to understand laughter we must "put it back in its natural environment, which is society, and above all we must determine the utility of its function, which is a social one". And fourth, it turns out that laughter "is above all a corrective. . . . By laughter society avenges itself for the liberties taken with it." It is remarkable, I repeat, how far these principles will go toward an understanding of laughter, and it is just as remarkable how much of the comic they leave untouched. They will do fairly well for the comedy of Greece and Rome, and for Molière, except when he is at his best; but they will not do for Shakespeare and the laughter of such literatures as those of Germany and Russia. Bergson's comic muse is French, and nothing alien is quite human to her. Near the end of his essay he almost realizes its limitations, and he makes some allowances for sympathetic laughter, "but", he quickly adds, "we rest only for a short time. The sympathy which is capable of entering into the impression of the comic is a very fleeting one. It . . . comes from a lapse of attention."

One of the things we miss in Bergson's idea of the comic is the sense of joy—the laughter of a baby, or a mother's joy in her child, or the laughter of lovers—the joy of everything which fulfills its own nature. The happiness of things in bloom is a very real matter, and it is central to much of comedy. It has nothing to do with morality, or society, or intellection of any sort, and it has no impulse whatever to correction. There is nothing corrective, or anti-Christian, or anti- or pro-anything in Sir Andrew Aguecheek's remark in *Twelfth Night:* "Methinks sometimes I have no more wit than a Christian or an ordinary man has; but I am a great eater of beef, and I believe that does harm to my wit." Sir Andrew is Shakespeare's most stupid character, and this statement is the supreme flowering of stupidity. We read it, and we find it good. When the Shandy family in *Tristram Shandy* are about to visit the catacombs of the Abbey Saint-Germain, someone tells Uncle Toby that the people they are going to see are all dead. "Then I need not shave", is his instant response. This may be a number of things, and one of the things which it certainly is is the essence of Uncle Toby, God bless his innocent heart. We tend to think that pain and grief have a greater reality than joy, because, I suppose, they triumph in the end, and because, in our Hebraic-Christian tradition, we are taught to. But Shakespeare always knew better. His darkest moments are often permeated with the joy arising from a sense of his own identity, of the self realized. As Sean O'Casey put it, "He heard music in everything, and where there was none, he put music into it." His vitality, in Shaw's phrase, kept him sweet.

Sir Andrew as we have viewed him is an instance of what Theodore Hoffman calls "the innocent comic", the comic which exists for itself, like beauty, and resists all attempts at analysis. So, perhaps, is the apotheosis of tact as recorded by Suetonius in "The Life of Passienus Crispus", the father-in-law of Nero. "When he was asked by Nero in a private conversation whether he had commerce with his sister, as the emperor had with his, he replied, 'Not yet.'" Or perhaps the conversation with Nero touches the grotesque, which is simply the innocent comic with a different subject matter. Baudelaire calls the grotesque "the absolute comic"; it simply *is*. When Falstaff, whose dread of death was the obverse of his love of life, was about to leave for yet another war in the second part of *King Henry the Fourth,* he spent the last evening at the Boar's Head Tavern. There had been a brawl, and when he returned to Doll Tearsheet, she asked, "Thou whoreson tidy little Bartholomew boar-pig, when wilt thou leave off fighting o' days and foining o' nights and begin to patch up thine old body for heaven?" And he replied, "Peace good Doll! Do not speak like a death's head: do not bid me remember mine end." The scene turns to lightness again, and then, a moment later while giving her "flattering busses", he is seized with the realization of mortality, and he calls out, "I am old, I am old!" though she is seated on his lap and his intentions are strictly dishonorable.

The alternation of the comic and the serious is as old as the English theater, but it remained for Shakespeare to make each a part of the other. A shaft of laughter brightens his darkest passages, and his gayest moments pass quickly into shadow. His was the broadest vision of life, and for the expression of it neither comedy nor tragedy was enough. In him the comic and the solemn stand side by side fortifying each other. I am sure that his own view of genres was that of Polonius: ". . . tragedy, comedy, history, pastoral, pastoral-comical, historical-pastoral, tragical-historical, tragical-comical-historical-pastoral; scene individable or poem unlimited". And this was so because he knew that the categories we impose on life in our attempts to understand it are, after all, impositions. He never confused the category with the thing itself. Categories make boundaries of nature's easy transitions. First Shakespeare saw clearly, and then he adapted the genre to what he had seen. He did not exclude subject matter because it was, as other writers might suppose, inappropriate to the kind of thing he was doing.

It has been customary since the time of Aristotle to say that follies and not crimes are appropriate to comedy, and by crimes Aristotle meant that which is productive of pain or harm to others. This is an excellent principle for the dramatist who wants popular success above everything else. Everyone is able to laugh at the foibles of others, and such laughter has always been a staple in the theater. Let us be grateful for it, and let us not in any sense undervalue it. But let us notice, too, that when the comic dramatist moves into serious subject matter, when the follies deepen into crimes and the laughter begins to strike home, the audiences begin to fall off. *Troilus and Cressida,* for instance, has never been a popular play. But if the dramatist writes tragedy on the one hand and only sure-fire comedy on the other, he leaves large areas of experience unexplored.

Shakespeare explored the whole range of comic expression. He began with *The Comedy of Errors* by writing farce. Farce is the comedy of action, of sudden and surprising action, and it is a little difficult to illustrate in words; but perhaps a scene from an old Marx Brothers movie which I saw on television not so long ago will do. The silent brother, Harpo, leans up against a building in ostentatious idleness, and he does not, of course, reply when a passing policeman asks him what he is doing. As this business repeats, the policeman grows angry and asks, "What do you think you are doing? Holding the building up?" Harpo nods vigorously, the policeman gives him a shove, and the building falls down. It is possible but not very sensible to be intellectual about this, to say, for instance, that our laughter is related to the resentment we all feel at the officiousness of the police; but surely the police themselves laughed at this scene, which is, essentially, the unexpected and meaningless translation of idiom into action. This is farce, and Shakespeare, basing his first comedy on a play by Plautus, doubled the action and reveled in action for its own sake. It is the efflorescence of high spirits. It is another manifestation of the absolute comic. And so, because it is an end in itself, is burlesque; but burlesque does not stand alone. It reduces *something* to absurdity, and only for the fun of doing so. In *As You Like It,* Rosalind reads the verses which Orlando, who was not a poet, had written to her:

> From the east to western Ind,
> No jewel is like Rosalind.
> Her worth, being mounted on the wind,
> Through all the world bears Rosalind.
> All the pictures fairest lined
> Are but black to Rosalind. . . .

And Touchstone improvises a burlesque of them:

> If a hart do lack a hind,
> Let him seek out Rosalind.
> If the cat will after kind,
> So be sure will Rosalind.
> Wint'red garments must be lined,
> So must slender Rosalind. . . .

And so on, to more joyous and explicit indecencies. The verses burlesqued are not worthy of criticism. Their worthlessness is only too apparent, and there is nothing in them to attack. Burlesque is a reduction to absurdity for its own sake.

But if a parody points out an essential weakness or absurdity of something taken more or less seriously, it becomes satire. Satire is corrective laughter. It calls attention to the absurdity of something in order to influence public opinion about it, laying bare the absurd so that we may see it for what it is and turn away from it. When Shakespeare was a young writer in the early 1590's there was an epidemic of sonneteering in imitation of Petrarch. The ladies of these sonnets were aloof and chaste. The poet lavished his devotion upon his lady, and she greeted him with disdain. She conformed to the Elizabethan ideal of blonde beauty, and she was described in what has come to be known as the descending description. Her hair was gold, her forehead ivory, her lips rubies, her teeth pearls, her neck alabaster, and so on. The poet began with her hair and was saved only by the happy brevity of the sonnet form. When Shakespeare wrote his sonnet sequence, his lady was of another sort. Her hair and eyes were black, her skin swarthy, and she was far from aloof. She was, to be brief about it, a charmingly unconventional beauty of no morals at all. On one occasion he refers to her in nautical terms as "the bay where all men ride". Yet he loved her. His love turned out to be an enslavement, but before he was aware of this he wrote,

> My mistress eyes are nothing like the sun,
> Coral is far more red than her lips red;
> If snow be white, why then her breasts are dun,
> If hairs be wires, black wires grow on her head.
> I have seen roses damask'd red and white,
> But no such roses see I in her cheeks;
> And in some perfumes is there more delight
> Than in the breath which from my mistress reeks.
> I love to hear her talk, yet well I know
> That music hath a far more pleasing sound;
> I grant I never saw a goddess go,
> My mistress, when she walks, treads on the ground.
>   And yet, by heaven, I think my love as rare
>   As any she belied with false compare.

This is at once both satire and high comedy. If it is considered in relation to the ladies of the Petrarchan tradition (and such a consideration would have been inevitable to a literate Elizabethan), it is satire. It corrects our notions of the ladies of the tradition. We think less well of them. We see that they have been built on "false compare". On the other hand, if we consider the poem apart from the tradition, it is pure comedy. The poet is aware of his lady's faults, but he loves her, faults and all. This is the essence of what we sometimes call high comedy; that is, that subdivision of the area of comedy which is neither farce nor burlesque nor yet satire. It differs from farce in that it has a certain intellectuality; it is about something. This intellectuality may be little or great. It differs from satire in that it does not ask you to think less well of the thing laughed at. You will find in George Meredith's essay on the comic spirit a test for determining to what degree the comic spirit inhabits you, and it is this: "If you can see the ridicule", as he puts it, of those you love without loving them less, then you have it. And he suggests something I wish he had said: if you can see the ridiculous in yourself without losing your self-esteem, you have a good share of the comic spirit in your soul. This is the spirit which animates the vast body of ne'er-do-wells who teem through Shakespeare's pages—Bottom, the early Falstaff, Pompey in *Measure for Measure,* and Autolycus, to name only a few. We do not take the moral view of them; we do not want them to be better than they are. We may in time learn a good deal from them, but while we are with them we know in our hearts that they and we are members in good standing in the universal brotherhood of folly. This is fun, and, I submit, it is good for us.

   We are aware of their faults. We know that Bottom is an ignorant egotist and Autolycus a thief, but in our complex response to them this is not uppermost in our consciousness. It has been customary for centuries to justify satire and high comedy by its corrective powers, and there is some just motivation to this. It is quite clear that satire makes its points and has its uses. It can correct manners. Meredith tells us that Molière's *Les Précieuses Ridicules* "ridiculed and put a stop to the monstrous romantic jargon made popular by certain famous novels". And I can be assured of the social uses of satire by my recollection of the effect of the writings of Sinclair Lewis on the thought and manners of his times. The Babbitts were made more conscious of their babbitry, and there were some signs of reform. Satire can enlighten its readers and move them toward good sense. It can humilitate its victims and perhaps chasten them. But this is not the heart of the matter; it does not account for the staying power of good satire. If satire were no more than this, *Candide* would have no more claim upon posterity than any good teacher. Although good deeds sometimes shine brightly in a naughty world, they do not shine for long. The satirist's job is always to do again. No, the real power of great satirists is, in Hoyt Hudson's words, "Positive rather than negative. They attract, if at all, by some steady light which burns in them, a light which is benevolent and grateful to the reader—yes, even in Swift. . . . The great satirist lifts the reader to his own plane of clear vision. . . . Good satire is an intrigue among honest men, a conspiracy of the candid." And this is true of good comedy, too, in Meredith's sense of the word. Good comedy creates a world into which we move and in which our experience is extended. And we cannot associate with the people of that world if, primarily, we take a moral view of them. A truly human association demands, if only for a time, a certain acceptance, a certain moral equality. This is a capacity Shakespeare had to an extraordinary degree. He was the opposite of Keats's friend Dilke, whom Keats described as "a Godwin perfectability man" and of whom he said, "He

will never come to a truth so long as he lives because he is always trying at it."
Shakespeare was, as Keats said, "capable of being in uncertainties, mysteries, and
doubts, without any irritable reaching after fact and reason". And this, as a
recent writer has it, is "the sovereign faculty of the creative mind. It was another
name for humility, and it enabled him to live in his world without ever becoming separated from it." And I suppose that this is why there is so little
satire in Shakespeare. There are, of course, satirical contemporary references in,
say, *Love's Labour's Lost,* but we know of them only through the footnotes.
The point of view of Shakespeare's works is never basically corrective. The
works may instruct, but the instruction does not begin with a separation from,
or a condescension to, the things depicted.

Shakespeare's recreations of life are many things, but they are first experience
for the spectator, an enlargement of his being. Of course we may learn from
comedies, and we often do. What are some of the things we may learn? But let
me say this first: I imagine that the simplest possible description of the average
play would say that it is a dramatic composition posing a situation from which
a conflict arises, and the action moves to a resolution of the conflict. When the
conflict is resolved, the play is done. In high comedy the conflict is between a
specious morality and what we may call a more deeply human one. In *Love's
Labour's Lost* four young noblemen, intent upon education, set up a school in
which for a number of years they will eat one meal a day, sleep only a few
hours a night, fast one day in seven, and see no women. Everyone who has
ever been to the theater before will know from the beginning how this will work
out. The young women, who represent life and good sense, inevitably appear
on the scene, and at the end of the play the young men move into the world to
live and love and suffer and learn. The theme of the play is that learning unrelated to experience is pedantry. The affected, the pretentious, the false are
shown up in the light of the reasonable, the sensible, the achievable, the human.
At the end of such a comedy the characters are more sensible than they had been.
Or if, like Malvolio, they are unchanged, their lack of good sense has been dis-
closed to us. The movement of the play is toward the achievable and the normal.
The comic muse is an earthly muse. What we may call the comic incongruity is
the gap between the affected and the unrealistic on the one hand, and the
sensible on the other. In Shakespearian tragedy the movement is toward the
ideal, toward the achievement of the heroic. It gives us a vision of greatness in,
very often, a neutral or hostile universe. And this is deeply gratifying because life
as we live it is often too small to be satisfactory. Shakespeare begins a tragedy
with characters who are in some way larger than life, and in the course of the
play he magnifies them further, and toward the end of the tragedy he leads us
into a realm in which the things of the world are dwarfed by things of the
spirit. Happiness and unhappiness, success and failure, no longer matter. The
one thing which the best tragedy must have, and which comedy cannot have,
is a basic sense of awe. The comic muse may scorn what she looks at; she may
condescend to it; she may view it with detachment; she may ally herself to it
and call it her own: but it is not in her nature to prostrate herself before anything. The genius of comedy and the genius of tragedy spring from the same
sources, but they move toward different ends. In *King Lear* tragedy moves into
a realm in which all that matters is love shining in the light of truth, and from

this vantage point it finds that the pageantry of kings and princes is no more than an engaging spectacle.

We may watch the tragic muse on her way. The grave-diggers' scene in *Hamlet* begins in comedy with the annoucement of the subject, the inevitability of death and its physical attributes. It begins lightly enough for such a scene, but it grows steadily more serious, more general, more personal—more personal to Hamlet, and through its increasing generality, more personal to us—until, in the end, it transcends the macabre. At the beginning the conversation of the grave-diggers discloses that someone is to be buried. She is not named, though we know who she is. There is some low comedy, and the scene moves quickly to some conundrums: "Who builds stronger than a mason, a shipwright, or a carpenter?" And the answer: "A grave maker. The houses he makes last till doomsday. . . . Fetch me a stoup of liquor." As the second grave-digger goes for the liquor, the first breaks into song, and Hamlet and Horatio enter and stand aside. The grave-digger digs up a skull. Hamlet comments on the skull: "That skull had a tongue in it and could sing once. . . . and now my Lady Worm's; chapless, and knocked about the mazzard with a sexton's spade." And while Shakespeare is thus generalizing upon the action, extending the realization of death until it reaches us, another skull is dug up, and the realization is pushed home: "This same skull, sir, was Yorick's skull, the King's jester." Hamlet takes the skull in his hands: "Alas, poor Yorick. I knew him, Horatio, a fellow of infinite jest. . . . Here hung those lips which I have kissed I know not how oft. Where be your jibes now, your gambols, your flashes of merriment. . . . Not one now to mock your own grinning." There are no conundrums, jokes, or songs now. And Shakespeare, who likes to be explicit when he can, has Hamlet say, "Now get you to my lady's chamber, and tell her, let her paint an inch thick, to this favour she must come. Make her laugh at that!" At this point we have passed beyond the realm of comedy. This personalized realization of death is then generalized further. Then the funeral procession enters, and Hamlet learns who is to be buried today. He has seen the body of an old friend dug up to make room for the body of the girl he loves. He has looked on death at what is for him its worst, and when we see him again, he is at peace. There is no more "fighting" in his soul, and although all is "ill about my heart", "it is no matter". It seems axiomatic that any horror looked squarely in the face becomes less horrible. It is not destroyed, it is rather that it tends to become bearable. With Hamlet this is not a simple matter. Events have also taught him that "there is a special providence in the fall of a sparrow". Nevertheless it is after the graveyard scene that the young man who had continually brooded on death is ready to face it. He can defy augury, for the augurs can foretell only such things as success or failure; but there is nothing, except himself, which can prevent a man from facing his private horror and rising above it. This is man's tragic freedom. So Hamlet says, "If it be now, 'tis not to come; if it be not to come, it will be now; if it be not now, yet it will come. The readiness is all."

All this is beyond the realm of comedy. Here in the contemplation of man's essential nature, risen now to grandeur, there is no room for man's follies, pretentions, ambitions, and crimes, for all that matters now is his at last triumphant spirit. But not all men can achieve greatness of spirit, even when confronted with situations demanding it, and shall not this, too, have a place in the theater? Shall the nontragic, the comic, restrict itself to the depiction of follies and leave large areas of experience unexplored? Shall not our "crimes", too, have a place in the nonheroic theater? Happily for all, it has been a long time since the muse of comedy was an Aristotelian. She seems to have very few principles indeed, but she has a keen mind, a knowing heart, perfect vision, and a sense of direction. And in Shakespeare she exercises all her talents. He seems never to have considered narrowing his vision in the interests of propriety, social or dramatic. Having treated the ridiculous in *Love's Labour's Lost* and *A Midsummer Night's Dream,* he went beyond it in *The Merchant of Venice,* almost wrecking the fragile, fairy-tale structure of his plot by locking the dynamic figure of Shylock in it. He went still further with Falstaff in both parts of *Henry the Fourth,* for the laughter darkens as the plays proceed. Then came *Hamlet,* where the laughter is often mordant and never merry. And then *Troilus and Cressida* and *Measure for Measure.*

Troilus and Cressida has never been popular, partly, perhaps, because of a certain grimness and an unrelenting tenacity to truth, but chiefly because it disappoints the average playgoer's expectation of what a play should be: the central conflict is never resolved, nor could it be, for the play shows us what happens when obligations demanding a measure of greatness are laid upon unheroic men. The dramatically important thing about Shakespeare's concept of "degree" and "order" is that high position both confers privileges and imposes obligations. Ulysses expounds this idea early in the play in the great speech on degree. And when these obligations are not met,

> Then everything includes itself in power,
> Power into will, will into appetite;
> And appetite, an universal wolf,
> So doubly seconded with will and power,
> Must make, perforce, an universal prey,
> And last eat up himself.

This is precisely what happens; this is the receipe for the play. The Greeks accept, or even wallow in, their privileges while refusing to acknowledge their obligations. In the council of the Trojan royal family Hector argues that the "moral laws of nature and of nations" demand that Helen be returned to Menelaus. The phrase is not accidental. He means that both natural law, which is the will of God implicit in nature, and human law require that she be returned. This he believes "in way of truth". He has already argued that all things are not relative, that there are absolute values. Yet he decides to keep Helen in order to save face. The play opens with Troilus' denial of his obligations:

> Call here my varlet, I'll unarm again:
> Why should I war without the walls of Troy,
> That find such cruel battle here within?

This is the central and unifying idea of the play: the denial of lawful and immutable obligations in favor of self-indulgence. In the central conflict Trojan and Greek are on the same side. They are sunk in war and lechery. They refuse to rise above either, and down they go. "Look, Hector", said Achilles before they fought, "How the sun begins to set." And after he had killed him: "The dragon wing of night o'er spreads the earth." At the end of the play Hector is dead, Achilles has triumphed dishonorably, Cressida is a strumpet, and Troilus is sadder but no wiser. His only hope is "hope of revenge". And for an epilogue Pandarus, who has given his name to a trade, wills us his diseases. Although the play is often funny, it is never merry. But how true it is! And remote as these people are from us in time and place and station, how much they are like us!

The play is a comedy, but such a comedy as had not existed before. It stands at the pole opposite the comedies with which Shakespeare began his career, and beyond the comedies of reconciliation which closed it. Here there is no reconciliation, for the "moral laws of nature" are immutable and cannot bow to man, and the Trojans, a lovable and self-indulgent people, cannot rise to them. Achilles and Thersites seem never to have considered them. It appears that the play did not succeed when it was new, and it is not popular now, although it is widely admired by the discerning. I do not think we need explain the play's intellectuality and its departure from normal dramatic structure by supposing that it was written for a private theater, although it may have been. All we need by way of explanation is an awareness of the breadth of Shakespeare's vision and his integrity as artist. Between *Troilus* and *The Comedy of Errors* ranges a panoply of comedy such as no one had imagined before and no one has achieved since.

Princeton University

Shakespeare's Comedies and the Critics

MILTON CRANE

S we approach the denouement of *Arms and the Man,* that delectable comedy written so long ago, in Shaw's and the world's youth, when war was still a subject to make light of, we find the admirable chocolate-cream soldier Bluntschli summing up the meaning of life for the romantic Sergius: "But now that youve found that life isnt a farce, but something quite sensible and serious, what further obstacle is there to your happiness?"[1] Obviously we are intended to smile at the simplicity of the sanguine, matter-of-fact Bluntschli, betrayed into the profession of arms by an "incurably romantic disposition", and now about to leave it for that most characteristically Swiss of professions: hotelkeeping. But, as Shaw teaches us again and again, we may soon find ourselves laughing out of the other side of our mouths. For the cream of Shaw's jest is precisely that life is indeed "something quite sensible and serious", something worthy of our laughter, something, in fact, whose seriousness and good sense we can perceive most fully through laughter, once we have rid ourselves both of illusions and of cynicism.

Now I am well aware that Shaw is a notoriously unreliable guide to the thought of Shaw, and that his obiter dicta are particularly misleading when one endeavors to apply them to Shaw's artistic achievement. Nevertheless, I submit that in the comic earnestness of Bluntschli's reasonable approach to the dashing Sergius we may find a key not only to Shaw's philosophy of comedy but also to the puzzling and indefinable practice—I dare not call it method—of an even greater writer of English comedies.

For, despite the many and obvious differences between their works, Shakespeare and Shaw, as comic dramatists, are exceedingly casual about freely mingling comic and serious matter, no doubt on the excellent principle that the best comedies must deal with serious themes, and consequently may well introduce scenes that border on the tragic. (We are familiar enough with comic relief; but let us remember that serious, and even tragic, relief also exists. Think of Barbara's terrible moment of decision at the end of Act II of *Major Barbara;* of the Hero-Claudio plot in *Much Ado About Nothing;* or of the Marschallin's profoundly moving soliloquy that ends Act I of Strauss's and Hofmannsthal's *Der Rosenkavalier.*)

The mixture of comedy and tragedy: the importance of the happy ending: these, as Dr. Johnson well understood, were problems not only to excite a Rymer or a Voltaire, but to give pause to the most passionate of Shakespeare's ad-

[1] Bernard Shaw, *Arms and the Man,* in *Selected Plays* (New York, 1948), III, 186.

mirers. And, as in so many things, Dr. Johnson's views continue to command our respectful attention:

> The players, who in their edition divided our author's works into comedies, histories, and tragedies, seem not to have distinguished the three kinds by any very exact or definite ideas.
>
> An action which ended happily to the principal persons, however serious or distressful through its intermediate incidents, in their opinion, constituted a comedy. This idea of a comedy continued long amongst us; and plays were written, which, by changing the catastrophe, were tragedies to-day, and comedies to-morrow....
>
> Through all these denominations of the drama, *Shakespeare's* mode of composition is the same; an interchange of seriousness and merriment, by which the mind is softened at one time, and exhilarated at another. But whatever be his purpose, whether to gladden or depress, or to conduct the story, without vehemence or emotion, through tracts of easy and familiar dialogue, he never fails to attain his purpose; as he commands us, we laugh or mourn, or sit silent with quiet expectation, in tranquillity without indifference.[2]

This leads to a remarkable judgment, which critics have more often quoted than endorsed:

> [Shakespeare] therefore indulged his natural disposition, and his disposition, as Rhymer has remarked, led him to comedy. In tragedy he often writes, with great appearance of toil and study, what is written at last with little felicity; but in his comick scenes, he seems to produce without labour, what no labour can improve. In tragedy he is always struggling after some occasion to be comick; but in comedy he seems to repose, or to luxuriate, as in a mode of thinking congenial to his nature. In his tragick scenes there is always something wanting, but his comedy often surpasses expectation or desire. His comedy pleases by the thoughts and language, and his tragedy for the greater part by incident and action. His tragedy seems to be skill, his comedy to be instinct.[3]

I cannot forbear to say how deep a note Dr. Johnson seems to me to strike in this extraordinary passage. Shakespeare's prevailing tendency is indeed toward the comic, whether or not the decorum or indeed the necessity of the particular play or scene points that way. What this means, I think, is that Shakespeare, like Tolstoy (among others), in contemplating the eternal disparity between man's aspirations and his limitations, could not but feel that the limitations carried the day. Man is *"demi-ange, demi-bête"*, and for some rare moments our attention is fixed on the angel, as Hamlet unforgettably tells us. But for the most part a sane man must admit that man's strivings are hopelessly inhibited by the shortcomings of man's own nature—by crassness, vanity, stupidity, and affectation, to remain only with the venial sins—and the end is inevitably laughter, not despair. I have not forgotten *Othello* or *Lear*, but at the same time I have not forgotten the grim comedy with which both plays are shot through. "The comedy of tragedy" is a term that had to be invented because of Shakespeare's achievement.

---

[2] *Johnson on Shakespeare*, ed. Walter Raleigh (London, 1929), pp. 17-18.
[3] *Ibid.*, pp. 18-19.

To return to Dr. Johnson, we must, I fear, admit that the great man, like many another critic, raised a basic problem of form without giving us a definitive ruling on the matter, which has remained to plague later generations of commentators. A valuable summary of many attempts to resolve the problem is to be found in John Russell Brown's admirable discussion of more than a half-century of criticism and analysis of Shakespeare's comedies—a sobering array of scholarly studies.[4] If it is true that when experts disagree the truth is not far off, then the truth about Shakespearian comedy must indeed be lurking hard by Mr. Brown's catalogue. For virtually every conceivable critical position is there represented, from suggestions that Shakespeare derived his plays from classical, Renaissance, or native English models, to the treatment of Shakespeare as a comic artist *sui generis,* equally remote from English and from classical tradition. Some, such as Northrop Frye [5] and C. L. Barber,[6] have seen in Shakespearian comedy a Jungian archetype of the "green world", in which Lords of Misrule (Falstaff, *par excellence*) frolic in a perpetual saturnalia. Others, such as Nevill Coghill,[7] have set Shakespearian (or "romantic") comedy off against Jonsonian (or "corrective") comedy, which is defined as performing the traditional comic functions of correcting folly and castigating vice. Perhaps the fullest statement of this view appears in H. B. Charlton's *Shakespearian Comedy* (London, 1938):

> To see [*As You Like It, Twelfth Night,* and *Much Ado About Nothing*] as a form of comedy, it is perhaps easiest to begin by realising that in kind they are essentially and obviously different from traditional classical comedy. Their main characters arouse admiration; they excite neither scorn nor contempt. They inspire us to be happy with them; they do not merely cajole us into laughing at them. Therein lies the fundamental difference between classical and Shakespearian comedy. Classical comedy is conservative. It implies a world which has reached stability sufficient for itself. Its members are assumed to be fully aware of the habits and the morals which preserve an already attained state of general well-being. The main interest is the exposure of offenders against common practice and against unquestioned propriety in the established fitness of things. Hence, its manner is satire, and its standpoint is public common sense. But Shakespearian comedy is a more venturesome and a more imaginative undertaking. It does not assume that the conditions and the requisites of man's welfare have been certainly established, and are therefore a sanctity only to be safeguarded. It speculates imaginatively on modes, not of preserving a good already reached, but of enlarging and extending the possibilities of this and other kinds of good. Its heroes (or heroines, to give them the dues of their sex) are voyagers in pursuit of a happiness not yet attained, a brave new world wherein man's life may be fuller, his sensations more exquisite and his joys more widespread, more lasting, and so more humane. But as the discoverer reaches this higher bliss, he (or rather she) is making his conquests in these realms of the spirit accessible not only to himself but to

[4] "The Interpretation of Shakespeare's Comedies: 1900-1953", in *Shakespeare Survey 8,* ed. Allardyce Nicoll (Cambridge, 1955), pp. 1-13.

[5] "The Argument of Comedy", *English Institute Essays 1948,* ed. D. A. Robertson, Jr. (New York, 1949), pp. 58-73.

[6] *Shakespeare's Festive Comedy* (Princeton, 1959).

[7] "The Basis of Shakespearean Comedy", *Essays and Studies* (London, 1950).

all others in whom he has inspired the same way of apprehending existence. He has not merely preserved the good which was; he has refined, varied, and widely extended it. Hence Shakespearian comedy is not finally satiric; it is poetic. It is not conservative; it is creative. The way of it is that of the imagination rather than that of pure reason. It is an artist's vision, not a critic's exposition. (Pp. 277-278)

This is followed by an even more extreme statement:

> Living is, indeed, not a colloquising with oneself on the top of Helvellyn, nor an exploring of the ultimate nature of matter in a laboratory. It is the setting up of harmonious and beneficent relationships with human beings. It is an active membership in the society of man. That, at all events, is what life is taken to be in Shakespeare's comedies. Of all virtues, that which best promotes its well-being is the passion for serving the world, the instinct for sacrifice in the cause of the general good, or, rather, for the good of Tom and Dick and Harry, of Maud, Bridget, Marian, Cicely, Gillian, and Ginn. ... (P. 292)

Consistent with this position, but presented in decidedly less rhapsodic terms, is the view of J. Dover Wilson, elegantly set forth in a book that is the worthy fruit of its author's eightieth year:

> We may note too [Shakespeare's] progress in the use of the critical elements of comedy. In my first chapter I distinguished Shakespearian comedy from the comedy of Jonson and later comic writers, as human and poetic as contrasted with critical. We have seen, however, that his comedy does not entirely lack critical elements. But they are always implicit and indirect rather than emphatic and forthright as in Ben Jonson. One never feels he is trying to teach, only that he derives ever keener amusement in contemplating the absurdities of the average human being. Indeed, it is always possible to watch and enjoy Shakespeare's comedies without noticing the critical aspects at all. And that was clearly what he intended. He wrote for two publics and mirrored life in his plays on two planes as it were: the surface plane of sheer entertainment, and a criticism of life below the surface for his own satisfaction and for the delight of the 'judicious' among his audience. There is something deeper too. Beneath that inexhaustible spring of geniality and fun, that prodigality of entertaining word-music, that tender and humorous observation of human frailty, that irresistible gusto and delight in every manifestation of life which we call Shakespearian comedy, we may hear, if we attune our ears, the still sad music of humanity. As I said in my first chapter, the tragic Shakespeare is implicit in the comic Shakespeare from the beginning. And after *Twelfth Night* the greatest spirit which ever spoke our tongue turned from the sunlit side of the garden to the other. He had enjoyed life, as few have ever enjoyed it, for ten years; he now set himself to face it.[8]

Another major group of critics, of whom John Palmer[9] is a distinguished representative, have concerned themselves almost exclusively with the analysis of Shakespeare's comic characters, paying scant or disrespectful attention to plays that seemed not to lend themselves readily to such examination.

The theme that runs through a great many of the studies that Mr. Brown

[8] J. Dover Wilson, *Shakespeare's Happy Comedies* (London, 1962), p. 183.
[9] *Comic Characters of Shakespeare* (London, 1953).

reviews is the rejection, explicit or implicit, of the view of Shakespearian comedy that would link it with the comic tradition of Aristophanes, Ben Jonson, Molière, Shaw, and other great practitioners of the art. The claim for the uniqueness of Shakespeare's comedies is based on the fact—alluded to by some of the critics I have cited—that, early and late, these comedies are often palpably different in conception and effect from *The Clouds, Volpone, Le Misanthrope,* or *Pygmalion* . . . as different, we may note in passing, as these admirable plays are from one another. What is this difference, and must we posit a wholly new genre in order to account for it? The difference appears to resolve itself into the statement that Shakespearian comedy belongs to the comic tradition by virtue of its movement toward a happy ending, but that it departs from the tradition because it is not consistently critical, punitive, or didactic. More important, it includes much matter that is far from comic.

I have argued elsewhere[10] for the view that Shakespeare as a comic dramatist was working within the great tradition of classical comedy, reconciling the demands of romance and comedy in a larger harmony. This still seems to me a useful way in which to think about Shakespeare's treatment of the matter of his comedies, whether in the early classical works, such as *A Midsummer Night's Dream,* the great mature comedies, such as *Twelfth Night,* or the late romantic plays, such as *The Tempest.* The late Roman and Renaissance theorists regarded comedy as essentially a love-story in which difficulties are overcome and vice exposed or folly corrected. Shakespeare's comedies in general may surely be said to conform to this description, although they admittedly diverge widely in conception, style, and comic effect. Why, after all, should we demand of Shakespeare a slavish adherence to a formula, when no other comic dramatist of the first rank is required to be so orthodox? If Shakespeare's way with comedy encompasses works as various as the Plautine *Comedy of Errors,* the knockabout Italianate *Taming of the Shrew,* the heroic *Henry IV,* the golden *As You Like It,* the dark *Measure for Measure,* and the sunset-touched *Tempest,* then spare a thought for Chekhov's *Sea Gull* or *Uncle Vanya,* for Shaw's *Heartbreak House* or *St. Joan.* Evidently Molière's *Misanthrope* is not the only comedy "qui fait rire dans l'âme".

Another, and profoundly interesting, group of writers on Shakespeare's comedies have addressed themselves to the search for underlying themes or patterns. Thus, John Russell Brown's thoughtful study concludes: "[Shakespeare's comedies] are in fact—against all immediate appearances—comedies designed around some theme of judgment, a weighing of this against that, and against those others."[11] Susanne K. Langer argues, in the rich and provocative statement of her aesthetic theory, for a view of comedy as ritualistic and "erotic, risqué, and sensuous if not sensual, impious, and even wicked"[12]— but not, oddly enough, necessarily humorous! While admitting that both Mr. Brown and Mrs. Langer have much justice on their side in seeking essentially serious explanations of comedy and its effects, I am not prepared to believe that *Le Misanthrope,* magnificent work that it is, represents the only true standard,

---

[10] *"Twelfth Night* and Shakespearean Comedy", *SQ,* VI (1955), 1-8.
[11] *Shakespeare and his Comedies* (London, 1957), p. 44.
[12] "The Great Dramatic Forms: The Comic Rhythm", in *Feeling and Form* (New York, 1953), p. 349.

the *beau idéal,* of the comic art. One may laugh in one's soul, but surely one is also permitted to laugh, without prejudice, with one's diaphragm. When Mrs. Langer finds that she must isolate something she calls "the comedy of laughter" (as distinguished from some higher form?), I must confess my skepticism.

The point cannot be made too strongly or too often that Shakespeare's comedies have lived because they have shown themselves capable, after nearly four centuries, of giving spectators and readers all over the world the true comic pleasure, which, however one explains it, expresses itself characteristically in laughter. Granted that laughter in general is so complex a phenomenon that we are still far from understanding it, and that laughter provoked by comic art is inextricably involved with convention,[13] it remains the only externalization of the comic response on which most observers can agree. The audiences that continue to find Petruchio, Launce, Falstaff, Rosalind, and Sir Toby Belch richly funny may be mistaken, poor things; but they are, happily, beyond our help.

Northrop Frye has given us, in his profound and comprehensive *Anatomy of Criticism,* an excellent approach to the problem of harmonizing the various elements of comedy within something that we may still call the comic form:

> Comedy usually moves toward a happy ending, and the normal response of the audience to a happy ending is "this should be," which sounds like a moral judgment. So it is, except that it is not moral in the restricted sense, but social. Its opposite is not the villainous but the absurd, and comedy finds the virtues of Malvolio as absurd as the vices of Angelo. Molière's misanthrope, being committed to sincerity, which is a virtue, is morally in a strong position, but the audience soon realizes that his friend Philinte, who is ready to lie quite cheerfully in order to enable other people to preserve their self-respect, is the more genuinely sincere of the two. It is of course quite possible to have a moral comedy, but the result is often the kind of melodrama that we have described as comedy without humor, and which achieves its happy ending with a self-righteous tone that most comedy avoids. It is hardly possible to imagine a drama without conflict, and it is hardly possible to imagine a conflict without some kind of enmity. But just as love, including sexual love, is a very different thing from lust, so enmity is a very different thing from hatred. In tragedy, of course, enmity almost always includes hatred; comedy is different, and one feels that the social judgment against the absurd is closer to the comic norm than the moral judgement against the wicked.[14]

Here is indeed a way of reconciling the many and various kinds of comedy in Shakespeare, the satirical comedy of *Twelfth Night*'s subplot, the romantic comedy of *Twelfth Night*'s principal plot, the comedy of intrigue of *The Taming of the Shrew* and *The Comedy of Errors,* the dark comedy of *Measure for Measure.* But there is something more, and I suggest that we can find it by returning to the challenge that Shaw put into the mouth of Bluntschli: "But now that youve found that life isnt a farce, but something quite sensible and serious, what further obstacle is there to your happiness?"

---

[13] See Langer, p. 348, and her citation of Francis Fergusson, *The Idea of a Theater* (Princeton, 1949), pp. 178-179.
[14] *Anatomy of Criticism* (Princeton, 1957), pp. 167-168.

Revelation, knowledge, and self-knowledge—in a word, wisdom—is the tie that binds Shakespeare's comedies together. The comic catharsis that is undergone by Berowne, Malvolio, Katherina, Benedick (not forgetting Beatrice), Olivia (and also Orsino)—the list stretches out to the crack of doom—is a catharsis that brings wisdom. Sometimes the wisdom is not desired (it has been observed that much knowledge brings sorrow), but Malvolio must be wise whether he will or no. The moment when wisdom comes to the comic protagonist is literally a moment of truth: disguises fall, illusions vanish, the lost is found, "journeys end in lovers' meeting". If wisdom entails further ironies and problems, they are for a Bradley to explore in a hypothetical sixth act.

Characteristically, Shakespearian comedy ends not in such wild discomfiture as Malvolio's but in a gentler resolution, accompanied by laughter, applause, and music. This has been exquisitely described by Lord David Cecil in the loveliest, wisest, and most persuasive essay ever written on Shakespeare's comedies:

> [Shakespeare's] gaiety is made poignant by a sense of its fleetingness, that sets our thoughts roving into darker regions far beyond the apparent compass of the play. As these bright figures and airy music will vanish, so, we perceive, will the carefree mood which they embodied. The pleasure of life is as ephemeral as a dream. All Shakespeare's comedies might be called 'Midsummer-Night's Dreams'; and its last speech might be the last speech in all of them:
>
> > If we shadows have offended,
> > Think but this, and all is mended,
> > That you have but slumber'd here
> > While these visions did appear.
>
> Such moments of realization are not harsh or discordant; the dance goes on, the pulsing lilting rhythm does not flag. But the melody modulates into a minor key to be touched with a wistful sadness. The fair faces grow pensive, as for an instant there passes over them the shadow of their mortality.[15]

George Washington University

[15] "Shakespearean Comedy", in *The Fine Art of Reading* (London, 1957), p 31

☞ The Public are refpectfully informed, that for the remainder of the feafon the Doors of the The will be open at half paft 5 and the curtain will rife at half paft 6 o'clock precifely.

United States' Theatre,
CITY OF WASHINGTON.

On Friday Evening, Sept. 5th 1800,

Will be prefented a TRAGEDY called

Romeo and Juliet.

Romeo,	Mr. *Cooper.*
Paris,	Mr. *Wood.*
Montague,	Mr. *L'Eftrange.*
Capulet,	Mr. *Morris.*
Mercutio,	Mr. *Bernard.*
Benvolio,	Mr. *Wignell.*
Tibalt,	Mr. *Francis.*
Friar Lawrence,	Mr. *Warren.*
Balthazer,	Mifs *Solomon.*
Apothecary,	Mr. *Milbourne.*
Peter,	Mr. *Bliffett.*
Page,	Mafter *Harris.*
Juliet,	Mrs. *Merry.*
Lady Capulet,	Mrs. *Salmon.*
Nurfe,	Mrs. *Francis.*

In Act I. A MASQUERADE, In which will be introduced the *Minuet de la Cour* and a *New Gavot* by Mafter Harris and Mifs Arnold.
In Act V. A FUNERAL PROCESSION and SOLEMN DIRGE.
The *Vocal Parts* by Meffrs. Darley, Francis, Bliffet, Robins, Mifs Arnold, Mifs Solomon, Mrs. Warren, Mrs. Stuart, &c.

To which will be added, a FARCE (in two acts) called

The Village Lawyer.

Scout,	Mr. *Warren.*
Snarl,	Mr. *Francis.*
Charles,	Mr. *Hopkins.*
Juftice Mittimus,	Mr. *Milbourne.*
Sheep Face,	Mr. *Blffct.*
Kate,	Mrs. *Stuart.*
Mrs. Scout	Mrs. *Francis.*

ADMITTANCE, One Dollar.
Places in the boxes to be taken at the Theatre from 10 to 2 o'clock on the days of Performance.
Tickets to be had at the office in the Theatre, at Way & Groff's Printing-Office, and at M'Laughlin's tavern, George-town.
Days of Performance, Monday, Wednefday, Friday and Saturday.
On *Saturday next, the COMEDY of the ROAD TO RUIN, with* Harlequin Hurry Scurry: or, the Rural Rumpus.

City of Wafhington: Printed by WAY & GROFF, North E Street, near the General Poft-Office.

Playbill for the performance of *Romeo and Juliet* at the United States Theatre in Washington, D. C., on 5 September 1800. 10¼″ x 16⅞″. Reproduced by permission of The Folger Shakespeare Library.

Shakespeare's Confluence of Tragedy and Comedy: *Twelfth Night* and *King Lear*

JULIAN MARKELS

In Memoriam Shepard Liverant

This cold night will turn us all to fools and madmen.

I am not mad, Sir Topas. I say to you this house is dark.

WELFTH *Night* and *King Lear*, evidently written within four or five years of each other, are often considered Shakespeare's greatest single achievements in the two genres of comedy and tragedy, and at very least they may be said to represent his maturest dramatic practice. Here I wish to argue that these two plays draw in large part upon a common body of intellectual and thematic material, which Shakespeare's mind shapes in each case to the forms and effects appropriate to comedy and tragedy. By examining his diverse use of this common material, we may hope to know better both the terrific centrifugal power of Shakespeare's imagination, and the process by which comedy and tragedy crystallize their distinctive structures out of a single substance.

An Elizabethan play is a life unto itself, of course, and any pursuit of differences between comedy and tragedy can easily become artificial and pedantic. Many of Shakespeare's solemn dramas have an admixture of comic stuff, and some of his ostensible comedies affright our risibility by their oblique seriousness. We find in the tragedies not only various shades and quantities of comic relief, but a comic posture in great men at their moments of intensest spiritual pain: Hamlet landing upright in Ophelia's grave with the announcement: "This is I,/Hamlet the Dane"; Othello eavesdropping on Iago and Cassio; or Lear bedecked with weeds speaking reason in madness. Comedies like *The Merchant of Venice* and *Measure for Measure,* on the other hand, are barely laughable and offer at best only cold comfort. And the humiliations of Shylock, Falstaff, and Malvolio are well-known instances where a comic perspective is threatened by a distorting pathos.

Tragedy and comedy also share many plot devices and situations. Both rely heavily upon intrigue; and the function of that old intriguer of the Moralities, the Vice, Shakespeare assigns indiscriminately to such as Puck and Iago. The customary apparatus of intrigue—the dropped handkerchiefs and forged letters and disguised madness, the indispensable arras and play-within-a-play, the slippings in and out of clothes to disguise sex and social status—all this provides as much of the framework of *Hamlet* and *Othello* as of *A Midsummer Night's Dream* and *The Tempest*. Character types which we habitually associate with one genre appear surprisingly in the other, Don John and Caliban in comedy, Mercutio and Oswald in tragedy. The device of the pretended death strategem, and its obverse, the hopefully drawn out actual death, are almost ubiquitous. The comic and serious elements so often overlap that on this subject it would be easy to say with some critics simply that Shakespeare is Shakespeare and the rest is silence.

But the relationship between *Twelfth Night* and *King Lear* goes significantly beyond this routine overlapping. One way in which *King Lear* surprises us is by its Fool, a figure whose presence we might have thought unbecoming to tragedy, especially one so bleak and bare as this. By logic and tradition the domestic fool belongs to comedy; and when Shakespeare introduces such a character in *Othello,* a tragedy whose thickly textured social surface reminds us of the comedies, even then the fool's part turns out fatally incommensurate with the size of the play, so insignificant that it seems to most producers hardly worth the trouble it takes to cast. But in *King Lear* Shakespeare goes right on, not only to discover by his art a truly functional part for a domestic fool, but to make the very word "fool" a blessing and a sanctification. All the good characters of the play, all who sooner or later stand up for Lear, in their purity or their purification are nevertheless called "fool". The Fool, who always speaks true, calls Lear "fool" for giving up his kingdom, and Kent for getting into the stocks. When Lear wakes up in Cordelia's tent, he confirms this judgment: in his earned humility he calls himself a fond and foolish old man. Goneril says of her husband Albany that her fool usurps her body. Lear in his madness and Gloucester in his blindness become "natural" fools unwittingly, and thereby are restored to bias of nature. Edgar, as if acting on their cue, wills himself a fool in order to preserve himself to life. The Fool leaves the play when its other truth-speaker, Cordelia, re-enters it; and when at last Lear comes on carrying her corpse, he cries that his poor fool is dead.

The word "fool" runs through a spectrum of meanings throughout the play, as when in successive speeches Lear calls the world a "great stage of fools" and himself "The natural fool of fortune". The Fool himself encompasses this range of meaning in a song that provides a microscopic statement of almost the whole idea of *King Lear:*

> That sir which serves and seeks for gain,
> And follows but for form,
> Will pack when it begins to rain,
> And leave thee in the storm.
> But I will tarry; the fool will stay,
> And let the wise man fly.
> The knave turns fool that runs away;
> The fool no knave, perdy.

Like the protean word "nature", "fool" is a major vehicle of thought in this most philosophic of Shakespeare's plays; and it is conceptually related to "nature" by inseparable bonds of meaning even at the farthest reaches of the play's doctrine. That is surely a large part for a comic concept in so terrifying a tragedy as *King Lear*.

The relation between Lear and his Fool which generates this meaning has been precisely anticipated in the opening dialogue between Olivia and her Fool in *Twelfth Night* (I. v). Lear's Fool bounces on to the stage offering his coxcomb to Kent for taking Lear's part, and then throughout two acts proposes a series of conundrums uniformly designed to show Lear a fool for giving his kingdom to his daughters. Olivia's Fool, who has absented himself from her household ever since she took a vow to mourn her brother's death for seven years, gets back in her good graces by proving her a fool:

> *Clown.* Good madonna, why mourn'st thou?
> *Olivia.* Good clown, for my brother's death.
> *Clown.* I think his soul is in hell, madonna.
> *Olivia.* I know his soul is in heaven, fool.
> *Clown.* The more fool, madonna, to mourn for your brother's soul, being in heaven. Take away the fool, gentlemen.
> *Olivia.* What think you of this fool, Malvolio? Doth he not mend?

Malvolio, of course, thinks not, and soon explains why:

> *Malvolio.* I marvel that your ladyship takes delight in such a barren rascal. I saw him put down the other day with an ordinary fool that has no more brain than a stone. Look you now, he's out of his guard already. Unless you laugh and minister occasion to him, he is gagged. *I protest I take these wise men that crow so at these set kind of fools no better than the fools' zanies.*
>
> *Olivia.* O, you are sick of self-love, Malvolio, and taste with a distempered appetite. To be generous, guiltless, and of free disposition, is to take those things for birdbolts that you deem cannon bullets. *There is no slander in an allowed fool, though he do nothing but rail; nor no railing in a known discreet man, though he do nothing but reprove.*[1]

This passage is packed with relevant matter. We may begin by reminding ourselves how it expresses the social function of the domestic fool, whom Olivia here calls "allowed" and Goneril in *King Lear* calls "all-licensed". He is a household servant whose address to his master is permitted a degree of freedom that would be considered slanderous in anybody else, because his purpose is to mend his master's follies. When Olivia asks whether the Fool does not "mend", probably she means improve in the performance of his vocation, although it has been suggested that she means "make amends" for his long absence from her household. But in either case the word in context means more than Olivia intends: in catechizing his mistress, the Fool attempts to mend her distempered appetite for mourning. He is trying to recall her from a violation of propriety, custom, and good sense, just as Lear's Fool does, and as Olivia herself is to do with Malvolio and Sir Toby.

In performing this corrective social function, the domestic fool wins the wise man's praise, a fact which Malvolio cannot understand. Olivia, having just been mended into "fool" herself, now undertakes the Fool's function with Malvolio. She affirms by implication that social custom and the cosmic scheme of life are consistent with one another, and that this harmony should be per-

[1] All italics within Shakespearian quotations are mine.

fectly evident to anyone not sick of self-love and thereby out of tune both with custom and with life. If there is no slander in an allowed fool, that is because of the artifice of social institutions whose creature he is: the Fool's words are licensed by the fiat of the social order. But there is no railing in a "known discreet man" only because his discretion has its source outside social institutions in what we can properly call Nature herself. If his reproofs cannot be mistaken for railing, that is not simply because society has so contrived the rules of the game. Society has not invented his wisdom, it has discovered it: the wise man's words are licensed because they are *known* to be discreet, because society looks beyond itself to discover a pattern of wisdom and hence of words by which to order itself. Thus the wise man's discretion guarantees society, whose custom licenses the Fool's words, which in turn aspire to keep custom aligned with discretion and the social fabric mended. "Marry, here's grace and a codpiece; that's a wise man and a fool."

This particular relation between the fool and wise man is one version of that parallelism of the social order and the cosmic order which has been the central issue in a series of Shakespeare's histories and tragedies culminating in *King Lear*. Shakespeare addresses himself preeminently in *King Lear* to the question of whether there is any reason in nature for the order and custom of society. Lear at the beginning, sick with self-love and a distempered appetite, wrenches apart custom and wise discretion by dividing his kingdom and making his daughters speak prettily for their portions. He divorces social form from the cosmic substance for which Cordelia stands, thereby making a breach in the social fabric through which now may pass all those who "seek for gain" and "follow but for form". Lear is chastised for his mistake first by the Fool, who seeks to mend him with the words licensed by society, and then, as society itself disintegrates, by Nature herself, in whom the principles of wise discretion are presumed to originate. Shakespeare goes on to ask in *King Lear* whether that presumption is justified, a question which, as I will indicate later, is proper to tragedy and not comedy. But now I want to look more fully at the way in which Lear's experience, as I have so briefly described it, bears a striking resemblance to Malvolio's.

Both men are punished for an affectation that threatens the order of rank and the stability of custom in society, and in both this affectation is expressed by conduct and imagery relating to clothes. Metaphorically speaking, Lear dresses falsely by inviting from his daughters flattering words unwarranted by his status either as king or father. The speeches he wants to hear, and with which his older daughters oblige him, violate social custom and basic human style in the same way as do the yellow stockings and cross-garters of Malvolio. But the sartorial consequences of Lear's mistake are not at all metaphorical. First he is stripped of his retinue of knights, and protests this act as a denial of clothing in his famous "reason not the need" speech:

> Allow not nature more than nature needs,
> Man's life is cheap as beast's. Thou art a lady:
> If only to go warm were gorgeous,
> Why, nature needs not what thou gorgeous wear'st,
> Which scarcely keeps thee warm.

When next he is denied even shelter, and he comes upon Edgar in the storm disguised by no clothes as Tom o' Bedlam (". . . he reserved a blanket, else we had all been shamed", says the Fool), Lear in his inspired madness questions whether all clothing is not affectation, and begins to disrobe in an effort to achieve the "unaccommodated" state in which he finds Edgar. This act is repeated by Lear in his right mind at the end of the play, when, thinking Cordelia dead and hence ready to give up his own restored life and accommodation, he says, "Pray you, undo this button."

From beginning to end, the idea of clothing is central to both Lear's and Malvolio's interpretation of their spiritual experience. In the full frenzy of his madness, Lear makes one speech—the one which Edgar calls "Reason in madness"—in which he describes how clothes may be used not to accommodate the bare forked animal which is natural man, but to cover by their gorgeousness discommoding violations of human justice and social order. This speech is equally a reflection upon Lear's "overdressing" at the beginning of the play, and upon Malvolio's fantasy of grandeur just before he picks up the fatal letter. I place Lear's and Malvolio's speeches together in order to illustrate the relationship:

> *Lear* . . . .
> Through tattered clothes small vices do appear;
> Robes and furred gowns hide all. Plate sin with gold,
> And the strong lance of justice hurtless breaks;
> Arm it in rags, a pygmy's straw does pierce it.
> None does offend, none—I say none! I'll able 'em.
>
> *Malvolio.* To be Count Malvolio. There is example for't. *The Lady of the Strachy married the yeoman of the wardrobe.* Having been three months married to her, sitting in my state—Calling my officers about me, *in my branched velvet gown;* having come from a day-bed, where I have left Olivia sleeping—*And then to have the humour of state;* and after a demure travel of regard, telling them I know my place, as I would they should do theirs, to ask for my kinsman Toby—Seven of my people, with an obedient start, make out for him. I frown the while, and perchance wind up my watch, or play with my—some rich jewel. Toby approaches; curtsies there to me—I extend my hand to him thus, quenching my familiar smile with an austere regard of control—Saying, 'Cousin Toby, *my fortunes having cast me on your niece, give me this prerogative of speech.* You must amend your drunkeness.'[2]

The "humour of state", as Malvolio imagines it, is capricious and arbitrary both in its acquisition and its exercise. It is conferred automatically upon him who wears the "branched velvet gown", and becomes a form of playacting designed to puff the ego. It alights upon Toby's drunkenness in order to satisfy Malvolio's vanity rather than any principle of decorum or justice. In a word, for similarly egotistical motives, Malvolio dreams himself into the exact situation and conduct of Lear in the opening scene. Lear exercises a capricious "humour of state" in demanding from his daughters protestations of love merely to please his personal vanity. We sympathize, of course, with his original wish to divide

---

[2] I have made Malvolio's discourse continuous by eliminating the various interruptions of the eavesdroppers.

his kingdom and live out his remaining life unburdened by public cares; and
Shakespeare has taken great pains to make us sympathize with Malvolio's underlying desire to correct Toby's conduct. But we have been persuaded to
approve their ends only so that we may perceive more clearly the error of their
means. Both men proceed on the assumption that "Robes and furred gowns
hide all." This assumption rips the social fabric, and forces both men eventually
to reap the whirlwind.

Beyond Lear himself, there is still another way in which a concern with
clothes links the two plays. When Lear encounters the half-naked Edgar on
the heath and asks him what he has been, Edgar replies:

> A servingman, proud in heart and mind; that curled my hair, wore gloves
> in my cap; served the lust of my mistress' heart, and did the act of darkness
> with her. . . .

To explain the cause of his undoing, Edgar attributes to his former self aspirations for which Malvolio becomes a comic butt. This former self is of course
fictitious; but in *King Lear* Shakespeare provides us with its living image in
Goneril's servant Oswald, a counterpart to Malvolio of whom Kent says, "A
tailor made thee". Oswald too is an *arriviste;* to the Elizabethan audience he
is the familiar type of the lower-class person on the make, and expressing his
upward social mobility by the clothes he wears. He is willing to cooperate with
Goneril's "humour of state" so long as it promises advancement to himself; and
in this he is carefully contrasted with Cornwall's servant who is never more loyal
than when he tries to prevent Cornwall from tearing out Gloucester's eyes.
While there is no direct suggestion of a sexual relationship between Oswald and
his mistress, something of the same taint is produced by Goneril's willingness
to have him witness her promising Edmund her sexual favors, and by Edgar's
remark after killing him:

> I know thee well. A serviceable villain,
> As duteous to the vices of thy mistress
> As badness would desire.

The relationship between Oswald and Malvolio suggests another important
connection between the two plays, less conspicuous than their mutual concern
with clothing, but at least equally important. That is their concern with the
effect upon the social order of a belief in Fortune's efficacy as an agent in human
affairs. Here again Malvolio provides the focus. When Maria announces the
prank she will play on Malvolio, she specifies in detail the qualities which make
him an eligible victim:

> The devil a Puritan that he is, *or anything constantly but a time-pleaser;
> an affectioned ass,* that cons state without book and utters it by great
> swarths; the best persuaded of himself; so crammed, as he thinks, with
> excellencies that it is his grounds of faith that all that look on him love him;
> and on that vice in him will my revenge find notable cause to work.

She announces her plan to her confederates; and in the great scene where the
plan is executed, she no sooner plants the forged letter and hides herself than
Malvolio comes on the stage speaking those words above all which make him
her legitimate victim: " 'Tis but fortune, all is fortune."

He reiterates almost tiresomely this belief in the supremacy of fortune through-out the scenes of his temptation and fall. In his imaginary address to Sir Toby that I have quoted, he claims that "my fortunes having cast me on your niece", he now has the right to correct Toby's conduct. The forged letter challenges him to be "worthy to touch Fortune's fingers". When he decides that the letter is in earnest and his lady loves him, he says, "Jove and my stars be praised". When he appears before his lady yellow-stockinged and cross-gartered, he man-ages wholly to misconstrue Olivia's unmistakable displeasure only because he believes that he is in friendly Fortune's hands:

> And when she went away now, 'Let this fellow be looked to.' 'Fellow.' Not 'Malvolio,' *nor after my degree,* but 'fellow.' Why, everything adheres together, that no dram of a scruple, no scruple of a scruple, no obstacle, no incredulous or unsafe circumstance—what can be said? Nothing that can be can come between me and the full prospect of my hopes. *Well, Jove, not I, is the doer of this, and he is to be thanked.*

Drunk with his delusion, he has forgotten what his "degree" really is. But that only leads him to believe that Olivia no longer thinks "degree" a relevant criterion of human conduct. When circumstances adhere together, degree and scruples may be forgotten. That is why only Jove is to be thanked.

Now as it is Malvolio's faith that all who look on him love him, he is like Lear at the beginning; as he is an affectioned ass, he is like Oswald; but as he is nothing constantly but a time-pleaser whose goddess is Fortune, he encompasses in one stroke the whole range of evil whose separate gradations are represented in *King Lear* by Oswald, Goneril, and Edmund. A faith in the rule of capricious fortune instead of stable customs with cosmic sanctions is the central offense and villainy of both plays. And it is a familiar fact that Shake-speare attributed the belief in Fortune's supreme power specifically to his vil-lains, from Richard III to Edmund, and that he consistently argued by his art that Fortune's devotees have room to get in the door of the social order only when degree goes out.

Lear himself opens the door in his opening scene. In this connection it is fruitless to argue whether Lear's error is dividing the kingdom or demanding flattering speeches. From the point of view of Shakespeare's dramatic structure rather than general ethics, these constitute a single act, which gives the oppor-tunity to all those who seek for gain and follow but for form, and Edmund principally among them. Like all of Shakespeare's Machiavels, Edmund be-lieves first of all in himself, in the self-sufficiency of the individual to go as far as his wits will carry him in the struggle to dominate a world organized upon the principles of free individual enterprise. In his famous opening soliloquy, he specifically rejects "the plague of custom" and "the curiosity of nations", with their correlative standards of legitimacy. But he clearly recognizes a supra-human limitation that is equivalent to Malvolio's "Jove":

> Well, my legitimate, *if* this letter speed,
> And my invention thrive, Edmund the base
> Shall top the legitimate. I grow, I prosper.
> Now, gods, stand up for bastards.

He will grow and prosper not by upholding custom and degree, but by a happy adherence of circumstances beyond the reach of scruples: his letter arriving swiftly, his wits remaining unimpaired, and the gods befriending him. He repeatedly manifests this dependence upon an accidental concatenation of circumstances not wholly within his control, as when he improvises his plan to have Edgar banished:

> My father hath set guard to take my brother,
> And I have one thing of *a queasy question*
> *Which I must act. Briefness and fortune, work!*

In his Machiavellian self-reliance, Edmund sums up a whole line of Shakespeare's villains; and it is especially striking that Shakespeare has Edmund repeatedly ask Fortune to bless his improvisations, and thereby qualify his own self-reliance. Shakespeare began his long encounter with the Machiavel by having Richard Crookback kill his king and announce, "I am myself alone". He climaxes it with Edmund, who says, in effect, "I am myself alone so long as Fortune is my friend"; and who ends by announcing, "The wheel has come full circle; I am here." From "I am myself alone" to "I am here" there lies an exciting intellectual development which cannot be discussed now. But it must be emphasized that for Edmund at the end, "here" is the place where he is not alone. It is the place where, unstrapped from the wheel of Fortune, he is free to remember that he was loved by Goneril and Regan, and able to take thought for Lear and Cordelia. Like Malvolio in his blindness to Olivia's displeasure, Edmund has been impervious to human contact so long as he has believed himself to be in touch with Fortune's fingers. In his amorous relations with Goneril and Regan throughout the play, he has been as mechanical and bloodless as Malvolio in cross-garters. It is a familiar fact that in *King Lear* evil is self-destructive; Edmund's evil wears itself out when he stops believing himself to be Fortune's darling, and thereby opens himself up to the currents of human sympathy that seek to flow in and out of him.

Edmund's "here", in short, is the place where Cordelia and other fools have stood from the beginning. It is the place presided over by custom and by Nature, the place where "the curiosity of nations" must govern the wearing of clothes, the uttering of vows, and the begetting of children. Cordelia stands for a hierarchy of custom patterned on the structure of created Nature, the Nature of the Chain of Being rather than the Struggle for Existence, so that both society and nature must either stand together or else relapse together into original Chaos. In this Cordelia has been anticipated by Olivia, when she chastises her uncle Toby for the disorders which are a comic counterpart to Edmund's villainy:

> Will it ever be thus? Ungracious wretch,
> Fit for the mountains and the barbarous caves,
> Where manners ne'er were preached! Out of my sight!

These women plead, as women should, for an idiom and a rhetoric of manners which alone make human love possible, and therefore human society. And Cordelia is aware that every idiom is limited and vulnerable, that Fortune does indeed play a role in human affairs. The difference between Cordelia on the one hand, and Malvolio and Edmund on the other, is not that Cordelia refuses to attribute power to Fortune; it is that she perceives clearly how the power of Fortune may work capriciously to produce disorder and push the world toward Chaos, and that she therefore refuses to hitch her wagon to erratically revolving stars or turning wheels. In *King Lear,* first Cordelia and then Kent and then again Cordelia risk their lives to stand fast in the face of adverse Fortune, because they know that only in this way may the structure of the whole Creation be sustained. Cordelia's very last words, when beyond expectation she has been defeated in battle and taken prisoner, are these:

> We are not the first
> Who with best meaning have incurred the worst.
> For thee, oppressed king, I am cast down;
> Myself could else outfrown false Fortune's frown.
> Shall we not see these daughters and these sisters?

Whatever else it may mean, her ability to outfrown false Fortune's frown must include the ability with best meaning to incur the worst, and thereby to *render* Fortune false by withholding her allegiance from it. Cordelia and Kent, and eventually Lear himself, become the natural fools of fortune in order to redeem Nature from the general curse to which the adherents of Fortune have brought her.

"Fortune" brings us inexorably back to "fool", where we began, and to the area where the two plays diverge in order to fulfill themselves respectively as comedy and tragedy. I have ignored some details of the relationship between *Twelfth Night* and *King Lear,* such as the way in which Sir Andrew and Sir Toby elaborate with variations the Malvolio-theme in *Twelfth Night,* and have their own interesting connections with Oswald and Edmund in *King Lear.* But I hope I have said enough to establish three points of similarity, all of which are essential to both plays. Both give a prominent part to a domestic fool, and incorporate the familiar social philosophy of degree and custom that is implied by the institution of the domestic fool. Both plays seek to validate that philosophy by applying it to the wearing of clothes. And both plays seek to defend that philosophy against a belief in the disorderly caprice of Fortune. Many of Shakespeare's plays are concerned with one or another of these ideas; but I do not think any show all three in such close combination, or that any other two plays are so strikingly similar in their use of a single combination.

An examination of the differences deepens our sense of the pervasive similarity; for the differences are what one might expect from the "comic" as against the "tragic" uses of a common material. "Comedy" and "tragedy" are vexed words, like "fool" and "fortune"; but we need be concerned here only with those general features of the two genres upon which reasonable men have been quick to agree. Comedy, says Aristotle, is an imitation of men worse than ourselves, whose mistake or deformity does not cause pain to others, and may therefore be chastised and purged by laughter. Tragedy is an imitation of men somewhat better than ourselves, whose errors of judgment cause pain to others, and who must therefore be chastised by dire events producing pity and fear and a catharsis of those emotions. The comic character's mistake affronts the values of society without undermining them: because he has brought pain to nobody else, nobody is moved to ask whether there is any reason either for his mistake or for the standard by which it is judged. Society can cure him of his error without examining its own conscience. It affirms its benign hegemony over human affairs first by laughing at him, and then by moving him offstage to make way for the marriages necessary to tighten the social fabric which his conduct has merely stretched. But the tragic protagonist tears the social fabric. His mistake is not innocent; it radiates pain and discord throughout the serried ranks of society, leaving society too shaken to reassert itself by its customary ceremonies. The tragic hero and his society force each other to a mutual reexamination of conscience, in order to justify either the alleged mistake of the one or the settled custom of the other. Where comedy is anthropological, tragedy is metaphysical. Comedy asks *how* the individual gets out of tune with society, and how society restores harmony. Tragedy asks *why* the individual behaves in this way, and why society insists upon its standards. Where comedy deals only with efficient causes, tragedy keeps asking whether there is any reason in nature.

Where *Twelfth Night* is concerned with a household, *King Lear* is concerned with a family; and ultimately with the family of man. To maintain a household, it is often enough to have a domestic fool policing the general poise. But to maintain a family it is sometimes necessary to go back to human beginnings in that created Nature which is the source of all poise. When a man becomes impervious to the ministrations of the domestic fool, he must descend into the destructive element and reconstitute himself by becoming a natural fool. That is what happens in *King Lear,* and conspicuously does not happen in *Twelfth Night*. The "natural fool", for the Elizabethans, is the person in a state of witlessness corresponding to the original Chaos of Nature before it has been shaped into Creation. Such a person can be an idiot or simpleton whose condition is irredeemable. Maria in *Twelfth Night* hints at this meaning when, Sir Toby having claimed for his friend Aguecheek "all the good gifts of nature", she says, "He hath, indeed, almost natural". But *King Lear* tells us that the natural fool can be in a condition of pregnant madness rather than impotent idiocy, in an amorphous condition amenable to society's shaping hands of custom and degree. Our humanity is imparted to us by those hands; and when we have twisted ourselves out of shape and place in Creation, we need to be returned to our original plastic character as natural fools in order to be sorted and shaped once more into men. Only by beginning again whenever necessary as natural fools may we end by becoming men. That is why the word "fool" acquires in *King Lear* a sacramental character.

The tragic movement of *King Lear* is toward the condition of the natural fool, and even its domestic fool participates in that movement. There is a striking difference in posture between the domestic fools in *Twelfth Night* and *King Lear*. Olivia and her Fool proceed in a ceremonious and highly structured pattern:

> *Clown.* Good madonna, why mourn'st thou?
> *Olivia.* Good fool, for my brother's death.
> *Clown.* I think his soul is in hell, madonna.
> *Olivia.* I know his soul is in heaven, fool.

The order and balance of their discourse maintain the poise of that society whose delightful ornament is the domestic fool. But Lear's Fool comes on the stage in the midst of social disorder already rampant—when Lear is rewarding Kent for tripping Oswald for being impertinent to Lear—and he contributes to the general confusion by offering Kent his cap. When he proves Lear a fool, as Olivia's Fool had done, Lear threatens him with whipping, whereas Olivia admitted that her Fool did mend. Too late to mend his master and maintain the social order, the Fool joins Lear in his downward course toward the "natural" condition. His riddles become increasingly functionless and distracted as he is pushed step by step out of doors, until he himself anticipates his own transformation from domestic to natural fool: "This cold night will turn us all to fools and madmen." Once this end is in sight, Lear's Fool has no more function in the play than in the society which has degenerated so far as not to need him indoors. For Lear himself is now a "natural", and must be recreated instead of merely contained. Stripped of clothes and wits, Lear does finally and perilously achieve that reason in madness which purges his pride and reconciles him to Cordelia in genuine contrition. By becoming a natural fool he renews himself as a man; and because this implies his acceptance of the shaping force of custom, we are reassured of society's continuance after his death. The confrontation of the tragic protagonist and his society has forced a mutual dissolution and reformation, which prophecies a spiritual renewal of the family of man.

The Fool in *Twelfth Night* is not allowed to become a "natural". And when in the guise of Sir Topas he tries to provoke Malvolio, Lear's counterpart in pride and clothes, to the same "natural" madness in which Lear outdistances his Fool, the sign of Malvolio's restoration as a man, and of his renewed adherence to custom and degree, is precisely that he does not yield to this provocation. Where Lear is chastised at the hands of Nature in the cold outdoors, Malvolio's society locks him indoors. Lear's daughters put him out with no concern for his wits one way or the other; for them his madness will be only a regrettable circumstance of Fortune. But Malvolio's tormentors try deliberately to persuade him that he is mad.

> *Malvolio.* I am not mad, Sir Topas. I say to you this house is dark.
> *Clown.* Madman, thou errest. I say there is no darkness but ignorance, in which thou art more puzzled than the Egyptians in their fog.
> *Malvolio.* I say this house is dark as ignorance, though ignorance were dark as hell; and I say there was never man thus abused. I am no more mad than you are. Make the trial of it in any constant question.
> *Clown.* What is the opinion of Pythagoras concerning wild fowl?
> *Malvolio.* That the soul of our grandam might happily inhabit a bird.
> *Clown.* What think'st thou of his opinion?
> *Malvolio.* I think nobly of the soul and no way approve his opinion.
> *Clown.* Fare thee well. Remain thou still in darkness. Thou shalt hold the opinion of Pythagoras ere I will allow of thy wits, and fear to kill a woodcock, lest thou dispossess the soul of thy grandam. Fare thee well.

Malvolio's wits are subjected to further trial before he is allowed back into the light, and they remain as clear and stable as we see them here. The Fool's joke at the end, which deflates Pythagoras' opinion and indirectly approves Malvolio's, reassures us that Malvolio has been cured at a stroke. Malvolio's firm resistance to continued attempts to undo him into a "natural" confirms our impression that his pride has been purged, and hence reassures us that his society does not need to be dissolved. In the dialogue quoted, Malvolio's return to normality is indicated by his clarity of mind and the correctness of his philosophic manners, but most of all by his ability to participate suavely with the Fool in just the same sort of set catechism by which we have already seen the Fool mend Olivia.[3] The artful formality of the discourse signifies the health and continuity of a society which has enabled this Fool to succeed in curing Malvolio where Lear's Fool had to fail.

This contrast in the form and extent of Lear's and Malvolio's chastisement for similar mistakes reflects a larger contrast in the structure of comic and tragic plots in *Twelfth Night* and *King Lear*. The concentrated power of *King Lear* carries us over some discrepancies in plotting that Shakespeare had many times before managed to avoid. In both its plots the play begins with incredible situations that make strenuous demands upon the audience's faith; and we are not at all rewarded by a closely plotted drama in which we had only to accept the major premise. In the remainder of the play there are not the probable connections among events, the intricately patterned reversals of our expectations, that Shakespeare had created so deftly in plays like *Hamlet* and *Othello*. One dire event is made to succeed another artificially, with such unchallenged force as to seem gratuitous. Shakespeare interrupts Lear's step by step descent into madness only in order to enhance its grim effect by showing us the "madness" of Edgar and the blinding of Gloucester. We and Lear are given no respite; our steadily mounting apprehensions are not relieved even momentarily—as we might expect them to be in life—not even in order to produce dramatic credibility and its correlative suspense. When Lear finds a hovel that promises shelter and restorative sleep, Edgar the Bedlam hops out raving and pushes him further into madness. When Lear and Edgar and the Fool have enacted the mock trial of Goneril and Regan, and Lear is asleep at last, Gloucester brings news of a plot upon the King's life, and Kent must wake him up unrestored and lead him to Dover. And at the end of the play the deaths of Cordelia and Lear are made to seem as much as possible fortuitous: they can be accounted for neither by ordinary considerations of human probability nor by any internal logic of the play itself.

The improbable sequence of this stark plot is produced by depriving the good characters of any influence upon events or our responses to events. It is incredible that Kent should not reveal himself to Lear, that Edgar should not reveal himself to his father when conducting him to Dover, or above all that the reformed Edmund should not bethink himself sooner to rescind his sentence of death upon Cordelia and Lear. These omissions deprive Shakespeare of many opportunities to produce in his audience feelings of relief and reassurance, those reversals of expectation that will make the final catastrophe, once it comes, seem inevitable rather than gratuitous. The characters are submitted

---

[3] Malvolio's clarity of mind and firmness under pressure in this scene make him a less pathetic figure than he is frequently taken to be. Since his sanity remains imperturbable despite his tormentors, and since he does not indulge in self-pity, we can go on laughing at him without being altogether hard-hearted.

to the gloomy provenance of the plot even at the expense of probability; and, as D. G. James has argued in his fine book, *The Dream of Learning,* Shakespeare's procedure here is deliberate: it serves to isolate, abstract, and allegorize the good characters into images of patient suffering:

> . . . it [Good] is made silent and patient; it is suffering love; it has little influence upon the executive ordering of the world; it merely *is* and suffers; it is not what it does but what it is, as is shown in a Cordelia and an Edgar, that we contemplate. Evil drives on, dynamic and masterful, but to its own destruction; Good is still, patient, and enduring, but it is also destroyed; no limit, not even that of death, is put to what it must endure.[4]

Men must endure their going hence even as their coming hither. That is what the plot itself of *King Lear* teaches us, in its improbable lack of a running dramatic conflict that actively opposes good to evil. The plot in its structure insists upon a motionless confrontation between the fool and Fortune, and is resolved when the fool of truth outfrowns false Fortune and thereby redeems the world.

Twelfth Night, on the other hand, is rightly said to be a superbly plotted play, by which we really mean that its plot never for a moment by the slightest lapse or oversight permits such an elemental confrontation. This plot submits its characters to a benign dispensation whose very intricacy of connection among events assures us that capricious Fortune cannot get her foot in the door of the social order. Instead of forcing its characters to suffer Fortune through, this plot forbids the encounter. I suppose that nothing in all of Shakespeare contrasts more sharply with Lear's descent into the "natural" condition, which is truly a sequence of one damned thing after another, than the sequence of events in *Twelfth Night* by which Sebastian arrives in the social condition just in the nick of time to prevent the duel which threatens it, and to lend himself to the marriage that knits the social fabric. Sebastian arrives on the scene just before Malvolio appears before his lady cross-gartered. Malvolio's challenge to the social order is no sooner met than Sir Toby and his cohorts pose a new threat by their plan for the duel. Viola is no sooner trapped by their plan than Antonio appears, and, supposing her to be Sebastian, forestalls the duel. But immediately Antonio is arrested, and his "betrayal" by Viola-Cesario-Sebastian encourages Sir Andrew to think his opponent a faithless coward and to attempt the duel again. He runs after Viola but encounters Sebastian, who cuffs Sir Andrew about and then is saved from Sir Toby's wrath by Olivia's mistaking him for Viola. Next we witness the restoration of Malvolio that I have described, and then we are ready for the triple marriage. Almost every episode in this series reverses the expectations aroused in us by the immediately preceding episode. The suspense is itchingly tight and delectable; and it keeps the characters locked inside the social order, protected from the risks which the unwound plot of *King Lear* insists upon. This plot, instead of stripping life bare to the gaze of Fortune and then Nature, clothes it in a magical intricacy of events that keeps the social world intact. Just as the catechism of Sir Topas certifies Malvolio's judgment, so the plot of the whole play polices the manners and judgment of that society for which the plot is a metaphor.

---

[4] (Oxford, 1951), p. 117.

One dimension of *King Lear* as Shakespeare's greatest tragedy is its bare and somber plot. One sign that *Twelfth Night* is his greatest comedy is its tight and bubbling plot. Both plots work upon the same thematic materials: the order of society threatened by furred gowns and false fortune. Both plots work out those materials to essentially the same conclusion: man in society must stand fast by custom even in the face of Fortune. To achieve that conclusion in any coherent and aesthetically satisfying form requires the highest intellectual powers. To confirm that conclusion again and again by reaching it in diverse forms equally coherent and satisfying each in its own way, is only to be Shakespeare and leave the rest to silence.

Ohio State University

'Twere Best not Know Myself: Othello, Lear, Macbeth

ROBERT B. HEILMAN

WHATEVER theoretical status may be assigned to self-knowledge in the tragic process, the historic fact is that major tragedies characteristically deal in some part with the action of the hero's mind as it turns upon, or toward, or away from, himself. It is this interaction of the hero's mind with the least yielding of all materials that contributes some of the necessary toughness of the tragic substance. If self does not surrender unconditionally to mind, mind, on the other hand, may be a fugitive from the very self that, in line of duty, it should be trying to imprison. Yet such a flight may be an inverted understanding, and evidence of power to understand. It is different from sheer incapacity of mind, which is not the material of tragedy at all, but of one kind of comedy. When we have to make do with a protagonist of so little intelligence as Willie Loman, it is hard to feel that the work is tragic. The substance lacks toughness. The world shown is rather a sad, pudgy, untonic one. We take it in at a glance, and we know that in it there is little to experience or learn. It offers little more than the pathos of a commonplace obtuseness.

Commonplace obtuseness is not held out as bait for our sympathy in Shakespeare's tragedies. These present, in their heroes, rather a misconstruction of reality, a resistance to the very enlightenment that seems unavoidable, a malorientation of view shored up or required by other motives. Not to have the talent for self-knowledge is one thing; to have the talent and be unable or unwilling to use it is another. It is somewhat standard praise of Oedipus that he unshirkingly seeks the facts, driving through to the truth regardless of cost. Here is the romantic adulation of the explorer: Tennyson on Ulysses. This modern interpretation, however, is less untrue than incomplete. As king, Oedipus is on the spot, and he has to produce—a situation conducive to unhesitant pursuit. Furthermore, the truth after which he relentlessly plunges has to do, he believes until late in the day, with someone other than himself. At the same time he is so sure of his own rightness, merit, and skill that he hardly follows the trail of the evidence: when the conduct of others does not accord with his own expectations or prejudgments, he assumes wilfulness, disobedience, or subversive activity. He is, that is to say, well equipped with the tools by which men resist truth. Technically, he is open to truth, or to what he takes to be truth; at the same time his own complacency closes off his vision of a particular movement of truth. Even when he sees, at last, that it is moving against himself, and accepts it, he believes that the damage will be in the realm of accident (birth) rather than of essence (moral action).

To say this is not to deflate Oedipus but to admire Sophocles on grounds somewhat different from the usual ones: he combined in one character both the will to pursue truth and the aspects of personality which help deflect, evade, and misconstrue it. Hence he created an archetypal pattern for the drama of self-knowledge: the hero has the capacity for knowing, but he has also other desires and needs that stand between him and what he can know. Or these desires and needs actually oblige him not to know what he might know or should know. Shakespeare repeatedly applies himself to this drama of consciousness, but always with a fresh sense of the interplay between the mind, knowing or unknowing, and the self to be known.

To speak of that which is to be known is to suggest the presence of an inert mass of the knowable to be taken in or rejected by the knower's mind. There is also an interesting alternative: truth can be presented as trying actively to break through to human consciousness. In *The Infernal Machine* Cocteau manages this assumption in a very clever theatrical fashion: not only the ambiguities of Tiresias, but the dreams of Jocasta and Oedipus, and indeed the ghost of Laius himself are crying out to Jocasta and Oedipus and imploring them to know what they are doing. It is an original way of dramatizing the impenetrability of a consciousness made rigid by commitments already undertaken in the heat of strong desires. What is novel in Cocteau is the ingenuity of the psychological detail and the bold mingling of the symbolic and naturalistic styles that has developed almost into a mode in the post-realistic theater. Yet his basic interpretation of reality makes little advance upon that dramatized by Marlowe, four centuries earlier, in the most remarkable parts of *Dr. Faustus*. Faustus' mind is wholly occupied, it appears, by the conviction that the cosmos is vulnerable to intellectual storming, and that any method of attack may be used with impunity. But the heart of the drama is the existence of, call it another Faustus, another part of the personality, another knowing, which is closer to the center of the self, and which embodies a more valid sense of reality. Faustus denies it, laughs it out of court, and feels ecstatically free to charge the heights and the depths. Hence arises the deadly battle between the upper mind, the maker of decisions and the determiner of action, and the old, knowing self, the residence of truth. This latter is ever trying to break through into full consciousness, to become known, and to influence action. Faustus "represses" it, and it is driven to oblique re-entries—in depressions, forebodings, apparitions, the psychosomatic stigmata on Faustus' arm. All this is perceptive enough to touch with greatness the drama of Faustus' resistance to saving knowledge. But Marlowe goes a step further and enters for a moment—a moment is enough, and is all that is possible—into an ultimately brilliant dramatization of transcendent moral reality trying to break into the closed consciousness: Mephistophelis himself, in a nostaligc flash superbly imagined by Marlowe, warns Faustus, ". . . leave these frivolous demands, / Which strike a terror to my fainting soul". Faustus' inaccessibility to truth leaps forth in jaunty insouciance, a boulevardier's version of Oedipus' complacency in a crisis. Eventually, of course, Faustus is overwhelmed by the truth that he has long held down; his mind coalesces with the original truly knowing self that he had denied, and in his recovered orientation he defines the nature of the partial self that was all his mind knew "for vain pleasure of twenty-four years".

What strikes Shakespeare is two main manifestations of that strange disastrous chasm, predictable yet irrational, between man as creature of will and as possessor of knowledge. There is the one chasm that man has to create to pursue an end; he denies, pushes back, closes off the knowing self and what it knows. Purpose needs ignorance; and the protagonist is driven to a quest for ignorance more taxing than the quest for knowledge, since for the tragic hero it means trying to deny a trait essential to the hero. It is the Faustus way and, with variations, the Macbeth way. The other chasm is created by the violent rush of emotion, a rush so powerful and self-justifying that it seems truth itself, and makes invisible the very chasm it creates; this chasm is not needed by the hero for his own protection, but rather has to be discovered by him as a shocking distortion in the terrain of existence that he knows and accepts. Slowly the mind discovers the split between action and reality, and gains, as well as it can, perspective on both. It is the way of Othello and Lear.

In the three dramas that, written in a relatively short time, bring the period of tragedies to a climax, Shakespeare makes increasingly extensive use of anagnorisis.[1] His interest grows in intensity, and his point of view changes. At no time does he cherish illusions about man's capacity for self-knowledge, but in *Macbeth* we find his most hardbitten view of man's resistance to knowing. The resistance is less compulsory and obsessive in *Othello* and *Lear*. But the slightly earlier dramas differ from each other too. In *Othello* Shakespeare is equally absorbed by the external agency that tortures the hero until he does evil; the dual focus extends the preparation for the main act of violence; and hence the period of illumination and retrospection has to be shorter. We might say that writing Act V, Scene ii of *Othello* really set Shakespeare's imagination off on the dramatic possibilities of anagnorisis, and that in *Lear* he explored these extensively: Lear explodes into injustice in the first scene, so that more than four acts are left for the drama of self-understanding. Macbeth, in turn, knows from the very beginning what is what, and his utterly different problem is to escape what he knows.

These different shadings of the light of self-knowledge reveal how the most comprehensive soul managed variations on a theme. It would be easy, for one who instinctively included anagnorisis in the tragic experience, to fall into a pat structure. Francis Fergusson's well known statement of the tragic rhythm of *Oedipus*—"purpose-passion-perception"—is so attractive a formulation that it would be easy to think it universal and obligatory, and to make a law of it, or a key for unlocking the inner pattern of all tragedies. The point is that these three Shakespeare tragedies do not fit into such a pattern. Purpose and passion are always there, but in *Othello* and *Lear* passion is the initiator, and purpose is secondary, an offspring of passion. Perception is always there too, but here the options are multiple. Perception is not inevitably a final grace; it may be reached only by paradoxical routes; it may be shunned, pushed away, pressed down. The very fighting off of a perception that is struggling to possess the protagonist may be the main source of tragic tension.

Although *Othello* is one of the "long" tragedies, only some two hundred

---

[1] In this essay the word is used for convenience in the restricted sense of "self-discovery" or the coming into moral knowledge of the self. The restriction is arbitrary. The wider original sense is not relevant to the present discussion.

lines are occupied with the illumination and self-inspection of Othello: this phase of the tragic process clearly did not at this time present itself to Shakespeare as substance that had to be fully expanded. Yet even in this brief treatment there are a dramatic vitality and a sense of ambiguity that foreshadow his much greater concern with anagnorisis in the next two tragedies. The clarification of Othello, as Shakespeare presents it, has both a psychological and a moral side. The psychological, which is traced in the middle third of V. ii, is the wrenching from disbelief to assent as his initial faith is breached by the inexorable pressure of facts. Othello's assurance in his error so resists correction that it takes all of Emilia's verbal violence and Iago's murderous attempt upon her to break Othello's set closure against the truth. Once he regains the power to grasp what others are, what they have been and have done, he must move on to the more punishing task—seeing what he has done and what he is. This moral side of his enlightenment, occupying the final third of a uniquely compressed scene, is the seat of ambiguity. In the traditional view, and probably the majority view, Othello nobly decrees justice against himself: "But why should honour outlive honesty?" (245)[2] . . . "This look of thine will hurl my soul from heaven, / And fiends will snatch at it" (274-275) . . . "An honourable murderer, . . ." (294). In executing himself, it is felt, Othello judges and identifies himself. But there have been various dissents, ranging from the argument that Othello is to be seen as a damned soul to the argument that he is far more bent on cheering himself up than on seeing himself in a moral glass. These conflicting interpretations reveal less an impasse than an ambivalence in the rendering of Othello's final hour, as if Shakespeare were hovering imaginatively over dual possibilities and in the end committed himself to something of both. To propose this is not to decry artistic uncertainty but rather to give credit for sense of ambiguity, that is, for full apprehension of latent meanings, of doubleness in the personality itself.

The more "modern" view of Othello is that he fails to think of himself as a vain and self-righteous man who has acted evilly, but appears in his own eyes as no more than a rather worthy fellow who has made a foolish mistake and thereby lost a valuable possession; that he is prone less to notice his shortcomings than to list extenuating circumstances; and that he is at some pains to make a histrionic exit, not as a criminal on the gallows, but as a substantial Venetian patriot. Against this view it is sometimes urged that whatever Othello says in his own behalf is to be attributed less to an unregenerate egotism than to the stage convention whereby the erring hero is free to do any case-making he can. Now one may have due respect for the influence of conventions upon literary structures and yet point to a certain rigidity in some conventionalist criticism. This is its tendency to regard all operations within a given convention as aesthetically equivalent or aesthetically neutral, precisely as if, let us say, all employments of a conventional greeting were indistinguishable reflex movements, revealing nothing of mood (apathy, tension, hostility, heartiness) or of basic style or personality (urbanity, breeding, gaucheness, slickness, self-centeredness). This assumption of parity begs the very question which must be

    [2] For ease of reference, all citations are from a single-volume edition: *The Complete Plays and Poems of William Shakespeare,* edited by William Allan Neilson and Charles Jarvis Hill (Cambridge, Massachusetts, 1942).

critically considered for each instance of conventional activity: is it the bare convention, with no more meaning than a formality normally entails, or is it also the instrument of some extraconventional illumination? Specifically, is Othello's picture of himself in the final hundred lines of V. ii, with its dominant insistence on honor, on himself as victim, on his grief, and on his public serv- ices, only a ceremonial exercise, as expectable and morally irrelevant as occasional oratory, or does it betray a limited personality that falls somewhat short of mature self-confrontation? Whoever believes that the latter reading embodies at least an important part of a complex truth will point, naturally, to the high incidence of defensive, self-explaining or self-lauding lines that Othello speaks and the relatively small number, and the rather unfocused, slanting vocabulary, of the lines that give him an opportunity to identify himself as a vengeful wife- murderer.

The situation is at least ambiguous; some of the internal evidence forces one to doubt the completeness of Othello's self-recognition. This doubt gains in probability if we look at external evidence: Othello acts like other Shakespeare heroes at the point where self-knowledge is a necessary or possible form of action. They do not easily experience anagnorisis. As early as Act I truth begins to "peep through the blanket of the dark" to Lear, but his confused struggle with the intruder goes on even into Act V. In simply getting the facts straight, in discovering the flimsiness of the retirement utopia that he had supposed he was creating by his offhand plunge into punishments and rewards, he has an unusual amount of help: Goneril and Regan are not much given to devious- ness and pussyfooting, and the Fool is an indefatigable preceptor. But even after a dream of such brevity, Lear's anguish in awaking into reality is in- juriously acute. Still greater is the suffering of the next step, of looking fully into the circumambient reality and saying, "It is I who brought this about", and "I brought this about because I am thus and so". Shakespeare is fascinated, surely, by the intensity of the human resistance to the white light of such moral realism, by the stubborn clinging to blinders. Lear's slip now and then, and there are moments of wider seeing: "Woe, that too late repents! . . . O most small fault, / How ugly didst thou in Cordelia show! . . . Beat at this gate, that let thy folly in / And thy dear judgment out!" (I. iv. 279 ff.). But, as with Othello, the greater outpourings of energy, the main burden of the speeches, show a different movement: bitter attacks on the offending daughters, sprinkled with cries of self-merit ("So kind a father!"—I. v. 35). In one fifty-line scene there is one faint flash of self-identification: "I did her wrong—" (I. v. 25). But this provides hardly a moment's distraction from the fierce conflict with the "unnatural hags", from the frenzied attacks of a frustrated will on the more obvious evil. Two polar terms of Yeats's come to mind here: "the quarrel with others" and "the quarrel with ourselves". Lear passionately pursues one, hur- ries over the other.

Lear carries the pursuit on into the storm, the "poor . . . old man" against "pernicious daughters" (III. ii. 20, 22), and even into madness itself, with un- flagging diatribes and the "arraignment" of Goneril and Regan. But again there is the fleeting interposition of the quarrel with himself: "O, I have ta'en / Too little care of this!" (III. iv. 32-33) The role of madness in Lear's protracted and tortured course toward anagnorisis needs clarification. Madness acts as something other than the paradoxical container of reason that Edgar identifies. Shakespeare presents it also as a necessary step in the progress toward self-knowledge. Its function is to make possible a catharsis of the quarrel with others that blocks off the quarrel with ourselves; in madness the quarrel explodes into an ultimate dimension, and then passes. Thus madness, regardless of how else it may function in the depths, contributes to understanding. In this sense Othello is less fortunate than Lear: he has never that acute disorder of mind that may be a prologue to clarity, and his quarrel with Iago goes on taking so much of his energy that, like most quarrels with others, it reinforces a combative stance not conducive to the full realization of his own spiritual shortcomings.

We should note the specific terms of the alteration in Lear after his illness: he no longer reviles his daughters, he is remarkably less assured, and above all he can say to Cordelia, "If you have poison for me, I will drink it. . . . You have some cause, . . . Pray you now, forget and forgive; . . ." (IV. vii. 72 ff.). Saying "forgive" is perhaps the most difficult way of acknowledging wrongdoing, of reducing the old ignorant and confident-striving self. Shakespeare shows how far Lear has come by making him repeat the word, more emphatically, several scenes later: "When thou dost ask me blessing, I'll kneel down / And ask of thee forgiveness" (V. iii. 10-11). To reach this point, Lear has traveled a long road, a road of ruinous hardship; in effect he has had to destroy a part of himself to understand himself. If Shakespeare found in man—at least in man as he is represented by Lear—the tardy ability to know himself, the dramatist was even more aware of man's almost demonic resistance to that all but unbearable knowledge. A good deal of the main plot of *Lear* exists because of that awareness in the dramatist. Suppose, for instance, that when Goneril and Regan show their hands, Lear were able to absorb the truth with the kind of realization that leads to action, and to throw himself upon the mercy of the Queen of France?

Finally, Shakespeare reverses the dramatic movement: if Lear yields to knowledge more and more, Macbeth yields to knowledge less and less, and Lady Macbeth seems impregnable to its attacks. Only in retrospect can we measure the pauperizing cost of her apparent invulnerability. When a protagonist "knows" that his course is morally intolerable, but strains frantically against that knowledge lest it impair his obsessive pursuit of the course, the tension between knowing and willing may itself destroy him. In Lady Macbeth Shakespeare catches the eventual psychic bankruptcy of the assured, plunging personality that can fight off, with a façade of nonchalance, all assaults of a saving self-knowledge, not only for herself but for her husband as well. There is a cumulative, but secret, drain of resources; the prodigal expenditure of will exhausts the soul. Lady Macbeth is the spiritual counterpart of the splendidly robust person who seems immune to all ailment and then, in a crisis apparently well within his powers, is suddenly, even mysteriously, overborne. Understandably, Shakespeare dealt with the type only once: it affords a hard, flaring brilliance during the high arc of its career, but then drops down and leaves the writer of tragedy nothing to go on with. Consciousness itself crumbles under the blows of the reality it will not admit, so that it can never reorient itself to the rejected truth; indeed it cannot even carry on with the programmatic action to which it has committed itself solely. The very arena for the climactic tragic action, the drama of seeing, is gone.

In Macbeth there is nothing of his lady's seemingly passionless closure against irruptive truth. From the beginning the troubles in the psyche break into open consciousness. They are pushed down, and then there they are again, up, pressing, twisting Macbeth into doubt or anguish or horror; and then gone, as if banished. The contrast between King and Queen invites us to suppose that a little knowledge is a saving thing: a touch of neurosis forestalls psychosis; a passing illness acknowledges symbolically a truth that, fought off unyieldingly, must in the end assert itself by blasting utterly the one who would exclude it utterly. Faustus and Macbeth both "see things"; yet this temporary ailing is a therapy for or preventive of a worse one, such as Lady Macbeth's; having survived it, each is able to go on in a chosen course, as if feverless, unweakened, safely beyond the challenges of knowledge. Lady Macbeth is a utopian of a sort; Faustus and Macbeth are politic men, freed from inner chains against action in the world; and to name their "success" is to acknowledge the subtle moral diminishment that is in the price.

With Macbeth, moments of acknowledgment bring guilt; yet his guilt can suddenly metamorphose into a sense of consequences, or a fear of them, or even a deflecting gesture. It is tempting to say that he is caught in a dilemma of truth or consequences: which shall he attend to? He might save himself by admitting what he knows instead of pushing it down below consciousness: "Our designs are evil; we cannot go on with them". Yet instead of asking "Is this course morally tenable?" he asks, "Can we get away with it?" "If the assassination / Could trammel up the consequence, and catch / With his surcease success; . . ." (I. vii. 2-4). "Bloody instructions . . . return / To plague th' inventor" (9-10). Duncan's "virtues / Will plead like angels, trumpet-tongu'd, against / The deep damnation of his taking-off" (18-20). Yet the soliloquy as a whole is fascinating because it reveals a sense of truth competing with a sense of consequences. The Macbeth who can cite Duncan's merits and his own obligations, who can speak of the "murderer", of "deep damnation", and of his own "vaulting ambition", has not yet won his quasi-victory against knowledge. Indeed his words to Lady Macbeth, "We will proceed no further in this business" (31), might imply the opposite: a surrender to knowledge. It is not that, however; it is a medley of moral acumen and practical misgiving, of "This may not be undertaken", and "This cannot be carried through". As soon as Lady Macbeth taxes him with a failure in manly resolution, he pushes knowledge away again, and asks only, "If we should fail?" (59). She can answer this, and he drifts into resolution. The play implicitly defines resolution: a denial of consequences and a narcotizing of what one knows. If narcosis were not needed or were totally effective, all we would have left would be bloody intrigue, the overt, visible mechanics of triumph or failure in the campaign. This is the kind of drama that Macbeth longs to find himself in; Shakespeare grasps this human lust for pure, insentient action, and tailors his drama to the long shrinking and hardening that must be undergone before one can get down to the tranquillity of bare life-and-death struggle. Resolution is not strong enough to enable Macbeth to use the dagger without first apostrophizing it, sighting "gouts of blood" upon it, and soliloquizing on the nocturnal moves of Witchcraft and Murder (II.i.34 ff). After he has done "it", he is almost beaten down by the resurgent knowledge that he has been fencing with and dancing away from; in a close parallel to Faustus' difficulty in sealing his blood-bond with the devil, Macbeth is physically unable to say "Amen" (II.ii. 32). Nurturing such thoughts, says Lady Macbeth, "will make us mad" (34); she knows more than she knows she knows. As she pulls Macbeth away from the dangerous abyss of insight, all her key terms show her tack to be the denial that his knowledge is knowledge. It is all an error, a "foolish thought" (22). "Consider it not so deeply" (30); don't be "brainsickly" (46); "Be not lost / So poorly in your thoughts" (71-72). So he does not stay lost in the realm of truth, but finds himself in action—in snatching the crown and averting consequences. In his next soliloquy the principal theme is success—"to be safely thus" (III.i. 49); then he coolly coaches the murderers. Still there are "terrible dreams" and "torture of the mind" (III.ii.18,21)—"scorpions", of truth, perhaps, but more likely of consequences. The fear of what one may do to others has turned into the fear of what others may do to one in return. The last flare-up of knowledge— knowledge forced away and then slipping back deviously as illness—is in Macbeth's hallucinations at the banquet: the Faustian brainsickliness, the moral malaise as nervous crisis. That surmounted, there is a kind of freedom for action, a release of all energies into program: for Faustus, traversing the world in quest and jest; for Macbeth, trying to insure his world with killings that can never quite stop. He is all caught up in fierce staff work. He finds the witches' heath less a Delphi, revealing a larger truth to man's dim consciousness, than a dopester's corner, with tips on how the different thoroughbreds will be running in the royal handicap. So Macbeth becomes more "resolute" than ever before, dynamically thrusting ahead in the tactics of surviving the field. Only in the few "I am sick at heart" lines (V.iii.19 ff.), reminiscent of Faustus' occasional moments of distress among popes and emperors, does Macbeth suffer, for a moment or two, the pangs of knowledge. For this corrosive, fighting is the required antidote.

Faustus ends in despair, somehow yielding to the horror of his fate through inability to repent: despair as passivity. Macbeth comes to despair too, the profound despair of activity. For both, the comparable and yet divergent movements of the soul are brilliantly done. In the end Faustus knows, only too well: "I know evil so great that I cannot escape it". Macbeth will not know: "I fight fiercely, and thus escape knowledge". The customary way of describing such a struggle as Macbeth's final one is to say that the protagonist "fought desperately": the very familiarity of the phrase reveals the representativeness of the situation, or at least the human mind's representative way of giving it moral form. "Desperately" implies a noble frenzy against excessive odds, an unconditional non-surrender. Yet the well worn adverb, which in popular usage carries a note of moral achievement, is exactly the word to expose a different inner truth. What on some occasions or to some eyes may appear a victory of spirit, a triumph of heart against destined victors, is at Dunsinane the kind of failure signified by the word *despair:* a failure to imagine any other course of action, a rejection of perceiving. Acting violently is not only a surrogate for knowing, but a barrier against knowing. Yet this acting is made obligatory, forced on one. "They have tied me to a stake" (V.vii.1)—*they:* others have put this upon me, and I will be brave, and claim the pity vouchsafed to the doomed. It is one more fold of insulation against the harsh air of truth. Courage to face others becomes equivalent to, perhaps finer than, the courage to face oneself.

Thus Shakespeare finishes off, very profoundly, his analysis of a basic kind of personality—of the man who can look at himself, who at first has to fight off the inclination to do so, who succeeds for practical purposes in not doing so, and eventually fights instead of doing so. Macbeth has got far away from anagnorisis; now he easily substitutes other modes of conduct that, in appropriate contexts, make a claim upon respect: philosophic reflections and heroic actions. He discourses on the absurdity of existence ("a tale / Told by an idiot") and vows a fight to the death ("I will not yield"). Early in the play he had to admit, "Look on [what I have done] again I dare not" (II. ii. 51-52); to cry, "Stars, hide your fires; / Let not light see my black and deep desires" (I. iv. 50-51; cf. Lady Macbeth's "Come, thick night, . . . That my keen knife see not . . ."—I. v. 51-53); and again to pray, "Come, seeling night" (III. ii. 46). The extensive imagery of seeing and night work together in constant reminders of the knowledge that continually breaks out into painful view, and of the perpetual need to shut it off. Twice Macbeth states his problem literally, explicitly: "False face must hide what the false heart doth know" (I. vii. 82) and "To know my deed, 'twere best not know myself" (II. ii. 73). Conceal knowledge, then eliminate it: it is a major theme of the play in which Shakespeare explores, for the last time in full scale, the complex subject of man's mingled openness to and resistance to self-knowledge.

"Know thyself", one of western man's oldest moral exhortations, comes easily and frequently into the preceptorial mouth; hence it may seem to name a routine obligation that, as long as it is not forgotten, may be easily fulfilled. To Shakespeare the dramatist, carrying out the command is indispensable to well being; yet carrying it out is so difficult as to border on the impossible. Three times in a two-year period he delineates tragic heroes in whom self-knowledge would be an appropriate magnanimity, a grace of spirit, or a mode of salvation; as he advances from one play to another, he derives an increasing amount of dramatic tension from the protagonist's resistance to this kind of knowing. It is almost possible to say, in truth, that at each return to the theme he has a stronger conviction of man's preferring or needing other satisfactions than those of mastering the truth of self. Some prior image of the self, some dream, some aspiration stands in the way of seeing what has really been felt and done. Not that what one has done and been does not get into the consciousness; Shakespeare never takes the cynical view that man is totally obtuse or insulated against self-knowledge. Rather he knows the difficulty of coming to it, and likewise of evading it. Othello appears to hurry over his evil act and to spend most of his few remaining words on sketching the most favorable possible portrait of himself. Lear needs a civil war, a terrible storm, and madness before he can shift from abuse of villains to acknowledgment that it is he who needs forgiveness; and even after that he cannot see that the death of Cordelia is due, ultimately, to the forces that he set in motion. Unlike the others, Macbeth does know himself from the start; for him the task is not slowly yielding to knowledge, but getting away from it, making it ever less effective, and escaping, as well as this may be done, into a frenzy of total action that will eventually relieve consciousness by destroying it. It would be supererogatory to praise these different dramatizations of a psychological realism whose validity we sense even more strongly, perhaps, after four hundred years.

University of Washington

"Yet am I inland bred"

MADELEINE DORAN

HEN in the Forest of Arden Duke Senior meets Orlando's threatening demand of food with the reproach,

> Art thou thus bolden'd, man, by thy distress,
> Or else a rude despiser of good manners,
> That in civility thou seem'st so empty?

the terms of Orlando's reply deserve attention:

> You touch'd my vein at first. The thorny point
> Of bare distress hath ta'en from me the show
> Of smooth civility; yet am I inland bred
> And know some nurture.
> $$(A.Y.L. \text{ II. vii. 91-97})[1]$$

The *OED* gives the sense of the adverb *inland* here as "in or towards the interior or heart of a country, as opposed . . . to wild outlying districts." What is important in the Shakespearian passage, of course, is not the bare geographical sense of the term, but the implication of good breeding it is made to bear. The word appears again in a later passage. Orlando, questioning Ganymede for the first time, remarks that "his" accent is "something finer" than "he" "could purchase in so removed a dwelling". Ganymede replies that "he" was taught to speak by an old religious uncle, "who was in his youth an inland man; one that knew courtship too well, for there he fell in love" (III. ii. 361-364). The *OED* glosses *inland* in this passage as "having the refinement characteristic of the inlying districts of a country". Shakespeare himself makes both the literal and the derivative sense abundantly clear, for *removed* is the opposite of *inland*, and *courtship* means "the ways of court" as well as "courting" in love. *Inland* with this implied sense of breeding does not appear to have been common, for the *OED* gives only the two Shakespearian passages as examples and Shakespeare nowhere else uses the word in just this way.

Since the action of the play is set on "the skirts of a wild forest" or within it, and since in some sense or other court and country are opposed throughout, it is well to see what bearing this unusual but precisely placed epithet may have on the central theme.

But first it will be necessary to make a rather long excursion into meanings. The defining terms in the first of Orlando's quoted speeches are "nurture" and "smooth civility" and one knows from these that the Duke's reproach of rudeness and incivility carries a deeper social implication than just bad manners in a modern superficial sense. *Inland* may be one of Shakespeare's uncommon words, but *civil, uncivil,* and *rude* are not; in fact, they are favorites with him.[2]

Civitas was defined in Elyot's *Bibliotheca*[3] (also in Cooper's *Thesaurus*)[4] as "a citee, properly it is the multitude of citesens gathered togyther, to lyue according to lawe and right". In Thomas Thomas' *Dictionarium,*[5] *civitas* is "A citee: the freedome of the citie; the companie or multitude of the citizens: a multitude or assembly of people, liuing vnder one and the same law: it is taken for the whole country". *Civilis* or "civil" meant first of all, therefore, what pertains to a *civis* or citizen ("our cuntry man, a Burgess, a freeman"—Thomas), a free man in a city or commonwealth living under law. But by implication, to be "civil" meant to be "civilized"[6] in the best sense, that is, brought up to be an orderly, responsible member of society, to behave with the self-control and the respect for others that life in society demands and that may be expected of rational men. To have *civilitas* was to have "curtesye, civilitee, gentylnesse, good humanitie" (Elyot, also Cooper); it was "The honestie, curtesie, and equalities, which citizens vse one to another: ciuilitie, humanitie" (Thomas). Just as with similar terms of social origin (such as *gentlemen, gentleness, generosity; urbanity; courtesy; clown; churl; villain*), the adjuncts, real or supposed, of the original social condition came by metonomy to take over the principal meanings of *civil* and *civility*. But it is evident, from common Elizabethan usage, with which Shakespeare's agrees, that the figurative sense had not wholly supplanted the literal one, only overlaid and enlarged it.

Note how the literal and the figurative senses enrich each other in such passages as the following, wherein savage beast and social man are opposed. Octavius comments on the reversal of order that might appropriately follow the death of so great a ruler as Antony—"The round world / Should have shook lions into the civil streets / And citizens to their dens" (*Antony* V. i. 15-17). When Othello says that "A horned man's a monster and a beast", Iago replies with two paradoxes, one in the form of an oxymoron: "There's many a beast then in a populous city, / And many a civil monster" (IV. i. 63-65). Again, the fully paradoxical effect of the antithesis in Northumberland's disingenuous speech to Richard II at Flint Castle, when Bolingbroke with his armed force waits below, comes only with an awareness of the whole range of meaning the terms may bear:

> The King of Heaven forbid our lord the King
> Should so with civil and uncivil arms
> Be rush'd upon!
> (III. iii. 101-103)

---

[2] My examples are severely culled from the total number.

[3] Thomas Elyot, *Bibliotheca Eliotae; Eliotis Librarie,* 1545, etc.; my quotations are from the edition of 1548.

[4] Thomas Cooper, *Thesaurus linguae latinae,* 1565, 1573, 1578, 1584, 1587; my quotations are from the 1565 edition. Cooper incorporates Elyot, but often adds a good deal by way of illustration.

[5] *Dictionarium linguae latinae et anglicanae,* ?1588, 1592, etc.; at least twelve editions by 1620. My quotations are from the edition of 1596. I have not often cited dictionaries other than Elyot, Cooper, and Thomas (such as Withal, Higgins, Huloet-Higgins, Florio, Cawdrey), since they are usually repetitious. It is instructive to look up in the sixteenth-century dictionaries generally all these terms of social origin and implication: *civil, urbane, rustic, rude, courteous, gentle, generous, humane,* etc.

[6] The verb and its participles, judging from the *OED,* had not yet come into English use. Florio, in *A Worlde of Wordes* (1598), glosses *Ciuilire* as "to growe ciuill, to tame, to make courteous".

The context nearly always points the direction of the intended meaning. The kerns of Ireland who are up in arms are "uncivil" (2 *H. VI*, III. i. 310), that is, barbarous and wild. Valentine has a hard time to keep the bandits from "uncivil outrages", which would be offenses against law and order; but at the end of the same scene he appeals for their pardon on the ground that they are "reformed, civil, full of good", that is, ready to live under law (*T.G.V.* V. iv. 17, 156). These are nearly primary senses of *civil* and *uncivil*.

A more personal sense of self-restraint, of sobriety in behavior, is suggested in Olivia's praise of Malvolio as "sad and civil" (*Twel.* III. iv. 5); in Juliet's personification of "civil night" as "thou sober-suited matron, all in black" (*Romeo* III. ii. 10); in Gratiano's promise, if he may but go with Bassanio to Belmont, to "put on a sober habit", "talk with respect", "look demurely", "Use all the observance of civility / Like one well studied in a sad ostent / To please his grandam". Gratiano, who has "a skipping spirit", seems to Bassanio "too wild, too rude, and bold of voice" to be taken along (*Merch.* II. ii. 189-206). The negative, *uncivil,* implies self-will as well as unsociability in Orsino's reproach to Olivia, who is "still so constant" in refusing his suit: "What, to perverseness? You uncivil lady" (*Twel.* V. i. 115). The passage which best defines this sense of *civil* as self-controlled and responsible behavior is Othello's rebuke of Montano after the "barbarous brawl" in the court of guard at Cyprus:

> Worthy Montano, you were wont to be civil;
> The gravity and stillness of your youth
> The world hath noted, and your name is great
> In mouths of wisest censure. What's the matter
> That you unlace your reputation thus
> And spend your rich opinion for the name
> Of a night-brawler?
>
> (II. iii. 190-196)

A good name, that most precious of Elizabethan commodities, can belong only to those who do not endanger civil order by heedless and self-indulgent passion.

Most of the passages just cited imply propriety of behavior as well as sobriety, Gratiano's lightly and mockingly, Othello's seriously and profoundly.[7] It is the lack of all apparent sense of the behavior appropriate in "a town of war, / Yet wild, the people's hearts brimful of fear", that most shocks Othello at the "private and domestic quarrel" between Montano and Cassio. Only Malvolio's civility need not imply more than sobriety. At least his sense of propriety is acquired and superficial, limited to dreams of his chance to impose proper behavior on others; he is a comic imposter, precisely because he is fundamentally blinded by self-love to what is becoming to himself and to others. Illiberal as he is, he cannot accommodate himself to civil society.

Propriety of course implies good manners, something more positive than just self-restraint. Manners can be assumed, as Gratiano's are to be. But Elizabethan "civility" in manners usually implies something deeply based. Iago intends to put the worst construction on Cassio's habitual good manners when he tells Roderigo that Cassio is "a knave very voluble; no further conscionable than in

---

[7] For an illuminating discussion of propriety or decorum and its place in civil society, see Cicero, *De officiis*, I. xxvii. 93-xlii. 151.

putting on the mere form of civil and humane seeming for the better compassing
of his salt and most hidden loose affection" (*Oth.* II. i. 243-246). But he knows
better, for it is he who tells us that Cassio "hath a daily beauty in his life" (V.i.
19) and therefore lets us know what Cassio's courtesy, his "civil and humane"
behavior, truly is. The equivalence of *civil* and *humane* is important. To be
"humane" is simply to be human in the best sense, for only a human being is
capable of kindness, of putting the welfare of others before his own selfish im-
pulses, hence capable of civility. These associations are fully stated under
Cooper's entry, *humanus,* and its derivatives. The adjective *humanus* is glossed
as "Humayne [i.e. 'human'], belongynge to man: gentill: courteys: tractable:
mercifull: friendly: learned: cunnyng"; the adverb *humanè,* as "courteisly:
mildly: like a man: as a man shoulde". The primary sense of *humanity* is given
in *communis humanitas,* "the state of humaine nature common to vs all". Derived senses are illustrated by these quotations from Cicero: "Humanus et
ciuilis cultus" ("Gentyll. courteyse, friendely"); "Humanitas & modestia";
"Singularis humanitas, suauissimi mores"; "Lepor & humanitas in omni vitae
tempore versetur" ("plesant behauour [*sic*] and courteisie"); "Immanitas &
Humanitas, contraria" ("Beastly crueltie, and courteous gentilnesse"); "Tol-
eranter & humanè ferre morbum" ("To suffer patiently and mildly"); "Hu-
maniter viuere" ("To liue in liberall sorte as a man should doo"). *Humanitas*
as learning or liberal knowledge is illustrated by the Ciceronian phrases "politior
humanitas" ("Fyne and cleane learnyng") and "Humanitas studia, artes ipsae
liberales dicuntur".

The opposite of *civil* is not only *uncivil* but *rude.* The word had a wide variety
of connotations. Elyot (followed by Cooper), glosses *Rudis* as "rude, ignoraunte,
vnlearned, vntaught, that knoweth nothynge, not exercised or traded in a thyng,
nothyng experte or counnyng. also rusticall". To these senses Thomas Thomas
adds "vnwrought, rough, not fashioned, homely, simple, plain, base, blunt, not
tilled or husbanded, not kembed, not picked or curious". In one place or another,
Shakespeare uses *rude* in nearly all these senses, literal and derived. Occasionally
he uses it in the sense of *rough* or *plain* with the praiseworthy implication of
artless, not sophisticated, "not picked or curious", as when Othello defends
himself from the charge of beguiling Desdemona: "Rude am I in my speech, /
And little bless'd with the soft phrase of peace" (I. iii. 81-82). But we are concerned with those more frequent examples of the word used pejoratively in
senses that oppose it to *civil.*

Just as "civil" behavior may have the sense of restraint of passion, so *rude*
may fitly be used as an epithet of *will* in the sense of selfish impulse. Friar
Lawrence, in his moral musings over his basket of herbs, tells us that "Two
such opposed kings camp them still / In man as well as herbs—grace and rude
will" (*Romeo* II. iii. 27-28). And self-will, leading to wild and irresponsible
behavior, may of course be a threat to civil order. Prince Escalus sentences Romeo
to banishment for the "rude brawls" which have resulted in the deaths of
Tybalt and Mercutio (III. i. 194). In the *Two Gentlemen,* when Proteus seizes
Sylvia to force her, Valentine charges him with two serious breaches of civility:
"Ruffian! let go that rude uncivil touch, / Thou friend of an ill fashion" (V. iv.
60-61). Proteus is rude and uncivil both in the violence offered to Sylvia and in
his betrayal of friendship, which is a fundamental social virtue.

Uncivil, as we have seen, meant to be in some way or other unfit for ordered society. The important idea that *rude* brings to this concept is that ignorance or lack of instruction is the cause of the unfitness, and that a man untaught is like a beast. When the Duke in *Measure for Measure* finds that Pompey the bawd is only too willing to argue away the filthiness of his profession, he orders him taken to prison: "Correction and instruction must both work / Ere this rude beast will profit" (III. ii. 33-34). He also calls Barnardine a "rude wretch", "unfit to live or die" (IV. iii. 85, 68), bestial in his ignorance of good and of his immortal soul. Rudeness may imply the savagery to be expected of a barbarous people, untamed and uninstructed in civilized decencies, as when King Henry describes the capture of Mortimer and the shameful mutilation of the bodies of his dead soldiers:[8]

> the noble Mortimer
> Leading the men of Herefordshire to fight
> Against the irregular and wild Glendower,
> Was by the rude hands of that Welshman taken,
> A thousand of his people butchered:
> Upon whose dead corpse there was such misuse,
> Such beastly shameless transformation,
> By those Welshwomen done as may not be
> Without much shame retold or spoken of.
> (*1 H. IV,* I. i, 38-46).

In a lighter vein, when Sir Toby falls on Sebastian (thinking him Cesario), Olivia finds her uncle only "Fit for the mountains and the barbarous caves, / Where manners ne'er were preach'd" (IV. i. 52-53). She orders him off— "Rudesby, be gone!"—and turns to the supposed Cesario with an appeal that makes the equivalence of *rude* and *uncivil* explicit:

> I prithee, gentle friend,
> Let thy fair wisdom, not thy passion, sway
> In this uncivil and unjust extent
> Against thy peace.

Rudeness may be expected, too, of the uneducated within a civilized society. In *2 Henry VI,* the commons are charged with being "rude, unpolish'd hinds" (III. ii. 271). And probably, when the "rude misgovern'd hands" throw dust on the head of the fallen Richard (*R. II.,* V. ii. 5), we are meant to think them uninstructed as well as capricious. There is, at any rate, no mistaking these connotations of *rude* (both rough and uncultivated, hence "uncivil") in the passages of *1 Henry IV* on Prince Hal's disorderly life (III. ii. 4-35). When the King charges his son with "such inordinate and low desires, / Such poor, such bare, such lewd, such mean attempts, / Such barren pleasures, rude society", he means the pursuit of disorderly, base, and fruitless pleasures with companions who are rough, wild, perhaps lawless, certainly ignorant, unbefitting a prince and uninstructive to him in his civil place. By such behavior he has "rudely lost" his place in council. The "rude society" remarked on here is glossed at the be-

---

[8] These implications are in the passage in spite of the picture of the courtly Glendower Shakespeare gives us later in the play.

ginning of *Henry V*, when the Archbishop speaks of the new king's former companions as "unletter'd, rude and shallow" (I. i. 55).

To return to our "inland" man, of whom civil behavior is expected. It would help us to know why Shakespeare used just this epithet if we were given an equivalent term for his opposite, the man who is expected to be rude. Our natural impulse is to supply "outland man". But *outland* and *outlandish* were commonly used in the sense of "foreign" or "strange", not implied here; the words did not necessarily connote "barbarous" in the sense of "savage". A "borderer", then? Kittredge's "frontiersman"? No doubt (if one can divest "frontiersman" of its anachronistic American associations). Any inhabitant of the "uncouth desert"? Orlando, surprised at meeting civility in a "wild forest", asks pardon for his rudeness: "I thought all had been savage here." A rustic, perhaps, or "uplandish" man? (*Upland* or *uplandish*, from *uppe-lond* 'on the land', was the commonly used English equivalent of *rusticus* or *agrestis*).[9] Indeed, the charge Orlando makes against his elder brother is that Oliver keeps him, unlike his brother Jaques, who is at school, "rustically at home" like an ox, without education; Orlando is no "villain" or base fellow, yet he is fed with the hinds, trained like a peasant, his gentility undermined, all gentlemanlike "qualities" or accomplishments hidden from him. His primary complaint is lack of education, and the boorishness that is the result. The usual dictionary connotations of *rustic* or *rustical* were rude, without courtesy, churlish. Under "Agreste per metaphoram" Cooper gives "Rude: homely: rusticall: carterlyke: without nourture or ciuilitee: without gentlenes: fierce" and he quotes several illustrative phrases from Cicero: "Indoctus & agrestis"; "Agreste & inhumanum"; "Animus agrestis ac durus". Thomas Thomas gives much the same list of epithets, but adds to "fierce" the phrase, "in whom is neither love nor humility". Florio, gathering up the accumulated synonyms from all the dictionaries, glosses *Rústico* as "rusticall, clownish, vplandish, homelie, churlish, plaine, loutish, that knowes no good fashions, rude, inciuill [*sic*], barbarous. Also a clowne, a swaine, a hinde, a countrieman, a rude fellow, a husbandman, an vplandish man, a rude bodie".

All these implications—remoteness from city or court, barbarousness, wildness, lack of education, rusticity—are present in what the "inland" man is not. "Removedness" from civil society (and all that that implies) seems to be the condition all these senses have in common; but in the play the removedness appears to be at least as much in social habits and in mental attitudes as in physical distance.

There is a partial parallel, and an amusing one, to Orlando's assertion of his gentility in the first book of the *Metamorphoses*, when Apollo, pursuing Daphne, pleads with her to stop running:

> cui placeas, inquire tamen: non incola montis,
> non ego sum pastor, non hic armenta gregesque
> horridus observo. nescis, temeraria, nescis,
> quem fugias, ideoque fugis: . . .
>
>   (i. 512-515)

---

[9] *Upland* and *uplandish* are common in the sixteenth-century dictionaries; *outland* and *outlandish* are occasional; *inland* I nowhere found.

He goes on to state his parentage and rehearse his many accomplishments in learning and in the arts. John Brinsley, in his translation of this passage in 1618,[10] and in his notes on it, makes use of some of the terms we have been looking at: "Yet take aduice, whom thou mayst please: I am no vplandish man. I am not a shepheard. I do not here clownishly tend herds or flocks. Thou knowest not, oh vnaduised soule, thou knowest not whom thou fliest, and therefore fliest thou me." "Non incola montis" is glossed as "I am not an inhabitour of the mountaine, or a rude fellow dwelling among the hils or crags".

Just to complete the social picture, there is in Orlando's charge against his brother an opposition implied not quite parallel to city or court versus country, and that is between the education due the gently born, and that due (or not due) the base born; gentlemen might, and often did, live in the country, but to be "rustical" meant being a hind, not just living in the country. Just as in the Renaissance *civility* and *courtesy* (the one concept having an origin in Greek and Roman society, the other in feudal society) were assimilated to one another, so also were *gentility* and *civility* (or *urbanity*). A characteristic resolution appears in Cooper: "*Praedia vrbana*. Vlpian. Gentilmens houses either in the citie or countrey. *Quia vrbanum praedium non locus facit, sed materia, inquit Vlpianus*". That Orlando is not in fact boorish in behavior despite his lack of proper education, that he can compose loverlike verses, and is said by Oliver himself to be "gentle; never school'd and yet learned; full of noble deuise" (I. ii. 172-173), comes in as a little cross current, reflecting the belief, always present in Shakespeare, that in spite of all, birth will tell, that the gently born, with or without nurture, are naturally gentle in behavior. In *Cymbeline* Belarius wonders how divine Nature blazons herself in Guiderius and Arviragus, the two princes raised in the mountains:

> 'Tis wonder
> That an invisible instinct should frame them
> To royalty unlearn'd, honour untaught,
> Civility not seen from other, valour
> That wildly grows in them, but yields a crop
> As if it had been sow'd!
> (IV. ii. 176-181)[11]

All this evidence of standard Elizabethan social theory and prejudice would not be remarkable if the action and the setting of the play did not invite us to entertain an apparently contrary idea, the idea that in the forest one may "fleet the time carelessly as they did in the golden world", finding the winter wind less unkind than man's ingratitude. In the two ideas, one taking for granted the superiority of civilized man to "rude" and uncultivated man, the other

[10] *Ouids Metamorphosis translated grammatically, and also according to the propriety of our English tongue, so far as grammar and the verse will well beare*. . . . London, 1618. The language of Brinsley's dedicatory epistle is amusingly pertinent to our discussion. He says the right use of translation is, first, "for all the ruder places of the Land. . . . Chiefly, for the poore ignorant countries of Ireland and Wales; . . . For . . . especially in those barbarous countries, the hope of the Church of God is to come primarily out of the grammar-schools, by reducing them first vnto ciuility through the meanes of schooles of good learning planted amongst them in euery quarter; whereby their sauage and wilde conditions may be changed into more humanity; according to the right judgement of our Poet, which the experience of all ages hath confirmed." One calls up a vision of the "rough rug-headed kerns" Richard II went to fight (II. i. 156).

[11] Cf. Spenser's Pastorella and even his "saluage man" in *F.Q.*, VI.

viewing civilized man as sophisticated and in some sense morally declined from an earlier stage of innocence and honest simplicity, one recognizes those familiar and opposite intuitions with which civilized men have always, apparently, responded to the evidence of man's alteration of his environment and of cultural changes in his own society. Logical consistency appears not to be necessary (any more than in awareness of time) when these responses, as they often seem to be, are emotional or temperamental. In one mood, we may castigate the degenerate times we live in and yearn for the good old days; in another, take it for granted that everything we do and have is superior to anything our ancestors did and had. The temper of some societies, too, may invite one response more than the other. These ideas may be found, however, fully developed as philosophies of history, giving different accounts of the origin and growth of human society: one, the idea of progressive advance, that man began as a brute and a savage and progressed, through the invention of language, the discovery of technical skills, and the development of social organization, to a state of civilization—that is, to a state in which there is time and freedom to put his mind to uses far beyond the satisfaction of merely physical needs; the other, the idea of primitivism, that man began in innocence and happiness, but that as he learned skills and began to live in society, his wants increased, and he grew ever more competitive and dissatisfied, so that civilization brought moral degeneration. I am not here concerned with the history of these ideas, with their various refinements, or with the ways in which they may be philosophically accommodated to each other—such as by the distinction between historical and cultural primitivism, the distinction between technical advance and moral decline, cyclic theories of progress and decline, and so on.[12] It is enough for my purpose to remind the reader of the wide currency of both these ideas in the Renaissance. They are to be met with, especially, in myths that everybody knew. It will be helpful to recall some of these myths briefly before we turn wholly to the play.

The idea of primitivism (either historical or cultural) was expressed in the myth of the Golden Age. Everyone knows how ubiquitous in the period the idea was, and to what varied poetic uses it might be put. But it may be pertinent here to mark the differences in the Ovidian and the Virgilian expression of it—the two most readily available to everybody. In the account of the Four Ages in the *Metamorphoses* (i. 89-150), the Golden or Saturnian Age is a state of changeless time, when "ver erat aeternum", a time when nature satisfied all wants without labor, and when men were perfectly innocent and perfectly happy. A change came with the rule of Jupiter, who introduced the year and a change of seasons, thus forcing men to seek shelter against the weather and to begin tillage that they might have food for the barren seasons. With these pursuits competitive trade, the enclosure of property, mining, and warfare

12 For such an account see J. B. Bury, *The Idea of Progress* (London, 1920); also Arthur O. Lovejoy and George Boas, *A Documentary History of Primitivism and Related Ideas* (Baltimore, 1935), Vol. I. In his rigorous sense of the idea of progress as an idea applied to the future as well as the past, Bury does not find it full-fledged in the sixteenth century, though he marks the seeds of it in Bodin, Le Roy, and Bacon; but there is hardly another phrase to suggest the opposite of the idea of degeneration, even if for a limited period of time. See also Erwin Panofsky, *Studies in Iconology* (New York, 1939), Chap. II, and W. K. C. Guthrie, *In the Beginning* (Ithaca, N. Y., 1957). For this last reference and very helpful criticism I am indebted to my colleague, Professor Friedrich Solmsen, of the Institute for Research in the Humanities, University of Wisconsin.

began; the Silver Age turned to Bronze, the Bronze to Iron. At this stage, men had become so savage and so impious that Jupiter destroyed them with a flood; and Deucalion and Pyrrha, the survivors, had to start a new race of men from stones. Virgil's fullest use of the myth is in the Fourth Eclogue, in which he sees already beginning the cyclical return of the reign of Saturn. In the new Golden Age of peace, about to be realized, the lion will not trouble the herds, there will be no commerce on the seas, "the earth shall not feel the harrow, nor the vine the pruning-hook":[13]

> omnis feret omnia tellus.
> non rastros patietur humus, non vinea falcem;
> . . . .   (iv. 39-40)

The brief account of the Ages in the first book of the *Georgics* (i. 121-146) makes the age "ante Iovem", when the realm slumbered in heavy lethargy ("torpore gravi"), less preferable, perhaps, than the Silver Age, in which men's wits were sharpened by the necessity of toil; this is what Lovejoy calls a "hard" as opposed to a "soft" primitivism. In any case the rural life set forth in the *Georgics* (and implied in the *Eclogues*) is a kind of Silver Age ideal. Away from the city and its splendors, but also free of its enmities and worries, the husbandman has repose without care ("secura quies"). His life is rich in treasures: the ease of the countryside with its broad fields, its caverns, its fresh lakes, its herds, its woods full of game; a hardy youth, inured to scanty fare; worship of the gods, reverence for age, and knowledge of justice (*Georgics*, ii. 458-476, 490-502). But Virgil likens this life to the Golden Age of Saturn (ii. 538), and to suggest the loveliness of early spring evokes the beauty of the first days at the dawn of the world: "ver illud erat, ver magnus agebat/ orbis" (ii. 336-339).[14] He has momentarily touched his picture of rural life with the mood of the Golden Age. This Virgilian mood is of course one of the moods of Renaissance pastoralism—the one which is expressed in the praise of the simple life of shepherds away from the intense competition of city and court.

> Who doth ambition shun
> And loves to live i' th' sun,
> Seeking the good he eats,
> And pleas'd with what he gets,
> Come hither, come hither, come hither!
>   Here shall he see
>   No enemy
> But winter and rough weather.

Lodge's Rosalynde, in disguise as a young swain, and "having but country fare and coarse lodging", every day led forth her flocks "with such delight, that she held her exile happy, and thought no content like to the bliss of a country cottage".[15]

The other idea of the origin of society, implying advance from a brutal stage, was expressed in a number of different myths, especially in the myths of Prometheus, of Amphion, and of Orpheus. The Promethean myth, in the form

---

[13] H. Rushton Fairclough's translation in the Loeb edition.
[14] "Springtime that was; the great world was keeping spring" (Fairclough translation).
[15] Thomas Lodge, *Rosalynde,* ed. Edward Chauncey Baldwin (Boston, 1910), pp. 40-41.

in which it was told by Plato in the *Protagoras* (320-322), is the fullest and most explicit. But Plato has Socrates less concerned with the advances men were able to make with Prometheus' gifts of fire and the mechanical arts than with their need for a second gift from Zeus, the gift of reverence and justice in order to govern themselves in the cities they had built. In the sixteenth century Louis Le Roy retold the myth from the *Protagoras* in *De la vicissitude ou variété des choses en l'univers* (1575).[16] He greatly elaborated it, especially with descriptions of the brutishness of primitive life and of the advances of civilization. The title to Book III, in Robert Ashley's English translation, is "Of the Vicissitude, and Invention of Arts, and How men from their first simplicitie and Rudenes, haue come to the present Commoditie, Magnificence, and Excellency." After recounting Prometheus' gifts to man of "artificial wisdom" and fire and the uses to which these were put, Le Roy abandons retelling for interpretation, with grafts from other familiar places, notably Cicero.[17] Man has three special helps, he says—reason to invent, speech to communicate, and hands to accomplish whatever he has invented or learned. Men have proceeded from the invention of necessary things to such things as serve for pleasure, ornament, and magnificence; they have given names to everything and invented letters and writing of all sorts; they have made all arts, both mechanical and liberal, proceeding so far as to measure the earth, the sea, and the heavens themselves. Only men participate with their souls in the divine nature; therefore even primitive men, by the aid of reason, thought there were gods and worshipped them. ". . . From thence, had religion her beginning, publicke gouernment, judgement, negotiation and traficke by Sea, and by lande, lawes were established, magistrates created, innumerable trades inuented, houses, villages, and townes builded, consequently cities, castles, and fortresses; and then kingdoms, and Empires erected; Where hence hath succeeded, the greatnes, and excellency of mankind such as we see it at this day" (fol. 27ᵛ). Le Roy, not concerned like Socrates to show the difference between the mechanical arts and the art of government, has no need for the second rescue of mankind with the gift of political wisdom from Zeus; he omits it and makes the progress of mankind from a brutish life[18] to the "sweetnes, and ciuilitie" of life in communities an orderly and steady one, found out by reason. Interestingly enough, a few pages further on (fols. 28ʳ-31ʳ), he almost insensibly shifts his point of view, and spends several pages condemning the multiplicity of wants and goods that modern man has; without any transition to prepare us for this changed emphasis, he adopts the view of present-day civilization as a moral deterioration from an early "hard" simplicity.

What happened in the interpretation of the myths of Amphion, said to have raised the walls of Thebes to the music of the lyre, and of Orpheus, said to have charmed the beasts, the trees, the stones, even the rivers and the mountains, by his singing, is instructive of contemporary attitudes and prejudices.

[16] Subsequent editions in 1577, 1579, 1583; translated into English by R. A[shley] as *Of the Interchangeable Course, or Variety of Things in the Whole World*, London, 1594.

[17] Cf. *De officiis*, I. iv. 11-14; *De re publica*, III. ii. 3.

[18] Similar views of the savagery of primitive life may be found in a number of places familiar to the Renaissance, as in the *Satires* of Horace (I. iii. 99-114). See Lovejoy and Boas for other references.

Orpheus with his lute made trees
And all the mountain tops that freeze
Bow themselves when he did sing.[19]
. . . .   (*H. VIII*, III. i. 3-14)

Occasionally these effects are allowed to stand simply for the power of music to move the minds of beasts and men.[20] But the commoner allegories read much more into the myths.

The most memorable passage, the one most often referred to by the mythographers, is in Horace, *Ars Poetica* (391-401):

> Silvestris homines sacer interpresque deorum
> caedibus et victu foedo deterruit Orpheus,
> dictus ob hoc lenire tigris rabidosque leones.
> dictus et Amphion, Thebanae conditor urbis,
> saxa movere sono testudinis et prece blanda
> ducero quo vellet.[21]

He goes on to say that in ancient times wisdom lay in drawing a line between public and private rights, between things sacred and common, in giving rules for marriage, in building towns, in graving laws on tables of wood. Because of their wisdom in these matters, honor and fame fell to bards and their songs as divine ("sic honor et nomen divinis vatibus atque/ carminibus venit"). In song, oracles were given and the way of life shown. Here Orpheus and Amphion are "vates", inspired teachers of mankind, like Musaeus, Homer, and Hesiod, who instructed men and hence civilized them through the special powers of poetry. Orpheus, as the supposed author of the *Argonautica* and the Orphic poems, fits the role of sage rather better than Amphion; he was thought to have first taught men the secrets of nature and instituted religious sacrifices. Sidney has it that poets went before other learned men (philosophers and historians) "as causes, to draw with their charming sweetnesse the wild untamed wits to an admiration of knowledge. So . . . *Amphion* was said to moove stones with his Poetry to build *Thebes*, and *Orpheus* to be listned to by beasts, indeed stonie and beastly people."[22]

Frequently, however, one finds the music and the poetry turned into oratory. The explanation of Amphion's feat given in Boccaccio's *Genealogia deorum*, for instance, is that with sweet harmony of words he persuaded the ignorant, rude, and hard men who lived scattered here and there to come together to live civilly, and for the sake of public defense to surround the city with a wall; that he had the cythara from Mercury is said because of the influence Mercury

---

[19] The primary passages in Latin literature are Horace, *Odes*, I. xii. 6-12, and Ovid, *Metamorphoses*, x. 86-105, xi. 1-2.

[20] As in Thomas Thomas, "Dictionarium propria locorum et personarum vocabula breviter complectens", appended to his *Dictionarium linguae latinae et anglicanae, op. cit.*

[21] "While men still roamed the woods, Orpheus, the holy prophet of the gods, made them shrink from bloodshed and brutal living; hence the fable that he tamed tigers and ravening lions; hence too the fable that Amphion, builder of Thebes's citadel, moved stones by the sound of his lyre, and led them whither he would by his supplicating spell" (Fairclough translation, Loeb edition).

[22] *Defence of Poesie*, ed. Albert Feuillerat (Cambridge, 1923), III, 4. Cf. full interpretation of the Horace passage in this sense in commentary of Sabinus (Georg Schuler) on *Met.* x. 86 ff. included in Thomas Thomas' edition of the *Metamorphoses* (Cambridge, 1584), a small (8ᵛᵒ) and useful school edition Shakespeare may have known.

had on eloquence.[23] Orpheus, too, was sometimes represented as an orator.[24] The fusion of poetry with oratory and the giving of persuasive eloquence a civilizing role is a commonplace of Renaissance thought.

The effect of Orpheus' eloquence may be seen as primarily ethical, as when the taming of the beasts is said to mean the taming of the passions.[25] But of course lawless passions must be controlled if men are to live together in mutual helpfulness. Hence the myth may receive a social, even political, interpretation like Amphion's. Horace, in the passage from the *Ars poetica,* does not say specifically that Orpheus brought men into towns, but Natalis Comes, explaining the myth with his eye on the passage, does: with the sweetness of his speech he prevailed on rude mortals, who lived without choice of customs and without laws, and who wandered in the fields without settled dwellings, to lead a gentler kind of life ("mansuetius vitae genus"); he called them into one place, taught them to establish communities ("civitates"), to submit to civil laws, and to observe marriage bonds.[26] It is Cicero who, without benefit of myth, best presents the view of the development of civilization with the establishment of community life:

> In all these respects [the arts of agriculture, engineering, navigation, medicine, etc.] the civilized life of man is far removed from the standard of the comforts and wants of the lower animals. And, without the association of men, cities could not have been built or peopled. In consequence of city life, laws and customs were established, and then came the equitable distribution of private rights and a definite social system. Upon these institutions followed a more humane spirit and consideration for others, with the result that life was better supplied with all it requires, and by giving and receiving, by mutual exchange of commodities and conveniences, we succeeded in meeting all our wants.
>
> (*De officiis* II. iv. 15)[27]

[23] *Genealogia deorum gentilium libri* (a cura di Vicenzo Romano, Bari, 1951), V. xxx: "Eum autem cythara mouisse saxa in muros Thebanos construendos dicit Albericus, nil aliud fuisse, quam melliflua oratione suasisse ignaris, atque rudibus et duris hominibus et sparsin degentibus, ut in unum conuenirent, et ciuiliter uiuerent, et in defensionem publicam ciuitatem menibus circundarent, quod et factum est. . . . Quod autem Mercurio cytharam susceperit, est quod eloquentiam ab influentia Mercurii habuerit, ut mathematici asserunt." Latin editions of the *Genealogia* (*ed. pr.* Venice, 1472) and of the Italian translation by G. Betussi (Venice, 1547) were numerous; French translation, Paris, 1498/9, reprinted 1531. This reading of the myth is the one to be found in Cooper's *Dictionarium historicum et poeticum* appended to his *Thesaurus* and in such a common reference book as Ravisius Textor's *Epithetorum opus absolutissimus* (Basel, 1541, etc.); I have consulted the Venice edition of 1588. A shorter form of the same work, called *Epithetorum Epitome* (Basel, 1540), was printed in England in ?1564, 1579, 1626, 1634; I have consulted the editions of 1579 and 1634.

[24] Boccaccio even derives his name from *aurea phoné* or "golden sound", that is "bona eloquentie vox", truly the daughter of Apollo, or wisdom, and Calliope, which means "bonus sonus"; the lyre given him by Mercury is the oratorical faculty (*Gen. deorum*, V. xii). See also ref. in n. 25, n. 26 below.

[25] Boccaccio says (V. xii) that only persuasive eloquence can move men of obstinate opinion (Orpheus' rooted trees), give stability to loose and lascvious men (the flowing streams Orpheus stayed), render gentle and humane choleric and rapacious men (the wild beasts). Geffrey Whitney (*Choice of Emblemes,* 1586) has it that Orpheus "with persuasions sounde" made the hearts of fierce and cruel men relent, "That meeke, and milde they did become, and followed where he wente" (No. 186, pp. 122-123).

[26] *Mythologiae sive explicationis fabularum, libri decem* (Venice, 1581, etc.), VII. xiv. I have used the Venice edition of 1581 and the Geneva edition of 1641.

[27] Walter Miller translation, Loeb edition.

Orpheus, a woodcut in *Accipe Studiose Lector P. Ouidii Metamorphosin. . .*
(Venice, 1509), courtesy of The Folger Shakespeare Library.

Orpheus, a woodcut in *P. Ouidio Metamorphoseos Vulgare* (Venice, 1522).
Courtesy of The Folger Shakespeare Library. The artist has reversed the picture
of 1509.

Orpheus, a woodcut in Lodovico Dolce: *Le Trasformationi* (Venice, 1558).
Courtesy of The Folger Shakespeare Library.

Vates en viduus, sed thua coniuge, supplet
lecti delirias ineripitante lyra

Mellitos cantus animalia suasa sequantur.
Aurem dic montes dic habuisse nemus.

Orpheus, this time with a harp instead of a violin, engraving by Crispijn van
de Passe: *Metamorphoseon Ouidianarum typi aliquot artificiocissime delineate,
ac in gratiam studiosae juuentutis edite* (1602). Courtesy of The Folger
Shakespeare Library.

Shakespeare's knowledge and use of these myths, except for that of the Golden Age, is not here in question. The interpretations of the other myths have been rehearsed because they express, in forms that were so universally available, common notions about the origin of society and the values attached to "civil" man. Shakespeare put Prometheus to other uses. Amphion he does not mention. And Orpheus he thought of, not as the teacher, but as the Thracian singer, able by his music to allay the savage passions. Even so, the civilizing connotations are not absent from Shakespeare's most explicit application of the myth. In the long discussion on the power of music in the garden at Belmont, Lorenzo tells how a wild herd of unhandled colts on hearing the trumpet or any air of music

> will make a mutual stand,
> Their savage eyes turn'd to a modest gaze
> By the sweet power of music. Therefore the poet
> Did feign that Orpheus drew trees, stones, and floods,
> Since naught so stockish, hard, and full of rage
> But music for the time doth change his nature.
> The man that hath no music in himself,
> Nor is not mov'd with concord of sweet sounds,
> Is fit for treasons, stratagems, and spoils;
> The motions of his spirit are dull as night,
> And his affections dark as Erebus.
> Let no such man be trusted.[28]
>
> (Merch. V. i. 71-88)

"Treasons, stratagems, and spoils" suggest the lawless, "uncivil" man rather more than the man simply angry or lustful or depressed in his private affairs. There is perhaps, also, an intimation of the Orpheus myth in the lovely passage in *A Midsummer Night's Dream* in which Oberon recalls to Puck the occasion on which he heard "a mermaid, on a dolphin's back,/ Uttering such dulcet and harmonious breath/ That the rude sea grew civil at her song" (II. i. 150-152.) At any rate, the values of "civil" and "rude" implied here are the same as in the common interpretations of the Prometheus, Amphion, and Orpheus myths. Music and poetry make the sea calm and tractable just as they render civil and humane the hearts of savage men. Whatever Shakespeare may have thought of the remote origins of society, he appears not to have questioned the fundamental assumption in the interpretation of these myths, namely, that "civil" man, living in an orderly society with its amenities, is superior to "rude" man. "Allow not nature more than nature needs,/ Man's life is cheap as beast's" (*Lear* IV. ii. 269-270). Ulysses, in his speech on degree, pictures a civilized society, with its regard for order and custom, its justice, its accord of honors to place and merit, returning to savagery as rude will takes over: "Strength should be lord of imbecility,/ And the rude son should strike the father dead" (*Troi.* I. iii. 115-116).

[28] With this passage cf. Sabinus' comment on *Met.* x. 86 ff. (in Thomas ed., *op. cit.*), pp. 387-388. Sabinus, like Sidney, attributes the civilizing effect of Orpheus to poetry and music rather than persuasive discourse, and gives special emphasis to music, which so penetrates the minds of men that if they are not moved, they are truly more rigid than wild beasts and trees: "Constat autem poëticam & musicam habere summam vim ad ciendos & permulcendos hominum animos. nulla enim res ita penetrat in animos, vt harmonia numerorum & vocum, qua qui non mouentur, nae illi rigidiores sunt feris & arboribus."

What, then, of *As You Like It,* where the main characters, all "inland bred", find themselves exiled from court and noble estate to the Forest of Arden? It was Lodge who skilfully grafted on the old tale of Gamelyn, the tale of noble outlaws, a pastoral setting in Renaissance style, pleasantly laced with reflections on the simple life. Shakespeare uses the pastoral–sylvan setting less conventionally than Lodge and so invites a more complicated response to it. He introduces it by a rumor early in the play:

> They say he is already in the Forest of Arden, and a many merry men with him; and there they live like the old Robin Hood of England. They say many young gentlemen flock to him every day, and fleet the time carelessly as they did in the golden world.
>
> (I. ii. 120-125)

This introduces a traditional mode of pastoral (for Robin Hood was easily assimilated to the pastoral), the mode of escape from sophistication;[29] but when we come with the characters to the forest, there are too many riffles and crosscurrents for the idyllic mood to be wholly ours. Were it not for the lioness, the palm tree, and the olive trees, we could almost believe in the English reality of the place. The characters respond to it according to their own natures. Duke Senior sustains the idyllic mood, finding the experience so instructive that he "would not change it". And his companions find hunting and rough weather at least temporarily attractive. It is worth noting, however, that the Duke is not indulging in a mood of escape, but is in truth making sweet the uses of adversity. Jaques finds occasion both for sentiment (as in his reflections on the weeping deer) and for mockery:

> If it do come to pass
> That any man turn ass,
> Leaving his wealth and ease
> A stubborn will to please,
> Ducdame, ducdame, ducdame!
> Here shall he see,
> Gross fools as he,
> An if he will come to me.
>
> (II. v. 52-59).

Touchstone makes the most of his unwilling exile among the Goths by exploiting the yokels, but never pretends he would not rather be at home. Rosalind, in love, is little concerned with her surroundings and does not moralize on them as does Lodge's heroine; but she gives tart and sound instruction to Phebe, the proud disdainful shepherdess. Orlando peoples the desert with his verses composed of "civil sayings"—the brevity of life, the violation of vows, and the praise of his lady:

> Why should this a desert be,
> For it is unpeopled? No!
> Tongues I'll hang on every tree
> That shall civil sayings show:

---

[29] Annotation is hardly necessary for so familiar a subject, but for especially informative and suggestive brief treatments, see Frank Kermode, Introduction to *English Pastoral Poetry* (London, 1952), and Hallett Smith, *Elizabethan Poetry* (Cambridge, Mass., 1952), Chap. I.

> Some, how brief the life of man
> ..., [etc.].

One may note, too, that though the forest presents the occasion for Oliver's repentance, it is hardly the cause of it. That lies in Orlando's kindness, "nobler ever than revenge,/ And nature, stronger than his just occasion", which led him to rescue his unnatural brother from the lioness.

We do not have pastoralism pure. But for all that, the object of criticism is not the "removed" country, but the court and the city. The play is not about shepherds and shepherdesses, but about the people who come among them. Thus, Shakespeare also uses (with a difference) the convention of the pastoral in its other mode, the mode of criticism of court and city seen from the vantage point of sheepcote and forest glade.

> Hath not old custom made this life more sweet
> Than that of painted pomp? Are not these woods
> More free from peril than the envious court?
> Here feel we but the penalty of Adam,
> The seasons' difference....
> (II. i. 2-6)

In the action of the play the courtly world shows up badly at first as a world of arbitrary and wantonly used power. Significant in the action is the relation of Adam and Orlando. In contrast to the flagrantly unnatural Oliver, who violates his responsibility to his younger brother, the old servant Adam behaves with perfect loyalty to his former master's son. Orlando comments:

> O good old man, how well in thee appears
> The constant service of the antique world,
> When service sweat for duty, not for meed!
> Thou art not the fashion of these times,
> Where none will sweat but for promotion,
> And having that, do choke their service up
> Even with the having. It is not so with thee.
> (II. iii. 56-62)

The times are degenerate. But are they, altogether? Orlando is a young man, from this newer world, yet as master to Adam his kindness and responsibility match Adam's loving service to him.

The forest is, then, a temporary place of escape where the characters from outside it take a look at their own permanent world. The temporariness is important. There is never any question that the exile will end as soon as Duke Frederick and Oliver have a change of heart. The sense one gets from Corin's conversation with Touchstone on why he was never in court (III. ii. 46-52, 76-81) is that each world has its own manners, each proper and right for itself. Nothing suggests that Shakespeare is a cultural primitivist. But neither is Duke Senior's finding "tongues in trees, books in the running brooks,/ Sermons in stones, and good in everything" mocked in the outcome. The stay in the greenwood has brought a temporary freedom, a lightening of cares, an invitation to reflection on the ways of men. It has brought an opportunity, on Orlando's part, to choose between revenge and forgiveness, and on Rosalind's to do her self and others good in matters of love. The Duke expresses no nostalgia for the past. His cheerfulness and hope are in the present and are not unjustified. The "fleeting of the time carelessly" is momentary, not a way of life; and Shakespeare's "golden world" is a timeless human dream of the possibility of innocence and happiness. The reality is Orlando's and the Duke's "civil" world on the one hand, Corin's world of sheep on the other; each belongs in his own. The "inland" man and his values are simply taken for granted. Perhaps the ideal of the Golden Age can only be held by civilized men who "can translate adversity/ Into so quiet and sweet a style" as Duke Senior's. There is, therefore, no contradiction in the play between Golden Age and "civil" man. Between dream and reality, two different modes of existence, there can be no logical contradiction.

This theme of civilized man, both in his own nature and in his relation to other men, is one of Shakespeare's most persistent themes, variously presented. Sometimes the terms are "nature" and "art" (as in *Love's Labour's Lost* and *The Winter's Tale*), sometimes "nature" and "nurture" (as in *The Winter's Tale, Cymbeline,* and *The Tempest*), sometimes order and disorder (as in the history plays, *Troilus and Cressida,* and *King Lear*), sometimes (as in *As You Like It, The Winter's Tale,* and *The Tempest*), the court and the "green world". But these terms are by no means interchangeable pairs; the terms alter as the focus shifts. If Shakespeare appears to be on the side of the "naturalists" against the "artsmen", he is not therefore on the side of primitive rudeness against civilization. To put him on one side or the other of any of these pairs (except order and disorder) is to miss the breadth of his vision and the depth of his perception.

The great tragic exploration of the theme of man in society is in *King Lear*. When, at the nadir of his experience, Lear confronts Poor Tom with the question, "Is man no more than this?" the seeming paradox of the speech is, within the frame of the action, profound. Shakespeare's final treatment of the theme, in *The Tempest,* is perhaps the clearest. Caliban, though imaginatively responsive through his senses and even capable of learning speech, is incapable of learning morality; he cannot answer Prospero's "humane care" with "gentle" behavior. He in his brutish way and Antonio and Sebastian in their sophisticated and vicious way are equally opposed to Gonzalo's naïve but warm vision of a Golden Age on the island (in the future rather than in the past). The existence of these three (Antonio, Sebastian, and Caliban) denies the possibility of Gonzalo's innocent society. Prospero, the wise man, man at his "humane" best, stands between. He is the "civil" man who puts his experience, his wisdom, and his art, to responsible and generous use:

> Though with their high wrongs I am struck to th' quick,
> Yet with my nobler reason 'gainst my fury
> Do I take part. The rarer action is
> In virtue than in vengeance.
>   (V. i. 25-28)

Without illusion, he is yet willing to put the future into the hands of the young lovers, for whom experience is still a wonder. Gonzalo's dream has its own validity, for the dream of the Golden Age is a dream of the heart, forever renewed.

The University of Wisconsin

Imagination in *A Midsummer Night's Dream*

R. W. DENT

OR many years editors and critics have customarily praised *A Midsummer Night's Dream* for its artistic fusion of seemingly disparate elements. Sometimes the praise involves little, really, beyond admiring the skill with which Shakespeare interwove the actions of the four lovers, the fairies, and the mechanicals in the first four acts of the play.[1] Usually, quite properly, it moves somewhat beyond this, relating this interwoven action to the thematic treatment of love in the play. But such praise has rarely concerned itself with the play's fifth act; it has tended to treat *A Midsummer Night's Dream* as essentially complete in four acts, but with a fifth act somehow vaguely appropriate in mood and content to serve as a conclusion. *Pyramus and Thisbe*, that rude offering of the mechanicals, has been briefly commended as loosely paralleling in action and theme the problems of the four lovers, and as delightful enough in itself to need no other artistic justification. Despite the consistency with which *A Midsummer Night's Dream* has been admired for its unity, in short, few critics have had much to say about the whole of the play.

The present essay seeks to reexamine the degree and kind of unity achieved by *A Midsummer Night's Dream*. Without pretending to be strikingly original, it approaches the play from a somewhat different angle, suggesting that the heart of the comedy, its most pervasive unifying element, is the partially contrasting role of imagination in love and in art. I do not mean to suggest for a moment that Shakespeare composed this play, or any play, as the result of a single governing conception to which every detail can be effectively related. But I do mean to suggest that *A Midsummer Night's Dream* has a dominant and premeditated conception. Thus, if my argument below appears guilty of the "intentional fallacy", it is so intentionally. Shakespeare's eye, in creating *A Midsummer Night's Dream,* did not "roll" in a "fine frenzy", and my point on imagination's role in the play demands my emphasis.

A prefatory word is necessary. Oversimply, to the Elizabethan the imagination ideally functioned as an essential servant to the understanding, whether as a reporter (the most emphasized function, that of transmitting accurate images of sense data, present or absent) or as a creator or inventor. When, as too fre-

---

[1] The frequency of such praise provoked R. A. Law's denial that the play had any organic unity whatever: "The Pre-Conceived Pattern of *A Midsummer Night's Dream*", *Texas Univ. Studies in English* (1943), pp. 5-14.

quently happened, it became dominated by passions in conflict with reason, it became a false reporter and/or inventor. In the case of passionate love, for example, one could not say that the imagination actually caused love, but rather that love so influenced the imagination as to have it misreport what it saw, thereby heightening the passion, thereby heightening the imagination, thereby . . . an endless chain reaction to man's ever-increasing peril. In watching the lovers of *A Midsummer Night's Dream,* we tend to be aware of the imagination's activity only when it is thus failing in its proper function. At such times we can scarcely attribute the folly to love or imagination alone, obviously; it derives from their interaction.

Nothing is more common than the observation that *A Midsummer Night's Dream* is a play "about love", about lovers' lunacy, where "reason and love keep little company together nowadays", where the follies of imagination-dominated Demetrius and Lysander are reduced to their essential absurdity by the passion of Titania for an ass. It is for the sake of this theme, surely, that Demetrius and Lysander are given so little distinctive characterization; they cannot contrast like a Claudius and a Benedick, so that a particular pairing of lovers is demanded by the characters of those involved. For the same reason, paradoxically, Hermia and Helena are differentiated, to heighten the puzzle of love's choices (as well as to increase the potentialities for comedy in the play's middle). By all conventional Elizabethan standards, tall fair gentle Helena should be the one pursued, and when Lysander eventually boasts his use of reason in preferring a dove to a raven his argument, by those standards, is indeed rational. Our laughter stems from recognizing that it is so only accidentally, as rationalization.

According to a good many critics, Shakespeare contrasts from the start the irrationality of the lovers with what these critics regard as the admirable rationality of Theseus-Hippolyta. The latter become a kind of ideal which the lovers approach by the end of the play. If so, the role of imagination in love is simple and obvious; it is a disrupting irrational influence which must eventually be purged, and will prove in simple and total contrast to the disciplined use of imagination essential to Shakespeare's art. But I cannot see that any contrast so mechanical as this is intended.

When, thanks to Dian's bud, Lysander returns to Hermia, his "true love", the return marks a release from dotage but no return to reason as such, any more than does Demetrius' return to Helena by the pansy-juice. Love's choices remain inexplicable, and the eventual pairings are determined only by the constancy of Helena and Hermia in their initial inexplicable choices. As so frequently in Shakespearian comedy, the men fluctuate before finally settling down to a constant attachment such as the heroines exhibit from the start. Men's "fancies are more giddy and unfirm, / More longing, wavering, sooner lost and won, / Than women's are." [2] In the case of true love, once stabilized— even as in the case of mere dotage—imagination cannot "form a shape, / Besides yourself to like of" [3]; it "carries no favour in't" but that of the beloved.[4] Unlike dotage, however, it is in no obvious conflict with reason, either in its

---

[2] *Twelfth Night* II. iv. 34-36.
[3] To use Miranda's words, *The Tempest* III. i. 56-57.
[4] *All's Well That Ends Well* I. i. 93-94.

object or its vehemence. By the end of the fourth act we are assured that Demetrius and Lysander have come to stability of this kind. But the terminus, I repeat, is not a rationally determined one. Like Theseus at the play's beginning, at the play's ending Demetrius and Lysander are settled. Jill has Jack, nought shall go back, and the prospect of happy marriage is before them all.

Thus in *A Midsummer Night's Dream* the origin of love never lies in reason. Love may be consistent with reason—e.g., Lysander is undeniably "a worthy gentleman"—and a healthy imagination, although influenced by love, will not glaringly rebel against reason. But as Hermia initially indicates, her choice is dictated not by her judgment but by her "eyes", by the vision of Lysander as her love-dictated imagination reports it. As Helena says at the close of this same introductory scene, love sees with that part of the mind that has no taste of judgment. Essentially this is as true for Hermia as for the others, although her choice conflicts with parental authority rather than with sound evaluation of her beloved's merits. Despite Egeus' initial disapproval, nevertheless, her choice is eventually confirmed. She is not compelled to "choose love by another's eyes" (I. i. 140), to see with her father's judgment (as Theseus at first demanded; I. i. 57), nor even to convert her love to one directed by her own judgment. Her love at the end is what it was at the beginning, with the obstacles removed.

Not even Egeus accuses her of dotage, although he does think her somehow "witched" in her refusal to accept his choice rather than her own. "Dotage", in this play, appears essentially reserved for two kinds of amorous excess approaching madness: the monomaniacal pursuit of an unrequited love (thus Helena "dotes in idolatry", Demetrius "dotes" on Hermia's eyes, and Lysander dotes for Helena in the night's comedy of errors), or the ridiculous bestowal of affection upon an obviously unworthy object (most grotesquely in Titania's passion for Bottom, but also in the gross excesses of Lysander and Demetrius during their "dream").[5]

In the middle of the play, then, when dotage grows most rampant, so too does imagination. The frenzied praises and dispraises of Lysander and Demetrius are exceeded only by Titania's infatuation for Bottom, her hearing beauty in his voice, seeing beauty in his ears, and so on. Were follies so excessive in the cases of the mortal lovers, we could never end as we do in marriage and lasting love. Yet by the end of Act IV, with all obstacles to happily paired marriages removed—no thanks to the behavior of the lovers—the lovers can sound, and behave, rationally enough. Their love, however, is in its essence as inexplicable as ever.

The inexplicability of love's choices was of course a favorite topic for discussion in the age and a favorite theme for Shakespearian comedy. Why should two particular people fall in love, often at first sight? Were they so destined by the stars, like Romeo and Juliet (but not Romeo and Rosaline)? Were they marked by peculiarly "correspondent qualytes of bloud"?[6]

[5] Helena is never so doting that she cannot recognize her apparent folly. Unlike the other victims of dotage, however, her foolish behavior has its root in a true love, once reciprocated and then unaccountably rejected. Thus only Helena can be cured of dotage by Oberon's curing someone else, rather than herself.

[6] Cf., for example, Boaistuau's *Theatrum Mundi* (ed. 1581), pp. 192-194, which treats both theories with equal seriousness. He concludes: "Others after that they had studied all that euer they

To this question *A Midsummer Night's Dream* perhaps suggests no kind of answer beyond the fact that such true loves do exist, are distinct from the fancy-dominated aberrations that mark inconstancy, and when properly terminating in marriage are part of the natural—and, in that sense, rational—order of things. From the start of the play, the mystery of love's choices (including the attendant male inconstancies) is stressed. Egeus, at least metaphorically, thinks Hermia "witched", and all Elizabethans would be reminded of disputes on whether love could be caused by witchcraft, or by philtres and charms, whether naturally or supernaturally administered.[7] When the fairies first appear (in II.i), and before ever they become involved with the lovers, Shakespeare skillfully prepares us for their role. First, the inexplicable fortunes and misfortunes of housewives are attributed to Puck—this may well receive first mention because it is drawn from folklore, is familiar to the audience, and thus allows the easiest transition into what follows. A few lines later, all the recently experienced disorders of the English-Athenian weather are similarly attributed to temporary discord in the fairy macrocosm:

> And this same progeny of evils comes
> From our debate, from our dissension.
>
> (II.i. 115-116)

For this night on which we can see fairies, we are allowed to understand, playfully, the cause for otherwise unaccountable phenomena. It is in such a context, too, that we hear the play's only reference to Theseus' well known infidelities preceding his "true love" marriage to Hippolyta; these too are charged to fairy influence (although Titania discounts the charge). In short, aspects of the inexplicable past, familiar to the audience, have been imaginatively explained as fairy-caused.

Within the play, thus far, we have one similarly puzzling phenomenon, Demetrius' desertion of Helena to pursue Hermia, as well as the less specific mystery of love's choices generally. We have by now a hint that such mysteries —at least that of Demetrius' infidelity—may be similarly explained. The play will never say, understandably. Instead it will allow us for one single night to witness, and thereby understand, "the mystery of things, / As if we were God's spies".

The magic charm by which love is to be manipulated on this single night is quite naturally a flower potion administered on the eyes.[8] From the play's beginning we are reminded of the commonplace that although the eyes are integrally involved in the process of inspiring and transmitting love, nevertheless "love sees not with the eyes"; instead, the eyes "see" what the lover's

---

coulde therein, and not finding the spring and original of this so furious an euill, haue said that Loue was one, I know not what, that came I knowe not how, and burned I know not how, a thing very certain and true. . . ."

[7] See Burton's voluminous annotation for *Anat. Mel.*, III. ii. V. iv, or the treatment in such familiar plays as *Endymion, Othello,* or *The Duchess of Malfi.* See also, in relation to Raleigh, Bruno, and Elizabethan preachers, T. Walter Herbert's "Dislocation and the Modest Demand in *A Midsummer Night's Dream*", *Renaissance Papers 1961* (Durham, N. C., 1962), p. 36.

[8] Not surprisingly, "eyes" appears far more frequently in *A Midsummer Night's Dream* than in any other of Shakespeare's plays (with *Love's Labour's Lost* second, for comparable reasons). Like the equally abundant use of "moon", this frequency is of course partly determined by the story, but the demands of the story are in turn determined by those of the theme.

imagination dictates. In *A Midsummer Night's Dream,* at least, this imagination does not misreport sense data, except in the sense that it selects from those
data and confers value accordingly. Hermia is never imagined as tall or blonde,
Bottom as hairless. Titania was "enamoured of an ass", and knew it, but her
selective imagination found beauty in its "fair large ears", "sleek smooth head",
even in its voice. Love, via imagination, transposes "to form and dignity" by
altering the normal evaluation, either in essence or in degree. At its extreme,
it sees beauty where others see "things base and vile", thus finding "Helen's
beauty in a brow of Egypt".[9] Conversely, it unwarrantedly makes "base and
vile" whatever object love causes it to reject. That the potion should be applied
to the eyes was inevitable.

The choice of flower for the potion was almost equally so. "Maidens call
it love-in-idleness." Perhaps it is foolish to labor over the implications of a
flower which the play avoids calling explicitly by its most familiar name. But
surely most of the audience would recognize the flower as the pansy, and "That's
for thoughts", as Ophelia says, as well as for relief of the heart. Cotgrave may
remind us of some of the usual associations:

> *Pensée:* f. A thought, supposall, coniecture, surmise, cogitation, imagina-
> tion; ones heart, mind, inward conceit, opinion, fancie, or iudgement;
> also, the flower Paunsie.
>
> *Menues pensées.* Paunsies, Harts-case, loue or liue in idlenesse; also idle,
> priuate, or prettie thoughts.[10]

However, although as Friar Laurence says,

> O, mickle is the powerful grace that lies
> In plants, herbs, stones, and their true qualities,

the true dispenser of grace in *A Midsummer Night's Dream* is Oberon. The
flower itself, wrongly applied by Puck, can make a hell of heaven rather than
a heaven of hell. Both the mispairings and the eventual proper pairings of love,

---

[9] That the love-stirred (or hate-stirred) imagination commonly distorted in this fashon, by
selection and erroneous evaluation, was a commonplace. Annotation is probably superfluous, but
see *Anat. Mel.,* III. ii. III. i, or Thomas Wright, *The Passions of the Minde* (1601), pp. 92-93: "Furthermore, the imagination representeth to the vnderstanding, not only reasons that may fauour the
passion [i.e., by selection], but also it showeth them very intensiuely, with more shew and ap-
parence than they are indeede; for as the Moone, when she riseth or setteth[,] seemeth greater
vnto us, than indeed she is, because the vapours or clowdes are interuerted betwixt our eyes and
her[,] euen so, the beauty and goodnesse of the obiect represented to our vnderstanding, appeareth
fairer and goodlier than it is, because a clowdie imagination interposeth a mist."

A useful survey of Renaissance thought on love generally, and on its relationship to imagination, appears in Chapter IV of Franklin Dickey's *Not Wisely but Too Well* (San Marino, Calif.,
1957). For the present point on the love-directed distortions of the imagination it is enough to
recall Sir Topas' praise of Dipsas in Lyly's *Endymion* (ed. Bond, III. iii. 50-60) or the parody
praise of Mopsa in Sidney's *Arcadia,* I. iii (ed. Feuillerat, I, 21).

[10] Necessarily, to remedy Puck's error with Lysander, Oberon must use Dian's bud, just as he
does for Titania. But the pansy influence, "Cupid's power", is clearly implied to have as lasting
an effect for Demetrius as "Dian's bud" for Lysander. Witness III. ii. 88-91 and V. i. 414-415, for
example. Shakespeare's working out of the love theme is perhaps a bit awkward here, but only if
we labor the play mechanically in a fashion contrary to is entire spirit. Yet we should not, I believe, do what several critics have done: treat the two flowers as representing opposed kinds of love,
irrational and rational, carnal and chaste, etc.

On the association of magic flowers with Midsummer Night, see Lou Agnes Reynolds and Paul
Sawyer, "Folk Medicine and the Four Fairies of *A Midsummer Night's Dream*", *SQ,* X (1959),
514-515.

on this single night, we can witness as produced by fairy influence. Oberon wishes true loves properly paired, and eventually sees that they are. Puck, while not wilfully mistaking, can delight in the consequences of his error, and we do too—the follies of mispaired doting lovers, their excessive praises and dispraises, their broken friendships, even the threat of bloodshed—potential tragedy were it not for Oberon's protection, of which we are so well aware that we can laugh at the folly they themselves take so seriously. The eventual pairings, then, are determined by Oberon, although always with the recognition that the heroines' choices are in some mysterious way right, that the pairings, to be "true loves", must correspond with their wishes. Oberon provides the remedy for the difficulties introduced at the beginning of the play and complicated by the subsequent action; the flower, like the eyes, is but his means.

The necessity of such "fairy grace" had been suggested from the start. Helena had asked in vain "with what art" Hermia won the heart of Demetrius. In love there is no art; imagination follows and encourages the mysterious dictates of the heart. Thus Lysander had appropriately wished Helena "luck" in gaining Demetrius, for only by such good fortune could she conceivably gain the man who found her every advance offensive (no more offensive, of course, than Lysander would later find Hermia, that dwarf, minimus, Ethiope). Helena had herself repeatedly lamented that her prayers were unanswered, that she somehow lacked the "grace" to be "happy", "fortunate", with "blessed and attractive eyes". On the night in the wood at last her prayers are answered. Like the rest of the lovers, including Theseus and Hippolyta, she is blessed, and an object of that "fairy grace" with which the chaos of the first four acts is ended and with which the play concludes (V. i. 406).

When initially Hermia defied her father's wishes, she said she knew not "by what power" she was "made bold". In similar terms, Demetrius later acknowledges being cured of his dotage for Hermia and restored to his true love for Helena: "I wot not by what power/ (But by some power it is)". The power is perhaps that mysterious source by which Hermia swore: "that which knitteth souls and prospers loves" (I. i. 172). "Fairy grace", certainly, removes the external obstacles to marriage for Hermia and Lysander, while at least assisting in the operation of knitting souls for all four lovers.

Initially, Hermia and Lysander had lamented that the course of true love never did run smooth. In the world of tragedy, whether for Romeo or for Pyramus, it does not. "A greater power than we can contradict" thwarts the plans of Friar Laurence, just as that same Heaven hath a hand in the tragic fortunes of Richard II. Within the complex world of these tragedies written approximately at the same time as *A Midsummer Night's Dream,* the divine will plays an essential role, as critics have long recognized. Within the comic world of *A Midsummer Night's Dream,* where Shakespeare of course avoids so sober an explanation of "events", we have "fairy grace".

In accordance with Oberon's plan, the four lovers awake harmoniously paired and think their whole experience of the night a dream,[11] although a

---

[11] Only Hermia has had an actual dream (II. ii. 147ff.), a prophetically accurate one to introduce the chaos into which she initially awakes. The love-threatening serpent of her dream, symbol of male inconstancy, proves more destructive than the literal "spotted snakes with double tongue" against which we have just heard the fairies sing. For spotted, double-tongued Demetrius see I. i. 110, III. ii. 70-73.

mystifying one with (as Hippolyta says) "great constancy". We know it was no dream, at least not in the sense they regard it as one; we have witnessed its entirety and have even better reason than Hippolyta to reject Theseus' dismissal of lovers' "shaping fantasies". What we have seen indeed "more witnesseth than fancy's images", partly because we are aware that we have been beholding the images of Shakespeare's "fancy" rather than that of the lovers. Yet we may well ask just how much it "witnesseth", and we may look to Bottom for a clue. When he awakes, he too thinks he has had a dream, and, as everyone knows, he soliloquizes in terms that echo *1 Corinthians* ii. 9-10.

> I have had a most rare vision. I have had a dream, past the wit of man to say what dream it was. Man is but an ass if he go about to expound this dream. . . . The eye of man hath not heard, the ear of man hath not seen, man's hand is not able to taste, his tongue to conceive, nor his heart to report what my dream was. I will get Peter Quince to write a ballet of this dream. It shall be call'd 'Bottom's Dream,' because it hath no bottom. . . .

> 9 But *we preache* as it is written, Things wᵉ eye hath not sene, & eare hath not heard, nether haue entred into mans mynde, which thinges God hath prepared for thē that loue hym.
> 10 But God hath opened *them* vnto vs by his Sprite, for the Spirite searcheth all thinges, yea, the botome of Goddes secretes.[12]

It used to be customary to see no significance whatever in this echo. One might merely observe, like Dover Wilson, "that Bottom was a weaver, and therefore possibly of a Puritanical turn of mind", apt to recall Scripture. Enticed by Bottom's suggestive malapropism a few minutes earlier ("I have an exposition of sleep come upon me"), it is tempting to look for more meaningful implications, ones that "expound" Shakespeare's *Dream* if not Bottom's. The lovers, of course, never saw the fairies; their "dreams" are only of the "fierce vexation" caused by Puck's mistakes in combination with their own folly. Bottom, in turn, had seen the fairies, had been the unappreciative, unimaginative object of Titania's temporary dotage and of the ministrations of her fairies.[13] Unlike either the lovers or Bottom, however, we have ourselves been admitted

---

[12] I cite the 1557 Geneva New Testament, which J. A. Bryant thinks "to have been the version that Shakespeare knew best" (*Hippolyta's View* [Lexington, Ky., 1961], p. 52). The 1557 version is like Tyndale and Coverdale in "the botome of Goddes secretes"; later 16th-century translations read "the deep things of God".

[13] Two recent critics have in their different ways been especially anxious to find meaning in Bottom's echo. See Paul Olson, "*A Midsummer Night's Dream* and the Meaning of Court Marriage", *ELH*, XXIV (1957), 95-119, and Frank Kermode, "The Mature Comedies", *Early Shakespeare* (Stratford-upon-Avon Studies, III, London, 1961), pp. 214-220. While very unlike one another in interpretation, Olson and Kermode agree in seeing the play as essentially serious and essentially about love, true and false, earthly and spiritual.

Kermode, p. 218, seems far-fetched in comparing Bottom's vision to that of Apuleius, who, "relieved by the hand of Isis from his ass's shape, has a vision of the goddess, and proceeds to initiation in her mysteries". Titania violently rejects her dotage when awakened, and Bottom certainly has not profited from any initiation. "Bottom's dream", Kermode argues, "is *oneiros* or *somnium;* ambiguous, enigmatic, of high import. And this is the contrary interpretation of blind love; the love of God or of Isis, a love beyond the power of the eyes. . . . Bottom is there to tell us that the blindness of love, the dominance of the mind over the eye, can be interpreted as a means to grace as well as to irrational animalism; that the two aspects are, perhaps, inseparable" (p. 219). If I understand Kermode, he appears to confuse Bottom's vision with that of Shakespeare's audience, and to make that vision a product of the "blindness of love" rather than the art of the poet.

to a more complete vision, though we may well be asses if we seek to infer from it more than the suggestion of a mysterious "grace" that sometimes blesses true love. Unlike the lovers and Bottom, we have been witnessing a play, a creation of Shakespeare's imagination. Only a part of the time have we watched imagination-dominated "dreams"; all of the time we have watched the product of Shakespeare's own imagination. If our attitude to art is that of Theseus, we may, as the humble epilogue encourages us to do, think we

> ... have but slumb'red here
> While these visions did appear.
> And this weak and idle theme,
> No more yielding but a dream.

But, being good Elizabethans, we may well remember that not all dreams are the product of disordered, passion-stimulated, never-sleeping imagination. Some dreams are divine revelations of truth, however difficult to expound, and we have already seen plays of Shakespeare where dreams contained at least a prophetic, specific truth, if not a universal one. Some dreams are yielding, and *A Midsummer Night's Dream*—although a poet's revelation rather than a divinity's—may be one of them.

At the same time, when we eventually hear the epilogue's modest disclaimer, we have seen much more than a treatment of "fairy grace" blessing true love. The "visions" we have beheld embrace far more than just the "visions" experienced by Titania, Bottom, and the four lovers. Our visions began with the first line of the play, and a good part of our time has been devoted to watching Bottom and his friends prepare and present a play of their own.

As I remarked at the beginning, few critics have had much to say about the relationship of *Pyramus and Thisbe* to the play as a whole.[14] Undoubtedly Shakespeare's reasons for including this farce were multiple and complex. For one thing, it is impossible to believe that *Pyramus and Thisbe* is only accidentally related to *Romeo and Juliet,* although we may never be certain which play preceded and provoked Shakespeare's contrasting treatment in the other.[15] Such considerations, however, are wholly external to our present concern with *A Midsummer Night's Dream* as an individual artistic entity. The play, if it was to be conventional, would of course include low comedy, and Shakespeare's problem was to determine what sort of low comedy would be most fitting. An ass like Bottom would serve to develop the love theme effectively, but such an ass could be easily introduced without his fellows. Why have a play-within-the-play, why give it the Pyramus-Thisbe plot, and why develop it in the particular way Shakespeare employed?

---

[14] Notable exceptions are Paul N. Siegel, "*A Midsummer Night's Dream* and the Wedding Guests", *SQ*, IV (1953), 139-144, and C. L. Barber, *Shakespeare's Festive Comedy* (Princeton, 1959), pp. 119-162. I am indebted to both, especially for their assuring me that my approach to the play is not wholly idiosyncratic.

[15] Not merely the play by the mechanicals but aspect after aspect of *A Midsummer Night's Dream* invites comparison, and contrast, with *Romeo and Juliet:* e.g., on Cupid's arrow versus Dian's wit, on doting versus loving, on love's "infection" through the eye, on oaths, inconstant moons, and male inconstancy, on "blind love" best agreeing with night, on dreams and fairies as "begot of nothing but vain fantasy". The relationship is too complex and too tangential to pursue here, but it once again suggests the need to treat *Pyramus and Thisbe* as an integral part of *A Midsummer Night's Dream.*

To begin with, within his play for a wedding occasion[16] Shakespeare apparently saw the advantages of introducing an inept production for a parallel occasion, the wedding of Theseus. Like Biron, he recognized " 'tis some policy/ To have one show worse than" his own offering.[17] Of course he could not decide what sort of plot to choose for this contrasting production without at the same time considering what development he would give it. But for the moment we can consider the two aspects separately. In contrast to his own play, the mechanicals should choose for Theseus a plot thoroughly inappropriate for a wedding: love tragedy. Only their ineptitude, and Shakespeare's skill, should make *Pyramus and Thisbe* fit pastime for a wedding night, both for the newlyweds within *A Midsummer Night's Dream* and those beholding it. Secondly, the plot should be one inviting comparison with the main plot of Shakespeare's play. The moment we meet the mechanicals in I. ii we learn they are preparing a play of Pyramus and Thisbe. Even without the early reminder that Pyramus would kill himself, "most gallant, for love", the audience would at once recognize in the familiar story parallels, actual and potential, to what had begun in I. i. Like Hermia and Lysander, Pyramus and Thisbe would run off to the woods in the night, frantically hoping to escape the obstacles to their true love. Unlike Hermia and Lysander (but at this point of the play the audience cannot know of the fairy grace to come), Pyramus and Thisbe, the audience knows, will find their "sympathy in choice" brought to such sudden catastrophe as Hermia and Lysander had expressly feared (I. i. 132ff.).[18]

Most critics who have related *Pyramus and Thisbe* to *A Midsummer Night's Dream* as a whole have largely confined themselves, very cryptically, to thematic implications of this partial parallel in the action. For E. K. Chambers, *Pyramus and Thisbe* is "but a burlesque presentment of the same theme which has occupied us throughout", that "lunacy in the brain of youth" which is "not an integral part of life, but a disturbing element in it".[19] For Arthur Brown, it is "an integral part of the main theme of the play, which seems to be concerned with gentle satire of the pangs of romantic love".[20] More soberly, for Frank Kermode it "gives farcical treatment to an important thematic element; for Bottom and his friends will perform a play to illustrate the disastrous end of doting".[21] For Paul Olson, most sober of all, it "fits into the total pattern" because "it is the potential tragedy of the lovers in the woods", reminding us of the probable consequences of the " 'headie force of frentick love' ".[22]

---

[16] Alfred Harbage has recently objected to interpreting Shakespeare on the basis of hypothetical occasions for which there is no external evidence ("*Love's Labour's Lost* and the Early Shakespeare", *PQ*, XLI [1962], 19-20). Nevertheless, the internal evidence that *A Midsummer Night's Dream* was either written or adapted for a courtly wedding seems to me, as to most, overwhelming.

[17] *Love's Labour's Lost* V. ii. 513-514.

[18] For reasons already indicated, I think Pyramus and Thisbe meant primarily to parallel Lysander and Hermia as examples of frustrated true love rather than as examples of folly. Lysander and Hermia may not behave rationally in their flight from authority, but only when misled by pansy–juice does Lysander approach the frenzied passion which so disturbed Friar Laurence. Even in that play, I believe, Shakespeare distinguishes between Romeo's doting for Rosaline and his true but frustrated love for Juliet.

[19] *Shakespeare: A Survey* (New York, 1926), pp. 87, 80.

[20] "The Play within a Play: An Elizabethan Dramatic Device", *Essays and Studies*, XIII (1960), 47.

[21] P. 216.

[22] P. 118.

Yet in the actual play as developed by the mechanicals, Shakespeare provides a focus that scarcely emphasizes any such parallel to the lovers. The thwarting parents are cast but never given even a line in rehearsal or production; they are referred to in neither Quince's argument nor in the lovers' speeches. In turn, the decision to run to the woods is presented in a single line, and the barrier wall is focused upon as farcical in itself rather than as a cause for action. Lastly, however ridiculous the love poetry of Pyramus and Thisbe, it scarcely seems focused for comic parallel and contrast to the speeches or actions of Shakespeare's four young lovers (except in one possible way, to be examined below).

For Shakespeare's actual development, few critics have much to say. They recognize such external considerations, all undeniably valid, as a possible light mocking of earlier plays, or the demonstration that a Romeo-Juliet plot could be converted to farce by its treatment, or the demands of the low comedy convention. More internally, they recognize the necessity that *Pyramus and Thisbe* be treated farcically if it is to harmonize in tone with *A Midsummer Night's Dream* as a whole.

But *Pyramus and Thisbe* is not merely a play about love with a partial resemblance to the love plot of *A Midsummer Night's Dream*. It is, as Shakespeare's original wedding audience would be inevitably aware, a play for a wedding audience. It provides a foil to the entire play of which it is a part, not merely to the portion involving the lovers. And not only Bottom's play, but his audience as well, invites comparison with Shakespeare's.[23]

It is time to turn to the principal member of Bottom's audience, and to his famous speech beginning Act V. Himself a creation from "antique fable" unconsciously involved in "fairy toys", Theseus believes in neither. His speech, without appearing improbable or inconsistent with his character, is obviously one demanded by Shakespeare's thematic development. Just as Theseus has no dramatically probable reason to refer to "fairy toys", so too he has no reason to digress on poetry while discussing the lunacy of love. But by his speech he can provide for Shakespeare a transition from the earlier emphasis of the play upon love to its final emphasis upon art. He can explicitly link the imagination's role in love with its role in dramatic poetry. For him, with his view that "the best in this kind are but shadows", pastimes to be tolerantly accepted when offered, the imagination of the poet commands no more respect that that of the lover.

Theseus' speech introduces the words "image", "imagine", "imagination", and "imagining" to the play. But of course it does not introduce the concepts involved. As we have already seen, and as Theseus reminds us, much of the play has thus far concerned the role of imagination in love. A subordinate part has similarly drawn attention to its role in drama, a role manifested by the entirety of *A Midsummer Night's Dream*.

The success of any play ideally demands effective use of the imagination by the author, the producers, and the audience. Perhaps through modesty, Shakespeare gives us little explicit encouragement to compare his own imaginative

---

[23] This point of view has been excellently advanced by Siegel (see note 14 above). My own emphases are somewhat unlike his, but his essay seems to me exceptionally illuminating, rivalled only by Barber's chapter on the play. That Siegel's view has received so little attention in the past decade leads me to hope that a partial repetition of his arguments is here excusable.

creation with that initially provided by Quince.[24] We hear nothing, strictly, of Quince's authorial problems prior to rehearsal. The sources of our laughter spring mainly from mutilation of his text in production, by additions and corruptions, rather than from the text with which the mechanicals began. Yet some measure of comparison of *A Midsummer Night's Dream* with their pre-mutilated text is inescapable. *Pyramus and Thisbe,* with nothing demanded beyond the simple dramatization of a familiar story, could at least have been given imaginative development in action, characterization, theme, and language. It has none. The first three are less than minimal, and the language—in its grotesque combination of muddled syntax, padded lines, mind-offending tropes, ear-offending schemes—does violence even to what would otherwise be woefully inadequate. We have:

> Anon comes Pyramus, sweet youth and tall,
>> And finds his trusty Thisby's mantle slain;
> Whereat, with blade, with bloody blameful blade,
>> He bravely broach'd his boiling bloody breast,

or

> O grim-look'd night! O night with hue so black!
>> O night, which ever art when day is not!
> O night, O night! alack, alack, alack,
>> I fear my Thisby's promise is forgot!
> And thou, O wall, O sweet, O lovely wall,
>> That stand'st between her father's ground and mine!
> Thou wall, O wall, O sweet and lovely wall,
>> Show me thy chink, to blink through with mine eyne!

Contrasting in every respect we have *A Midsummer Night's Dream,* perhaps the most obviously "imaginative" of all Shakespeare's plays before *The Tempest:* we have the poetic fusion of classical and native, remote and familiar, high and low, possible and "impossible", romance and farce—all controlled by a governing intention and developed in appropriately varied and evocative language. Unlike Bottom, if not unlike the Quince who calls his play a "Lamentable Comedy", Shakespeare knows what is appropriate for his purposes. He will have infinite variety, but not merely variety as an end in itself. Bottom wishes to have a ballad written of his dream, and "to make it the more gracious" he will sing it over the dead body of Thisbe at the tragedy's end. Shakespeare, very literally "to make it the more gracious", will end his comedy with a song bestowing fairy grace. The contrast needs no laboring.

The contrast in authorial imagination, however, is not the principal cause for turning *Pyramus and Thisbe* from tragedy to farce. In the first appearance of the mechanicals, the largely expository casting scene, we get a hint of the aspect that receives subsequent emphasis: author-director Quince warns that if the lion roars "too terribly" it will "fright the Duchess and the ladies", and Bottom proposes as a solution to "roar you as gently as any sucking dove" (a remedy almost as sound as the later suggestion to "leave the killing out"). What

---

[24] Quince is perhaps the one who most invites contrast with Shakespeare, while his fellows contrast with the remainder of the Lord Chamberlain's Men. Yet Bottom by his irrepressible initiative tends to usurp even the authorial role. He is indeed the play's "weaver", effectively intertwining the thematic threads of love and art in the play.

the mechanicals fail to understand, obviously, is the audience's awareness that drama is drama, to be viewed imaginatively but not mistaken, in any realistic sense, for reality. The idea that these clowns could conceivably create a terrifying lion is in itself ridiculous, but the basic folly lies in their supposing that their prospective intelligent audience will have the naiveté of Fielding's Partridge. And it is this aspect that receives all the emphasis of the mechanicals' rehearsal scene. Except for a very few lines of actual rehearsal, enough to heighten our expectation of the eventual production as well as to allow Bottom's "translation" to an ass, the whole rehearsal is concerned with how the mechanicals abuse their own imaginations by a failure to understand those of the audience. On the one hand they fear their audience will imagine what it sees is real, mistaking "shadows" for reality; on the other, they think the audience unable to imagine what it cannot see. Paradoxically, although they lack the understanding to think in such terms, they think their audience both over- and under-imaginative, and in both respects irrational. For each error Shakespeare provides two examples. More would render the point tedious rather than delightful; fewer might obscure it. Thus, to avoid the threat of over-imagination, they resolve by various ludicrous means to explain that Pyramus is not Pyramus and that the lion is not a lion; then, to counteract the audience's under-imagination, they will create Moonshine and Wall. In a play where Shakespeare's audience has been imagining moonshine since the beginning, Bottom and Quince can conceive only of real moonshine or a character to "disfigure" it. Of course they choose the latter. So too they can think only of bringing in a real wall, weighing tons, or another disfiguring personification.[25]

Significantly, Shakespeare opens the rehearsal scene as follows:

> *Bottom.* Are we all met?
> *Quince.* Pat, pat; and here's a marvail's convenient place for our rehearsal. This green plot shall be our stage, this hawthorn brake our tiring house. . . .

The stage is a stage, not a green plot; the tiring house is a tiring house, not a hawthorn brake. The Lord Chamberlain's Men ask us to imagine a green plot and hawthorn brake, just as they ask us to imagine nonexistent fog or, on the other hand, imagine the invisibility of an obviously visible Oberon.[26] The play perpetually makes such demands upon us, and even greater ones. It asks us not only to accept mortal-sized actors as diminutive fairies but even to let them be bi-sized, sleeping in flowers and yet engaging in intimate association with ass-headed Bottom. Most basic of all, it asks us to enter imaginatively into a world dominated by fairies, and to accept them as the ultimate source of disharmony and of harmony, while at the same time not asking us to "believe" in them at all.

[25] Shakespeare wisely avoided much use of "Antigonus pursued by a bear" on the stage of his plays, but, as several critics have pointed out, the wall for *Romeo and Juliet* II. i may have posed momentary staging problems which find their reflection here.

[26] Modern productions of *A Midsummer Night's Dream*, admittedly magnificent spectacles, often seem to have more in common with the mechanicals than with Shakespeare. Such productions obscure, if not destroy, thematic implications of the kind discussed here. Readers of the play are sometimes subjected to a similar disservice by editors—e.g., the New Cambridge stage direction opening II. i: "The palace wood, a league from Athens. A mossy stretch of broken ground, cleared of trees by wood-cutters and surrounded by thickets. Moonlight[.]"

When we next see the mechanicals (except for their brief transitional appearance in IV. ii) it will be after Theseus' speech, with its condescending attitude toward poetry, and after the prefatory discussion by the court concerning the "tedious brief . . . tragical mirth" they wish to enact.[27] The emphases in the actual production—including both the production itself and the asides by the audience—are just what we have been prepared for in the rehearsal: not the follies of love but the follies of abused imagination in the theatre. When, for example, Quince concludes his Argument,

> For all the rest,
> Let Lion, Moonshine, Wall, and lovers twain
> At large discourse while here they do remain,

Theseus cannot yet believe that Quince literally means "discourse":

> *Theseus.* I wonder if the lion be to speak.
> *Demetrius.* No wonder, my lord. One lion may, when many asses do.

But before ever they hear the talking lion they listen to "the wittiest partition that ever I heard discourse", that "courteous wall" which provides the "chink to blink through", only to receive the curses of frustrated Pyramus.

> *Theseus.* The wall, methinks, being sensible, should curse again.
> *Pyramus.* No, in truth, sir, he should not. 'Deceiving me' is Thisby's cue. She is to enter now, and I am to spy her through the wall. You shall see it will fall pat as I told you. Yonder she comes.

As Theseus says, a few lines later,

> If we imagine no worse of them than they of themselves, they may pass for excellent men.

There is no danger of wounding the feelings of a Bottom by letting him overhear an aside. His imagination, devoid of understanding, can as easily create beauty in his own mind as it can create unintended farce on the stage. Titania's folly, if possible, was less than what we are now witnessing.

Wall's eventual exit provokes further satiric asides, followed by the primary thematic dialogue of the play:

> *Hippolyta.* This is the silliest stuff that ever I heard.
> *Theseus.* The best in this kind are but shadows; and the worst are no worse, if imagination amend them.
> *Hippolyta.* It must be your imagination then, and not theirs.

While a successful production depends on the imaginative cooperation of playright, producers, and audience, Bottom's group has placed the entire burden on the audience. Theseus' group quite naturally makes no effort to "amend them". The tragedy is too entertaining as farce, too fitting for their nuptial spirits, and, besides, it would take an imagination transcending Shakespeare's own to give "form and dignity" to this *Pyramus and Thisbe*.

What follows demands no further elaboration. The lion proves "a goose

---

[27] This includes, of course, Theseus' comments on how a noble host should accept any well intended offering, however incompetent. Surely the host of the Lord Chamberlain's Men, especially if a greater admirer of poetry than Theseus, would recognize the implications as to how he should receive their humbly presented masterpiece.

for his discretion"; the moon, appearing "by his small light of discretion" to be "in the wane",[28] ridiculously exits on command from Pyramus. And so on, until "Moonshine and Lion are left to bury the dead". "Ay, and Wall too."

But we may return to Theseus' comment that "The best in this kind are but shadows". In a sense he is obviously right, as Shakespeare never ceases to remind us, but his estimation of such "shadows" is consistently deprecating. A noble governor, quite willing to accept poetry for a wedding-night pastime and to acknowledge it as the well-intended offering of his faithful subjects, he at no time implies any respect for it. Shakespeare's entire play implies a contrary view, despite the humility of its epilogue.

Just how contrary a view is open to question. In his "Imagination in the English Renaissance: Psychology and Poetic",[29] William Rossky usefully surveys in detail the reasons for imagination's "general disrepute" in Elizabethan England, and the response it produced from defenders of poetry. His basic thesis is well summarized in his concluding paragraph:

> Thus laboring to free the poetic imagination from the current disrepute of the faculty, Elizabethan poetic responds to the very bases of the disrepute. Although instrumental to the healthy operation of the soul, imagination, according to the psychology, is a faculty for the most part uncontrolled and immoral—a faculty forever distorting and lying, irrational, unstable, flitting and insubstantial, haphazardly making and marring, dangerously tied to emotions, feigning idly and purposelessly. And from the attempt to combat these grounds of disrepute through the adoption and adaptation of materials which were an absorbed part of every educated Elizabethan's background—materials often from the very psychology itself—there evolves a concept of poetic feigning: that poetic feigning is a glorious compounding of images beyond life, of distortions which are yet verisimilar imitations, expressing a truth to reality and yet a higher truth also, controlled by the practical purpose, the molding power, and, in almost every aspect, by the reason and morality of the poet.

The age's defenders of poetry—whether in extended defenses like Sidney's, or in prefaces like Chapman's or Jonson's, or even in passing (like Hamlet's)—inevitably stressed the high moral function of poetic imagination. One seldom finds so modest a defense as that prefacing *The Shoemakers' Holiday:* "Take all in good worth that is well intended, for nothing is purposed but mirth, mirth lengthneth long life." Yet, after all, as Theseus implied, there is a time for "pastime", and only the most vigorous precisian would have denied it. *A Midsummer Night's Dream* could have been defended as indeed a pleasant pastime, especially appropriate for a wedding occasion but fitting for any moment of merriment. It could be further defended, unmistakably, as a delightful exposition of the follies produced by excessive imagination in love and the pleasures produced by controlled imagination in art. Only the most stubborn

---

[28] It is fanciful, perhaps, to see parallel implications in the opening of Shakespeare's play, where "O, methinks how slow/ This old moon wanes" before the new "moon, like to a silver bow/ New-bent in heaven" can appear. Certainly while the old moon wanes we behold the inconstancies and indiscretions of lovers, the "lunatic" aspect of love. With the new moon comes harmonious marriage, and the "silver bow" with its Diana associations (witness the later *Pericles* V. i. 249) may well suggest this alternative aspect of the moon, the prevalent one in the play.

[29] *Studies in the Renaissance*, V (1958), 49-73.

precisian could have thought poetry the "mother of lies" after witnessing Shakespeare's thematic distinction, however ambiguous in its ultimate implications, between the worlds of imagination and of "reality". Thus in offering a defense for its own existence the play simultaneously offers us Shakespeare's closest approximation to a "Defense of Dramatic Poesy" in general.

In some measure, surely, *A Midsummer Night's Dream* is such a defense, although one that expresses its view by indirection and without the emphasis upon strictly moral edification one commonly finds in more formal defenses. More legitimately than Greene, Shakespeare might well have appended to his play: *Omne tulit punctum qui miscuit utile dulci*. Theseus links lunatic, lover, and poet indiscriminately. Shakespeare, by contrasting the role of imagination in love with that in dramatic poetry, discriminates. As the play delightfully demonstrates, and lightly satirizes, the imagination in love often operates in defiance of "discretion", especially in creating beauty observable by no one but the creator. Poetic art, distinct from that of a Quince or Bottom, is in accord with discretion, and its creations are capable of universal appreciation, both as beautiful and as meaningful. In love, the ridiculous results from the dominance of imagination over reason, and the lover is unaware of his being ridiculous. In good art, the ridiculous (if it exists) is the product of imagination's cooperation with reason, occurs only when the dramatist intends it, and is subordinated to a purpose which in some degree, at the least, combines *utile* with *dulci*. Rather than being a foe to good living, poetic imagination can be its comfort and its guide, far "more yielding" than most dreams. Whether *A Midsummer Night's Dream* has an unplumbed "bottom" as well as its inescapable Bottom I hesitate to say. But it provides us "a most rare vision", one that offers us a disarmingly unpretentious defense of poetry by the greatest of England's poets.

University of California (Los Angeles)

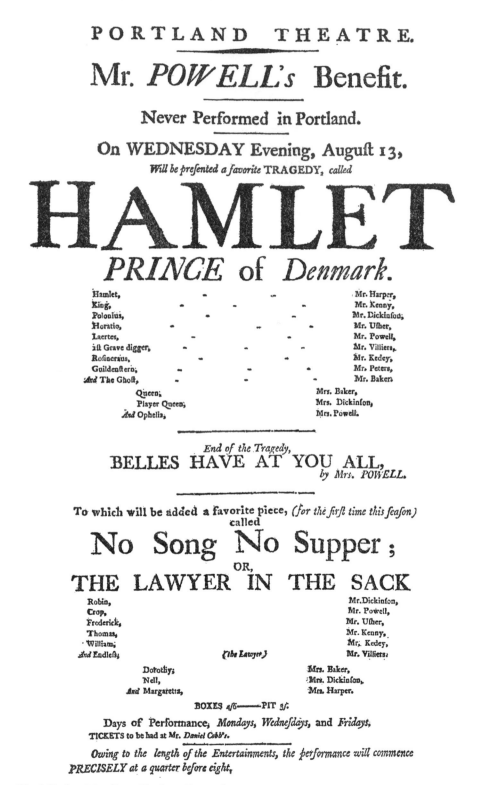

PORTLAND THEATRE.

Mr. *POWELL's* Benefit.

Never Performed in Portland.

On WEDNESDAY Evening, Auguſt 13,
Will be preſented a favorite TRAGEDY, *called*

HAMLET
PRINCE of *Denmark.*

Hamlet,	Mr. Harper,
King,	Mr. Kenny,
Polonius,	Mr. Dickinſon,
Horatio,	Mr. Uſher,
Laertes,	Mr. Powell,
iſt Grave digger,	Mr. Villiers,
Roſincraus,	Mr. Kedey,
Guildenſtern,	Mr. Peters,
And The Ghoſt,	Mr. Baker,
Queen,	Mrs. Baker,
Player Queen,	Mrs. Dickinſon,
And Ophelia,	Mrs. Powell.

End of the Tragedy,
BELLES HAVE AT YOU ALL,
by Mrs. POWELL.

To which will be added a favorite piece, *(for the firſt time this ſeaſon)*
called
No Song No Supper;
OR,
THE LAWYER IN THE SACK

Robin,	Mr. Dickinſon,
Crop,	Mr. Powell,
Frederick,	Mr. Uſher,
Thomas,	Mr. Kenny,
William,	Mr. Kedey,
And Endleſs, *(The Lawyer)*	Mr. Villiers,
Dorothy,	Mrs. Baker,
Nell,	Mrs. Dickinſon,
And Margaretta,	Mrs. Harper.

BOXES 4/6———PIT 3/:

Days of Performance, *Mondays, Wedneſdays,* and *Fridays,*
TICKETS to be had at Mr. *Daniel Cobb's.*

Owing to the length of the Entertainments, the performance will commence
PRECISELY *at a quarter before eight.*

Playbill for Mr. Powell's benefit performance of *Hamlet* on 13 August 1800 in
Portland. 10¼″ x 17″. Reproduced by permission of the Harvard Theatre Collection.

George Whetstone and the Sources of *Measure for Measure*

CHARLES T. PROUTY

EORGE Whetstone's two-part play *Promos and Cassandra* (1578) is generally regarded as the principal source of *Measure for Measure*, although Professor F. E. Budd lists some seven dramatic and eight nondramatic versions of the basic story plus derivations from some of these, written before Shakespeare's play.[1] Of these Professor Geoffrey Bullough prints passages from a sermon by St. Augustine, an original translation of a tale by Cinthio, a summary of Cinthio's dramatization of this tale, *Epitia,* the complete text of *Promos and Cassandra,* as well as condensed versions of analogues by Thomas Lupton and Barnaby Riche.[2] In common with all previous versions, Whetstone's wicked magistrate, Promos, seduces the sister of a condemned man, but she is made an honest woman through marriage to Promos by decree of

---

[1] Quoted by Thomas C. Izard, *George Whetstone* (New York, 1942), p. 53:

> The basic plot of *Promos and Cassandra* had a wide currency during the Renaissance period, appearing in numerous versions shortly after the middle of the sixteenth century. A number of Shakespearean scholars or historians of literature have compiled lists of these variants; among these lists are those of Dunlop, Douce, Creizenach, and Foth. The best survey of the story is that of Frederick E. Budd in his 'Material for the Study of the Sources of Shakespeare's *Measure for Measure*.'2 [2 *Revue de littérature comparée,* October-December, 1931, pp. 711-736.] Professor Budd includes eight nondramatic and seven dramatic pre-Shakespearean versions, exclusive of many which vary only slightly from other accounts and are listed by him under the main versions from which they seem to be derived.

Actually Professor Budd lists six, not seven, dramatic versions and three of these are Commedie dell' Arte of uncertain date. Professor Bullough increases the total number of sources and analogues by two: St. Augustine and Barnaby Riche.

W. W. Lawrence has an interesting discussion of the source materials available to Whetstone wherein he emphasizes the "realistic character of this theme". In particular Lawrence calls attention to a letter in the Hungarian Public Record Office written in 1547 from Vienna by a young Hungarian student, Joseph Macarius, to a relative living at Sárvár in Hungary. This tells of an incident which took place near Milan in 1547. A wife, to save the life of her husband who had committed murder, pleaded with the chief justice—called "the Spanish count"—who promised pardon at the price of her honor. The wife yielded; but her husband was beheaded, so she journeyed to Milan to complain to Don Ferdinando Gonzaga. The wicked justice was forced to marry the widow, to pay her three thousand ducats as a dowry, and on the following day was executed. Almost exactly the same story was told in 1607 by Goulart in his *Histoires Admirables et Mémorables advenues de Nostre Temps* (Hazlitt, *Shakespeare's Library,* III, 167-168). The date is the same (1547), the town is Como, the villain is a Spanish Captain, the source of justice is the Duke of Ferrara and the sum of money nine hundred ducats. Goulart adds another version dealing with the Provost la Vouste who had the woman's husband in prison, but here there is no justice for the violated widow. (W. W. Lawrence, *Shakespeare's Problem Comedies,* New York, 1931, pp. 86-87.)

[2] Geoffrey Bullough, ed., *Narrative and Dramatic Sources of Shakespeare* (London, 1953), II, 418-530.

Corvinus, King of Hungary, who ultimately spares Promos' life. In Cinthio's *novella,* Vico, the condemned man is actually executed, while in *Epitia* he is spared by the substitution of another criminal who is his double. In the earlier versions there are other variations: the magistrate's victim is the wife of the condemned, while later she becomes his sister.

There are, however, innovations in Whetstone's play which were taken over by Shakespeare, and a major one is the introduction of a world of whores, shyster lawyers, and various criminals. This world and its characters occupy a large part of Whetstone's play exactly as they do in Shakespeare's, but critical consideration of the reasons for such a combination of a traditional story with the low-life of London—and it is the low-life of London in Whetstone's "Cyttie of Julio" just as it is in Shakespeare's Vienna—seems to have been neglected or treated most casually. In my judgment it is of prime importance to ascertain why Whetstone introduced this world into his play; particularly since Shakespeare took it over, and since Whetstone himself omitted it in his prose redaction published in 1582, some four years after the play, in *An Heptameron of Civil Discourses.*[3]

In other words since Shakespeare knew and used Whetstone's play, he presumably had some idea of the assumptions, dramatic and ethical, upon which Whetstone was operating. And a specific indication of Whetstone's thought is found in his second invocation, the ethical and moral one of justice administered not only to a corrupt magistrate but to other wrongdoers as well. The source of this particular interest is found in the dedication of *Promos and Cassandra:* "To his worshipfull friende, and Kinesman, *William Fleetwoode Esquier, Recorder* of London".[4] Whetstone's fourth major work, *A Mirour for Magestrates of Cyties* (1584), was dedicated "To the Right Honorable, Sir Edward Osburne, Knight, Lord Maior, of the famous Cittie of London: To the Right Worshipfull, his assistantes, the Aldermen: And to their learned Counseller, M. Seriant [Sergeant] Fleetwood, Recorder of the same Citie: his approved Good Frende and Kinsman".[5]

Now William Fleetwood was a very important man in the affairs of the City of London because of his legal position as Recorder, which means that he was the secretary to the Court of Alderman and was in effect the equivalent of a prosecuting attorney. In the words of the *D.N.B.,* he was "famous for his rigorous enforcement of the laws against vagrants and papists". He was also famous for his vigorous enforcement of all laws concerning the moral behavior of the citizens of London, as may be seen from the various City records printed by Sir Edmund Chambers in that section of *The Elizabethan Stage* entitled "Documents of Control". For example, on 18 July 1578 Fleetwood wrote the Lord Treasurer, Lord Burghley, telling of a meeting with the Lord Mayor and others where ". . . I shewed unto my Lords our Assistaunts those pointes that your honour in tyme paste gave us for good order; plaies, unlawful games, ffensse skoles, vacaboundes and suche like to be suppressed, with a vigilant eye to the plage, to the watches, and to laye often privie searches".[6]

---

[3] W. C. Hazlitt, ed., *Shakespeare's Library* (Second Edition, London, 1875), pp. 155-166.
[4] Bullough, II, 442.
[5] Izard, p. 134.
[6] E. K. Chambers, *The Elizabethan Stage* (Oxford, 1923), IV, 277. The phrase "ffensse skoles"

Through the diligent research of Professor Franklin B. Williams, we now learn of several interesting books which were dedicated to Fleetwood.[7] Among them are Johannes Ewick's *Of the duetie of a magistrate in the time of the plague* (1583);[8] and John Field's *A godly exhortation by occasion of the late judgement of God at Parris garden* (1583).[9] This divine judgment on the spectators at a Sunday's bear-baiting is thus described by the Lord Mayor in a letter to Lord Burghley, dated 14 Jan. 1582/3.

> It maye please your Lp. to be further advertised (which I thinke you have alredie hard) af a greate mysshappe at Parise gardeine, where by ruyn of all the scaffoldes at once yesterdaie a greate nombre of people are some presentlie slayne, and some maymed and greavouslie hurte. It giveth greate occasion to acknowledge the hande of god for suche abuse of the sabboth daie, and moveth me in Consciens to beseche your Lp. to give order for redresse of suche contempt of gods service. I have to that ende treated with some Iustices of peace of that Countie, who signifie them selfes to have verye good zeale, but alledge want of Comyssion, which we humblie referre to the Consideracion of your honorable wisedome.[10]

Stowe writing of the same disaster says it was "a friendly warning to such as more delight themselves in the cruelty of beasts, than in the works of mercy, the fruits of a true professed faith, which ought to be the Sabbath day's exercise".[11] Dr. John Dee concurred in this view, as did Fleetwood, in a letter to Lord Burghley on 19 January 1582/3.[12]

Clearly Fleetwood would have been a willing recipient of a moral play dedicated to him wherein was

> showne, the unsufferable abuse, of a lewde Magistrate: The vertuous behaviours of a chaste Ladye: The uncontrowled leawdenes of a favoured Curtisan. And the undeserved estimation of a pernicious Parasyte. In the second parte is discoursed, the perfect magnanimitye of a noble Kinge, in checking Vice and favouring Vertue: Wherein is showne, the Ruyne and overthrowe, of dishonest practises: with the advauncement of upright dealing.[13]

As a diligent magistrate, Fleetwood would also have been gratified by the description on the title page of *A Mirour for Magestrates of Cyties* outlining the formidable tasks confronting Alexander Severus and those found in sixteenth century London.

> Representing the Ordinaunces, Policies, and Diligence, of the Noble Emperour, Alexander (surnamed) Severus, to suppresse and chastise the

---

refers to the practice of holding fencing exhibitions in public places to which the public was attracted by the often fatal results which ensued.

[7] Franklin B. Williams, Jr., *Index of Dedications and Commendatory Verses in English Books Before 1641* (London, 1962), p. 69. "FLEETWOOD, William, *Recorder of London (DNB)*. 886, *10607, *10845, *25341 [cf. 25335], 25347, J. Danyel, *Jehovah, [1576]-L²; epistle 20109 by editor; verse 4938, 15175; indexes 20041, 20042; see 18773."

[8] *S.T.C.* 10607, *tr.* J. Stockwood.

[9] *S.T.C.* 10845.

[10] Chambers, IV, 292.

[11] Chambers, II, 462.

[12] Chambers, II, 462.

[13] Bullough, II, 442.

notorious Vices noorished in Rome, by the superfluous nomber of Dicing-houses, Tavarns, and common Stewes: Suffred and cheerished, by his beastlye Predecessour, Heliogabalus, with sundrie grave Orations: by the said noble Emperor, concerning Reformation. And hereunto is added, *A Touchstone for the Time*: Containyng: many perillous Mischiefes, bred in the Bowels of the Citie of London: by the infection of some of thease Sanctuaries of Iniquitie.[14]

As we have observed, others besides George Whetstone were much interested in the activities of magistrates, but Whetstone had a particular, personal interest in the "many perillous Mischiefes, bred in the Bowels of the Citie of London". These "many Mischiefes" Whetstone had known at first hand as he tells us in the autobiographical portions of his first book, *The Rocke of Regard* (1576).[15] This work is divided into four sections whose titles indicate something of the nature of their contents: "The Castle of Delight", "The Garden of Unthrifti-nesse", "The Arbour of Vertue", and "The Ortchard of Repentance". Of this final section he writes in the Epistle dedicatory "To all the young Gentlemen of England":

> *The fourth is, the* Ortchard of Repentance, *the which for the most part, I planted with experience: the fruits therin growing (think I) be hoalsome, although to curious appetites, not greatly toothsome. But what for that? the smarting wound is cured with fretting plaisters. Even so, abuse is to be refourmed with sharpe reprehension, then sure it were not* Decorum, *in inveying against a* Cousener, Cheter, Dicer, Quareler &c. *(who for the most part) live without good order, to use any milde and plausible kinde of writ-ing. The inconveniences that rise of these professions, are the fruites of forewarning, that my Orchard (gallant Gentlemen) affordeth: and yet to afforde you a good peniwoorth, it marreth the markets of a great many. The Cousner will chafe to see his practises published: the Cheter will fume, to see his crosbiting and cunning shiftes decyphered: the Dicer will sweare to heare his cogging & foysting advantages discovered: the Quareler will stampe to heare his braules and brables bayted at: the Merchaunt will storme to see his new kinde of Usuries revealed: the Lawyer wilbe in a wonderfull heate, to heare his double dealings, his dilatorie delayes, and unconscionable advantage disclosed: al these mens displeasures have I hazarded, in opening (for your behoves) their mischiefous subtilties: and trust mee, not one of these sortes of men, but his teeth watereth with the desire of your lyvinges, yea hee daily studieth to bring you in lash: so that it behoveth you to looke warily into your estates, else you shall light into the smarts, of some of their daungers.* (¶ 2ᵛ-3ʳ)

Long before Robert Greene, Whetstone was giving to the world a first-hand account of the low-life of London which he had known through personal experience, and if we read a few of his comments on persons and practices, it is not difficult to understand whence came the vivid and dramatic characters and events which appear in *Promos and Cassandra* and reappear in *Measure for Measure.*

---

[14] Izard, p. 132.

[15] I am using my own photostat of the Huntington Library original. Each section has separate pagination. The only alterations made here and elsewhere are "s" for long "s" and "u" and "v" according to modern usage.

Like many another young Elizabethan gentleman Whetstone had first sought favor at Court, but with his money gone he discovered himself deserted by his erstwhile friends and utterly cast out. Like his good friend and fellow poet, George Gascoigne, Whetstone decided to try his fortunes in foreign wars, and incidentally for the second time as he tells us. Yet even here, in spite of initial success, he soon found "The sowre sauce of swete reported war".

> When thus of warres, I felt the sower taste,
> Which seemed sweete, by speach I heard of yore,
> Forworne with toile, I homewards trudgst in haste,
> My skinne well paide, with woundes and bruses sore,
> But sure of pence, I had but slender store,
> Thus did I spend the time that servde for thrift,
> And left old age in drowping dayes to shift.[16]

Returned home he tried his hand at farming but was again unsuccessful and thus met his final temptation in the form of a false friend who advised him of the means necessary for advancement in the world.

> But listen well, and I will shortly showe,
> How that thy want in drowping dayes shall die,
> The way I know, how every state doth growe,
> From base degree, to wealth and honour hie,
> Thy conscience yet, must beare with briberie,
> With falsehoode, fraude, feare not to use deceites,
> To fishe for wealth, those are the sweetest baites.
>
> If thou doest love, a faithlesse priest to bee,
> If Courtiers life, in thee hath lyking wrought,
> In merchauntes fraude, if thou wouldst deeply see,
> If Lawyers gaine, doth tempt thy greedie thought,
> If through the warres, aloft thou wouldst bee brought,
> In countrie cares, if thou wouldst beate thy braine,
> If Cheters craft, thou weanst, is full of gaine. (Sts. 36, 37)

As this advice continued, Whetstone's latent virtue caused him to reject the false friend and to embark upon a lengthy and detailed exposition of just how the evil ones operated in a sub-section entitled, "A Larges to the world", since "The knowledge of deceite is necessarie for the good".

> My knowledge yet, unto the world y knowne,
> May haply warne, my friends to shunne this baite,
> Amonge the lewde, this seede is hugely sowne,
> They daily take, this bitter sweete receite,
> For why their foode, is rapine and deceite,
> My larges yet, to all I franckly give,
> Within this world, that have desire to live. (St. 42)

The marginal notations of this section, which is composed of 77 rhyme-royal stanzas, will give some indication of Whetstone's familiarity with his subject matter:

The Courtier
The Lawyer

---

[16] "Ortchard of repentance", p. 10, st. 28.

Physicians
The practise of a lewde Physician
Officers [Officials]
One officer by honestie discovereth the deceites of
    the lewde
A notable cloake [Provide a cloake, to couler stil
    your crime, / Then worke your will . . .]
Gaylors
Younge Gentlemen
Merchaunts
Religion without devotion
Crosbytinge, a cusnage under the couler of friendship
Note this policie [feign friendship]
Be dangerous to enter into a statute to a marchaunt
Burgoses [shopkeepers]
To take ware on trust, a notable usurie
A worthie custom in London
Selling wares on credite, collusion
Scriverners
Monie takers
Cousiners
Note this policie [To make false deedes, let maister
    Lawyer see, / To get them seald, use scriveners
    policie . . .]
By the imprisoning of the complainant, the cousiner
    agreeth without open shame
Right Cousiners stand upon their credite
Make shiftes
Counterfet Astronomers
Phisitians
Baudes
Courtesans
Painting, may helpe a courtesan, but ther end is a
    baude and a begger
His farewell to the world, a degression that shewes a
    [sic] of al this covetousnesse
Arbitriment, best for poore men
Usurie, a newe trade of merchandise
Cousiners not without friends of calling
A comfort to the godly in miserie
A bolde challenge.[17]

It is tempting to quote in detail what Whetstone has to say about bawds, courtesans, cozeners and in particular his description of an honest official who discovered the knavery of the wicked; but enough has been said to show Whetstone's first-hand knowledge of London which constitutes the more entertaining parts of *Promos and Cassandra* and of *Measure for Measure* as well.

Further details of his own personal experiences with the low-life of London are found in the autobiographical poem "The Inventions of P. Plasmos", the

---

[17] *Ibid.*, pp. 15-28. A detailed personal account of such experiences is found in the "Inventions of P. Plasmos", pp. 79-121.

final piece in this fourth section of *The Rocke of Regard*. Here the hero falls in love with a light woman, Laymos, and to please her gets into great financial difficulties and is cheated out of some property by counterfeit deeds and cozeners such as we have had described. From this experience Whetstone evidently learned a bitter lesson and he never again gives any indication of relapsing into the ways of his youth.[18]

All his literary efforts from this time forth were devoted to moral and didactic subjects with a few elegies designed not only to memorialize the deceased but perhaps to earn a reward, a kind of writing which Thomas Churchyard practised so well. Unlike Greene, who repented for profit more than once, it would seem that Whetstone was a sincere moralist of the Puritan persuasion with his work on marriage, *An Heptameron of Civil Discourses* (1582); *A Mirour for Magestrates of Cyties* and *A Touchstone for the Time* (1584), whose titles are indicative of their purpose, as is that of *The Honorable Reputation of a Souldier* (1585); and *The English Myrror* (1586), made up in part of the preceding two works plus some new material, the whole designed to bring the best possible government to England.[19] A part of *The English Myrror* was devoted to various treasonable conspiracies directed against Queen Elizabeth, but with the Babington plot coming just after publication of that work, Whetstone covered this new material in *Censure of a Loyall Subject* (1587).[20]

It is obvious that this interest in proper government by just and uncorruptible magistrates was what led Whetstone to *Promos and Cassandra,* and certain details of that play emphasize that interest. Chief of these is the scene of the action and the name of the King, who in Part Two administers justice to all the evildoers. The setting is *"the Cyttie of* Julio *(sometimes under the dominion of* Corvinus *Kinge of Hungarie and Boemia. . .) . . .".*

Both facts—the name of the city and that of the King—are historically accurate. Corvinus, or to use his real name Matthias Hunyadi, was known as Matthias Corvinus because of the raven on his coat of arms; he became King of Hungary in 1458, and by military conquest gained the kingdoms of Austria, Bohemia and the territories of Wallachia, Croatia, and Dalmatia. Thus his rule extended from the Black Sea to the Adriatic, so that he was the most important monarch in Central Europe.

The fact that Corvinus controlled a large section of the Adriatic coast and that at least a portion of this area was held by his successors is of at least passing interest. Not only Corvinus is referred to as King of Hungary and Bohemia; his successors from Ferdinand of Austria through Rudolph (died 1608) were known as Kings of Bohemia and Hungary, and Archdukes of Austria. The distinct possibility exists that the title King of Bohemia could include within its compass all the territories ruled by these monarchs. Thus Robert Greene's *Pandosto, King of Bohemia* could have had a seacoast, and it may be that the many jests about "the seacoast of Bohemia" as found in *The Winter's Tale*

---

[18] *Ibid.,* p. 79. "Inventions of P. Plasmos touching *his hap and hard fortune, unto the which* is annexed the sundrie complaintes of foure notable couseners, the instrumentes of his greatest troubles: which in the prime of their mischievous enterprises, with soudaine death and vexation were straungelie visited. At the end of every of the said inventions, for the more plaine knowledge of them, is the reporters admonition in prose both pleasant and profitable."

[19] Izard, pp. 8ff., 131ff., 162ff.

[20] Izard, pp. 219ff.

will have to be discarded, since Greene and Shakespeare may have been correct according to the geographical definitions of their time.

Of particular importance for our purpose is the general opinion of Corvinus as an administrator of justice. After his untimely death in 1490, "Mathias is dead and justice is fled the earth", became a proverb,[21] and this great attribute of the monarch is echoed in all subsequent accounts. The most recent account of his reign gives us this significant statement:

> He simplified the administration and made it more efficient, and carried through a grandiose reform of the entire judicial system, abolishing many anachronisms and abuses and introducing a simplified and accelerated procedure which was of particular benefit to the small man. He encouraged the towns, especially the smaller market towns, and while not alleviating the legal position of the serfs, in fact greatly improved their condition by the even-handed justice which he enforced, so that when he was dead they mourned: 'King Mátyás is dead, justice is departed.'[22]

In the 19th century Chambers' *Encyclopædia* (V, 298) said of him, "Justice was strictly administered to peasant and noble alike". The famous 13th edition of the *Encyclopedia Brittanica* observes, "Though naturally passionate, Matthias's self-control was almost superhuman, and throughout his stormy life, with his innumerable experiences of ingratitude and treachery, he was never guilty of a single cruel or vindictive action."[23]

These attributes, plus his cultural activities in establishing the famous library of 55,000 volumes, almost completely MSS with some books from the printing presses of Europe, which he began in 1466, and his establishment of a press in Buda in 1473 made him a famous man throughout Europe. Aeneas Silvius mentions him at length in his *De Historia Bohemia,* and two of his contemporaries, Galeotto Marzio and Antonio Bonfini, wrote biographies praising his cultural achievements.

The importance of all this for our purpose is that Whetstone chose this king and his realm for the play. Justice was a rare commodity in the Renaissance world, and such a king well-known to all Europeans was the perfect example for the agent of justice who dominates the second part of Whetstone's play.

The city of Julio is almost certainly that which is called variously "Jula", "Gyula", and "Iula", located in eastern Hungary on the border of present day Roumania, or in the words of a 17th-century Englishman, "on the borders of Transylvania".[24] Whetstone might have known of this city from a work printed in 1566, *Newes from Vienna of Jula in Hungary assaulted by the great Turke.*[25] Suleiman began a war against Maxmilian II in 1563 and a peace was concluded

---

[21] C. M. Knatchbull-Hugessen, *The Political Evolution of the Hungarian Nation* (London, 1908), I, 52. There is a full account of the reign of Matthias Corvinus in *The Cambridge Medieval History,* VIII, 611-619.

[22] C. A. Macartney, *Hungary A Short History* (Edinburgh, 1962), p. 57.

[23] *Chambers' Encyclopædia* (revised edition, New York, 1894), V, 298. *Encyclopedia Brittanica* (13th edition), XVII, 901. G. G. Zerffi, "Hungary Under King Matthias Hunady, Surnamed 'Corvinus' ", *Trans. Royal Hist. Soc.,* New Series (London, 1884), I, 271-272.

[24] *A Prospect of Hungary, and Transylvania, With a Catalogue of the Kings of one, and the Princes of the other; Together with an account of . . . the chiefest Cities, Towns, and Strong-holds, Rivers and Mountains. . . . A brief description of Bohemia* [etc:] *contained in a Mapp affixed hereunto: . . .* London, 1664. Wing, P3808, p. 5.

[25] *S.T.C.* 24716.

in 1567. Sometime during this campaign Gyula was betrayed by its Governor Kereshen, who was well rewarded for his treachery by Selimus who "caused him to be shut up in a Barrel, knocked full of nails, with the points inward, and so to be tumbled up and down until he died most miserably. On the Barrel there was this inscription written: *Here receive the reward of thy Covetousness and Treason:* Gyula, *thou soldest for Gold. If thou beest not faithful to* Maxmilian, *thy Natural Lord, neither wilt thou be true to me.*"[26] Justice is vividly connected with this particular city.

Finally, and of importance for *Measure for Measure,* is the fact that Corvinus conquered Vienna and made it the seat of his government. Thus the step from Julio in Hungary to the Vienna of Shakespeare's play is not such a strange alteration as might superficially appear.[27]

Whatever meanings have been read into Shakespeare's play, it is clear that Whetstone was primarily interested in the impartial administration of justice, and he therefore chose as the agent that monarch who had the highest reputation for justice in Europe. We have only to look again at the title-page of *Promos and Cassandra* to realize this point: "In the second parte is discoursed, the perfect magnanimitye of a noble Kinge, in checking Vice and favouringe Vertue. . . ." And we should remember that it is only in Whetstone's play that there is any "vice" to be checked. In all other versions of the story, there is only one wicked character, the magistrate who uses his office to obtain his unlawful desires; there is no world of vice populated by bawds, whores, and cozeners.

Whetstone's preoccupation with virtue and justice is the determining factor in the structure of his play and this also accounts for his inclusion of Lamia, Rosko, Gripax, Rapax, Prisoners, Hacksters, and other rogues. This much we learn from the dedication wherein the author explains his reasons for dividing "the whole history into two Commedies. . . ." But what Whetstone does not explain is his precedent or authority for presenting in dramatic form, even though in two parts, the theme of a good magistrate (king) righting the wrongs of a wicked magistrate and, as well, punishing a large number of evildoers. Discussion of this latter point must be postponed for a time, since Whetstone's observations on drama require consideration, because Shakespeare ignores the central precept of Decorum as it is clearly defined by Whetstone, who invokes the authority of Plato and the Roman dramatists.

> I devided the whole history into two Commedies: for that, *Decorum* used, it would not be convayde in one. The effects of both, are good and bad: vertue intermyxt with vice, unlawfull desyres (yf it were possible) queancht with chaste denyals: al needeful actions (I thinke) for publike vewe. For by the rewarde of the good, the good are encowraged in wel doinge: and with the scowrge of the lewde, the lewde are feared from evill attempts: maintayning this my oppinion with *Platoes* auctority. *Nawghtinesse, commes of the corruption of nature, and not by readinge or hearinge the lives of the good or lewde (for such publication is necessarye,) but goodnesse (syth he) is beawtifyed by either action.* And to these endes: *Menander, Plautus,* and *Terence,* them selves many yeares since intombed, (by their Commedies) in

---

[26] *A Prospect of Hungary,* p. 5.

[27] In fact Vienna remained the capital of Hungary for some time after the death of Corvinus and the accession of the Hapsburgs, who lost most of Hungary itself to the Turks.

> honour live at this daye. The auncient *Romanes*, heald these showes of suche prise, that they not onely allowde the publike exercise of them, but the grave Senators themselves countenaunced the Actors with their presence: who from these trifles wonne morallytye, as the Bee suckes honny from weedes.[28]

Thus, to separate the evil from the good:

> In the fyrste parte is showne, the unsufferable abuse, of a lewde Magistrate: The vertuous behaviours of a chaste Ladye: The uncontrolled leawdenes of a favoured Curtisan. And the undeserved estimation of a pernicious Parasyte. In the second parte is discoursed, the perfect magnanimitye of a noble Kinge, in checking Vice and favouringe Vertue: Wherein is showne, the Ruyne and overthrowe, of dishonest practises: with the advauncement of upright dealing. (II, 442)

Such a division is also necessary because of the sad state of contemporary drama, which Whetstone views with as severe an eye as Gosson or Sidney. As we know, Ben Jonson also took a harsh look at the popular drama of his own time, and although he does not survey continental drama in the famous prologue to *Every Man in his Humour,* he certainly does echo the complaints against the English stage which Whetstone voices in the latter part of his dedication:

> But the advised devises of auncient Poets, disc[r]edited, with the tryfels of yonge, unadvised, and rashe witted wryters, hath brought this commendable exercise in mislike. For at this daye, the *Italian* is so lascivious in his commedies, that honest hearers are greeved at his actions: the *Frenchman* and *Spaniarde* folowes the *Italians* humor: the *Germaine* is too holye: for he presentes on everye common Stage, what Preachers should pronounce in Pulpets. The *Englishman* in this quallitie, is most vaine, indiscreete, and out of order: he fyrst groundes his worke on impossibilities: then in three howers ronnes he throwe the worlde: marryes, gets Children, makes Children men, men to conquer kingdomes, murder Monsters, and bringeth Gods from Heaven, and fetcheth Divels from Hel. And (that which is worst) their ground is not so unperfect, as their workinge indiscreete: not waying, so the people laugh, though they laugh them (for theyr follyes) to scorne: Many tymes (to make mirthe) they make a Clowne companion with a Kinge: in theyr grave Counsels, they allow the advise of fooles: yea they use one order of speach for all persons: a grose *Indecorum,* for a Crowe wyll yll counterfet the Nightingales sweete voice: even so, affected speeche doth misbecome a Clowne. (II, 443)

The proper decorum to be observed in the writing of a comedy is next carefully defined:

> For to worke a Commedie kindly, grave olde men should instruct: yonge men should showe the imperfections of youth: Strumpets should be lascivious: Boyes unhappy: and Clownes, should speake disorderlye: enterming-ling all these actions, in such sorte, as the grave matter, may instruct: and the pleasant, delight: for without this chaunge, the attention would be small: and the likinge, lesse. (II, 443-444)

Certainly Whetstone would have regarded *Measure for Measure* as utterly

[28] Bullough, II, 443.

lacking in decorum and fully as lascivious as anything perpetrated by those Italians who metamorphosed Englishmen into incarnate devils.

While the theme of part one of *Promos and Cassandra* is almost exclusively the sin of lust, Whetstone makes very clear the heinous nature of this sin and the lewdness of those who engage in it. We first hear of Andrugio's (Shakespeare's Claudio) forthcoming punishment from a soliloquy delivered by his sister Cassandra, and there is no mistaking her view of the situation.

> Foule fall thee love, thy lightning joyes hath blasted my welfare.
> Thou fyerest affection fyrst, within my brothers brest.
> Thou mad'st *Polina* graunt him (earst) even what he would request:
> Thou mad'st him crave and have a proofe of Venus meede,
> For which foule act he is adjudgd, ere long to lose his heade. (II, 450-451)

Unlike Isabella, who thinks that a marriage between her brother Claudio and the pregnant Juliet will settle the matter, Cassandra has no such illusions even though she does think the law "wrest much amis".

> Faults should be measured by desart, but all is one in this.
> The lecher fyerd with lust is punished no more
> Then he which fel through force of love, whose mariage salves his sore: . . .
> (II, 451)

Earlier in this speech Cassandra has upbraided Lust in these lines:

> O blynde affectes in love, whose torments none can tell,
> Yet wantons wyll byde fyre and frost, yea hassard death, nay hell,
> To taste thy sowre sweete frutes, digested styll with care. (II, 450)

The behavior of wantons is the major sin exemplified in Part One, and we are shown three other examples, aside from that of Andrugio and Polina.

After a brief interview in which Cassandra pleads for her brother, Promos is entrapped, for "Her bewtie lures, . . .", and in their next encounter Promos quite early announces his feelings and his intentions.

> *Cassandra* in thy brothers halfe, thou hast sayde what may be
> And for thy sake it is, if I doe set *Andrugio* free:
> Short tale to make, thy beauty hath surprysed mee with love,
> That maugre wit I turne my thoughts as blynd affections move.
> And quite subdude by *Cupids* might neede makes mee sue for grace
> To thee *Cassandra*, which doest holde my freedome in a lace.
> Yeelde to my will, and then commaund, even what thou wilt of mee,
> Thy brothers life and all that else may with thy liking gree. (II, 459-460)

Phallax, Promos' secretary, acting as a deputy to the magistrate, is presented with the courtesan Lamia, but instead of passing sentence on her, falls in love, with fully obvious intentions which Lamia welcomes and celebrates in a song that closes the scene.

> Adue poore care, adue,
> Go, cloye some helples wretche:
> My life, to make me rue,
> Thy forces do not stretche.

Thy harbor is the harte
Whom wrong hath wrapt in woe:
But wrong doth take my parte,
With cloke of right in sho[w]e.

My faultes inquirie scape,
At them the Judges winke:
Those for my fall that gape,
To showe my lewdnesse shrinke.

Then silly care go packe,
Thou art no Geast for mee:
I have, and have no lacke,
And lacke is shrowde for thee. (II, 466-467)

Lamia's maid, Dalia, achieves a sordid conquest of her own with Grimball, a character of her own class, and Whetstone's attention to decorum of speech is apparent in their dialogue and their song.

Other criminals do appear and there are other scenes of low life, but these are more in the nature of interpolations, since they do not involve the characters of the three major episodes illustrating the workings of lust. In one case we have a group of prisoners being led to the gallows and in another a slapstick scene in which Grimball's purse is cut, but nothing in this has anything to do with his affair with Dalia.

Part One concludes with the deflowered Cassandra singing a doleful song invoking Death to end her woes, and Part Two begins with another sorrowful female, Polina (Shakespeare's Juliet), who laments that she cannot die and so resolves to endure God's penance. She ends her solitary appearance with a doleful song invoking Care to "feede on my life thy fyll", with the hope that eventually she may waste away and that Death will then throw his lure, and thus destroy her.

At once, however, we know that all will be well, for a Messenger announces the coming of King Corvinus. Although the lower classes do appear in Part Two, the action is concerned with the punishment of the wicked. Phallax escapes with the loss of all his property and his office; Cassandra is forgiven for her "forced fault" by the King; Promos is ordered to marry Cassandra but is to be executed on the next day as payment for the death of Andrugio; and Lamia is arrested. The sudden appearance of Andrugio—Andrugio had been smuggled out of prison by a sympathetic jailor who had substituted the head of another prisoner for that of the intended victim—makes it possible for the King to spare Promos' life and to pardon Andrugio if he marries Polina; Promos, of course, must marry the seduced Cassandra. Cassandra, who has had no success in attempting to save the life of her new husband, is of course overjoyed and when Promos asks "Cassandra, howe shall I discharge thy due?", she replies quite simply, "I dyd but what a Wife shoulde do for you".

So the package is neatly wrapped up and only the captious will wonder why Whetstone omitted any account of the punishment of Dalia, Rosko, Rowke, Grimball, et al. The major personages have been taken care of, and the moral lesson of true justice administered by an upright King (magistrate) is indubitably clear.

Thus Whetstone has fulfilled his purpose as announced in the dedication and has managed to create a definitely dramatic work into the bargain. Judged by the standards of its own time, *Promos and Cassandra* is certainly superior to other works, say such a play as Richard Edwards' *Damon and Pithias* of 1571. There is a quick movement of action, particularly in Part One; the moralizing and didactic passages are reasonably brief; we are spared the static debate on such topics as good and bad counsellors, false and true friendship, and the like; Phallax is a rather amusing character; and the scenes of low-life have a real vitality. In particular the varied use of songs, from the sorrowful to the bawdy, gives still another dramatic value to the play. We can only wonder at the marginal note in *An Heptameron of Civill Discourses* which tells us that it had "never yet been presented on the stage". We may understand that the Master of the Revels might not regard it highly for Court performance because it does lack the rhetoric of wit which seems to have been highly valued in Edwards, and, later, in the plays of John Lyly. Perhaps the scenes of low-life would not have been regarded as proper for performance either at Court or at any of the Inns of Court, where high seriousness of the *Gorboduc* variety prevailed. The only play of a lighter nature which we know to have been presented in these sophisticated haunts was George Gascoigne's *Supposes,* presented at Gray's Inn in 1566, but this of course had the sanction of Ariosto's original authorship, and no such characters as the unsavory denizens of the city of Julio make an appearance.

We can find a ready enough example of such characters in the plays of the popular theater of the wandering groups of actors. *Hickscorner* gives us a lively and vigorous picture of life in the stews, brothels, and prisons of early 16th-century London. No other Tudor interlude quite equals this for the frank realism of both character and dialogue, but in others the Vices are always interesting if not so particularly bawdy.[29]

While the moralities do contain characters representing the Virtues as well as the Vices, they do not present the character of the King or Magistrate who administers justice and corrects the wrong perpetrated by evil doers. It is only in the highly specialized dramatic form of the Prodigal Son play which had some popularity on the Continent that we find punishment of offenders carried out by a magistrate or a ruler. In particular the only one of these plays to introduce this character and the characters of a whore, a bawd, a pimp, and a parasite is George Gascoigne's *The Glasse of Government* (1577).[30] Although Whetstone's friendship with Gascoigne is reasonably well known, largely by reason of his obituary of his more gifted contemporary, Whetstone's almost slavish imitation of Gascoigne seems to have escaped notice and it is my belief that *The Glasse of Government* was clearly in Whetstone's mind when he wrote *Promos and Cassandra.*

[29] Reality often exceeded the fictitious. Cf. Fleetwood's account of a school for pickpockets, *Original Letters,* ed. Henry Ellis (London, 1825), II, 297-298.

[30] *The Complete Works of George Gascoigne,* ed. J. W. Cunliffe (Cambridge, 1910), II, 1-90. In *The Nice Wanton* (1560), a judge, Daniel, makes a brief appearance and condemns to death Ismael, who is guilty of felony, burglary, and murder (*Early English Dramatists,* ed., John S. Farmer, London, 1905, pp. 107-110). A corrupt judge, Sisamnes, is the center of the first action in *Cambyses.* While the King is absent, Sisamnes heeds the advice of Ambidexter and demands a bribe of Small Habilitie. The King, informed by Commons Cry, has Sisamnes executed.

A noteworthy feature of *The Glasse of Government* is the harsh and un-relenting administration of justice which completely lacks any quality of mercy or compassion. Severus, the Markgrave, hears Fidus' account of the execution of the wicked younger brother in the very sight of the virtuous elder brother and observes,

> It is a happy common wealth where Justice may be ministered with severitie, and where no mediacions or sutes may wrest the sentence of the Lawe. (II, 86)

For his own part Severus has no mercy for Ambidexter and Eccho, who are sentenced to be whipped about the town for three days and then banished. Since a similar three days' whipping in Geneva has left the second wicked younger brother at death's door, a similar fate obviously awaits these two rogues. Although Lamia and Pandarina get off with three days of public display in the "Cucking stoole" and subsequent banishment, there is no suggestion of mitigation in this sentence.

Whetstone, as we have seen, presents in the judgments of Corvinus, a con-siderable mitigation and mercy. Phallax, Promos' venial secretary, loses his goods and his office but not his life. Gonsago, a rich man charged with un-specified wrongs, is given a warning of future punishment if he reverts to his evil ways. While Lamia is presumably to suffer a whipping, her cohorts are not even mentioned. The only execution is to be that of Promos, not for his violation of Cassandra but because he had caused her brother Andrugio to be executed. With the fortunate reappearance of Andrugio this crime is eliminated so that Promos may live happily ever after with his loving wife, Cassandra.

In marked contrast with this tone of mercy is the frequent insistence on a strict and severe justice in Shakespeare's play. The Duke, in conversation with Friar Thomas (I. iii), says that Angelo will strike home and enforce the laws which he (the Duke) has allowed to slip. Angelo insists on the letter of the law and the Duke visiting Claudio in prison offers no hope; instead he delivers a homily on death. Granted that all turns out well in the end, the theme of the severe magistrate is represented in *The Glasse of Government* as it is not in *Promos and Cassandra.*

We know that Shakespeare used Gascoigne's *Supposes* as the subplot of *The Taming of the Shrew,* and since he also knew Whetstone, it is probable that he would have known *The Glasse of Government* as well. It is too easily forgotten that Gascoigne and Whetstone, but particularly the former, were the chief poets of England during the youth of Marlowe and Shakespeare. Thus it seems to me both pertinent and valuable to consider *The Glasse of Govern-ment* when one approaches *Measure for Measure* through its immediate source, *Promos and Cassandra.*

In his friend's play Whetstone had the example of a good magistrate and a world of low-life, but its static and didactic nature were poor stuff for the stage and I could well wish that those who have heaped such scorn on *Promos and Cassandra* might be induced to read *The Glasse of Government.* What was needed was something of dramatic value and that Whetstone found in the well-known story of the lustful magistrate who is finally brought to justice by the good magistrate. Secondly, Whetstone saw the dramatic possibility of incorporating other instances of lust (on varying social levels) and of unifying the entire subject through the integration of the underworld with the main action. By such amalgamation Whetstone was following that important critical doctrine of Imitation, according to which an author did not invent, instead he developed the source materials according to his own ability or in the words of Count Lewis in *The Book of the Courtier* who emphasizes the necessity for reinterpretation as "wading further":

> An if Virgill had altogether folowed Hesiodus, he should not have passed him nor Cicero, Crassus, nor Ennius, his Predecessors. . . . And truly it should be a great miserye to stoppe without wading any farther then almost the first that ever wrote. . . .[31]

Shakespeare in his turn waded further, but now that we know a bit more about Whetstone's play and its background in European history, the underworld of London, and Whetstone's interest in good and bad magistrates, we are in a somewhat more certain position from which to examine *Measure for Measure*. If we today can reconstruct something of Whetstone's world and his literary principles, we must realize that Shakespeare knew both at first hand and in more detail than we can recover. What is now necessary is a critical examination of *Measure for Measure* with its manifold alterations of the old play and the incorporation of new elements, particularly in respect to the concept of justice. Vincentio, Duke of Vienna is no counterpart of Corvinus, King of Hungary and Bohemia, but there are close similarities. Corvinus, coming to Julio, has issued a proclamation promising justice to any citizen who has been wronged; the Duke sends word to Angelo charging him "to proclaim it an hour before his entering, that if any crave redress of justice, they should exhibit their petitions in the street". Cassandra and Isabella both make their pleas for justice openly before the ruler. Even as the resolution of the two plays uses the same device, so too they have similar opening scenes. Corvinus' proclamation read by Phallax appoints Promos as Judge of the city of Julio, "to weede from good the yll,/ To scoorge the wights, good Lawes that disobay."[32] The Duke appoints Angelo his deputy "to enforce or qualify the laws/ As to your soul seems good" (I.i. 66-67). Shakespeare's "wading further" between such borrowed opening and closing scenes will be the subject of a future study.

Yale University

[31] Baldassare Castiglione, *The Book of the Courtier*, trans. Sir Thomas Hoby, 1561, ed. Walter Raleigh (London, 1900), pp. 74, 76.
[32] Bullough, II, 446.

CHARLESTON THEATRE.

This Evening, Friday, December 20,

WILL BE PRESENTED

(By Particular Desire,) Shakspeare's Celebrated *TRAGEDY* of

HAMLET;
PRINCE OF DENMARK.

KING,	Mr. TURNBULL,	PLAYER KING,	Mr. SIERSON,
HAMLET,	Mr. JONES,	LUCIANUS,	Mr. SULLY,
HORATIO,	Mr. STORY,	GHOST,	Mr. WHITLOCK,
POLONIUS,	Mr. DYKES,	GRAVE DIGGERS,	Meſſrs. BATES, and HAYMAN.
LAERTES,	Mr. CROMWELL,		
ROSENCRAUS,	Mr. CLAUDE,	QUEEN,	Mrs. HOGG,
GUILDENSTEAN,	Mr. CLARK,	OPHELIA,	Mrs. OLDMIXON,
OSTRICK,	Mr. WILSON,	PLAYER QUEEN,	Mrs. DYKES.

TO WHICH WILL BE ADDED,

The Musical Entertainment, of

The PRIZE;
Ten Thousand Pounds!!
O R,

2, 5, 3, 8.

DOCTOR LENITIVE,	Mr. SULLY,	JUBA,	Mrs. CLAUDE,
MR. CADDY,	Mr. DYKES,	MRS. CADDY,	Mrs. TURNBULL,
HEARTWELL,	Mr. CLAUDE,	CAROLINE,	Mrs. OLDMIXON.
LABEL,	Mr. WILSON.		

DOORS to be opened at half paſt five, and the curtain to riſe at half paſt ſix o'Clock, preciſely.

BOX and PIT, 4s. 8d.—GALLERY, 2s. 4d.

TICKETS and places for the BOXES to be had at Mr. G. G. Bailey's, Meeting-Street; where Subscribers for the Season, are requested to send for their Tickets, *before Dusk.*

☞ *The Proprietors are requested to send for their Tickets, to Mr. W. P. Young's,* before Dusk.

People of Colour cannot be admitted to any part of the Houſe.

Smoaking in the Theatre, Prohibited.

PRINTED BY W. P. YOUNG, No. 41, BROAD-STREET.

Playbill for the performance of *Hamlet* at the Charleston Theatre on 20 December 1805. 12″ x 21½″. Reproduced by permission of The Folger Shakespeare Library.

The Tempest and the Renaissance Idea of Man

JAMES E. PHILLIPS

OST students of *The Tempest* are agreed that there is more to Shakespeare's last play than charms the eye and delights the ear.[1] Some have regarded its deeper meaning as autobiographical in nature, communicating Shakespeare's view of his own art and announcing his withdrawal from active professional life. Others have found it a covert commentary on England's colonizing efforts in the New World, or more generally, on the impact of civilization on primitivism. Some have explained its significance in terms of Christian concepts of ethical and political morality, some in terms of neoplatonic doctrine, and some in terms of Renaissance ideas about white and black magic. Almost all concur, however, in a general feeling that beneath its splendid surface of poetry and theater *The Tempest* is somehow concerned with man's effort to overcome his worser self. Or as John Middleton Murry put it, "The Island . . . is what would be if Humanity—the best in man—controlled the life of man. And Prospero is a man in whom the best in man has won the victory: . . ."[2]

In their efforts to define "the best in man" as exemplified in *The Tempest,* all but a few commentators have tended to ignore ideas on the nature of man widely held in Shakespeare's day and frequently expressed in treatises on moral philosophy, learned and popular alike. Theodore Spencer, among the few, has suggested that Renaissance ideas about the animal, human, and intellectual elements in man can be made to account respectively for the character and actions of Caliban, of the conspirators, comics, and lovers, and of Prospero. Ariel is not clearly incorporated into this scheme.[3] With similar reference to sixteenth-century thought about the nature of man, Donald Stauffer equated Caliban with "instinct and passion", Ariel with "Imagination", and Prospero with "Noble Reason" in interpreting *The Tempest* as a drama symbolically portraying (among other autobiographical and moral concerns) the ultimate triumph of ethical control over passion.[4]

---

[1] For a review of interpretations to 1954, see *The Tempest,* ed. Frank Kermode (The Arden Shakespeare, London, 1954), pp. lxxxi-lxxxviii. To these should be added the general discussions of the play in Donald Stauffer, *Shakespeare's World of Images* (New York, 1949), pp. 301-311; D. C. Allen, *Image and Meaning* (Baltimore, 1960), pp. 42-66; and Leo Kirshbaum, "*The Tempest*—Apologetics or Spectacle?", *Two Lectures on Shakespeare* (London, 1961), pp. 19-41. All Shakespeare quotations are from Kermode's text in the new Arden edition.

[2] *Shakespeare* (New York, 1936), p. 332.

[3] *Shakespeare and the Nature of Man* (New York, 1945), p. 195.

[4] *Shakespeare's World of Images* (New York, [1949]), pp. 304-305.

Neither critic, however, nor any other that I know of, has observed the striking similarity between the functions of Prospero, Ariel, and Caliban in the play and the functions of the three parts of the soul—Rational, Sensitive, and Vegetative—almost universally recognized and described in Renaissance literature on the nature of man. Upon closer examination, this similarity appears to be more than coincidental. The parallels which I propose to point out suggest, I think, a way of looking at the activities and relationships of the island trio that might contribute ultimately to a more complete understanding of the play as a whole. They cannot be made to account for every detail of the history and character of Prospero and his two aides, nor can they be extended, directly at least, to the other characters and incidents of the play. As Frank Kermode admonishes us in his introduction to the Arden text of the play, the temptation to allegorize Shakespeare is strong but to be resisted; on the other hand, Theodore Spencer, echoing other critics, acknowledges that *The Tempest* is "a play with so many layers of meaning that no single interpretation can do it justice". A brief reminder of Renaissance thought about the nature of man and his soul will provide, I hope, an adequate basis for suggesting one more element of meaning in the play.

I

Studies by Lily B. Campbell, Ruth Anderson, Lawrence Babb, and others have made generally familiar to students of Shakespeare a concept of the tripartite soul widely accepted in his day and expounded in such discussions of moral philosophy as *Batman uppon Bartholome* (1582), Sir John Davies' *Nosce Teipsum* (1599), Philippe de Mornay's *The True Knowledge of a Mans Owne Selfe* (1602), and Pierre de la Primaudaye's *The French Academy* (1618).[5] Ultimately derived from Plato and Aristotle, the concept was also indebted to Galen, Augustine, Avicenna, and Aquinas. In the sixteenth century the soul of man, which animates the body and directs its activities for good or ill, was usually described in terms of three sub-souls, to each of which particular functions were attributed. The lowest of these was known variously as the vegetative or quickening soul. To this soul or power, which man has in common with vegetable and animal life, were ascribed the faculties of nourishment, growth, elimination, reproduction, and the other instinctive physiological processes. Often referred to as the "housekeeper of the body", charged with supplying the basic needs, the vegetative soul, as Sir John Davies described it, "doth employ her *oeconomicke art,* /And busie care, her household to preserue".[6] The second sub-soul or power, possessed by man in common with animal life, was known as the sensitive or sensible soul. It includes the faculty of knowing, in the sense of perceiving and apprehending, and the faculty of moving, in the sense of physical and emotional activity alike. The faculty of knowing includes, in turn, the activities of the five senses, and the activities

---

[5] In the following summary I have relied mainly on Ruth L. Anderson, *Elizabethan Psychology and Shakespeare's Plays* (Iowa City, 1927); Lily B. Campbell, *Shakespeare's Tragic Heroes* (Cambridge, 1930), pp. 51-72; and Lawrence Babb, *The Elizabethan Malady* (East Lansing, 1951), pp. 1-20. The last contains a useful bibliography of primary and secondary works on the subject (pp. 189-197).

[6] *Nosce Teipsum* (1599), ed., from the 1622 edition, by A. B. Grosart, *The Complete Poems of Sir John Davies* (London, 1876), I, 63. Subsequent quotations are from this edition.

of common sense, imagination or fantasy, and memory. The faculty of moving includes in its turn the power of bodily movement and the power of the passions or affections, as the emotions were termed. The third and highest of the sub-souls, in the possession of which man is unique among all worldly creatures, was variously termed the intellectual power or rational soul. As Professor Babb describes the concept of it generally held in the Renaissance:

> It has two divisions—intellectual and volitional, that is, *reason* and *will*. The former . . . is capable of perceiving the essence, not merely the appearance [of things]. It seeks truth through a logical train of thought. It draws conclusions regarding truth and falsehood, good and evil; in other words, it is capable of judgment. The reason determines what is good and what is evil and informs the will of its conclusions. The will because of an instinct implanted in it by God, desires the good and abhors the evil which the reason represents to it. . . . When the will conceives a desire or aversion, a corresponding passion normally arises in the sensitive soul. Thus the will causes physical action indirectly through the sensitive passions.[7]

Or as Miss Campbell puts it, "The rational soul has two great powers: . . . It knows what 'twere good to do and has the power of desiring to do that which it judges good to do."[8]

When these three sub-souls or powers operate together in the way God originally designed them to operate, man lives virtuously and knows true happiness in this world. The vegetative soul keeps the organism running. The knowing power of the sensitive soul collects the impressions of experience through the senses and identifies the data by means of the common sense; with the imagination it forms the data into images or transforms them by its creative ability, then evaluates them as pleasurable or painful; and with the memory it retains the data for future use. At this point, the rational soul takes over the data thus processed. Reason proceeds to evaluate it, determining general principles from the particulars, judging what is true and what is false, and above all, distinguishing between good and bad. It so informs the will, which, with its God-given instinct to choose good, decrees man's action accordingly by directing the sensitive soul, in its function of moving, to provide the appropriate emotional response (desire for good, for example, or hatred of evil), and to effect the appropriate physical action through the muscles, sinews, and tendons.

Unfortunately, however, man's tripartite soul does not always function in the way that God intended. As a result of the Fall, man's life and happiness are constantly threatened by a persistent tendency in the soul to short-circuit itself. Or as Davies put it, a "declining *pronenesse unto nought,* / Is euen that sinne that we are borne withall" (p. 57). That is, the sensitive soul collects and processes the data as it should, but then it by-passes the rational soul and sends the data directly to the motive faculties of the sensible soul. The passions, with no control by the judgment of reason or the moral choice of will, are aroused by what is pleasurable or what is painful, not by what is true or false, good or bad, and they direct action accordingly. And that way lie madness, misery, and death. Consequently, man since the Fall has faced a constant struggle to keep his vegetative and sensitive souls the servants of his rational soul, and

---

[7] *The Elizabethan Malady,* pp. 4-5.
[8] *Shakespeare's Tragic Heroes,* pp. 66-67.

above all to keep the passions subject to the control of his reason. In this control lies the essential humanity that distinguishes man from all other creatures. The man who achieves this victory is the virtuous man and therefore, inevitably, the happy man. As Professor Babb concludes, quoting Pierre Charron's *Of Wisdom* from the English translation of 1606:

> The *summum bonum,* the greatest good possible to man in his earthly life, is 'tranquillitie of the spirit. . . . This is that great and rich treasure, which . . . is the fruit of all our labors and studies, the crowne of wisdome'. To achieve this enviable condition, the reasonable soul must keep continual watch over the sensitive powers and must continually exert itself in curbing them.[9]

Such, then, is the concept of the nature of man's soul which, even in the latter days of the Renaissance when disturbing doubts were already beginning to be expressed, was still widely accepted.[10] Re-examined in the light of this concept, the functions and relationships of Caliban, Ariel, and Prospero take on new meaning.

II

Caliban has been interpreted by commentators in different ways too numerous to be conveniently detailed here.[11] All agree, however, that in Caliban Shakespeare intended to represent some form of life or activity below that of civilized man, whether it be the primitive savage encountered in England's colonial ventures, the monster frequently described in contemporary travel literature, the devil-daemon of black magic and medieval Christian tradition, or the cannibal, from which his name seems to be derived. Many critics see in Caliban a symbol of the brutish or animal element in human nature, a representation of the instincts and passions in man. John E. Hankins, for example, has argued that he is Aristotle's "bestial man", possessing the attributes of the sensible soul but not those of the intellectual.[12]

If we regard only the history, the appearance, and the drunken, conspiratorial character of Caliban, each of these suggested interpretations appears plausible. But when we regard the function of Caliban on the island and his relationship to Prospero, his activities are remarkably like those attributed in the Renaissance not to the sensitive or animal soul, but instead to the vegetative or quickening power. Sir John Davies, it will be recalled, in describing the quickening power as it should function ideally, wrote:

> Her *quick'ning* power in euery liuing part,
>   Doth as a nurse, or as a mother serue;
>   And doth employ her *oeconomicke art,*
>   And busie care, her household to preserue.

[9] *The Elizabethan Malady,* p. 19.
[10] Cf. Spencer, pp. 1-50.
[11] Cf. note 1, above, to which should be added J. E. Hankins, "Caliban as the Bestial Man", *PMLA,* LXII (1947), 793-801, and N. Coghill, "The Basis of Shakespearian Comedy", *Essays and Studies* (1950), pp. 1-28.
[12] "Caliban as the Bestial Man", p. 799.

> Here she *attracts,* and there she doth *retaine,*
>> There she *decocts,* and doth the food prepare;
>> There she *distributes* it to euery vaine,
>> There she expels what she may fitly spare.
>
> This power to *Martha* may compared be,
>> Which busie was, the *household-things* to doe;
>> Or to a *Dryas,* liuing in a tree:
>> For euen to trees this power is proper too. (Pp. 63-64)

Like the vegetative part of man's soul, Caliban is the "housekeeper" of the is-land. Only at the end, of course, does Caliban come to regard his duties with anything like an attitude that might be called "busie care". But from the be-ginning the activities expected of him are consistently similar to those assigned to the vegetative soul. Like this lowest power in man, Caliban is regarded as essential to simple existence on the island. When Miranda exclaims of him at the outset, " 'Tis a villain, sir, I do not love to look on", her father replies:

> But, as 'tis,
> We cannot miss him: he does make our fire,
> Fetch in our wood, and serves in offices
> That profit us. (I. ii. 311-315)

Soon these "offices" are more specifically indicated. It was Caliban, we learn, who first provided nourishment for Prospero and Miranda when they arrived on the island, showing them "all the qualities o'th'isle, / The fresh springs, brine-pits, barren place and fertile" (I. ii. 339-340). Later, Prospero commands him, "Fetch us in fuel, and be quick, thou'rt best, / To answer other business" (I. ii. 368-369). Even when he would change masters, Caliban speaks of his service function in terms of providing heat, drink, and nourishment. He promises Stephano:

> I'll show thee the best springs; I'll pluck thee berries;
> I'll fish for thee, and get thee wood enough.
> A plague upon the tyrant that I serve!
> I'll bear him no more sticks, but follow thee,
> Thou wondrous man. . . .
> I prithee, let me bring thee where crabs grow;
> And I with my long nails will dig thee pig-nuts,
> Show thee a jay's nest, and instruct thee how
> To snare the nimble marmoset; I'll bring thee
> To clustering filberts, and sometimes I'll get thee
> Young scamels from the rock.   (II. ii. 160-172)

Caliban summarizes the housekeeping duties which he has performed for Prospero (and will perform again) when he sings:

> No more dams I'll make for fish;
>> Nor fetch in firing
>> At requiring;
> Nor scrape trenchering, nor wash dish.   (II. ii. 193-196)

Finally brought to recognize his true master and his true function, Caliban willingly accepts Prospero's order to trim the cell handsomely (V. i. 290-295).

It is possible that we are also meant to identify Caliban with the generative or reproductive functions of the vegetative soul, as well as with its maintenance functions. It does not appear to be the passions of love or lust in the sensitive soul that motivate Caliban's attempt to violate the honor of Miranda, but simply the instinctive urge to reproduce his own kind. As he tells Prospero:

> O ho, O ho! would't had been done!
> Thou didst prevent me; I had peopled else
> This isle with Calibans.   (I. ii. 351-353)

Apparently he is incapable of thinking of the relationship of man and woman in any other than these fundamental terms, for he later tells Stephano, with reference to Miranda, "she will become thy bed, I warrant, / And bring thee forth brave brood" (III. ii. 102-103). But be that as it may, in all the services that Caliban can and does perform on the island, his powers are consistently limited to those attributed in Renaissance moral philosophy not to the knowing and moving power of the sensitive or animal soul, but to the quickening powers of the vegetative.

As in his functions, so in his relationship to Prospero does Caliban resemble the vegetative soul in its relationship to the nature of man as a whole. A more pertinent examination of this resemblance can better be made when Prospero himself has been considered later. Suffice it to say for the moment that the Renaissance moral philosophers repeatedly insisted that, insofar as man is concerned, the vegetative soul is simply the servant of the higher human powers. As Davies put it, "The best the service of the least doth need" (p. 80). To enumerate Prospero's frequent references to Caliban as "slave" and "servant", or Caliban's references to the "master" he serves, is probably unnecessary. To this ordained servant, even freedom itself means only that "Cacaliban / Has a new master". His relationship to Prospero further resembles the Renaissance concept in the fact that, just as man's vegetative soul, like his sensitive soul, must constantly since the Fall be kept under control by man's rational soul, so also Caliban must constantly, and often by vigorous means, be kept under control by Prospero. Howsoever we may regard Prospero in the Renaissance scheme at this point, the fact in itself that Caliban must be controlled from above in performing his "housekeeping" functions completes the striking similarity to the vegetative or quickening power of man's soul.

III

Ariel, like Caliban, has been subject to almost as many different interpretations as there are commentators on the play.[13] He has been variously explained as Shakespeare's own poetic imagination or, more generally, a symbol of man's higher imaginative powers; as the beneficent spirit or daemon of the elements in Hebrew or Neo-platonic tradition; and as the fairy creature sometimes reported in the travel literature of the period. All agree, however, in identifying him with the spiritual and intangible, in contrast to the earthiness of Caliban. But again, if we regard the activities of Ariel and his function in relation to Prospero, as distinct from his history and character, his similarity to the sensi-

---

[13] Cf. note 1, above, to which should be added W. Stacy Johnson, "The Genesis of Ariel", *SQ*, II (1951), 205-210.

tive soul in Renaissance man appears to be more than coincidental. Not all of the powers ascribed to the sensitive soul by the moral philosophers of Shakespeare's day can be found in Ariel, perhaps, but all of Ariel's functions can indeed be found in contemporary descriptions of this aspect of man's nature.

The sensitive soul, it will be recalled, was regarded in the Renaissance as possessing two classes of powers, the knowing or apprehending and the moving or feeling. In the first of these are found the activities of the senses, which enable man to receive impressions from the world outside himself. As Sir John Davies wrote of man's soul:

> She hath a power which she abroad doth send,
> Which views and searcheth all things every where.

> This *power* is *Sense,* which from abroad doth send
> The *coulour, taste,* and *touch,* and *sent,* and *sound;*
> The *quantitie,* and *shape* of euery thing
> Within th'Earth's center, or Heauen's circle found.

> This power, in parts made fit, fit objects takes,
> Yet not the things, but forms of things receiues;
> As when a seale in waxe impression makes,
> The print therein, but not itselfe it leaues. (Pp. 64-65)

And he concludes, with particular reference to the eyes and ears, "These conduit-pipes of knowledge feed the Mind" (p. 68).

One of Ariel's principal functions in *The Tempest* is reporting to Prospero what he sees and hears, for Prospero himself does not always see or hear the crucial actions he controls. Ariel describes for him the sights and sounds of the storm and the wreck. He announces that he will report to his lord what he has observed of the conspiracy against Alonso (II. i. 321), and what he has overheard when Caliban, Stephano, and Trinculo are hatching their plot (III. ii. 113). Later, he describes for Prospero the discomfiture of the comic plotters, even to the point of suggesting the smell of "the foul lake" that "O'er-stunk their feet" (IV. i. 182-184). And finally, it is Ariel who reports the helpless state of the aristocratic prisoners which is the basis of Prospero's crucial decision to forgive (V. i. 7-18).

In addition to the sensory faculties, Renaissance moral philosophers also assigned to the sensitive soul the faculty of imagination, both in its power to retain and recreate images received through the senses, and in its power to create new images. As Professor Babb summarizes the commonly received opinion on this point:

> Sensory impressions are next conveyed to the imagination. This faculty can retain and consider them for some time. It evaluates them as pleasant or painful. It has the power of conceiving circumstances and situations other than those existing at the moment and of forming synthetic images from disparate elements as it pleases (hence, centaurs, griffons, and chimeras). This is the creative power of the imagination. It is a faculty which never rests; even when the other sensory and intellectual powers are in repose,

a stream of images flows aimlessly through the imagination, and when one
is asleep, this stream continues in his dreams.[14]

This is the faculty which enables man's soul to achieve the remarkable feat of
traveling outside the body to any point in time or space. In *Nosce Teipsum*
Sir John Davies marvels at this power:

> When she, without a *Pegasus,* doth flie
>   Swifter then lightning's fire from *East* to *West,*
>   About the *Center* and aboue the *skie,*
>   She trauels then, although the body rest. . . .
>
> She is sent as soone to *China* as to *Spaine,*
>   And thence returnes, as soone as shee is sent;
>   She measures with one time, and with one paine,
>   An ell of silke, and heauen's wide spreading tent.
>   (Pp. 31, 45)

Several of Ariel's powers and functions are similar to these attributed to
the imaginative faculty in the sensitive soul. In fact, the first thing we hear of
him is his sleepless ability to travel instantaneously to any point in space. When
Prospero summons him at the outset of the play, Ariel responds:

> All hail, great master! grave sir, hail! I come
> To answer thy best pleasure; be't to fly,
> To swim, to dive into the fire, to ride
> On the curl'd clouds, to thy strong bidding task
> Ariel and all his quality. (I. ii. 189-193)

And a few moments later he recalls

>   the deep nook, where once
> Thou call'dst me up at midnight to fetch dew
> From the still-vex'd Bermoothes, . . . (I. ii. 227-229).

Prospero acknowledges this power, somewhat backhandedly, perhaps, when
in rebuking Ariel for ingratitude he charges that the sprite

>   think'st it much to tread the ooze
> Of the salt deep,
> To run upon the sharp wind of the north,
> To do me business in the veins o'th'earth
> When it is bak'd with frost, (I. ii. 252-256)

a charge, incidentally, which Ariel promptly denies with "I do not, sir". Some
of Ariel's most important activities in the play, however, are those associated
in Shakespeare's day with the creative function of the imagination. Prospero
usually wills the poetry, music, and drama that are part of the action, but Ariel
is charged with producing the works themselves. He creates the lyric poetry
which leads Ferdinand to Miranda (I. ii. 377-405), and the song which alerts
Gonzalo to Antonio's conspiracy (II. i. 295-300). He performs, and presumably
composes, the music which puts the stranded aristocrats to sleep (II. i. 177-180).
He designs, directs, and participates in the lavish spectacle of the banquet, rich

---

[14] *The Elizabethan Malady,* p. 3. Babb cites M. W. Bundy, *The Theory of the Imagination in
Classical and Medieval Thought* (Urbana, 1927), Chap. IX, as a fuller account of the subject.

in settings, music, and dance, whereby the crimes of the aristocrats against Prospero are revealed to themselves. So effective is Ariel in this particular creative achievement that Prospero compliments him:

> Bravely the figure of this Harpy hast thou
> Perform'd, my Ariel; a grace it had devouring:
> Of my instruction hast thou nothing bated
> In what thou hadst to say: . . . (III. iii. 83-86)

And finally, of course, at Prospero's command Ariel creates, and acts a principal role in, the masque of Iris and Ceres, a production where, in accordance with Renaissance theories, the arts of music, dance, and poetry are made to serve a moral function by instructing Ferdinand and Miranda in proper pre-nuptial conduct (IV. i. 34-138).

In addition to these functions which Shakespeare's contemporaries associated with the knowing and apprehending part of the sensitive soul, Ariel demonstrates others that are similar to those assigned to the moving and feeling part. In Renaissance moral philosophy, as Miss Campbell has observed, "The sensible soul . . . is also generally regarded as the soul that has the moving power which resides in the sinews, muscles, ligaments, etc., by which power the soul [i.e., the rational soul] effects its purposes" (p. 67). Or as Davies describes this power in the sensitive soul:

> This makes the pulses beat, and lungs respire,
>   This holds the sinewes like a bridle's reines;
> And makes the Body to aduance, retire,
>   To turne or stop, as she them slacks, or straines.

> Thus the *soule* tunes the bodie's instrument;
>   These harmonies she makes with *life* and *sense;*
> The organs fit are by the body lent,
>   But th'actions flow from the *Soule's* influence.
>   (Pp. 74-75)

One of Ariel's principal functions in *The Tempest* is, of course, to effect the purposes of Prospero. From the raising of the storm in the beginning to the calming of the seas at the end, Ariel regularly puts into action the judgment and will of his master. Again it is worth noting that just as Prospero sees and hears little of the crucial developments directly, so he does little directly in actuating the developments he decrees. It is Ariel who brings Ferdinand to Miranda, leads the conspirators, noble and comic alike, to their respective confusions, brings the mariners back to Prospero, and effects the release of Caliban and his companions—to cite only a few of the ways in which he translates Prospero's will into action. The relationship is epitomized, perhaps, in the dialogue between the two when Prospero suddenly recalls Caliban's proposed rebellion. He summons Ariel: "Come with a thought". Ariel immediately responds: "Thy thoughts I cleave to. What's thy pleasure?" "We must prepare to meet with Caliban", his master answers, and Ariel proceeds to carry out the order to fetch the "trumpery" of royal vestments that will trap the conspirators (IV. i. 164-166). So Ariel, like the motive power of the sensitive soul, promptly gives each proportioned thought its act.

With one notable exception there is little evidence in *The Tempest* to suggest that Ariel, in addition to his sensory, imaginative, and motive powers,
possesses the power of feeling or passion attributed by Shakespeare's contemporaries to the moving part of the sensitive soul. As a result, commentators who
have concerned themselves with the matter are inclined to deny to Ariel any
capacity for feeling or emotion at all.[15] But at a critical juncture in the play,
Prospero himself seems to attribute such a capacity to his sprite. At the beginning
of the fifth act, when Ariel reports that the aristocratic conspirators are now
under Prospero's control, he adds:

> Your charm so strongly works 'em,
> That if you now beheld them, your affections
> Would become tender.
> *Pros.*   Dost thou think so, spirit?
> *Ari.* Mine would, sir, were I human.
> *Pros.*   And mine shall.
> Hast thou, which art but air, a touch, a feeling
> Of their afflictions, and shall not myself,
> One of their kind, that relish all as sharply
> Passion as they, be kindlier mov'd than thou art?
>   (V. i. 17-24)

This passage suggests that Ariel may feel less deeply than Prospero, but nonetheless possesses a capacity for feeling. In this connection we recall the insistence
of Renaissance moral philosophers that man's tripartite soul, when it functions
as it was designed to function, brings the passionate potential of the sensitive
soul into action only after the rational soul has determined that a true and good
cause for an emotional response exists. More will be said on this subject below in
connection with Prospero. But at least Ariel's one expression of feeling, as
qualified by his master, is not inconsistent with contemporary ideas of the
powers of the sensitive soul. Ariel's reiterated demands for freedom, like Caliban's, can perhaps also be better understood when Prospero's function in the
scheme is considered. Suffice it to observe for the moment that Ariel's desire
to be free of Prospero is in general agreement with the Renaissance view of
the sensitive soul as constantly seeking to escape from rational control.

IV

Prospero, variously identified as Shakespeare himself, a magician, a theurgist,
a civilizing influence in the colonies, a symbol of art or nurture as opposed to
nature, and a representation of higher reason, is recognized by all commentators
to be the power controlling all that is and all that happens on the island.[16] For
many of Prospero's attributes and much of his history, Shakespeare apparently
drew on contemporary knowledge of magical art. But whatever the sources of
the character, the fact remains that at least some of his more significant functions and relationships on the island are remarkably like those assigned by the

[15] Cf., for example, Stauffer, *Shakespeare's World of Images*, p. 305: "Ariel has no human
feelings, though he can observe them clearly".

[16] Cf. note 1, above, to which should be added F. D. Hoeniger, "Prospero's Storm and Miracle",
SQ, VII (1956), 33-38; G. H. Durrant, "Prospero's Wisdom", *Theoria*, VII (1955), 50-58; and
Harold Wilson, "Action and Symbol in *Measure for Measure* and *The Tempest*", *SQ*, IV (1953),
375-384.

Renaissance to that highest of the three faculties in man, the rational soul.

The rational soul, it will be recalled, was thought by Shakespeare's contemporaries to consist of two powers, the reason or wit, and the will, both of which are sustained by the vegetative soul and served by the sensitive. On the basis of impressions collected and processed by the apprehending faculty of the sensitive soul, the reason determines the true and the good, and informs the will accordingly, whereupon the will directs the moving part of the sensitive soul to effect an appropriate action. Enough has perhaps been said above to suggest that the similarity between Prospero's employment of Ariel and the rational soul's employment of the sensitive provides in itself some basis for identifying Prospero's function with that of the rational soul. Also, as we have seen, his constant struggle to keep Caliban and Ariel under his control is consistent with the stuggle which the rational soul has had since the Fall to keep the lower faculties in check. But Prospero's relationship to both Caliban and Ariel also recalls the insistence of Renaissance moral philosophers on the interdependence of the three component powers when man's soul functions as it should. As Davies concluded:

> This is the *Soule,* and these her vertues bee;
>   Which, though they haue their sundry proper ends,
>   And one exceeds another in degree,
>   Yet each on other mutually depende.
>
> *Our Wit* is giuen, *Almighty God* to *know;*
>   Our *Will* is giuen to *loue* Him, being *knowne;*
>   But God could not be *known* to vs below,
>   But by His *workes* which through the sense are shown.
>
> And as the *Wit* doth reape the fruits of *Sense,*
>   So doth the *quickning* power the *senses feed;*
>   Thus while they doe their sundry gifts dispence,
>   The best, the seruice of the least doth need.
>   (Pp. 79-80)

Prospero's reiterated gratitude to Ariel and, at the end, his willingness to pardon Caliban, suggest a similar recognition of the indispensability of these lower powers to the higher when man is demonstrating his true humanity.

Other aspects of Prospero's role strengthen the parallel with the function of the rational soul. He distinguishes between good and evil, then wills the action necessary to repulse the evil and advance the good. His function in this respect is generally exemplified in the complete direction which he exercises over all three of the principal plot threads in the play—aristocratic conspiracy, comic conspiracy, and love story. He orders the storm which precipitates the action of each. To achieve his virtuous ends he frustrates the aristocrats, misleads the servants, and imposes the test of log-carrying on Ferdinand. Finally, he effects a resolution for all that is just and happy. Even Prospero's deep learning, howsoever we may describe its content, is reminiscent of the fact that Renaissance moral philosophers insisted on the education of the rational soul, particularly in self-knowledge, if it is to achieve the control that God designed it to exercise.[17]

Although many of his activities and functions thus resemble those attributed

---

[17] Cf. Babb, *The Elizabethan Malady,* p. 19.

to the rational soul alone, Prospero emerges, by the end of the play, as the complete Renaissance man within whose own character the rational will directs all the faculties of the soul toward the attainment of true felicity in this life. It may be worth noting in this connection that Sir John Davies, in describing the three powers of the soul, also recognized three types of men, or creatures, whose basic natures are determined by the domination in each of one of the three sub-souls:

> And these three powers, three sorts of men doe make:
> For some, like plants, their veines doe onely fill;
> And some, like beasts, their senses' pleasure take;
> And some, like angels, doe contemplate still. (P. 80)

But throughout his account Davies is mainly concerned with defining the three faculties as parts of one soul, the soul of man. As he insists at the end:

> Yet these three powers are not three *soules,* but one;
> As one and two are both contained in *three;*
> *Three* being one number by itself alone:
> A shadow of the blessed Trinitie. (P. 81)

In the soul of Prospero it is the triumph of reason over passion that most clearly links him with the contemporary view of the nature of man and human happiness. As Sir Thomas More had observed of his Utopians, they thought true felicity to consist in virture, and virtue to be defined as the governance of reason in human behavior, as nature had ordained.[18] More concretely, Juan Luis Vives, in *An Introduction to Wisedome,* had warned the age with reference to the perturbations, or passions:

> As it is . . . a poynt of treason, that suche lewed perturbations . . . should rage rebell & take vpon them the rule of the hole man, contemptuously despysynge the auctorytie of the mynde, so it is extreme foly for the mynde, to be slaue vnto fonde affections, and to serue at a becke, the vyle carkeys, neyther the dignitie of nature, neyther the expresse lawe of god, any thyng regarded.[19]

It has already been suggested, with reference to Ariel, that Prospero keeps under his control and service that faculty in which the passions were thought to reside. But on more than one occasion he demonstrates a considerable capacity for passion in himself. He reveals anger against the complaining Ariel that mounts to fury against the rebellious Caliban, and at the end of the masque he is so perturbed that Ferdinand says to Miranda, "Your father's in some passion / That works him strongly", to which she replies, "Never till this day / saw I him touch'd with anger, so distemper'd" (IV.i. 143-145). But in all these instances, the passion is made to serve, as passion should, the reasonable ends which Prospero pursues. His triumph is finally, and much more dramatically, illustrated, appropriately enough, at the very climax and turning point of the whole play. Informed by Ariel at the beginning of Act V that his enemies are now completely within his power, Prospero faces the choice of letting his pas-

---

[18] *Utopia* (London, 1910, "Everyman's Library"), p. 73.
[19] Translated by Rycharde Morysine (London, 1540), sigs. Dii-Diii, quoted in Babb, *The Elizabethan Malady,* p. 17.

sion or letting his reason direct and determine his action. His decision is the one which Shakespeare's contemporaries would have regarded as the truly virtuous one, and therefore the only one conducive to felicity. Thus he replies to Ariel:

> Though with their high wrongs I am struck to th' quick,
> Yet with my nobler reason 'gainst my fury
> Do I take part: the rarer action is
> In virtue than in vengeance: they being penitent,
> The sole drift of my purpose doth extend
> Not a frown further. Go release them, Ariel:
> My charms I'll break, their senses I'll restore,
> And they shall be themselves. (V. i. 25-32)

When, shortly thereafter, the conspirators do indeed become themselves again, Prospero describes their recovery in terms of their return to reason's control. "The charm dissolves apace", he says,

> And as the morning steals upon the night,
> Melting the darkness, so their rising senses
> Begin to chase the ignorant fumes that mantle
> Their clearer reason. (V. i. 64-68)

And a few moments later he observes again:

> Their understanding
> Begins to swell; and the approaching tide
> Will shortly fill the reasonable shore,
> That now lies foul and muddy. (V. i. 79-82)

Prospero is thus not only the reasonable man himself, but he is also the cause of reason in others. And from a Renaissance point of view, men in whom the rational soul has been restored to its proper function can truly be regarded as goodly creatures in a brave new world, and mankind as beauteous indeed.

University of California (Los Angeles)

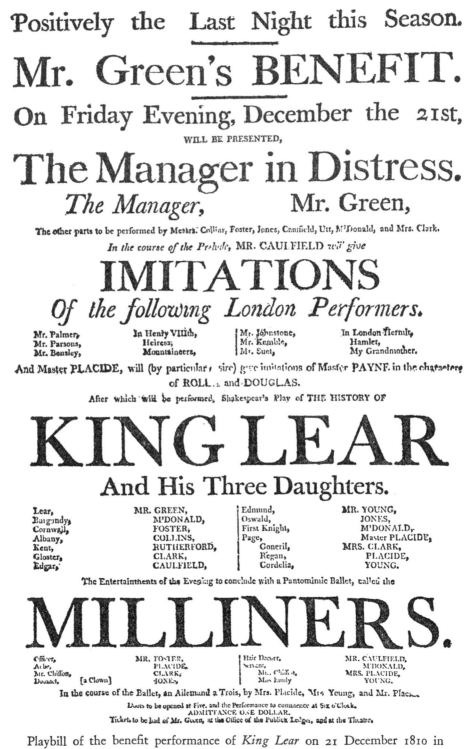

Playbill of the benefit performance of *King Lear* on 21 December 1810 in Richmond. 11⅝" x 18¼". Reproduced by permission of The Folger Shakespeare Library.

Richard II at Covent Garden

JAMES G. McMANAWAY

NE of the minor treasures in the Folger Shakespeare Library from the Warwick Castle collection of Shakespeariana is what at first glance seems to be a theatrical promptbook, bound into which are the two earliest extant sketches of stage settings for one of Shakespeare's plays. The play is *Richard II;* the period is early eighteenth century; and the transcriber, John Roberts, who also made the sketches. Only one of the drawings has been reproduced,[1] and there has been no discussion of the theatrical problems involved in the production or of the prompt text.

The book consists of leaves of *Richard II* abstracted from a copy of the Second Folio of 1632, with manuscript changes in diction, passages marked for omission, and a number of lines of text supplied in manuscript that are wanting in the print.[2] On a fragment of the original cover, the transcriber has written boldly, "K. Rich^d: 2^d. Correct' cum Libr'Theatr', Jn°. Roberts."

Before identifying Roberts or proceeding further into stage history, it is desirable to describe the book and trace its history. It is a blank book consisting of 27 unnumbered leaves of heavy paper, with the margins ruled in red. There is a flyleaf, front and back, of lighter paper. The leaves are approximately 10″ × 11¾″ in size. The nineteenth-century binding is three-quarter red morocco with a dark brown cloth resembling watered silk. Tipped in on the rectos of twelve leaves are the leaves of the Second Folio bearing the text of *Richard II.* Since these are about 12½″ tall, each one is folded over at the top or the bottom and so are the sketches. Pasted on fol. 3^r is a Drury Lane play-bill for the performance of *Richard II* on 23 October 1815. On the verso is a colored print of Edmund Kean as Richard II, published on 26 June 1815 by T. Palsor. The next leaf is made up as a title-page, "The play / of / Richard ye II. / Original edition / 1623. / T. Purland. / " The ornamental capitals T, P, O, O, and E and the owner's name, printed in several colors, have been cut out and pasted in position, with the other letters supplied in manuscript. There is a fancy border of baroque design printed in red and gold, cut out and pasted down like the initials. In the lower left corner is the memorandum, "Done in a day Sep.: 11: 1847", in Purland's hand. On leaves 7 and 8 respectively are pasted reproductions of the

---

[1] In W. M. Merchant's *Shakespeare and the Artist* (1959), p. 41—see also p. 181 for comment; and again in the festival program of the American Shakespeare Festival Theatre and Academy (1962), p. 28.

[2] It will be recalled that the text of the play in F 1 was printed from one of the later quartos, with the abdication scene supplied from an authentic manuscript. Some revisions were made in the text, and eight passages, totalling fifty lines, were cut. See W. W. Greg, *The Shakespeare First Folio* (1955), pp. 236 ff., for details.

Shakespeare arms and signatures and of scenes in Stratford. On leaf 9, within double rules of red ink, is inlaid part of the original heavy gray paper cover of Roberts' transcript, measuring 7 5/16″ × 4 7/16″. It bears the title supplied by Roberts and quoted above. (On the verso of the fragment, in Purland's hand: "N. B. — by Shakespear. / the 1st Edition — / a prompter's Book —".) Above the inlay are two clippings from newspapers, one dated in manuscript "Aug. 2, 1729" and the other "Sept. 4, 1731". Their contents will be considered later. At the foot of the page Purland has written:

> The prompter's book of Drury Lane Theatre 1727. Roberts was Cibbers prompter, and also an Actor and Commentator of Shakspeare: His name appears in Fieldings company at Bartholomew Fair in 1731; and that of his wife in 1729. Their names are frequent in 1730 at Drury Lane, and 1733 at the Hay-Market, and Goodman's-Fields 1734.

The first leaf of text (pp. 23-24 of F 2) is tipped along its inner margin to fol. 11. On the verso of fol. 12 is Roberts' sketch of the Combat Scene, titled and marked for insertion facing page 25 of F 2. The leaf bearing pp. 25-26 is on fol. 13. The other leaves of text follow in order until fol. 20, which bears the sketch of the setting for the Parliament Scene, marked for insertion facing page 38. The last leaf of F 2 text, pp. 45-46, is on fol. 24, leaving foll. 25-27 blank.[3]

A label of the Warwick Castle Shakespeare Library is pasted inside the front cover. In the upper left corner is a printed slip from a bookseller's catalogue; and on the recto of the flyleaf is an unsigned memorandum by James Orchard Halliwell-Phillipps:

> The text of this prompt copy is from the second folio of 1632, not from the first of 1623. It is rendered particularly curious by the insertion of the old rough drawings of the stage dispositions of the Combat Scene & the Parliament Scene, showing exactly how they were placed on the stage in Roberts' time, 1727. These are the earliest relics of the kind I know of.

Theodosius Purland (6 Jan. 1805—16 Aug. 1881), who put the book in its present form, was a London dentist with antiquarian interests, particularly in places of amusement. According to the sale catalogue of Puttick and Simpson for 20 August 1852, "the greater part of [his] Library and Literary curiosities" were to be sold by auction because their owner was "leaving England".[4] Lot 134 in the 1852 sale is Roberts' *Richard II,* sold to "Boone" for 14/-. The clipping pasted inside the front cover is from a Puttick and Simpson catalogue. Apparently the book passed from Boone to Halliwell-Phillipps to the Earl of Warwick, and thence to Marsden J. Perry and ultimately to Henry Clay Folger.[5]

---

[3] In F 2, the text of *Richard II* ends on p. 45, and *1 Henry IV* begins on p. 46. It may be re-marked that the sketch of the Parliament Scene actually faces the blank verso of fol. 19, not p. 38, which is on the recto of fol. 19.

[4] I am greatly indebted to Miss Eleanor Pitcher for examining this and a later catalogue (Puttick and Simpson, 16 March 1882) at the British Museum for me and for hunting out at Hodgson's in Chancery Lane their catalogue of Purland's dramatic and miscellaneous books auctioned on 14-17 March 1882.

[5] The biographical information about Purland has been collected from *N and Q,* ser. 6, V, 168-169, 293, 317; VI, 154-155. A note in ser. 15, CLXXXVI, 96, describes a neat little engraving of Purland in costume of *c.* 1855, on the back of which are the words, "Theodosius Purland Esq., Member of the B.A.A." [British Archaeological Association]. The initial inquiry of 4 March 1882 by "J. R. D." describes Purland as "Ph.D. M.A. &c." and calls him a friend of William Upcott,

Presumably Purland acquired the marked copy of *Richard II* in the process of forming his theatrical library and in 1847 mounted it in a scrapbook, as described above.[6] And for doing this he may be forgiven several inaccuracies. Purland erred, for example, in stating that the printed text Roberts marked was from the First Folio. He erred also in stating that Roberts was prompter at Drury Lane and that the promptbook he transcribed was used at that theater. It is less easy to forgive him for failing to record how *Richard II* came into his possession or the names of previous owners (if he knew them). There is a gap of a century between the making of Roberts' transcript and Theodosius Purland.[7]

Where was *Richard II* actually presented about 1730? How came it to be revived? And who was Roberts? The early stage history of *Richard II* is sketchy. After the performance by the King's Men at the Globe on 12 June 1631, there is no record of the play on the stage until Nahum Tate's alteration was produced about 1680-1.[8] In 1719-20, Lewis Theobald's alteration was presented at Lincoln's Inn Fields seven times, and during the next two seasons was revived for three performances. The production Roberts was concerned with was at Covent Garden in 1738, the first known attempt to perform Shakespeare's unaltered text in over one hundred years. As Prof. Emmett L. Avery has related,[9] credit for John Rich's revival of *Richard II* was given at the time to the unknown members of the Shakespeare Ladies Club. In the three preceding seasons, their insistence had increased the number of performances of Shakespeare's plays at Drury Lane, Covent Garden, and the New Haymarket until they comprised 14.0%, 17.0%, and 22.2% of the total. In 1737-8, after the Licensing Act had closed all the playhouses except Drury Lane and Covent Garden, 27.7% of the performances at Covent Garden were Shakespearian. *Richard II* was brought out on 6 February 1738 and repeated nine times in little more than a month; a

---

J. J. Fillinham, Thomas Wright, Roach Smith, and F. W. Fairholt. Frederick Boase replied that Purland practised as a dentist from 1830 to 1881, residing for the last 30 years in Mortimer Street, Cavendish Square. "Calcuttensis" reports that he saw an *os calcis* of Edward IV in Purland's possession, and "A. H." adds that he knew Purland when in Wilson Street, Finsbury, where he distracted young patients with ingenious gadgets moved by clockwork.

[0] The identification of Purland's hand is confirmed by notations in *Alsatian eccentricities, 1700-1782, collected by T. Purland*, "Being a collection of cuttings from newspapers, containing relations of murders and robberies, reports of trials, dying speeches, together with portraits of celebrated criminals, views etc.", British Museum shelflist 1243.k, 2 vol. 4°. Apparently the Museum did not purchase Purland's collection of water colors of Vauxhall Gardens or his notes thereon.

[7] On the scrap of the original cover is a scrawl that Miss Laetitia Kennedy-Skipton of the Folger staff doubtfully reads as "Rob[t] Attkin". Another scrawl, occurring on the back of the sketch of the Combat Scene, suggests "Rob[t] Atkin" or "Atkins". On page 33 in the white space to the left of the center rule is more scribbling, this time in pencil and in a different hand. The only word may possibly be "Ireland". The writing differs greatly from that of W. H. Ireland, the forger. The same hand has doodled in the bottom margin of the page: "dp", "dper", "d". At the foot of p. 45, the hand has written "d O[?]d" and "d&", and in the top margin of p. 32, several forms of ampersand. In the left margin of p. 32 are "ds" and more doodling. There was a Mrs. Atkins (sometimes called Widow Atkins) at Covent Garden, the Haymarket, and Lincoln's Inn Fields in various capacities in the 1720's and 1730's; and in the 1750's there was a dancer named Atkins at Drury Lane; but there is no traceable connection between these people and *Richard II*. The scribbles do not look like the work of the kind of person who would pay to have a promptbook transcribed.

[8] See below for comments on its suppression.

[9] "The Shakespeare Ladies Club", *SQ*, VII (1956), 153-158. Scouten, *The London Stage, Part 3* (1961) I, cxlix-clii, discusses the Shakespearian revivals, names the plays that were revived with the number of performances, and in his calendar gives the casts; see also his "The Increase in Popularity of Shakespeare's Plays in the Eighteenth Century", *SQ*, VII (1956), 189-202.

benefit performance on 2 May was the last in that season. In the following year, there were four revivals. After the next revival, on 23 October 1739, the play vanished from the boards until Macready appeared in a more or less faithful version at Newcastle in 1812-3.[10]

John Roberts deserves a few words. On the testimony of Thomas Davies, it has been customary to identify him as the author of *An Answer to Mr. Pope's Preface to Shakespear . . . By a Stroling Player* (1729).[11] There is no doubt that Davies, who was an actor at the Haymarket in 1736 and was always closely connected with the stage, had opportunity to know Roberts, and there is no reason to question his attribution of the pamphlet.[12]

If Roberts wrote *An Answer,* he must have had good store of audacity, for he begins his attack with a clever misquotation of the *Dunciad Variorum,* I, 5-6, and gives his readers considerable amusement by his mock-modest ridicule of Pope's judgment in the matter under discussion. Roberts' defense of actors reveals that he had used a Shakespeare Folio, a Jonson Folio, Heywood's *Apology for Actors,* Gerard Langbaine, and Sir Richard Baker—to name some of the more important sources of his information about Tudor and Stuart actors. He was surprisingly well read in seventeenth-century drama.

In the years between 1721 and 1750, there were several men named Roberts in the London theaters: a box keeper at Goodman's Fields in 1731; a dancer at Covent Garden in 1736 and a singer there in 1743 and afterwards; a singer named Ellis Roberts[12a] at Drury Lane, who is named in the same bill as "Mr. Roberts" for 5 May 1733. Usually it is possible to distinguish between these people and the Mr. J. Roberts who had a benefit at Covent Garden on 17 May 1739 and whom I take to be "Roberts the player" of Davies and the scribe of *Richard II.* He is first named among actors at Drury Lane in 1721-2, but the first named role recorded is that of Roberto in *Love in a Forest* on 9 January 1723 at Drury Lane.[13] He was a minor actor, moving from Drury Lane for a season to Hay-

[10] See A. H. Scouten, *Part 3,* II, 701-706, for a notice derived from the *London Daily Post* of 6 Feb., which states that the play had not been acted "these Forty Years" and promises "proper decorations. Likewise a New Prologue address'd to the Ladies." This is probably the prologue printed in the *Daily Post* of 10 Feb. Scouten gives the original cast: King—Delane; York—Stephens; Gaunt—Johnson; Bolingbroke—Ryan; Norfolk—Walker; Carlisle—Chapman; Aumerle—Hallam; Salisbury—Lyon; Scroop—Aston; Bushy—Rosco; Bagot—Salway; Green—Arthur; Northumberland—Bridgewater; Piercy—Hale; Ross—Ridout; Willoughby—A. Ryan; Surry—Houghton; Fitzwalter—Stevens; Earl Marshall—Mullart; Queen—Mrs. Horton; Dutchess of York—Mrs. Hallam; Dutchess of Gloster—Mrs. James. To these, Thomas Davies adds three other names: Richard Yates as the attendant who fetches a mirror, Michael Stoppelaer as the Abbot of Westminster, and Nathanael Clarke as the Groom (*Dramatic Miscellanies,* I (1784), 175, 180, 192).

[11] Writing of the London theaters during the time when Wilks, Booth, and Cibber were managing Drury Lane, Davies describes the indignation of the public that Wilks should advance his protege, John Mills, at the expense of older and better actors, such as Booth and George Powell, and records that "Roberts the player, author of a letter to Mr. Pope concerning some passages in his protege, John Mills, at the expense of older and better actors, such as Booth and George Powell, (*Dramatic Miscellanies,* II, 132).

[12] Some difficulty arises, however, in the acceptance of Roberts as an eyewitness of the event recounted by Davies. Though Mills lived until 1736, Powell's last season was 1714, and it is easier to believe that Roberts (who first appears in theatrical records in 1721) handed on to Davies a story that circulated among theatrical people than that, as a boy, he should have heard the outburst.

[12a] This is perhaps the Roberts who sang at Covent Garden on 26 Oct. 1737, 3 Jan. 1738, etc, but Scouten lists no singer of this name at *Part 3,* II, 680.

[13] Emmett L. Avery, ed., *The London Stage, Part 2* (1960), II, 638, 704 and *passim.* See also Scouten, *Part III, passim,* and George Winchester Stone, ed., *Part 4* (1962), *passim.* Prof. Avery, who has ransacked his notes in my behalf, directs attention to a passage on p. 6 of *The Theatric*

market (before 9 Nov. 1730), then back to Drury Lane in 1731, and after March 1734 to Covent Garden; in 1735-6 he went to the New Haymarket. Here, surprisingly enough, Fielding assigned him comic leads in such plays as *Pasquin*. It is unnecessary to follow his career in detail. There are intervals when his name is not to be found in the casts of any of the theaters, and it has been suggested that he had accidents or misfortune or sickness.[14] Perhaps it was during one of his periods of inactivity on the stage that Roberts marked the copy of *Richard II* and copied the two diagrams. Roberts is listed at Covent Garden from 1737 to 1743, but Prof. Avery informs me that by 1740 he was being paid only 5/- each acting day. The last notice of him is his inclusion in a company of London actors performing at Richmond and Twickenham in the summer of 1750.[15]

Roberts' wife was an actress. Her maiden and baptismal names are unknown, and she may have been on the stage earlier than the first performance recorded under her married name. This was at Richmond on 29 June 1724, when she had the very small part of Cherry in *The Beaux Stratagem*—Roberts was at the same theater in three plays in July. She may also have been a dancer in her early years (see the Drury Lane season for 1730-1). The couple appeared frequently, but not always, at the same theaters. They also played in the booths during Bartholomew Fair and the Southwark Fair.[16] And they were from

Squabble; or, the P—ntees (1733):
> Next *Rob—ts* grave, and slow, moves surly on
> With Arms across, and damns th'ungrateful Town:
> Dull, droning, one long irksome Stile he keeps,
> Drawling he dreams, and the tir'd Audience sleeps;
> Imperfect too, with Spleen and Vapours vext,
> He gravely asks the Prompter—*What is next?*

This is less favorable than the estimate in Thomas Cooke's *Comedian, or Philosophical Enquirer* (Oct. 1732, p. 39), which calls him "a just Speaker, but he seems to want Strength of Voice to go thro a passionate Part". For this reference and several others about Roberts and his wife, I am indebted to Prof. Philip Highfill. Aaron Hill entertained enough hope for Roberts to address one of his Original Letters to him on 3 Nov. 1733. This praises his carriage, the harmony, distinctness, and articulation of his speech, and his gravity but suggests that he improve his breathing to avoid a cracking voice, advises him to acquire "the musical variation, which will flow from a change, with the changing passions", and urges "a gayer, shorter, less deliberate, and more lively *tread*, according to the spirited fierceness, or soft amorous vivacity, of the part" he acts in (*Works* (1753), I, 168-170).

[14] A benefit performance was given for him at Drury Lane on 28 Jan. 1732, he being then "Confined in the Fleet Prison" (*London Stage, Part 3*, I, 186). See also a letter in *The Daily Advertiser* of 2 May 1737:

> Sir,
> As at every one of our Theatres this Day, there is a Benefit for Persons under Misfortune, 'tis humbly hop'd that the more humane Pursuers of Pleasure will suspend their Curiosity for Vaux Hall for one Day, (out of a hundred) in Favour of so many Unfortunates, who have but the Chance of one single Night to relieve them from Afflictions which perhaps they have long labour'd under. And, as I have somewhere read,
> > So humane Worth to God like Heights they'll raise,
> > For the Preserver shares the Maker's Praise
> I believe it is fully known, without troubling you with farther Particulars, that among the Number above mention'd, is included
>
> Hay-Market   Sir,
> Theatre   Your very humble Servant,
>   John Roberts.

The New Haymarket bill for 2 May offers *The Fatal Curiosity*, etc., "For the Entertainment of the Antient and Honourable Society of Non-Common Pleas." For the Benefit of Mr. J. Roberts.

[15] Sybil Rosenfeld, *Strolling Players & Drama in the Provinces 1660-1765* (1939), p. 296.

[16] One of the clippings pasted into *Richard II* gives notice that Mr. Fielding of Drury Lane

time to time strolling players. The Swansea Corporation collected 5/- from "Mr. Roberts the player" in 1732-3 for the use of the upstairs room in the Town Hall.[17] In 1733, he was with a mixed company from the London theaters at Canterbury; and in 1740 he appeared there in such roles as Macbeth and Lear. He was with the Duke of Grafton's company at Norwich in 1735, playing Othello and similar roles, and he returned to Norwich in 1743. In one visit to Norwich, Mrs. Roberts played Anne to his Richard III.[18] In London, Roberts never had roles that equalled in importance those assigned to his wife at the height of her career. Between 1737 and 1744, for example, she was appearing at Drury Lane as Belvidera in *Venice Preserv'd*, as Andromache in Ambrose Philips' *Distrest Mother*, and as the Queen in *Richard III* opposite David Garrick.[19] When a group of players revolted from Drury Lane in 1744, Mrs. Roberts remained loyal and even secured a substantial loan for Fleetwood the manager. When order was restored, Fleetwood attempted to weasel out of paying the debt, refused to allow Mrs. Roberts her articled benefit, denied her payment of a large amount of back salary, and then fired her. For his ingratitude and dishonesty, he was attacked bitterly in two pamphlets of 1744, both of which pay high tribute to Mrs. Roberts' abilities as an actress, and one of which advocates casting her as Lady Macbeth, the Queen in *Hamlet*, etc.[20] During the next season, Mrs. Roberts made a single recorded appearance with Theophilus Cibber's short-lived company at the Haymarket, "her 1st appearance there for 12 years".[21] She is next heard of among a large group of minor actors in 1748-9;[22] and the last trace that I have found of her is in a company brought from London to Maidstone by Wignall in June 1757.[23]

The revival of *Richard II* at Covent Garden in 1738 is generally attributed, as we have seen, to the mysterious Shakespeare Ladies Club. But with all the canon to chose from, why did John Rich select *Richard II*, a play whose history

---

plans to present *The Beggar's Wedding* at his booth in the George Inn Yard at Smithfield during Bartholomew Fair and names Mrs. Roberts in the cast (cf. *London Stage, Part 2*, II, 1042, for 23 August 1729). The other news clipping announces that Fielding's, Hippisley's, and Hall's booth at Smithfield will continue performances of *The Emperor of China* "till Tuesday next", with Roberts playing Emperor (cf. *London Stage, Part 3*, I, 153, for 8 Sept. 1731). See also Sybil Rosenfeld, *The Threatres of the London Fairs in the 18th Century* (1960), *passim*. She finds Roberts and his wife at Penkethman's booth at Smithfield in 1724 (p. 28). They disappear from her records after 1734 until Roberts is named to play King Henry in *Fair Rosamond* for Adam Hallam at Bartholomew Fair in 1741 (see Scouten, *Part 3*, II, 920).

[17] Cecil Price, *The English Theatre in Wales* (1948), p. 7.

[18] Rosenfeld, *Strolling Players*, pp. 58, 60, 225, 226, 234, 235. Miss Rosenfeld notes than an actress named Anne Roberts died in Norwich in 1740; her relationship to John Roberts is unknown.

[19] During this flourishing period, Mrs. Roberts had her own house in Duke Street, near Lincoln's Inn Fields as we learn from the announcements of her benefits on 30 April 1739, 16 March 1742, and 24 March 1743. In the first of these, she was Mary Queen of Scots in *The Albion Queens*; in the second, Berinthia in *The Relapse*; and in the third, Calista in *The Fair Penitent* to Garrick's Lothario. The receipts in 1742 were £130, strong testimony to her popularity. See Scouten, *Part 3*, II, 772, 976, and 1043-1044. Prof. Avery writes me that Mrs. Roberts was the subject of a poem in *The London Daily Post* of 26 Sept. 1737. But when she appeared as Queen Elizabeth in *Richard III* on 1 Oct. 1737, she was "hiss'd", Scouten, *Part 3*, II, 684.

[20] *The Disputes between the Directors of D--y, and the Pit Potentates* (1744), pp. 16-19; *An Impartial Examen of the Present Contests between the Town and the Manager of the Threatre* . . . (1744), pp. 16, 18, 19.

[21] John Genest, *Some Account of the English Stage* (Bath, 1832), IV, 169. The date was 20 Oct. 1744.

[22] Stone, *Part 4*, I, 61.

[23] Rosenfeld, *Strolling Players*, p. 254.

was so tumultuous? He can hardly be supposed to have known that in the time of Queen Elizabeth "this tragedy was played 40[tie] times in open streets and houses", "the Erle [of Essex] himself being so often present . . . with great applause giving countenance and lyking to the same"[24] or that on the eve of Essex's attempted rebellion his followers paid a bounty to Shakespeare's company for a performance of the play. There may have been no one to tell Rich that on 14 December 1680, in a time of violent political controversy, a version of *Richard II* by Nahum Tate was forbidden performance by the Lord Chamberlain. Undeterred, Tate changed the locus of action (much as Massinger had done with the play now called *Believe as you List*), and it was given under a new name, *The Sicilian Usurper,* and performed twice (18 and 19 Jan. 1681) before authority penetrated the deception and stopped the production.[25] Tate's introductory letter in the quarto of 1681 disclaims awareness of any parallels between the current political situation and events in the play, but G. C. D. Odell[26] was not the only reader to feel that the author did protest too much. In a later period of political disturbance, Lewis Theobald made an adaptation of *Richard II* that managed to escape governmental censure. It opened on 10 December 1719 at Lincoln's Inn Fields and was acted for the last time in the autumn of 1721 (see above).

During the next twenty or thirty years, England was in political turmoil, and dramatic and journalistic attacks upon the government exceeded in ferocity and brutality—but also in wit—anything published today.[27] Fielding's *Pasquin* (5 March 1736; 60 performances by 26 May) and *The Historical Register* (21 March 1737) burlesqued and satirized the government so pointedly that during one performance Sir Robert Walpole went back stage and "corrected" one of the comedians "with his own Hands very severely".[28]

In the following summer, the five hundred and seventy-fourth number (2 July 1737) of *The Country Journal: or, the Craftsman,* featured a letter by "C. C. P. L." to the pseudonymous editor, Caleb d'Anvers, with a sharp attack on the government in the guise of advice about enforcing the Bill for Licensing the Stage. Ostensibly the author was Colley Cibber, Poet Laureate, but within a short time the writer was identified with almost certainty as Nicholas Amhurst. The course of events may be followed in the pages of *The Gentleman's Magazine.* The number for July 1737 gives the Earl of Chesterfield's speech against the Licensing Bill (pp. 409-411), notices and abstracts in cautious terms the letter of C.C.P.L., and adds that the printer of *The Craftsman* is in custody (p. 430). Before 23 July, the premises of the printer were seized, including his account books, publication of *The Craftsman* was stopped for a week, and several people were imprisoned (*G.M.,* pp. 437-438).

Subjected to vitriolic attack in the columns of *The Daily Gazetteer* and *The Gentleman's Magazine,* the writers in *The Craftsman* protested the innocence

[24] E. K. Chambers, *William Shakespeare* (1930), II, 326-327, 323. The Deposition Scene was not included in the three quartos printed in the lifetime of the Queen but appeared in the second issue of Q 4 (1608).

[25] William Van Lennep and E. L. Avery, edd., *The London Stage, Part 1,* under date.)

[26] *Shakespeare from Betterton to Irving* (1921), I, 56-59.

[27] For a summary account of the fermenting theatrical situation, see Scouten, *Part 3,* especially "The Licensing Act", "Repertory", and "The Shakesperian Revival", I, xlviii ff., cxxxviii ff., and cxlix ff.

[28] Scouten, *Part 3,* I. l.

of their intentions (*G.M.,* pp. 499-500) and named Sir Roger L'Estrange (1616-1704) as the type of minister who endangers liberty (*G.M.,* pp. 500-501). Then they entered a general defense of liberty of the press (*G.M.,* Sept., pp. 551-552) and proceeded to a discussion of the abuse by Princes of their authority, with pointed quotations from *Measure for Measure* ("O 'tis excellent To have a giant's strength; but it is tyrannous To use it like a giant. . . .) (pp. 557-559). As Haines, printer of *The Craftsman,* Amhurst, the reputed author of the offending letter of 2 July 1737, and John Kelly, supposed author of *Fog's Journal,* waged their battles in the courts, *Old Common Sense* (No. 45, 10 Dec.) reported at length the trial in New York of Peter Zenger and printed the arguments of his attorney, Andrew Hamilton, in defense of freedom of the press (*G.M.,* Dec. 1737, pp. 749-750), and *The Craftsman* devoted its No. 602 (21 Jan. 1738) to Zenger, with a recommendation of the relevant tracts just published in London (*G.M.,* Jan. 1738, pp. 35-36). Such were the laws of the land that Amhurst, the author, was released after a short imprisonment, but Haines, the printer, was found guilty of printing a libel and sentenced to imprisonment for a year and to a fine of £200 and was required to find security for his good behavior for seven years (*G.M.,* May 1738, p. 274). Amidst the war of the journals, *The Gentleman's Magazine* reported the opinion of *Common Sense* (No. 65) that Haines's attorneys had "not much strengthened the arguments used by Mr. Hamilton "for Mr Zenger the Printer of New-York; whose Tryal, therefore, no Printer ought to be without. . . ." It continued:

> If the Judges make new Laws by an ill Construction, or an ill Execution of old ones, I conclude, that Parliaments will soon be found useless, and the Liberty of the People an inconvenience to the Government. ('*G.M.,* April 1738, p. 208)

As You Like It and *King John* were quoted, and even some of the "political aphorisms of my Lord Bacon" were reprinted "to keep awake the Anger of the Gazeteers, so much offended with some quotations from Shakespeare" (*G.M.,* June 1738, pp. 297-298, 308-309).

Just what had the author of the letter of 2 July 1737 written that it started such a controversy, and what was his method of attack? He took the position that once a statute is on the books it should be enforced and then set out to demonstrate his qualifications to serve as licenser of plays. Old plays and new, he argued, were likely to offend chiefly in the areas of Politics, Divinity, and Bawdry; he chose Politics for his domain, and gave a series of passages apt for inclusion in an *Index Expurgatorius.* The plays quoted from were Jonson's *Sejanus,* Dryden's *Don Sebastian* and *All for Love,* Lee's *Rival Queens, or Alexander the Great,* George Sewell's *Sir Walter Raleigh,* and three plays by Shakespeare: *King John, 2 Henry IV,* and *Richard II.* Several of these had not been seen on a London stage for many years: *Sejanus, Don Sebastian,* and *Sir Walter Raleigh.* There had been seven performances of *The Rival Queens* in the previous season; six of *All for Love;* nine of *King John;* and one performance of Betterton's (?) adaptation of *2 Henry IV.* All four were performed in the 1737-8 season while the trial of Haines was in progress. As for *Richard II,* the announcement of its revival on 6 February 1738 stated that it had "not [been] acted these forty years". Perhaps, as the management claimed, the cause of the revival was the "Desire of several Ladies of Quality", but I suggest that Rich expected audiences to flock into the theater to see the play that had had a crucial role in the events leading to the prosecution of *The Craftsman* and its printer.

Shakespeare's *King John* is the first play to be examined in C.C.P.L.'s letter in *The Craftsman,* possibly on the assumption that Londoners might be expected to remember something of it from the nine performances earlier in the year. The writer continues:

> The next Play, that falls under my Consideration, is *the Life and Death of King* Richard *the 2d,* written by the *same Author;* which hath not been acted within my Memory, and I think never ought, without considerable Castrations and Amendments; for it not only represents an *obstinate, misguided Prince* depos'd by his *People,* which is agreeable enough to the Principles of the *Revolution;* but likewise contains several Passages, which the *disaffected* may turn to their Account.—I will mention only two or three.
>
> The *King,* speaking of the Duke of *Hereford,* (his Successor, by the Name of *Henry* the *4th)* makes the following Reflection upon his *Popularity.*
>
> > —Bagot and Greene
> > Observ'd his Courtship to the common People;
> > How He did seem to dive into their Hearts,
> > With humble and familiar Courtesie;
> > What Reverence He did throw away on Slaves,
> > Wooing poor Craftsmen with the Craft of Souls,
> > And patient under-bearing of his Fortune.

It is to be observed that the *King* had used the *Duke of Hereford* very ill; and though He was neither his *Son,* nor his *lawful Heir,* malicious People may apply it to *Princes,* between whom there is a much nearer Relation. I need say no more; but shall leave it to your Judgment whether this Passage ought not to be expunged, as well as the whole first Scene of the second Act; particularly where *John of Gaunt,* Duke of *Lancaster,* foretels the Fate of the King, his Nephew, just before his Death. As You formerly quoted this prophetical Speech in one of your Papers, I shall, repeat only the Conclusion of it.

> This Land of such dear Souls, this dear-dear Land,
> Dear for her Reputation through the World,
> Is now leas'd out, (I dye pronouncing it)
> Like to a Tenement, or pelting Farm.
> England, bound in with the triumphant Sea,
> Whose rocky Shore beats back the envious Siege
> Of watery Neptune, is bound in with Shame,
> With INKY BLOTS, and ROTTEN PARCHMENT BONDS.
> That England, that was wont to conquer others,
> Hath made a shameful Conquest of itself.

This is such a general Reflection upon my *dear Country,* and the whole Mystery of *Treaty-making,* that I think it ought not to be suffer'd to appear even in *Print,* much less to be pronounced upon the *Stage.*

In another Part of the same Scene, *old Gaunt* addresses the *King*, in this licentious Manner, which will likewise admit of very bad Constructions.

> Thy Death-bed is no lesser than the Land,
> Wherein Thou lyest in Reputation sick,
> And Thou too careless, patient as Thou art,
> Commit'st thy annointed Body to the Cure
> Of those Physicians, that first wounded Thee;
> A thousand Flatterers sit within thy Crown,
> Whose Compass is no bigger than thy Hand,
> And yet incaged in so small a Verge,
> The Waste is no whit lesser than thy Land.

At the latter End of this Scene, the following Dialogue passes between *Northumberland, Willoughby* and *Ross;* which is more intolerable than all the rest.

> Nor.   The King is not Himself, but basely led
>   By Flatterers, and what They will inform
>   Meerly in Hate 'gainst any of us all,
>   That will the King severely prosecute
>   'Gainst us, our Lives, our Children and our Heirs.
> Ross.   The Commons hath He pill'd with grievous Taxes,
>   And quite lost their Hearts. The Nobles hath he fin'd
>   For antient Quarrels, and quite lost their Hearts.
> Will.   And daily new Exactions are devis'd;
>   But what O'God's Name doth become of this?
> Nor.   Wars have not wasted it; for warr'd He hath not,
>   But basely yielded upon Compromise
>   That, which his Ancestors atchiev'd with Blows.
>   More hath He spent in Peace than They in Wars.

This wants no Comment. . . .

All the lines quoted in *The Craftsman* were spoken in the 1738 revival except the first seven (those at I. iv. 23-29).

The absence of contemporary reviews of the production of *Richard II* in the journals is partly compensated by the report of Thomas Davies:

> When this play was revived at the theatre in Convent-garden, about forty years since, the ancient ceremony which belonged to the single combat was very accurately observed, with all the decorations and arrangements proper to the appellant and respondent, the spectators and the judges. Amongst the latter, the king was seated in a throne of state. The combatants were dressed in complete armour. Two chairs, finely adorned, were placed on opposite sides of the lists: to these they retired after each of them had stood forth and spoken. Bolingbroke was acted by Ryan. Walker personated Mowbray. His helmet was laced so tightly under his chin, that, when he endeavoured to speak, nobody could understand him; and this obstacle occasioned a laugh from the audience: however, this was soon removed, and the actor was heard with attention. In their persons, dress, and demeanour, they presented something like an image of the old trial of right by duel. (*Dramatic Miscellanies*, I, 124-125)

As soon as Richard, intent upon his Irish expedition, had left the stage, the author introduces a political scene between the earl of Northumberland and the lords Willoughby and Ross, full of severe reflections upon the king's misconduct. The writing is not singularly good, but it was greatly distinguished by the particular behaviour of the audience, on the revival of this play, who applied almost every line that was spoken to the occurrences of the time, and to the measures and character of the ministry. (I, 150-151)

Davies then summarizes conditions in the quarrel with Spain and gives Sir Robert Walpole's fears of an insurrection in Scotland by the Scottish and English Tories and Jacobites, predicting, before his death in 1744, that the King would have to fight for his crown.

The more reluctant Walpole appeared to second the wishes of the merchants in commencing hostilities, the more clamorous the people were for letting loose the vengeance of the nation against the Spaniards. When this tragedy was, after being long forgotten, revived, the cry for war was the highest, and the spectators were ready to apply all that was uttered in the theatre to the transactions of the day and to the ministry. The dialogue of Northumberland and his friends furnished ample materials for political innuendo and application. There was in Bridgewater, who personated Northumberland, a most grave and solemn manner of delivering a sentiment, which dwelt fully upon the attentive hearer. When he pronounced the following words,

> The king is not himself, but basely led
> By flatterers,—

the noise from the clapping of hands and clattering of sticks was loud and boisterous. And when Ross said,

> The earl of Wiltshire hath the state in farm, —

it was immediately applied to Walpole, with the loudest shouts and huzzas I ever heard. Likewise the following observation of Northumberland, that the king's revenue was not diminished by war, was met, by the audience, with redoubled shouts—

> War hath not wasted it; for warr'd he hath not.
> More hath he spent in peace than they in war.

The two following remarkable lines, spoken by Willoughby and Northumberland, were heard with a dead and respectful silence:—
WILLOUGHBY. The king's grown bankrupt, like a broken man.
NORTHUMBERLAND. Reproach, and dissolution, hangeth over him.
(I, 152 ff.)

Davies' description of the audience reaction to the topical hits of the play seem ample confirmation of the hypothesis that the choice of *Richard II* for revival was not an accident. The Covent Garden management were venturing greatly in giving the public opportunity to echo the attacks of *The Craftsman*.[29]

What text was used in the revival of *Richard II* at Covent Garden? The pre-Wars promptbook of the King's Men can hardly have survived, and so the

---

[29] This attack at Covent Garden must have seemed the basest ingratitude to Walpole, for his government's Licensing Act had given the two patent theaters a monopoly.

promptbook of 1738 must have been a marked copy or a transcript of one of the editions of the play—a quarto, a folio, Rowe, Pope, or Theobald, or one of the inexpensive reprints of Pope's text issued between 1734 and 1736. A clue is provided at I. iii. 268 in a marginal note by Roberts: "Desunt 14 lines vide Pope's Edition."[30] And sure enough, the text used proves to be that of Pope. In general, his emendations are accepted, his wording of the stage directions is adopted, lines that he relegated to footnotes are often marked for omission, and twice (at I. iii. 129 and II. ii. 76) lines that Pope had restored from Qq 1-5 are transcribed in the margin. At I. iii. 267, however, Roberts did not insert the fourteen lines referred to in his marginal note, despite his interlinear memo quoted above, nor did he insert four lines Pope had restored from the early quartos at III. iii. 29. There is no comment at I. iii. 238, where Pope had restored two out of four lines missing from Ff Q 6.

The acting version is considerably shorter than the text of the Folios. Three scenes are omitted entirely: I. iv, in which Richard, Aumerle, Greene, and Bagot jest about Bolingbroke's departure and Richard goes to visit the dying Gaunt with the wish that "we may make hast, and come too late"; II. iv, where a Captain tells Salisbury of the dispersal of the Welsh troops; and V. iv, in which Exton decides to murder Richard. Approximately 285 other lines are marked for omission. Sententious passages, speeches of passion that do not forward the action (e.g., I. ii. 58-74, V. i. 37-50), couplets—especially those concluding a speech or a scene—, word-play (as where Gaunt rings changes on his name at II. i. 73-93), and verses rich in imagery make up the bulk of the deletions. At V. iii. 111, Bolingbroke puts an end to the pleas of the Duchess of York with the words, "Good Aunt, arise, I pardon him" (borrowing from line 131) and continues as in line 137. The omission of the Groom's visit in V. v speeds the play towards its close and also eliminates one speaking part (as Exton is eliminated at V. iv and V. v. 113-118, and a servant-messenger at the end of II. ii). The adaptation was made by a practised hand for the purpose of pruning whatever might retard the action or sound antiquated to the audience.

Most of the changes in diction are the substitution of *Heaven('s)* for *God('s)*. There are a few modernizations (*unavoydable* for *unavoyded*); where Pope has restored a reading from the early quartos or corrected grammar, the acting text often agrees.

One minor change remains for consideration. An entrance direction at II. iii. 67 names "Barkely", and Northumberland says, "It is my Lord of Barkely, as I ghesse." The newcomer, *"Bark."*, speaks only twice, at II. iii. 69 and 74. In Roberts' transcript, "Surrey" and "Sur." are substituted. Since Barkely appears nowhere else, the change may have been made to eliminate a speaking part, for Surrey has a prominent place in IV. i (where, however, he is linked with Richard's party). If this were the reason, Northumberland's line should have been altered correspondingly. Perhaps Roberts overlooked the changed reading.[31]

---

[30] Actually Qq 1-5 supply 26 lines that are not in Ff Q 6; Pope disregarded 12 of these.

[31] It seems unlikely that there were political reasons for the change in 1738, for James, the third earl of Berkeley, had died in 1736 and his son Augustus, the fourth earl, does not appear to have gained prominence until 1745, when he held a command against the rebels. It is true that an uncle of the third earl, George Berkeley, was a member of Parliament for many years; of him, the *DNB* states that "He voted against the measures of Sir Robert Walpole." Could there have

It has already been mentioned that the stage directions have generally been altered to agree with Pope. The only innovation is, I think, at II. iii. 80, where York enters "attended". This wording occurs in print first in Capell (*Comedies, Histories and Tragedies,* 1767-8). Readers who are familiar with promptbooks of the eighteenth century will not be surprised to find a scattering of specific indications for entrances. Thus, after I. i. 19, Roberts has written "M.D.P.S."— Middle Door, Prompt Side (*S* is covered by a blot of ink). After the initial stage direction at II. ii is "P.S."; after line 40, "O.P.", and again after the stage direction at line 71, "O.P." At the opening of II. iii, Bolingbroke and Northumberland enter "O.P."

There are two changes of importance. The heading of I. iii, *"Scaena Tertia",* is altered to *"Scaena* The Lists at Coventry."; and the initial scene of Act IV is marked: *"Actus Quartus, Scaena Prima.* Parliament Scene." (The unitalicized words are in manuscript.) To right and left of the added words at IV. i (but not at I. iii) is a circle with dot in the center to indicate a change of scenery.

The sketches by Roberts that face these two pages of text are the earliest of their kind, and they have an authority far greater than the engraved illustrations in Rowe's edition of Shakespeare in 1709 or those in the similarly illustrated editions of other Elizabethan and Jacobean playwrights published about this time.[32] Some of these have been thought to derive from sketches made during rehearsals or performance, and this may well be the case; but all have suffered an inevitable sea change (great or small) at the hands of engravers.[33]

In both of the sketches of settings at Covent Garden, the chair of state occupies the center of the back stage. Davies spoke with approval of the historical accuracy of the Combat Scene (see p. 170). The arrangement was traditional. The setting of the Parliament Scene has high documentary support. At back stage center is the canopied chair of state, approached by three steps. A Cardinal sits on a stool at each side of the bottom step. Extending down stage is a long table, on which rest the Purse and the Mace, symbols of Majesty, with the Chancellor at the upper end, a Secretary at the lower, and a Judge seated on a cushion on either side. Along a diagonal line from near the foot of the dais to the outer front of the stage are ranged, on one side, the robed figures of Bolingbroke, Northumberland, Percy, and Fitzwater, and then 12 Bishops and 25 Civilians. Opposite, in similar formation, are Aumerle, Surrey, Willoughby, and Scroop, robed; then Carlisle, the Abbot of Westminster, and Civilians; next to the Civilians are Fryars with crosses, and at lower left are Gentleman Usher and Black Rod. This was such a sight as was familiar to those who had sat in Parliament or had seen the engraving of Queen Elizabeth seated in Parliament that faces page 126 of Robert Glover's *Nobilitas Politica vel Civilis* (1608) or the revised plate with James I substituted for Elizabeth, facing page 68 of

---

been a desire to avoid implicating him? The name "Surrey" was innocuous, the last holder of that title having died in 1554.

[32] More authoritative, too, than the engraved frontispieces to the contemporary plays published separately in the first half of the eighteenth century.

[33] See Merchant, pp. 20-55, for a discussion of theatrical elements in engraved illustrations of English plays before 1740. See also A. C. Sprague, *Shakespeare and the Actors* (1945), especially pp. 162-169, for some of the illustrations in Rowe's Shakespeare. The Henry Peacham drawing of some of the *dramatis personae* of *Titus Andronicus* however suggestive of stage costume, cannot be considered to represent any stage setting seen by an Elizabethan audience (see Chambers, I, 312ff., and Plate XI).

Thomas Milles, *The Catalogue of Honor* (1610). The same setting was perhaps more readily accessible in the engraved frontispiece of Sir Simon D'Ewes, *The Journals of All the Parliaments During the Reign of Queen Elizabeth . . .* (1682).[34] What the theater provided, and what the audience expected, was a traditional setting. And its focus was the chair of state, the throne. Its position was central and dominating, and placed elsewhere it would, I think, have invited criticism.

Comment on the location of the thrones leads inevitably into a discussion of their use and placing on the English stage, not only at this time but during the Restoration period and, earlier, in the Elizabethan. It is not difficult to establish the fact that during the last decades of the seventeenth century and afterwards the front curtain was often lowered to cover the setting of the stage for formal scenes. Thrones could in these conditions be brought on and removed at will. There was no need to let them stand on the stage throughout a performance, ignored alike by actors and audience except when in use. The practice may have been different on the earlier platform stages. Jonson's reference to the coming down of a creaking throne has influenced some writers to argue that such chairs of state were always, or customarily, lowered through the trapdoor in the heavens to a place at the center of the back stage. Others think that they were placed on stage before a play began, there to remain unnoticed save when required in the business of a scene. Yet others think that thrones were ordinarily placed in the closed inner stage before the opening of a scene and removed after the curtains closed at the scene's ending. It has also been suggested than on occasion they appeared in the upper stage or atop the (perhaps temporary) structure that extended forward from the façade of the tiring house.[35] I find especially cogent Prof. Beckerman's discussion of the staging of group scenes at the Globe:

> It is apparent . . . that in the case of 156 of the 166 group scenes, the organizing principle is ceremony or duty. Movement and arrangement, though not formal, are not artificial. Rather, they reflect circumstances of Elizabethan life. (P. 171)

And so I like to think that the attempt in 1738 to recapture the ceremonial effects of the Combat and Parliament Scenes is a continuation of an age-old stage tradition. In the Elizabethan productions of *Lear* I. i, of *Hamlet* I. ii, II. ii, and V. ii, of *Henry V,* I. ii, of *Merchant* IV. i, and elsewhere, the throne, the chair of state, should have been upstage center, flanked by appropriate dignitaries and attendants, as represented in Glover and Milles and D'Ewes—and in the sketches of the Covent Garden stage for *Richard II* in 1738. These are a reflection of some of the circumstances of Elizabethan life, and by their very ceremoniousness they lend an awful dignity: trial by combat, with an appeal to Heavenly Justice; and the impious uncrowning of an anointed king, God's vicegerent in England.

---

[34] It served also as the frontispiece of his *A Compleat Journal of the Votes, Speeches and Debates, Both of the House of Lords and House of Commons . . .* (1693).

[35] See, for example, George F. Reynolds, *The Staging of Elizabethan Plays at the Red Bull Theater, 1605-1625* (1940), and "*Hamlet* at the Globe", *SS 9*, pp. 49-53; John C. Adams, *The Globe Playhouse* (1943), pp. 192, 335-339; C. Walter Hodges, *The Globe Restored* (1953); Irwin Smith, *Shakespeare's Globe Playhouse* (1956), p. 111; Bernard Beckerman, *Shakespeare at the Globe* (1962), pp. 165, 171, 209, and Appendix C, ii; and Merchant, pp. 180-181.

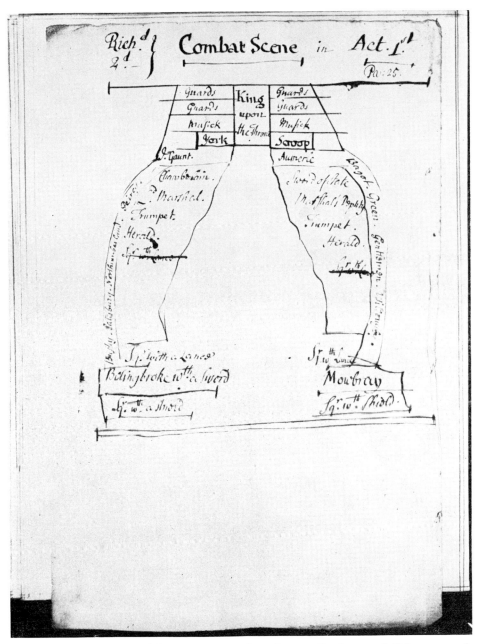

The Combat Scene in *Richard II* as staged at Covent Garden on 6 February 1738.
Courtesy of The Folger Shakespeare Library.

But since correction lyeth in those hands
Which made the fault that we cannot correct,
Put we our quarrell to the will of heaven,
Who when they see the houres ripe on earth,
Will raine hot vengeance on offenders heads.

Dut. Findes brotherhood in thee no sharper spurre?
Hath love in thy old blood no living fire?
Edward's seven sonnes (whereof thy selfe art one)
Were as seven vialles of his Sacred blood.
Or seven faire branches springing from one roote:
Some of those seven are dride by natures course,
Some of those branches by the destinies cut:
But *Thomas*, my deere Lord, my life, my Gloster,
One Viall full of *Edwards* Sacred blood,
One flourishing branch of his most Royall roote)
Is crack'd, and all the precious liquor spilt:
Is hackt downe, and his summer leaves all vaded
By Envies hand, and Murders bloody Axe.
Ah *Gaunt*? His blood was thine that bed, that wombe,
That mettle, that selfe-mould that fashion'd thee,
Made him a man: and though thou liv'st, and breath'th,
Yet art thou slaine in him: thou doest consent
In some large measure to thy Fathers death,
In that thou seest thy wretched brother dye,
Who was the modell of thy Fathers life.
Call it not patience (*Gaunt*) it is despaire,
In suffering thus thy brother to be slaughter'd,
Thou shew'st the naked pathway to thy life,
Teaching sterne murther how to butcher thee:
That which in meane men we intitle patience
Is pale cold cowardise in noble brests:
What shall I say, to safegard thine owne life,
The best way is to venge my Glosters death.

Gaunt. Heavens is the quarrell: for heavens substitute
His Deputy annoynted in his sight,
Hath caus'd his death, the which if wrongfully
Let heaven revenge: for I may never lift
An angry arme against his Minister.

Dut. Where then (alas) may I complaine my selfe?

Gau. To heaven, the widdowes Champion to defence.

Dut. Why then I will: farewell old *Gaunt*.
Thou go'st to Coventry, there to behold
Our Cosine Hertford, and fell Mowbray fight:
O sit my husbands wrongs on Herefords speare,
That it may enter butcher Mowbrayes brest:
Or if misfortune misse the first carreere,
Be Mowbrayes sinnes so heavy in his bosome,
That they may breake his foaming Coursers backe,
And throw the Rider headlong in the Lists,
A Caytiffe recreant to my Cosine Hereford:
Farewell old *Gaunt*, thy sometimes brothers wife
With her companion Greefe, must end her life.

Gau. Sister fare well: I must to Couentrie,
As much good stay with thee, as go with me.

Dut. Yet one word more: Greefe boundeth where it
Not with the emptie hollownesse, but weight: (falls,
I take my leave, before I have begun,
For sorrow ends not when it seemeth done.
Commend me to my brother *Edward Yorke*.
Loe, this is all: nay yet depart not so,
Though this be all, do not so quickly goe,
I shall remember more. Bid him, Oh, what?
With all good speed at Plashie visit me.
Alacke, and what shall good old *Yorke* there see
But empty lodgings, and unfurnish'd walles,
Vn-peopel'd Offices, untroden stones?

And what heare there for welcome, but my grones?
Therefore commend me, let him not come there,
To seeke out sorrow that dwels every where:
Desolate, desolate will I hence, and dye,
The last leave of thee, takes my weeping eye. *Exeunt.*

Scæna Tertia.

The Lists at Coventry.

Enter Marshall, and Aumerle.

Mar. My L. *Aumerle*, is *Harry Hereford* arm'd?

Aum. Yea, at all poynts, and longs to enter in.

Mar. The Duke of Norfolke, sprightfull and bold,
Stayes but the summons of the Appealants Trumpet.

Au. Why then the Champions, are prepar'd, and stay
For nothing but his Majesties approach. *Flourish.*

Enter King, Gaunt, Bushy, Bagot, Greene, & others: Then Mowbray in Armor, and Herauld.

Rich. Marshall, demand of yonder Champion
The cause of his arrivall heere in Armes,
Aske him his name, and orderly proceed
To sweare him in the justice of his cause.

Mar. In Gods Name, and the Kings, say who thou art,
And why thou com'st, thus knightly clad in Armes?
Against what man thou com'st, and what's thy quarrell,
Speake truely on thy knighthood, and thine oath,
As so defend thee heaven, and thy valour.

Mow. My name is Tho. *Mowbray*, Duke of Norfolke,
Who hither come engaged by my oath
(Which heaven defend a knight should violate)
Both to defend my loyalty and truth,
To God, my King, and his succeeding issue,
Against the Duke of Hereford, that appeales me:
And by the grace of God, and this mine arme,
To prove him (in defending of my selfe)
A Traitor to my God, my King, and me,
And as I truly fight, defend me heaven.

Tucket. Enter Hereford, and Herauld in Armor.

Rich. Marshall: Aske yonder Knight in Armes,
Both who hee is, and why he commeth hither,
Thus placed in habiliments of warre:
And formaly according to our Law
Depose him in the justice of his cause.

Mar. What is thy name? & wherefore com'st thou hither
Before King *Richard* in his Royall Lists?
Against whom com'st thou? and what's thy quarrell?
Speake like a true Knight, so defend thee heaven,

Bull. Harry of Hereford, Lancaster, and Derbie,
Am I: who ready here do stand in Armes,
To prove by heavens grace, and my bodyes valour,
In Lists, on *Thomas Mowbray* Duke of Norfolke,
That he's a Traitor foule and dangerous,
To God of heaven, King *Richard*, and to me,
And as I truely fight, defend me heaven.

Mar. On paine of death, no person be so bold,
Or daring hardie as to touch the Listes,
Except the Marshall, and such officers
Appointed to direct these faire designes.

Bull. Lord Marshall, let me kisse my Soveraigns hand,
And bow my knee before his Majestie:
For *Mowbray* and my selfe are like two men,
That vow a long and weary pilgrimage,

Then

C

A page of text in John Roberts' "transcript" of the Covent Garden prompt-book (1738). Courtesy of The Folger Shakespeare Library.

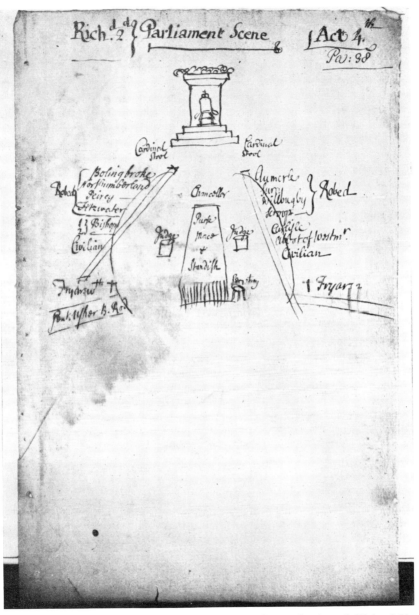

The Parliament (i.e. the Deposition) Scene in the production of *Richard II* at Covent Garden in 1738. Courtesy of The Folger Shakespeare Library.

Queen Elizabeth and Parliament, engraving in Robert Glover: *Nobilitas Politica vel Civilis* (1608). Courtesy of The Folger Shakespeare Library.

In recollecting the production, Davies emphasizes the use of "complete armour" by the two champions. Whence it was borrowed or whether it was authentic of the late fourteenth century is not known (Froissart tells that Bolingbroke's armor was made by Milanese smiths and Norfolk's by German craftsmen), but this must be recognized as a conspicuous example of the attempt at historical costume. As such, it lends weight to the arguments of Mr. Hal H. Smith that from Elizabethan times the theaters often used national or historic or emblematic costume to enhance dramatic effects.[36] When the Duke's company presented the Earl of Orrery's *Henry V* in 1664, "This Play", writes John Downes, "was Splendidly Cloath'd: The King [Harris], in the Duke of York's Coronation Suit: Owen Tudor [Betterton], in King Charle's [*sic*]: Duke of Burgundy, in the Lord of Oxford's, and the rest all New."[37] The verisimilitude was, I fancy, a continuation of Elizabethan stage practice and a striking anticipation of the ceremoniousness in Covent Garden's *Richard II*.

In its several ways, the 1738 revival of *Richard II* was an important event, and we may feel grateful to the unknown lover of the stage that employed John Roberts to prepare a text "Correct cum Libr' Theatr'".

The Folger Shakespeare Library

---

[36] "Some Principles of Elizabethan Costume", *Journal of the Warburg and Courtauld Institutes*, XXV (1963), 240-257.

[37] *Roscius Anglicanus* (1709), pp. 27-28.

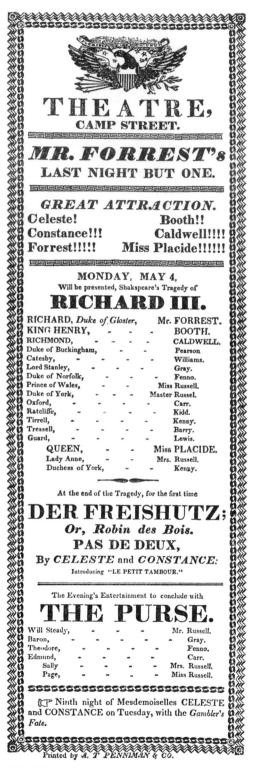

Playbill of the Camp Street Theatre, New Orleans, for 4 May 1829, featuring Edwin Forrest in *Richard III*, 5¼″ x 14⅛″. Reproduced by permission of The Folger Shakespeare Library.

Shakespeare's Revisions in
Titus Andronicus

JOHN CRANFORD ADAMS

HE "titus & ondronicus" entered by Henslowe as "ne" when acted by the Earl of Sussex's men on January 23, 1594, is almost certainly a revised version of an earlier play.[1] It can be demonstrated, I believe, that this earlier play had been designed for a stage consisting of a Platform and Gallery (substantially as shown in DeWitt's well-known sketch of the Swan), but in its extant form, preserved in Quartos of 1594, 1600, and 1611, and in the First Folio, a curtained rear stage also is required for several major episodes.

Titus Andronicus is composed in twelve scenes (fourteen in F1), all located in Rome and its immediate environs. The beginning action is longer, more varied, and theatrically bolder than anything Shakespeare had written previously. It is probably the first action in English dramatic history to employ three stages simultaneously.[2] Here is the opening direction:

> *Flourish. Enter the Tribunes and Senators Aloft And then enter Saturninus and his Followers at one doore, and Bassianus and his Followers at the other, with Drum & Colours.*[3]

This eye-filling spectacle is soon augmented by yet another Tribune:

> *Enter Marcus Andronicus aloft with the Crowne.*

At the lowest count, there are now five persons in the Gallery overlooking the two rival candidates and their cohorts on the main stage below. But there is to be a delay in the selection of the new emperor. The people of Rome have named Titus Andronicus as a third candidate, and in consequence the Senate has

---

[1] The complex textual history of this oft performed and much amended play is analyzed in detail by E. K. Chambers in *William Shakespeare*, I, 312-322, and more recently by W. W. Greg in *The Shakespeare First Folio*, pp. 203-209. The bibliographical assumptions in this present paper are based on Greg: specifically (1) that the newly revised prompt-book of 1594 may have contained a leaf that was not among Shakespeare's foul papers when these were supplied as copy for Q1, (2) that between 1600 and 1611 this prompt-book was replaced—"destruction through constant use . . . would be likely enough in the case of a manuscript that had been through the hands of four different companies", (3) that the substituted prompt-book was an annotated copy of Q2, and (4) that the Folio was printed from a copy of Q3 corrected by a scribe who manifestly had access to the second prompt-book, and may have had access to the original. As to the last point, Greg comments elsewhere (*ibid.*, p. 160): "If the prompt-book were only damaged or worn it would doubtless be preserved, even if it could not be used, for the sake of the license."

[2] *The Jew of Malta* (written *c.* 1589), V. v, requires a Platform, Gallery and curtained rear stage, but it exposes the rear stage only after emptying the Gallery.

[3] Stage directions are copied from the First Folio (see Greg, p. 205) unless otherwise noted; but dialogue and line numbering from *The Complete Works of Shakespeare*, edited by G. L. Kittredge (Boston, 1936).

ordered his return from the land of the Goths. Saturninus and Bassianus, sons
of the late emperor, therefore dismiss their followers; and after their departure
Saturninus demands:

> Open the gates and let me in.
> *Bass.* Tribunes, and me, a poor competitor.
> *Flourish.* They go up into the Senat house.

This clears the Platform and places at least seven in the Gallery.

A Captain enters to announce the imminent arrival of Titus; six lines later
(after line 69) appears the direction:

> *Sound Drummes and Trumpets. And then enter two of Titus Sonnes; After
> them, two men bearing a Coffin covered with blacke, then two other Sonnes.
> After them, Titus Andronicus, and then Tamora the Queene of Gothes, &
> her two Sonnes Chiron and Demetrius, with Aaron the Moore, and others,
> as many as can bee: They set downe the Coffin, and Titus speakes.*

As the text unfolds we discover the *"others"* to include Alarbus, oldest of
Tamora's sons, and Gothic prisoners brought in chains to Rome. It is hardly
surprising that before the entrance of this great procession the followers of
Saturninus and Bassianus were dismissed and sent off stage where they could
shift to other coats and join the Titus cortege.

Titus, the aging famous warrior, greets the Tribunes of Rome whose
victories he has wrought in distant lands; he calls on all Romans to cherish his
four living sons and to mourn with him the two whose bodies he now brings to
Rome for burial. At line 81:

> Behold the poor remains, alive and dead!
> These that survive let Rome reward with love;
> These that I bring unto their latest home,
> With burial amongst their ancestors . . .
> Make way to lay them by their bretheren.
>   *They open the Tombe.*
> There greet in silence, as the dead are wont,
> And sleep in peace, slain in your country's wars.

At this point all three stages are in use at once: the Gallery lined with Saturninus, Bassianus, three Tribunes, and two or more Senators; the Platform filled
with Romans and Goths; and the rear stage or Study exposed as a "Tomb" to
receive the coffin.[4]

Once the Tomb is open, Lucius calls (at line 96) for a sacrificial slaying of
Tamora's oldest son "before this earthy prison" of his brothers' bones. Tamora

---

[4] In other plays produced in the years 1588-1594 the opening of the rear stage is occasionally
marked by the direction *"The Arras is drawen . . ."* or *"He draweth a curten . . ."* or *"the
Queenes Tent opens"*.

A rear stage 12-14 feet wide and 8-9 feet deep was large enough, I believe, to accommodate any
"discovery" prior to 1595, and a stage of such width, flanked on either side by a Platform door,
would have taken up the greater part of the scenic wall below the Gallery in the De Witt sketch
of the Swan.

In this first scene of *Titus Andronicus* the two stage doors are twice mentioned by name; one
probably served actors going to and from the Senate House, the other as a general entrance to
the Platform. Neither door could have been pre-empted for use as the Tomb, a fact established
beyond question by lines 385-398.

frantically protests, but the proposal is approved notwithstanding and swiftly carried out. *"Exit Sonnes with Alarbus."* Twelve lines later the sons return— *"Enter the Sonnes of Andronicus againe"*—and Lucius relates that the sacrifice was successfully performed.

Q1 contains a passage, beginning at line 35, irreconcilable with lines 96-149 and with all subsequent stage business involving the Tomb. In it Marcus Andronicus reports that earlier this same day, before his arrival at the Senate House, Titus had already visited the Tomb and there had sacrificed Tamora's eldest son.[5] This passage, omitted in later texts, indicates that in the original play no attempt was made to represent the Tomb on stage. This is but the first of several indications—at least one in each of the five Acts—that the stage management of *Titus Andronicus* was recast, together with relevant dialogue, to take advantage of a curtained rear stage. This third major unit of the Elizabethan multiple stage came into general use in London playhouses after 1587.[6]

Lucius continues (at line 146) with the matter in hand:

> Remaineth naught but to inter our brethren
> And with loud 'larums welcome them to Rome.
> *Tit.* Let it be so, and let Andronicus
> Make this his latest farewell to their souls. *Flourish.*
> *Then Sound Trumpets, and lay the Coffin*
> *in the Tombe.*
> In peace and honour rest you here, my sons; ...

The Gallery used in *Titus Andronicus* as the Senate House is, of course, directly over the Study used as the Tomb, hence no one "aloft" can see into it. Here lay a minor problem of versimilitude that Shakespeare overcame by developing considerable activity *in front* of the Tomb—the call for a sacrifice, the naming of Alarbus, the protests of Tamora, and so forth—and by limiting all business *inside* the Tomb to the single act of depositing the coffin. Presumably this took no more time than the sounding of the trumpet fanfare; and the episode was concluded, as Titus ended his benediction, by closing the curtains.

The second movement of Scene 1 begins with the entrance of Lavinia, daughter of Titus and the beloved of Bassianus. She greets her father and kneels for a moment before the Tomb. Marcus Andronicus the Tribune informs his brother that the citizens of Rome have chosen him as their candidate for the emperor's crown; but this honor Titus declines on the grounds of age and the fact that Saturninus and Bassianus are sons of the late emperor and should

---

[5]   and at this day,
     To the monument of that [*read* the] Andronicy
     Done sacrifice of expiation,
     And slaine the Noblest prisoner of the *Gothes.*

The slaying of Alarbus earlier that day explains the absence of his name in the direction at line 69.

[6] One recalls that Marlowe's first play, *1 Tamburlaine* (1587), made no demands on a rear stage, but that his *2 Tamburlaine* (1588) and all other plays did; and furthermore that plays of 1588-92 used by companies on tour, such as *The Troublesome Reign of John* or *The Taming of a Shrew*, made few if any demands on a rear stage. On the other hand, in Shakespeare's *The Taming of the Shrew* (1594) the rear stage is indispensable.

inherit; in the end it is decided that Titus shall name the new emperor. A supporter of the rights of eldest sons, he chooses Saturninus. Marcus announces the choice officially (at line 230):

> With voices and applause of every sort,
> Patricians and plebeians, we create
> Lord Saturninus Rome's great Emperor
> And say, 'Long live our Emperor Saturnine!'
> *A long Flourish till they come downe.*

With all actors brought together on the Platform, the third movement begins. Saturninus hypocritically thanks Titus, and declares his intention of making Lavinia Empress of Rome. This so gratifies Titus that forthwith he makes him a present of Tamora, her sons, and the other captured Goths. But Bassianus loves Lavinia and takes prompt steps to carry her off. In this rescue he is aided by Titus' sons, one of whom, by name Mutius, attempts to thwart his father and is slain at the "gate". While this melee is taking place on one side of the Platform, Saturninus, whose lustful eyes had already noticed Tamora, leads her out at the Senate House door. At line 295 the Gallery fills for the second time:

> *Enter aloft the Emperour with Tamora and*
> *her two sonnes, and Aaron the Moore.*

Safely out of reach in the Senate House, Saturninus openly declares his hatred of Titus, his detestation of Lavinia, and his determination to make Tamora his wife and Empress. Tamora swiftly abases herself to Saturninus and vows all love and duty. He lifts her up:

> Ascend, fair Queen, Pantheon.[7] Lords, accompany
> Your noble Emperor and his lovely bride, . . . *Exeunt.*[8]

The old man is stunned, his hopes all overthrown:

> I am not bid to wait upon this bride.
> Titus, when wert thou wont to walk alone,
> Dishonoured thus and challenged of wrongs?
> *Enter Marcus and Titus Sonnes.*

All four beg Titus to permit the burial of Mutius in the family tomb. It is some time before Andronicus yields. At line 383:

> *Tit.*   Rise, Marcus, rise . . .
> Well, bury him, and bury me the next.
> *They put him in the Tombe.*
> *Luc.* There lie thy bones, sweet Mutius, with thy friends,
> Till we with trophies do adorn thy Tomb!
> *They all kneele and say.*
> No man shed tears for noble Mutius!
> He lives in fame that died in virtue's cause.[9]

---

[7] This byplay of Tamora's kneeling suggests that by 1593 the Gallery parapet was similar to the inconspicuous guard rail used in later playhouses.

[8] I.e., *Exeunt, all but Titus.*

[9] Modern editions add: "*The Tomb closes.*"

The fourth movement of Scene 1 begins at line 393:

> *Flourish. Enter the Emperor, Tamora, and her two sons, with the Moore
> at one doore. Enter at the other doore Bassianus and Lavinia with others.*

Saturninus jeers at his brother and his bride, Lavinia; he takes no pains to conceal his deep hostility to them both and to Titus also despite the latter's part in naming him Emperor. Tamora shares her new husband's hatred to the full—she intends to have her revenge for the slaying of Alarbus—but she urges him to pretend forgiveness and to gloss over insults until his crown is more securely on his head. At line 479:

> *Tam.* Nay, nay, sweet Emperor, we must all be friends.
> The Tribune and his nephews kneel for grace.
> I will not be denied! Sweet heart, look back.

Saturninus professes to forgive them and condescends so far as to invite everyone to his wedding feast for Tamora. In the Folio, Act I ends on this note and a promise to join Titus in a hunting party the following day. *"Exeunt."*

In the undivided Quartos, on the contrary, the direction reads:

> *Exeunt. Sound trumpets, manet Moore.*

This continuation is theatrically logical, for it will complete the expository themes of the play's first day by showing that Tamora's sons are already quarreling over the chaste Lavinia notwithstanding her marriage to Bassianus. In addition, the continuation is technically correct, for at this point a clear stage (the Folio's editorial Act division followed by its *"Enter Aaron alone"*) would violate the "law of re-entry" inasmuch as Aaron was present to the very close of the preceding scene.[10]

Classical allusions and Latin phrases bedeck the text of *Titus Andronicus* and attest its early date. Numerous passages of verbal scenery reveal Shakespeare's efforts to localize his scenes, for example (II. ii):

> *Enter Titus Andronicus and his three sonnes, making
> a noyse with hounds and hornes, and Marcus.*
> *Tit.* The hunt is up, the morn is bright and grey,
> The fields are fragrant, and the woods are green.
> Uncouple here, and let us make a bay,
> And wake the Emperor and his lovely bride, ...
> *Here a cry of houndes, and winde hornes in a peale,
> then enter Saturninus, Tamora, Bassianus, Lavinia,
> Chiron, Demetrius, and their Attendants.*

Thirteen or more actors are now present on the Platform; greetings are exchanged; it is time to mount horses and chariots and begin the hunt. All these details launch the action on its second day and, of course, point to an outer-stage scene.

Scene 3 (II. iii) contains another extensive revision to introduce a Study setting furnished with property trees[11] and a concealed pit, all indispensable to the plot. *"Enter Aaron alone"*.[12]

---

[10] For discussion of this Elizabethan stage convention see C. M. Haines, "The Law of Re-entry in Shakespeare", *RES*, I (1925), iv. 449-451.

[11] Kyd had employed an "arbor" setting with telling effect in *The Spanish Tragedy* (1589).

[12] Modern editions add: *"with a bag of gold"*.

> *Aar.* He that had wit would think that I had none
> To bury so much gold under a tree
> And never after to inherit it. . . .
> Know that this gold must coin a stratagem,
> Which, cunningly effected, will beget
> A very excellent piece of villainy.
> And so repose, sweet gold, for their unrest
> That have their alms out of the Empress' chest.[13]
>
> *Enter Tamora to the Moore.*
>
> *Tam.* My lovely Aaron, wherefore look'st thou sad? . . .
> The birds chaunt melody on every bush;
> The snake lies rolled in the cheerful sun;
> The green leaves quiver with the cooling wind
> And make a checker'd pattern on the ground
> Under their sweet shade. Aaron, let us sit.

Tamora opens her arms to him, but for the moment his concern is with his stratagem, and after outlining his plans for the murder of Bassianus and the rape of Lavinia, he proceeds (at line 45):

> Seest thou this letter? Take it up, I pray thee,
> And give the King this fatal-plotted scroll.
> Now question me no more. We are espied.
> Here comes a parcel of our hopeful booty,
> Which dreads not yet their lives' destruction.
> *Enter Bassianus and Lavinia.*
> *Tam.* Ah, my sweet Moor, sweeter to me than life!
> *Aar.* No more, great Empress. Bassianus comes.
> Be cross with him; and I'll go fetch thy sons
> To back thy quarrels, whatso'er they be.[14]
> *Bas.* Who have we here? Rome's royal Emperess? . . .
> Why are you sequest'red from all your train, . . .
> And wand'red hither to an obscure plot,
> Accompanied but with a barbarous Moor,
> If foul desire had not conducted you?

Tamora sees to it that the quarrel grows. Her sons Chiron and Demetrius arrive (at line 88):

> *Dem.* How now, dear sovereign and our gracious mother?
> Why doth your Highness look so pale and wan?
> *Tam.* Have I not reason, think you, to look pale?
> These two have 'tic'd me hither to this place.
> A barren detested vale you see it is;
> The trees, though summer, yet forlorn and lean,
> O'ercome with moss and baleful mistletoe.
> Here never shines the sun; here nothing breeds,
> Unless the nightly owl or fatal raven . . . .
> No sooner had they told this hellish tale
> But straight they told me they would bind me here . . .

---

[13] Modern editions add: *"He hides the gold".*
[14] Modern editions add: *"Exit Aaron".*

> And leave me to this miserable death....
> Revenge it, as you love your mother's life,
> Or be ye not henceforth call'd my children.
> *Dem.* This is a witness that I am thy son. *stab him.*
> *Chi.* And this for me, struck home to show my strength....[15]
> Drag hence her husband to some secret hole,
> And make his dead trunk pillow to our lust.

Lavinia's protests and pleas go unheeded; eventually she is seized by Chiron (at line 185)

> *Chi.* Nay then, I'll stop your mouth.—Bring thou her husband.
> This is the hole where Aaron bid us hide him.[16]
> *Tam.* Farewell, my sons. See that you make her sure....
> Now will I hence to seek my lovely Moor
> And let my spleenful sons this trull deflow'r. *Exit.*

It will have been noticed that the text is again highly inconsistent: in Chiron's first passage, echoing Aaron's proposals at the close of II.i, the "secret hole" in which Lavinia is to be ravished and the body of Bassianus hidden is manifestly off stage, whereas in his second it is on stage. This inconsistency arises from an extensive recasting of the text to take advantage not only of the rear stage wherein a woodland glade can be discovered, but also of the distinctive inner stage trap, which came into use about 1592.[17]

As Tamora leaves the stage on one side, to seek out Saturninus and deliver the scroll, Aaron leads in Quintus and Martius on the other. At line 191:

> *Enter Aaron with two of Titus Sonnes.*
> *Aar.* Come on, my lords; the better foot before.
> Straight will I bring you to the loathsome pit
> Where I espied the panther fast asleep....

The drowsy Martius unheedingly falls into this pit.

> *Quint.* What, art thou fallen? What subtile hole is this,
> Whose mouth is covered with rude-growing briers,
> Upon whose leaves are drops of new-shed blood? ...
> Speak, brother. Hast thou hurt thee with the fall?

Martius' reply indicates that he is seriously injured; Aaron slips away to bring the Emperor; and Martius renews his cries for assistance:

> *Mart.* Why dost not comfort me and help me out
> From this unhallowed and blood-stained hole? ...
> To prove thou hast a true-divining heart,
> Aaron and thou look down into this den
> And see a fearful sight of blood and death.
> *Quint.* Aaron is gone.

By now there can be no question but that the "pit" exists in some part of

---

[15] Modern editions add: *"Chiron also stabs him"*.

[16] No early text contains a direction here, but modern editions uniformly supply the following: *"Demetrius throws the body of Bassianus into the pit: then exeunt Demetrius and Chiron, dragging off Lavinia"*.

[17] For a description of this trap and its characteristics see the author's *Globe Playhouse*, pp. 209-216.

the stage visible to all spectators. Furthermore, certain important details have been established by the dialogue: (1) the trap in the stage floor has been open at least since line 98, and probably from the start of the scene; (2) it has some sort of screen over it that can be described as "rude-growing briers"; (3) it is large enough to receive the body of Bassianus who is pushed into it, and that of Martius who falls into it; and (4) it is seemingly deep enough that Martius cannot climb out without assistance or look out to observe that Aaron had gone. Later in the scene Martius reaches up to grasp his brother's hand, but in his efforts to get out (at line 245), he drags Quintus over the edge. The Folio direction reads: *"Boths fall in"*.

Aaron returns with the Emperor in time for them to see Quintus fall. On hastening to peer into "this gaping hollow", Saturninus learns from Martius that Bassianus' body is down there also. Tamora, with Attendants, Titus, and his third son Lucius now enter, and she presents her husband with the "fatal writ":

Saturninus reads the Letter

> ... 'Look for thy reward
> Among the nettles at the elder tree
> Which overshades the mouth of that same pit
> Where we decreed to bury Bassianus. ...'
> *Sat.* O Tamora! was ever heard the like?
>   This is the pit, and this the elder tree ....
> *Aar.* My gracious lord, here is the bag of gold.

Since the manipulated evidence points to Martius and Quintus as the murderers of the Emperor's brother, orders are given for their immediate arrest. Titus offers bail but is refused. At line 299:

> *Sat.* Thou shalt not bail them. See thou follow me.
>   Some bring the murthered body, some the murtherers.
>   Let them not speak a word—the guilt is plain;
>   For, by my soul, were there worse end than death,
>   That end upon them would be executed.
> *Tam.* Andronicus, I will entreat the King.
>   Fear not thy sons; they shall do well enough.
> *Tit.* Come, Lucius, come! Stay not to talk with them. *Exeunt.*

What does *"Exeunt"*—i.e., *Exeunt Omnes*—mean in this situation? It appears to mean that as the Emperor with Tamora departs through one of the two Platform doors, and Titus with Lucius departs through the other, the inner-stage curtains close, shutting off the audience's view of the pit with Martius, Quintus, and the body of Bassianus yet inside and with Attendants grouped about the pit as if about to carry out the Emperor's order.

However we may blench at the piling up of horrors in this scene, we must grant that from beginning to end it is contrived with technical skill of a high order. It suggests a playwright intent on exploiting to the full a stage innovation capable of imparting new twists and turns to his dramatic theme. The distinctive quality of the rear trap arose from its location in a curtained stage: it could be made ready in advance with auxiliary properties—here a cover of "briers" framed by "elder trees"—apt for the business in hand. Further, and also distinguishing it from the Platform trap, it could be kept open indefinitely.

Scenes 4 and 5 next following pile horror on horror, but present no problems of staging: (II. iv) *"Enter the Empresse Sonnes, with Lavinia, her hands cut off and her tongue cut out, and ravisht";* her rescue by Marcus and return to Rome; (III. i) the procession over the stage of Judges and Senators conducting Martius and Quintus *"to the place of execution, and Titus going before pleading";* the banishing of Lucius for trying to rescue his brothers; the chopping off of Titus' hand as the price of freeing his condemned sons—only to have Aaron's messenger return with *"two heads and a hand";* and at last the resolve of Titus, Marcus, and Lucius to submit no further—instead to seek revenge.

All three Quartos next introduce as Scene 6 the dramatic episode (IV. i, in the Folio) in which Lavinia manages by writing in sand to inform her father and uncle of the names of her ravishers—*"She takes the staffe in her mouth, and guides it with her stumps and writes"*[18]—the turning point in the play. The Folio, on the other hand, introduces ahead of Scene 6 eighty-five lines of an alternate and far less dramatic episode (III. ii) in which, during a repast in the Gallery (?)[19], the lamentations of III. i, are resumed and the killing of a fly debated. The episode ends with the proposal that Titus read aloud to Lavinia and his grandson, young Lucius—a step that presumably would have led to some clue as to Lavinia's destroyers. This resort to books is the opening gambit in the revised scene (IV. i) as prelude to the writing in the sand. The Quartos correctly omit III. ii, for, quite apart from its ineffectiveness, its presence in the Folio[20] creates major difficulties of two kinds, the one a violation of the law of re-entry and the other a pronounced *non sequitur* in the unfolding of the action, as follows:

The Folio's Act III, scene ii, concludes with Titus leading Lavinia and his grandson, young Lucius, off stage as if to another room in his house:

> *Tit.* Come, take away. Lavinia, go with me.
> I'll to thy closet and go read with thee
> Sad stories chanced in the times of old.
> Come, boy, and go with me. Thy sight is young,
> And thou shalt read when mine begin to dazzle. *Exeunt.*

[18] A sandbox was often used in Elizabethan schools for instruction in writing. For details see James G. McManaway, "Writing in Sand in *Titus Andronicus,* IV. i", *RES,* IX (1959), 172-173.

[19] For similar stage usage see *The Taming of a Shrew* (1592), Scene 2, and *The Taming of the Shrew* (1594), Induction ii. Both *Shrews* are based (independently) upon a yet earlier original, no longer extant.

[20] Of all the textual problems in *Titus Andronicus* none has proved more baffling than the Folio's introduction of a complete scene not given in any antecedent text. At first glance it might seem that the episode in question was a late addition by Shakespeare or some other to rival the additions to *The Spanish Tragedy.* But if Greg is right (see above, note 1), the scene may have been copied from the original prompt-book, preserved for the sake of its license, by the scribe employed *c.* 1622 to assemble copy for the Folio. In that event III. ii—whether acted or cut in revivals of *Titus* in the period 1594-1611—must date from the earliest years of the play. This is the opinion of a number of scholars, among them H. T. Price, who (in *Adams Memorial Studies,* p. 102) calls attention to Aaron's lines in Q1 (V. i. 141-142)—

> So I have done a thousand dreadful things,
> As willingly as one would kill a fly—

and concludes: "This clear echo in Q1 of the incident with the fly makes it certain that III. ii, is not a later addition."

The Folio's next scene (IV. i), Scene 6 in all Quarto texts, opens:

> *Enter Young Lucius and Lavinia running after him, and the Boy flies from*
> *her with his bookes under his arme. Enter Titus and Marcus.*[21]

> Boy. Help, grandsire, help! My Aunt Lavinia
> Follows me everywhere, I know not why.

Obviously these two scenes were never performed as printed, for too many
details are at loose ends. Whereas III. ii, showed all four Andronici toying with
food in some room in Titus' house, IV. i, introduces Lavinia chasing young
Lucius across the Andronici courtyard in an effort to seize his books (and
thereby spell out her ravishers' names), and by his cries attracts Titus and
Marcus. The mood and pace of the two scenes are in sharp contrast: in the one
Titus is exhausted and senile, in the other vigorous and alert; the one fails to
advance the plot, the other not only exposes the criminals but also leads to the
first steps of revenge. The spectacular business of writing in the sand is the clue
to the employment of the inner stage for this episode, for the making ready
of the bed of sand as well as its subsequent removal are details best performed
out of sight of the audience. A seven-line soliloquy by Marcus—required by the
law of re-entry—brings IV. i, to a close.

Scene 7 (IV. ii) opens on the Platform, as if close by the Palace.

> *Enter Aron, Chiron and Demetrius at one dore: and at another dore young*
> *Lucius and another, with a bundle of weapons, and verses writ upon them.*

After presenting his grandfather's gifts—larded with bitter asides—to Tamora's
sons, young Lucius leaves. The sons are puzzled, but Aaron perceives that
Titus has discovered their guilt. There follows word that the Empress has been
delivered of a child, and the Nurse's bringing this "blackamoor" infant to its
father, Aaron; then the killing of the Nurse and the involving of Tamora's
sons in the plan to supply Tamora with a fair-skinned substitute child.

Scene 8 (IV. iii) follows on the Platform, also beneath the Palace walls.

> *Enter Titus, old Marcus, young Lucius, and other gentlemen with bowes,*
> *and Titus beares the arrowes with Letters on the end of them.*

At line 52 Titus supplies his comrades with arrows and orders them to shoot
his messages high in the air (to ensure their carrying over the walls into the
Palace yard?). Dialogue makes clear that these arrows were in fact discharged—
a business that recalls an episode in 2 *Tamburlaine* (1588), III. ii, in which
soldiers are ordered to shoot and kill the captive Governor of Babylon suspended in chains upon his city's walls. Differences in detail do not obscure the
fact that in both episodes the actors launched their shafts into the stage Gallery—the only reasonably safe target afforded by playhouse design.[22] If visual
reinforcement is considered necessary for the ensuing dialogue which describes
in detail where the arrows struck, one might conjecture that a painted cloth
depicting the Olympian gods—akin to the painted cloth of Hell displayed in
Dr. Faustus (c.1590)—was suspended in the Gallery as a backdrop.

---

[21] Titus and Marcus presumably enter after line 1.
[22] Even so a child in the audience was killed by an arrow during a performance of 2 *Tambur-*
laine (1588); see the *TLS.*, 28 August 1930.

Scene 8 concludes with the entrance of a Clown bearing pigeons in a basket and his employment to carry from Titus to the Emperor yet another written message, this time wrapped round a dagger.

Once again *Titus* offers a seeming redundancy of parallel episodes: (1) Lucius delivering the weapons to Chiron and Demetrius; (2) Titus and others shooting the arrows over the walls; and (3) the Clown hired to carry the knife. May it be that the first dates from the first version of the play and the other two, which alone are developed in Scene 9, are early additions?

Scene 9 (IV. iv) carries the action inside the Palace to some room where seats for the Emperor (and his Queen?) are provided—"yonder sits the Emperor"—and where messengers and patricians are received. These indications of an audience chamber in all extant texts suggest that the rear stage, pre-set with suitable furniture, has been brought into use. The opening direction reads:

> *Enter Emperour and Empresse, and her two sonnes, the Emperour*
> *brings the Arrowes in his hand that Titus shot at him.*
> Sat. Why, lords, what wrongs are these! Was ever seen
> An emperor in Rome thus overborne.

Tamora uses all her skill to calm the Emperor's fears, first after his alarm caused by the arrows, a second time after the Clown has delivered Titus' message, and yet a third time after Æmilius has brought word that Lucius is advancing on Rome with an Army of Goths. Hers is the proposal of a meeting between Saturninus and Lucius to be held "at his father's house, the old Andronicus". Her schemes prevail, and the scene closes.

Scene 10 (V. i) opens on the Platform—"*Flourish. Enter Lucius with an Army of Gothes, with Drum and Souldiers*"[23]—another reason for assuming that the scene immediately before was mounted in the rear stage (by 1594 Elizabethan dramatists were beginning to adopt a convention prompted by theatrical logic, namely that a distinct change of place is made obvious to the audience by a change of stage. Shakespeare never violates this convention in plays written after 1595).

Except that Aaron, escaping from Rome with his infant son, is captured and all but hanged from a "tree" (i.e., one of the two large posts that supported the stage ceiling?), the scene is more full of speeches than action. It closes after the arrival of Æmilius and his inviting Lucius to attend the parley at his father's house.

Scene 11 (V. ii) opens with Tamora and her two sons—all three wearing disguises—entering to the door of Titus' house. At line 5:

> *Tam.* Knock at his study, where they say he keeps
> To ruminate strange plots of dire revenge. . . .
>   *They knocke, and Titus opens his study dore.*
> *Tit.* Who doth molest my contemplation?
> Is it your trick to make me ope the door? . . .
> *Tam.* Know, thou sad man, I am not Tamora; . . .
> Come down and welcome me to this world's light;
> Confer with me of murder and of death. . . .

---

[23] The Quartos' and Folio's misprint for "*and Colours.*"

> *Tit.* Art thou Revenge? and art thou sent to me
>> To be a torment to mine enemies?
> *Tam.* I am; therefore come down and welcome me.
> *Tit.* Do me some service ere I come to thee. . . .

But at line 69 he makes his exit. During the eleven lines that he is descending off stage Tamora explains her plans to her sons; then as Titus reappears:

> *Tam.* See, here he comes, and I must ply my theme.

The reiterated "come down . . . come down" in all texts makes it evident that Titus, on emerging from his "study", first appeared aloft in the Gallery—and one recalls that Henry VI was found reading there in *3 Henry VI* (1591), V. vi. It makes a better stage tableau, of course, to involve the Gallery in this byplay, and his position aloft no doubt helped convey the fact that Titus, closely scrutinizing the disguised trio in the street below, came to perceive exactly who they were.[24]

The remainder of the scene advances Tamora's plans for inducing Titus to invite Lucius to a parley and banquet, but her leaving Chiron and Demetrius as hostages with Titus gives him the chance to have them seized and killed.

In Scene 12 (V. iii), the play's finale, many characters are involved: at Tamora's suggestion Titus has invited Marcus, Lucius, and "the chiefest princes of the Goths". Tamora herself has come bringing the Emperor, Tribunes, *"and others"*. Aaron has been brought on stage, but is led off, guarded, before the feast begins; an Attendant, holding Aaron's child by Tamora, remains.

In the temporary absence of the host, Marcus, brother of Titus and himself a Tribune, invites the Emperor and chief guests to sit to the feast (at line 24):

> *Marc.* Please you therefore draw nigh and take your places.
>> *Sat.* Marcus, we will.
>>> *Hautboyes. A Table brought in. Enter Titus like a*
>>> *Cooke, placing the meat on the Table, and Lavinia*
>>> *with a vale over her face.*

This is the Folio direction. The Quartos uniformly omit *"A Table brought in,"* and substitute *"dishes"* for the Folio *"meat"*.

Chairs and tables are freely moved about in real life to meet the needs of the occasion, and there is abundant evidence that Elizabethan stage practice followed suit. But it is difficult to determine to what part of the stage this table was *"brought in"* or how many were asked to sit at it. If only four or five—those guests of highest rank or deepest involvement in the crimes against Titus—then the table could be small; and Marcus' invitation to "draw nigh and take your places" could be taken to mean an opening of the stage curtains and a discovery of the table being made ready in the rear stage. An inner-stage setting would accelerate matters here and would serve later in the scene as a suitable exit for those carrying off the dead bodies of Titus and Lavinia.

Titus urges his guests to eat of his food; but once they have begun he interrupts to ask the Emperor's opinion on the fable of Virginius who with his

---

[24] The *"door"* of the direction is an interesting detail: if it opens to the Gallery it indicates the stage feature that made plausible the "locked Gallery" episode of *The Spanish Tragedy* (1589).

own hand slew his ravished daughter. On hearing the Emperor's commendation of that deed, Titus produces a dagger and stabs his daughter Lavinia.

> *Tit.* Die, die, Lavinia, and thy shame with thee!
>   And with thy shame thy father's sorrow die! *He kils her.*
> *Sat.* What hast thou done, unnatural and unkind? ...
>   What, was she ravish'd? Tell who did the deed.
> *Tit.* Will't please you eat? Will't please your Highness feed?

But a moment later he names Chiron and Demetrius as the villains and, when ordered to send for them, replies:

> Why, there they are both, baked in that pie,
> Whereof their mother daintily hath fed....
> 'Tis true, 'tis true! Witness my knive's sharp point!
>   *He stabs the Empresse.*
> *Sat.* Die, frantic wretch, for this accursed deed![25]
> *Luc.* Can the son's eyes behold his father bleed?
>   There's meed for meed, death for a deadly deed![26]

Lucius then relates the high crimes that have destroyed his father's family; and Marcus, at line 119, continues the account, including the evil part played by Aaron. At the close he asks:

> Now you have heard the truth, what say you, Romans?
> Have we done aught amiss? Show us wherein,
> And, from the place where you behold us pleading,
> The poor remainder of Andronici
> Will hand in hand all headlong hurl ourselves
> And on the ragged stones beat forth our brains.

These last four lines constitute the only evidence the text affords for the traditional assumption that Marcus, Lucius, and young Lucius escaped during the melee to the safety of the upper gallery of the Andronici house, the place to which Titus first entered in the preceding scene. If this assumption is correct, their elevated position considerably enhances the stage grouping of the finale (in which Lucius is acclaimed emperor) and creates a tableau reminiscent of the first scene of the play—a resemblance that is yet closer if the inner stage is used here for the fatal banquet as it was used there for the Tomb.

The problem of removing so many bodies had of course to be resolved, and once again the Study may have been helpful. Lucius (at line 190) gives directions:

> Some loving friends convey the Emperor hence
> And give him burial in his father's grave.
> My father and Lavinia shall forthwith
> Be closed in our household's monument.
> As for that ravenous tiger, Tamora,
> No funeral rite, ...
> But throw her forth to beasts and birds of prey.

---

[25] Modern editions add: "*He stabs Titus*".

[26] Following this couplet modern editions supply the direction: "*He stabs Saturninus. A great tumult. Lucius, Marcus and their Friends go up into a gallery.*"

Six lines later there is the final *"Exeunt omnes"*. All four bodies and the guarded Aaron may have been carried off in a single procession, but the more probable management, based in part on the lines just quoted, is (1) that Titus and Lavinia were dutifully conveyed into the Andronici courtyard after which the curtains were closed—thus also clearing the stage of the table and chairs—(2) that the body of the Emperor was carried with pomp and circumstance out through one stage door, and (3) the sentenced and shackled Aaron, together with the body of Tamora, were dragged off through the other.

* * * * *

Differences, omissions, contradictions, additions, redundancies (and in the Folio violations of the law of re-entry) in the early texts of *Titus Andronicus* indicate a full-scale revision of an older play before its production as a "new" play on January 23, 1594. An uncancelled passage in the Q1 text of Scene 1 makes clear that in the original *Titus* the Andronici Tomb was off stage. The visible opening of the Tomb in all texts makes equally clear that the revision introduced the Tomb as a "discovery" in the rear stage. Moreover, all texts preserve in Scene 3 the unambiguous reference to an off-stage pit as well as the complex sequence requiring a visible pit. These marked differences in staging help to explain the Folio's preservation of the cancelled Fly Scene for which all three Quartos substitute the vivid episode of writing on a bed of sand. In short, the original *Titus* appears to have been written for a stage of two units (the Platform and Gallery), whereas the revised *Titus* was written for three (Platform, Gallery, and Inner Stage). As a consequence three scenes were radically recast and others modified to take advantage of improved stage resources.

The revised *Titus Andronicus* made theatrical history. It was the first Elizabethan play to begin and end with episodes involving three stages at once, and its major revisions establish Shakespeare as a theatrical innovator already greater than any of his contemporaries.

Hofstra University

Romeo and Juliet: The Source of its Modern Stage Career

GEORGE WINCHESTER STONE, JR.

HE third quarter of the eighteenth century, notable as marking the watershed towards a more expressive emotionalism and sense of imagination in art, music, and poetry than had, perhaps, existed earlier, showed a veritable burst of these qualities in performances of Shakespeare's plays, and especially of *Romeo and Juliet*. From 1748 to 1776 in the two major London theaters alone over 329 performances of the play occurred—a record second only to the run of *The Beggar's Opera*. These came after Theophilus Cibber's revival of the play in 1744 for six performances at the Little Theatre in the Haymarket, to which a halt had to be called because he was playing at an unlicensed location. He had advertised his revival 28 August 1744 as the first performance of *Romeo and Juliet* for one hundred years.[1] It had, indeed, been replaced on stage in October 1679 for some forty scattered performances of Otway's *Caius Marius*—an adaptation of the plot to a Roman setting—during the Restoration period and the early eighteenth century.

Theophilus Cibber worked hard to gain the contempt of his own generation and still receives so little credit, and probably deserves so little for a generally misspent life, that one is glad to yield him a compliment where compliment is due, as it is for reviving *Romeo and Juliet*, 11 September 1744. He played Romeo, and Jenny, his daughter by a first wife, played Juliet. He piqued London curiosity by advance advertising, played three nights to standing room only, "at the particular Desire of several Ladies of Quality", and "Persons of Quality . . ." "to great applause, . . ." and "with an extraordinary fine appearance of Ladies in the boxes". After the eighth performance his play was interdicted, but allowed a ninth on 13 December as a "Benefit for Miss Jenny".[2] Cibber commented on the circumstances in his *Serio-Comic Apology*, published in Dublin in 1748.

Examination of the Cibber text, published in octavo (n.d.) probably in 1748, reveals customary use of a free hand in stage adaptation, yet shows remarkably close adherence to the Shakespeare play. It was paced for Cibber's stage, borrows occasionally from Otway's play, takes a soliloquy from Shakespeare's *Two Gentlemen of Verona*, omits some scenes, shortens others, adds some lines, and, as in Otway, has Juliet awaken before Romeo expires. Genest in his *Account of the English Stage* (IV, 167-168) summarizes in briefest fashion the major changes, and gives a favorable account. But the nine per-

[1] A. H. Scouten, *The London Stage, 1660-1800, Part 3*, II (Carbondale, Ill., 1961), 1117.
[2] John Genest, *Some Account of the English Stage*, IV (Bath, 1832), 167-171 *passim*.

formances seem to have ended the Cibber influence save that they may have planted a thought or two about the potential of the play in the fertile mind of David Garrick.

During the early months of the season 1748-49, after Garrick had successfully managed Drury Lane for a season, he prepared *Romeo and Juliet* for presentation there, instructing Spranger Barry and Mrs. Cibber, Theophilus' estranged second wife, in the title roles. The play was first acted 29 November 1748 and proved to be successful enough to run nineteen more times during the season. It grossed the managers about £3,000.[3] The playbill announcing the first performance stated, truly, that it had never been acted at Drury Lane Theatre.

As usual, it was Garrick's version which impressed the mid-eighteenth-century audiences and which held the stage for ninety-seven succeeding years.[4] The play must be called Garrick's "version" instead of Garrick's "restoration" of Shakespeare's play, for, aside from the cuts in the text, it contains transpositions, emendations, and additions which depart rather widely from his customary principle, evident in his handling of other plays, of preserving the bulk of Shakespeare's text intact. Here he worked with a freer hand than his closest admirers of late years might wish. Shakespeare idolators of the nineteenth and twentieth centuries have not missed a single chance to condemn him his freedoms. Joseph Knight, writing in 1894, remarked with rising indignation:

> One or two special features mark this season [1748]. First of these comes the production of *Romeo and Juliet* in Garrick's mangled version, the earliest of these perversions of Shakespeare's texts which are Garrick's crowning disgrace and cast something more than doubt upon his much vaunted reverence for Shakespeare....[5]

F. A. Hedgcock, writing in 1912, analyzed the play with considerable scorn for the actor, and concluded:

> Garrick wanted a piece free of all fancy and of purely poetical declamation, a piece in which the dialogue should be as natural as possible giving free scope to the actor; he wished, moreover, to make Shakespeare's tragic force yet more powerful and to create for himself an opportunity of playing one of those terrible scenes of passion and death in which he excelled. To reach these ends he sacrificed the poet to his own pretensions. He was neither the first nor the last actor manager to do so; may these pages be a warning to his successors.[6]

[3] G. W. Stone, Jr., *The London Stage, 1660-1800, Part 4,* I (Carbondale, Ill., 1962), 78-108 *passim*. For 39 performances of *ten* Shakespearian plays in the preceding season the managers grossed £5,227, according to Treasurer John Powel's account, see pp. 7-56.

[4] G. C. D. Odell, *Shakespeare from Betterton to Irving,* II (London, 1921), 191, 266, mentions Madam Vestris' unsuccessful attempt to remove it; see pp. 271-272 for Charlotte Cushman's restoration of Shakespeare's text in 1845.

[5] *David Garrick* (London, 1894), pp. 115-117.

[6] Hedgcock illustrates Garrick's method of emendation by instances such as substituting *hate* for *love* in Tybalt's fine antithesis (*David Garrick and his French Friends,* London, 1912, p. 70):

> Romeo the *love* I bear thee can afford
> No better term than this—thou art a villain!

as being more readily intelligible to the pit; and changing Juliet's "every day in the hour" to the

One notes, however, that these academic protests were made more than a century and a quarter after Garrick's death and in the wake of a shift in taste. His contemporaries judged differently. They liked his play and thought his alterations both justifiable and effective. Thomas Davies, Garrick's friend and biographer, went a thought far in praise of Garrick's ending as being "written with a spirit not unworthy of Shakespeare himself", and Francis Gentleman outdid himself, perhaps, in his peculiar kind of plantigrade criticism when he wrote:

> The whole dying scene does Mr. Garrick great credit as being worthy the matchless author he has furnished it to, and we must venture to affirm that his prejudice in favor even of Shakespeare's faults was the only reason why he did not retrench and add more, which in particular places he ought certainly to have done.[7]

One expects a measure of praise from these men who were at various times in their lives under obligations to the actor. But it is more than interesting to note the reaction of one of Garrick's opponents, MacNamara Morgan, who praised Barry as "the greatest tragedian in England", and who, in 1753, published his *Letter to Miss Nossiter; occasioned by her First Appearance on the Stage: in which is contained Remarks upon her playing the Character of Juliet.* After a delightfully detailed account of Miss Nossiter's every tone and gesture in her performance of Juliet at Covent Garden, he observes as follows upon Garrick's much disputed last act:

> Nothing was ever better calculated to draw tears from an audience than this last scene, when it is happily performed. The circumstance of Juliet's waking from her trance, before Romeo dies, and he in excess and rapture of his joy, forgetting he had drank poison,
>   "She speaks, she lives, and we shall still be bless'd!"
> is perhaps the finest touch of nature in any tragedy ancient or modern.

Morgan is unwilling, however, to credit Garrick with any of this, for he continues:

> It is very strange, therefore, that it has not been inquired into who the author was that made so happy an alteration. I have heard it attributed to one of the players; and it passes current that his knowledge of the stage enabled him to do it. But that we may not learn to set too small a value on the tragic Genius, by imagining that every little smatterer can with such delicacy touch the human heart; know that none but that Genius who comes next to Shakespeare's self cou'd draw so fine a stroke. It was Otway altered it. Compare the Tomb scene in *Romeo and Juilet* with that in *Caius Marius* . . . and there you will find this noble incident, and the very words of the whole scene, with very little alteration. (Pp. 50-56)

That Morgan in his enthusiasm is certainly overstating his case, one may judge by comparing the two endings. The development of the scene is original with Garrick, and hunters for plagiarism can find no more than five lines

---

more customary "every hour in the day". The examples are unfortunate since they seem not to have been made in the 1748, 1750, 1763, 1774 texts which I have been able to collate.

[7] *The Dramatic Censor,* I (London, 1770), 187-188.

taken over from Otway.[8] This letter, however, did produce Garrick's acknowledgment of his reliance upon the Restoration dramatist, which he expresses
in his advertisement to the 1753 edition of his play, and which he turns neatly
upon the author of the *Letter*.

Garrick had first published his *Romeo and Juliet* in 1748, the very year in
which he altered it. There he included the following advertisement:

> The alterations in the following play are few and trifling except in the last
> act; the design was to clear the original, as much as possible, from the jingle
> and quibble, which were always thought the great objections to reviving it.
> Many people have imagin'd that the sudden change of Romeo's love from
> Rosaline to Juliet was a blemish in his character, but an alteration of that
> was thought too bold to be attempted; Shakespear has dwelt particularly
> upon it, and so great a judge of human nature, knew that to be young and
> inconstant was extremely natural: Romeo in the third scene of the second
> act makes a very good excuse to the Friar for the quick transition of his
> affections:
>
> > —She whom now I love,
> > Doth give me grace for grace, and love for love.
> > The other did not so—
>
> However we shall leave this to the decision of abler criticks; those, I am sure,
> who see the play will very readily excuse his leaving twenty Rosalines for
> a Juliet.
> The favourable reception the new scene in the fifth Act has met with,
> induc'd the writer to print it, and if he may be excus'd for daring to add
> to Shakespear, he shall think himself well rewarded in having given
> Romeo and Juliet an opportunity of shewing their great merit.

In 1750 a second edition was called for during the time when sentiment was
running high over the rival performances of Barry and Garrick in the role of
Romeo. Its advertisement was brief and to the point:

> The alterations in the following play are few, except in the last act; the
> design was to clear the original as much as possible, from the jingle and
> quibble which were always thought a great objection to performing it.
> When the play was reviv'd two winters ago, it was generally thought, that
> the sudden change of Romeo's love from Rosaline to Juliet was a blemish
> in his character, and therefore it is to be hop'd that an alteration in that
> particular will be excus'd; the only merit that is claim'd from it is, that it
> is done with as little injury to the original as possible.

For the edition of 1753, after the appearance of Morgan's *Letter*, Garrick
continued his statement concerning the chief design of the alteration, but
lengthened his explanation in his advertisement:

> The sudden change of Romeo's love from Rosaline to Juliet, was thought
> by many, at the first revival of the play, to be a blemish in his character;
> an alteration in that particular has been made more in compliance to that

---

[8] See below, note 26, for Otway's lines, Genest's vague statement that the line, "O let me
hear some voice besides my own in this drear vault of death Or I shall faint", is derived from
Congreve's *Mourning Bride* is unsubstantiated. Only the following lines by Almeria in any way
resemble it: ". . . let me hear thy voice, Nay quickly speak to me and let me hear thy voice, my
own affrights me with its echoes. . . ."

opinion, than from a conviction that Shakespeare, the best judge of human Nature, was faulty.

Bandello, the *Italian* novellist, from whom Shakespeare has borrow'd the subject of this play, has made Juliet to wake in the tomb before Romeo dies: this circumstance Shakespeare has omitted not perhaps from judgment, but from reading the story in the French or English translation, both which have injudiciously left out this addition to the catastrophe.

Mr. Otway in his *Caius Marius,* a tragedy taken from *Romeo and Juliet,* has made use of this affecting circumstance, but it is a matter of wonder that so great a Dramatic Genius did not work up a scene from it of more Nature, Terror and Distress—Such a scene was attempted at the revival of this play, and it is hop'd, that an endeavour to supply the failure of so great a master will not be deem'd arrogant, or the making use of two or three of his introductory lines, be accounted a plagiarism.

The persons who from their great good nature and love of justice have endeavour'd to take away from the present editor the little merit of this scene by ascribing it to Otway, have unwittingly, from the nature of the accusation, paid him a compliment which he believes they never intended him.

This advertisement appeared in the many subsequent editions. The demand for the play was so steady that a new printing appeared on the average of every three years from 1748 until 1787.[9]

During the season 1749-50 Mrs. Cibber, Garrick's first Juliet, failed to appear owing to a dispute with Garrick. Barry refused to play Romeo to Mrs. Ward's Juliet, whom Garrick planned to substitute for Mrs. Cibber. So the play was not acted in his repertory that year. Barry and Mrs. Cibber went over to Covent Garden in 1750-51 and planned to capture the town by repeating there their former triumph in *Romeo and Juliet.* The play suddenly became the focus of a theatrical contest to decide the merits of the rival houses. Garrick himself secretly undertook the part of Romeo, instructing lovely Miss Bellamy as Juliet, and was prepared,[10] after Rich had announced the play for Covent Garden for the night of 28 September, to offer the same thing at Drury Lane.

The contest became the talk of the town. After the twelfth consecutive performance Mrs. Cibber fell ill and Rich was forced to advertise another play for the night of 12 October. Garrick continued in Romeo for one more night to mark his triumph. "Though the public ran in crowds at first", says Davies, "to decide upon the merits of the actors of this tragedy; yet many were justly angry at being obliged either to see one play repeatedly, or give up the diversions of a theatre for almost a fortnight. It was observed that the managers got no emolu-

---

[9] 1748, 1750, 1753, 1756, 1758, 1763, 1766, 1769, 1770, 1773, 1774, 1775, 1778, 1780, 1784, 1787, etc.

[10] Garrick's preparation, begun in July before the season opened was, as usual, long and careful. Both this fact and the conscious rivalry with which he undertook the part are attested in his letter to James Lacy 27 July 1750:

> I shall soon be ready in Romeo, which we will bring out early: I have altered something in the beginning and have made him only in love with Juliet—I believe you'll like it—if Bellamy agrees with us, she may open with it: Then if we can get our *King John* before 'em (as we certainly may) and dress the characters half old English half modern as in *Edward the Black Prince,* we shall cut their combs there too. (first publ. *Public Advertiser,* 31 Aug. 1786)

ment by the contest for they often played to thin audiences, or such as were made up by art."[11]

The disappointment of the public in the lack of variety in the theatrical offerings during this contest received neat expression in the verse of I. H—tt, which appeared on the front page of the *Daily Advertiser* for 12 October 1750:

> "Well what's tonight?" says angry Ned,
>   As up from bed he rouses;
> "Romeo again!" and shakes his head;
>   "Ah, Pox on both your houses!"

But that the managers received little emolument for their efforts must not be taken too seriously. Garrick played only twice to houses of less than £100, and made £1,610 during the thirteen nights of competition.[12] He repeated the play six more times during the year and brought his total receipts for nineteen performances to £2,760.

Many criticisms appeared which attempted to prove the superiority of one or the other Romeo. "Parties", says Cooke in his *Memoirs of Charles Macklin*, "were much divided . . . but the critics seemed to be unanimous in favor of Barry. His fine person and silver tones, spoke the very voice of love. The *Lover* was likewise his predominant character in private life, whilst Garrick wanted these requisites, at least in that eminent degree. 'The Drury Lane hero (said they) is the *modern,* the Covent Garden hero the Arcadian wooer:' and indeed those who saw him in the several tender interviews with his beloved Juliet, (even many years after this contest) must confess he was the Romeo which Shakespeare drew...."[18]

Francis Gentleman, attempting to be balanced in his judgment, leaned toward Garrick as his favorite:

> As to figure, though there is no necessity for a lover being tall, yet we apprehend Mr. Barry had a peculiar advantage in this point; his amorous harmony of features, melting eyes, and unequal plaintiveness of voice, seemed to promise everything we could wish, and yet the superior grace of Mr. Garrick's attitudes, the vivacity of his countenance and the fire of his expression shewed there were many essential beauties in which his great competitor might be excelled; those scenes in which they most evidently rose above each other are as follows—Mr. Barry in the Garden scene of the second act—Mr. Garrick in the Friar scene in the third—Mr. Barry the garden scene in the fourth—Mr. Garrick in the first scene, description of the Apothecary &c fifth act—Mr. Barry first part of the Tomb scene, and Mr. Garrick from where the poison begins to operate to the end.[14]

He decided after seeing three performances at each house that Barry drew more tears and Garrick more applause, ascribing as a reason an astonish-

---

[11] *Life of Garrick,* I (London, 1808), 162-163.

[12] 5 October, £90; 10 October, £90; Stone, *The London Stage,* pp. 210-211.

[18] But Macklin in a rather backhanded compliment praised Garrick's naturalness in the Garden Scene, when he noted that Barry swaggered into the garden talking so loudly of his love that Capulet's servants, were we not to suppose them dead with sleep, must surely have tossed the fellow in a blanket, while Garrick, sensible that the family were at enmity with him, came "creeping in upon his toes, whispering his love, and looking about him just like a *thief in the night*". William Cook, *Memoirs of Charles Macklin* (London, 1804), pp. 205 ff.

[14] *The Dramatic Censor,* I, 189-190.

ment in Garrick's performance which checked tears, "by a kind of electrical merit Mr. Garrick struck all hearts with a degree of inexpressible feeling, and bore conception so far beyond her usual sphere that softer sensations lay hid in wonder".[15]

Mrs. Pritchard said that if she were acting Juliet to Mr. Garrick's Romeo, so hot and passionate were his words in the Garden scene that she would have expected him at any moment to climb right up to her balcony, while if she were playing to Barry's Romeo, so sweet and seductive were his words that she was sure she would have gone down to him.[16]

Criticism spread to the character of Juliet as performed at the two houses also. The *Gentleman's Magazine* for October 1750 carried a full-length article distinguishing the different merits of Mrs. Cibber and Miss Bellamy, and, though on the whole favorable to the former, it concluded in this manner:

> [Mrs. Cibber's] judgment greatly fails her in the Tomb scene, when she rises as it were instantaneously which prevents a great part of that alarming distraction which Romeo discovers in finding life returning to his Juliet by slow degrees. Miss Bellamy rises more gradually, she keeps the audience longer in astonishment while the astonishment of Romeo rises in proportion and is finely heightened and wonderfully affecting as perform'd by Mr. Garrick, whose attitudes throughout the whole play are so inimitably excellent as to bid defiance to the other Romeo. . . . Upon the whole, Romeo is better performed by Garrick; Juliet tho' not better at least more affectingly by Mrs. Cibber. Mercutio in the New House is not acted but burlesqued by Macklin; Paris is better done in the New; Capulet and Tibalt better in the Old; and Shakespeare is under greater obligations to the Old than to the New House. Another critic gives this short decision: "At Covent Garden I saw *Juliet and Romeo;* and at Drury Lane *Romeo and Juliet."* (Pp. 437-438)

But the weighing and balancing of prejudiced viewpoints is little to the purpose save to point out that under Garrick, for he was as much responsible for Barry's Romeo as his own, Romeo and Juliet returned to life, and walked from the printed page into the eyes, and minds, and arguments of the men and women of the eighteenth century. To what extent they were Shakespeare's characters will be seen by a careful examination of the Garrick text.

It is a matter of more than antiquarian interest on the occasion of celebrating the four-hundredth anniversary of Shakespeare's birth to pause about midway to consider the life-giving quality which one of England's greatest actors gave to a play of undoubted poetic quality, of universal emotional appeal to youth, tinged with a note of fatalism, frustration, despair, unmerited pain, amid lush fulfillment of primal urges beautifully and chastely expressed, a play in which age matures in wisdom, and youth snuffs out, where the pomp of villainy and the gravity of humor both lie stretched in blood on Verona's pavements. More than antiquarian interest, because those three hundred performances in the eighteenth century established a stage tradition and in a real sense gave a propulsion to the play which has carried on to our times!

[15] Cooke noted the custom of some to leave the performance at Covent Garden after the third act to attend Drury Lane to see Garrick in the last two. *Memoirs of Charles Macklin,* p. 160.
[16] Percy Fitzgerald, *The Life of David Garrick,* I (London, 1868), 257.

Garrick's great love was Shakespeare. One of his artistic challenges was to fit his plays to the mid-century stage and so act in them as to persuade his audiences of their greatness. Shakespeare's plays had never been played, as far as we can discover, in complete and perfect accord with any ideally perfect text that scholars can construct. For plays are not books but promptbooks. Shakespeare doubtless overwrote his plays to indicate character development for his actors— all of whom he knew. As a man of the theater he knew also what the actor could be counted upon to do beyond the limits of language to bring the text to life on stage. Garrick, and Cibber, and Otway before him, men of the theater, knew likewise what actors could do, what they must do, what their stage limitations were, and what audience expectations were, and how far they might be led into new responses. Action upon this knowledge constitutes the dynamic and fluid nature of drama as a plastic art, unique among its sister arts.

What were some of the pressures, some of the currents, some of the topics uppermost in the minds of the audiences in the 1748-49 season, and again in the 1750-51 season, and again in the 1753-54 season to which the theaters might well respond, not just in an adaptation of a Shakespearian play, but in all plays? For the theater was one of the most sensitive sounding boards of the age, not only to topical events, but also to the flow of basic ideas, as witness any dozen *prologues,* or the interpolations of incidental lines in any dozen different types of play or afterpiece, or the constant change of entr'acte pieces, or the fresh creation of afterpieces, or the lines marked for excision by the licenser in the Larpent play-manuscripts in the Huntington Library.

Pope and Swift had died in the mid-forties. The two great symbols of neoclassical law, order, rational analysis, the common-sense view, and the satirical approach were no more. James Hervey's *Meditations among the Tombs* had appeared in 1746, preceded by Mark Aikenside's "Pleasures of the Imagination", 1744; Young's "Night Thoughts", 1742-4; Joseph Warton's "Enthusiast", 1744; Thomas Warton's "Pleasures of Melancholy", 1747; Richardson's *Clarissa,* 1748 (with the subtitle "the distresses that may attend the misconduct both of parents and children in relation to marriage"); Johnson's "Vanity of Human Wishes", 1749; Dodsley's *Collection* of many of these poems in 1748. The Wesleyan movement with its personal, more emotional relationship of the individual to his maker was growing against the deistic tendency to generalize seen earlier in the period. Walpole was out. Political stagnation for some twenty years was about over, a Jacobite rebellion had been put down. Between 1748 and 1756 a complete change in the grouping of the European powers took place, Prussia maintained itself, British sea power extended itself, and Pitt and the British people emerged as the firm controlling power in England. New forces were stirring. New releases, especially for the emotions, on stage were welcomed, consonant with those finding expression in other forms of art.

Garrick, not unaware of the atmosphere intellectual, emotional, artistic in which he lived, knew for certain what a steady source of income Shakespearian performances contributed to Drury Lane. During his season 1747-48, thirty-nine of his one hundred seventy-two nights of performing had been given over to ten different Shakespeare titles. Combined income from these nights amounted to £5,710 in round figures, according to the sums listed in the *Diary* of Richard Cross, prompter, or about twenty-five per cent of the total season's income, the thirty-nine performances representing about twenty-two per cent of the performances of mainpieces for the season.[17]

Cibber's success at the Haymarket four years earlier with *Romeo* was a good omen, and would provide a pattern of novelty similar to that of the *Twelfth Night* which Garrick had put on 6, 7 January 1748, but which had not been done there for two years. *Romeo and Juliet* was instinct with youth and with melancholy; with rebellion, and with retribution; with poetry and with didacticism; with braggadocio and with sophistication. The echoes of the graveyard, the vanities of human wishes, the folly of zealots, and the sad personal consequences of warring houses were impressively carried across the footlights by means of incomparable poetry. The age was ready for it, in Renaissance English garb—not in the togas of *Caius Marius*.

Garrick outlines clearly in his various *Advertisements* the nature of his alterations. In the first place he made certain structural changes concerned almost entirely with the excision of Rosaline in Act I (as had Cibber) and with the addition of his death scene to Act V. In the second place throughout the play he sought to reduce "quibble", the endless puns and plays upon words that crop up in the speeches of the main as well as the subordinate characters. Deference to eighteenth-century "Taste" which in the wake of Addison condemned the pun as the lowest form of wit and thought it highly inappropriate in serious drama led him to do this. In the third place he made some, though not extensive, effort to reduce the "jingle" in the play. This term referred to the use of rime in certain passages instead of blank verse. The motive seems to have been, as Hedgcock states, to obtain a piece in which the dialogue should be as natural as possible. Injury done to the play on this score is not great, inasmuch as Garrick's emendations of riming words amount to less than twenty-eight throughout the whole play. The usual process may be exemplified as follows:

> *Friar Lawrence:* Young son it argues a distemper'd head
> So soon to bid good morrow to thy *bed:*
> Care keeps his watch in every old man's eye,
> And where care lodges, sleep will never *lie;*
> But where unbruised youth with unstuff'd brain
> Doth couch his limbs, there golden sleep *doth reign.* (II. ii. 32-38)

Garrick substituted the words *pillow* and *bide* for *bed* and *lie,* and rearranged the last two lines to read:

> But where with unstuff'd brain unbruised youth
> Doth couch his limbs, there golden sleep *resides.*

Later, when Benvolio speaks:

> O noble Prince! I can discover all
> The unlucky manage of this fatal *brawl*
> That slew thy kinsman, brave Mercutio.
> *Lady Cap.:* Tybalt, my cousin! O my brother's child!
> O Prince! O cousin! husband! O the blood is spill'd
> Of my dear kinsman. Prince as thou art *true,*
> For blood of ours shed blood of Montague. (III. i. 148-155)

---

[17] Stone, *The London Stage,* 1747-48 season. Receipts by Cross differ slightly from Powel's.

Garrick changes *brawl* to *quarrel,* and rearranges Lady Capulet's speech, which he gives to Capulet, as follows:

> *Cap:* Unhappy sight alas! the blood is spill'd
> Of my dear kinsman. Now as thou are *Prince*
> For blood of ours shed blood of Montague.

The "jingle" has been removed but not much poetry that would feed the waters of the spirit has been sacrificed. Garrick did not comb through the play to break up all the rimes. He altered enough to satisfy the average playgoer of the century. When, however, he came upon such a speech as Friar Lawrence's at the opening of Act II, scene iii, "The grey-eyed morn smiles on the frowning night, Chequering the eastern clouds with streaks of light . . . etc.," he made no attempt to regulate it: he merely cut the eight lines referring to a drunkard and to the "womb" of nature, and left the remaining twenty intact. It was Francis Gentleman who wanted to dignify this speech by turning it into blank verse, and did so in his *Dramatic Censor.*

Garrick made such use of shears and paste in his altering of the first act that, for all practical purposes, it had to be printed anew to be read by any other than the actor himself. In the Shakespearian text it is composed of five scenes containing in all 719 lines. Garrick with some rearrangements and with many cuts turned the material into an act of 451 lines divided into six scenes. To these lines of Shakespeare he added forty-two lines of his own which were necessary either to bridge gaps or to effect proper transitions for his new arrangement.

With the *Prologue* and almost one-third of the act cut, Garrick's revision proceeds in the following manner: in scene i, the underlings brawl in Verona's streets and the Prince rebukes both Montague and Capulet; in scene ii, the Montagues discuss Romeo with Benvolio, discovering in him symptoms of the moon-calf lover; in scene iii, Capulet discusses Juliet with Paris; in scene iv, in a wood near Verona, Mercutio, Benvolio, and Romeo meet, information is given concerning the feast to be held that evening at the house of Capulet, Romeo discloses his love (and knows it is with Juliet), and Mercutio gives his "Queen Mab" speech; in scene v, Lady Capulet, the Nurse, and Juliet talk of marriage and of Juliet's babyhood; the sixth scene presents the ball at Capulet's house, where Juliet falls in love with Romeo and learns his identity.

All reference to Rosaline, of course, is omitted; several dozen lines of "quibble" and bawdry amongst the servants and amongst Mercutio, Benvolio, and Romeo are cut; Juliet, to suit the change of times, is described as eighteen years old instead of fourteen; Lady Montague is cut from the play and what lines of hers remain are given to her husband; a scene entirely made up of servants' preparations for the feast at Capulet's is left out, and the guests all receive invitations offstage; Mercutio's "Queen Mab" speech is pushed forward in the play; Romeo's questioning speeches as to the identity of Juliet at the masquerade ball are given to Benvolio; and the whole verbal scene of the ball is much shortened.

The additions become dramatically necessary, but are not poetically significant.[18] Emendations are typical of mid-century decorum and rationalism. The

---

[18] For example, Mercutio informs Romeo of the banquet to be held at Capulet's:
> . . . I warrant thee if thou'lt but stay to hear
> Tonight there is an ancient splendid feast
> Kept by Old Capulet, our enemy,
> Where all the beauties of Verona meet. . . . (I. iv. 243ff.)

Nurse speaks not of her *dugs,* but of her *breasts;* Capulet generalizes the location of the *ladies' corns,* putting them merely on their *feet,* instead of on their *toes;* Romeo is said to bear himself like a *courtly,* instead of a *portly* gentleman; and Mercutio informs Benvolio that Queen Mab is *fancy's midwife,* instead of the *fairies' midwife;* as Juliet is given four more years in age so the Nurse is given four more teeth to swear by. Decorum dictated not only the excision of bawdry but of certain references unpleasant to the eighteenth-century sensitivity as well, such as Mercutio's elaboration upon the tainted breath of the maids who eat sweetmeats before retiring (I. iv. 75-76).

Lady Capulet loses much by the cuts. Lady Montague loses all. But Romeo still loves, Mercutio cracks wise, Tybalt is hasty and ill-tempered, Capulet and Montague are as typical Italian fathers as in the Shakespearian version. Benvolio is an even pleasanter companion, and servants are still louts. The Nurse is still garrulous and risqué if not bawdy in her reminiscences. The beauty of Juliet still "hangs upon the cheek of night like a rich jewel in an Ethiop's ear". The act gains speed and clarity of movement. The serious loss to the lover of words is, perhaps, found only in the shortening of the delightful verbiage in the love scene between Romeo and Juliet at the masquerade ball. In reducing the "quibble" Garrick lost some pretty love-making which turns upon the wordplay concerned with *Saint, Pilgrim, Lips,* and *Sin.* Even Gentleman was forced to comment upon the swiftness of Juliet's falling in love as a result of excision in this scene. He condemned her character rather than Garrick's shears:

> This masquerade scene is well disposed to give Romeo an opportunity of *unfolding himself:* but we rather think the lady's catching fire so very suddenly, shows her to be composed of tinder-like material.[19]

The significant phrase here is "opportunity of unfolding himself". We must remember that we are looking now not at a text to be studied in the library, but at a prompt-book for actors upon stage. The play was revived for a first performance on Tuesday, 29 November 1748. The play notice for Thursday, 1 December 1748, adds significantly "with a new *Masquerade Dance* proper to the Play". And every advertisement hereafter makes a special feature of the masquerade scene, which involved a large part of the acting company and pleased the audience with special music, choreography, and costume. Time was elongated for this. The text was made lean, but the burden of responsibility was not removed from the main actors. At this point *they* had opportunity for unfolding themselves in their growing youthful love by pantomimic action, in a location of prominence on stage against the background of the dancers and soft music. The evidence? A set of five prints on "superfine paper of the Five Principal Scenes in *Romeo and Juliet* designed, and engraved by Mr. Ant. Walker . . ." advertised in the *Public Advertiser* of 21 January 1754 as "serving for Mr. Pope's edition of Shakespeare in Quarto, Sir Thomas Hanmer's edition, 6 Vols quarto, or for any of the folio editions, and may be framed and glazed for furniture". One of the five principal scenes from *Romeo and Juliet* is the Masquerade Scene, which suggests the stage grouping, quite possibly from the Barry-Nossiter performance.[20]

[19] His note in the Bell 1774 edition of *Shakespeare's Plays as They are Perform'd at the Theatres Royal in London,* II, 98.

[20] An original set is in the possession of the Folger Shakespeare Library, from which the Masquerade Scene has been reproduced in Stone, *The London Stage,* I, 176-177.

Garrick's alteration of the second act is marked chiefly by his cuts, and by the attempt mentioned before to reduce "quibble" and "jingle". The high point is the Garden Scene. Of its 189 lines he cut twenty-six, twenty-two of which were from Romeo's speeches. Some poetry is lost—Romeo no longer compares Juliet's eyes to the stars in heaven, he is content to say in combined Garrick-Shakespearian phrase:

> O *were those* eyes in heaven,
> *They'd* through the airy region stream so bright
> That birds would sing and think it were *the morn.*[21]

His lines, "I have night's cloak to hide me from their eyes; And but thou love me, let them find me here; . . ." etc., are omitted along with the couplet, "Love goes toward love, as schoolboys from their books But love from love, toward school with heavy looks." Romeo must *vow* not *swear,* and his reference to being new *baptiz'd* under another name is changed lest the Church be offended.[22] Otherwise the scene stands in its Shakespearian glory filled with poetry, love, and beauty.

Garrick omitted the sonnet which serves as a prologue to the act, as it contained information unnecessary in his development of the play. The remainder of his excisions had to do with a long passage of word-play between Benvolio, Mercutio, and Romeo in the fourth scene, and the shortening of some of the Nurse's teasing discourse with Juliet in the fifth. The act is one-third shorter than the original.

The third act is about half the length of the original. A good deal of emendation in single words or phrases reduced the rime. Mercutio's pun on being a "grave man" is cut, and his "plague o' both your houses" becomes "A pox on both your houses". Juliet's lines are retrenched in that she poetizes less on "civil night, the sober-suited matron", brings fewer imprecations upon Romeo's head for killing Tybalt,[23] and is so stunned by "that word 'banished'", that she cannot elaborate upon it in the succeeding thirteen lines of Shakespearian text. The scene between Friar Lawrence and Romeo is shortened. The one raves less, the other comforts him more quickly. There is no bedroom scene, but the parting of Romeo and Juliet takes place in the garden with very little excision. The final scene at the Capulet household in which Juliet learns she is to marry Paris is shortened, and a piece of excellent dramatic irony is lost thereby when Juliet is not allowed to tell her mother:

> . . . I never shall be satisfied
> With Romeo, till I behold him—dead. . . .
> Madam, if you could find out but a man
> To bear a poison I would temper it,
> That Romeo should, upon receipt thereof
> Soon sleep in quiet . . . .

21 Italicized words represent Garrick's changes.
22 Shakespeare: Call me but love, and I'll be new baptiz'd;
          Henceforth I never will be Romeo
    Garrick: Call me but love, *I will forsake my name*
          And never *more* be Romeo.
23 No longer does she cry: "O serpent heart, hid with a flowering face / Did ever dragon keep so fair a cave?" etc.

The fourth act in this version was also reduced by half. Servants, musicians, Capulet, Paris, and the Friar suffered loss, but nothing vital to the clear movement of the plot was omitted.

At the opening of the fifth act, after the year 1750, a funeral procession for Juliet was introduced in which appeared the following dirge written by Garrick:

> *CHORUS*
> Rise, rise!
> Heart-breaking sighs
> The woe-fraught bosom swell;
>   For sighs alone
>   And dismal moan
> Should echo Juliet's knell.
>   *AIR*
> She's gone—the sweetest flower of May
>   That blooming blest our sight;
> Those eyes which shone like breaking day
>   Are set in endless night.
>   *CHORUS, etc.*
>   *AIR*
> She's gone, she's gone, nor leaves behind
>   So fair a form, so pure a mind;
> How couldst thou, Death, at once destroy
>   The lover's hope, the parent's joy?
>   *CHORUS, etc*
>   *AIR*
> Thou spotless soul, look down below
>   Our unfeign'd sorrow see;
> O give us strength to bear our woe,
>   To bear the loss of thee.
>   *CHORUS, etc.*

The circumstances of the introduction of this procession again bear witness to the competitive pressures of stage managership. The bare statement of the situation is made by Cross in his *Diary,* 2 October 1750:

> Both ye Houses play'd on ye same day Romeo & Juliet, Mr. Barry & Mrs. Cibber at Covent Garden against Mr. Garrick & Miss Bellamy at Drury Lane—Miss Bellamy never apear'd upon this stage before; & was greatly receiv'd—both Houses too added a Scene of Juliet's funeral. (Folger Shakespeare Library)

The funeral procession involved the composition of a Solemn Dirge, for which Garrick wrote the words and for which he asked Dr. William Boyce to compose the music. At least seven vocal parts were involved.[24] The demand seems to have been forced upon Garrick by news that Rich at Covent Garden was instituting such a procession and Solemn Dirge at his house, with music composed by Dr. Thomas Augustine Arne. Thereafter playbills for performances for both houses featured not only the Masquerade Scene but also the Funeral *Procession* and

---

[24] The play notice in the *Public Advertiser* for 20 October 1760, and often thereafter, lists as many as 12 singers for the Dirge.

Solemn Dirge. This sort of thing was partial evidence of the stage's response to the graveyard atmosphere of a dozen poems and meditations such as those mentioned above. The music for Garrick's Dirge has been discovered recently by the research of Mr. Charles Haywood.[25]

One hundred and sixty-six lines were cut from this last act, mainly from the parts of the Friar, Paris, and those people—watchmen, a page, etc.—who appear in the massing of characters at the tomb in the end.

Just after Romeo drinks the poison Garrick added his new seventy-five line death scene which so thrilled eighteenth-century audiences.

> *Rom: . . . seal with a righteous kiss.*
> Soft—soft—she breathes, and stirs[26] [Juliet wakes]
> *Jul:* Where am I? defend me powers!
> *Rom:* She speaks, she lives; and we shall still be bless'd![26]
> My kind propitious stars o'erpay me now
> For all my sorrows past—rise, rise my *Juliet,*
> And from this cave of death, this house of horror,
> Quick let me snatch thee to thy Romeo's arms,
> There breathe a vital spirit in thy lips,
> And call thee back to live and love! [Takes her hand.]
> *Jul:* Bless me! how cold it is! Who's there![26]
> *Rom:* Thy husband.
> It is thy *Romeo,* Love, rais'd from despair
> To joys unutterable! quit, quit this place
> And let us fly together— [Brings her from the tomb.]
> *Jul:* Why do you force me so—I'll ne'er consent
> I'll not wed *Paris—Romeo* is my husband—[26]
> *Rom:* Her senses are unsettled—Restore 'em Heav'n!
> Romeo is thy husband; I am that Romeo,
> Nor all th' opposing pow'rs of earth or man
> Can break our bonds, or tear thee from my heart.
> *Jul:* I know that voice—Its magic sweetness wakes
> My tranced soul—I now remember well
> Each circumstance—O my lord, my Romeo!
> Had'st thou not come, sure I had slept forever;
> But there's a sovereign charm in thy embraces[26]
> That can revive the dead—O honest *Friar!*
> Dost thou avoid me *Romeo?* let me touch
> Thy hand and taste the cordial of thy lips—
> You fright me—Speak—O let me hear some voice
> Besides my own in this drear vault of death,
> Or I shall faint—support me—
> *Rom:* O I cannot,
> I have no strength, but want thy feeble aid,
> Cruel poison!
> *Jul:* Poison! What means my lord; thy trembling voice!
> Pale lips! and swimming eyes! death's in thy face!
> *Rom:* It is indeed—I struggle with him now—
> The transports that I felt, to hear thee speak,

---

[25] "William Boyce's 'Solemn Dirge' in Garrick's *Romeo and Juliet* Production", *SQ*, XI (1960), 173-188.
[26] A line almost verbatim from Otway's *Caius Marius.*

And see thy op'ning eyes stopt for a moment
His impetuous course, and all my mind
Was happiness and thee; but now the poison
Rushes thro' my veins—I've not time to tell—
Fate brought me to this place—to take a last,
Last farewell of my love and with thee die.
Jul: Die! was the Friar false!
Rom: I know not that,
I thought thee dead! distracted at the sight
(Fatal speed) drank poison, kiss'd thy cold lips
And found within thy arms a precious grave—
But in that moment—O—
Jul: And did I wake for this!
Rom: My powers are blasted,
Twixt death and love I'm torn—I am distracted!
But death's strongest—And I must leave thee, Juliet!
O cruel, cursed fate!—in sight of heav'n—
Jul: Thou rav'st—lean on my breast—
Rom: Fathers have flinty hearts, no tears can melt 'em
Nature pleads in vain—children must be wretched
Jul: O my breaking heart—
Rom: She is my wife—our hearts are twin'd together
Capulet forbear—Paris loose your hold—
Pull not our heartstrings thus—they crack—they break—
O Juliet! Juliet
Jul: Stay, stay for me Romeo—a moment stay; fate marries us in death
And we are one—no pow'r shall part us. [Faints on Romeo's body.]

Hereupon the text returns to Shakespeare where Friar Lawrence enters and speaks:

Saint Francis be my speed! How oft tonight
Have my old feet stumbled at graves! Who's there?
Alack! what blood is this which stains [twenty-one lines cut]
The stony entrance of this sepulchre?
Ah Juliet awake, and Romeo dead. What Paris too
Oh what an unkind hour
Is guilty of this lamentable chance!

Then follows the remainder of Garrick's addition:

Jul: Here he is still, and I will hold him fast,
They shall not tear him from me—
Friar: Patience Lady—
Jul: Who is that! O thou cursed Friar! Patience!
Talk'st thou of patience to a wretch like me!
Friar: O fatal error! rise thou fair distrest
And fly this scene of death!
Jul: Come thou not near me
Or this dagger shall quit my Romeo's death. [Draws dagger.]
Friar: I wonder not thy griefs have made thee desp'rate.
What noise without? sweet Juliet, let us fly—

At this point the text returns again to the Shakespearian one where the Friar offers to dispose her "amongst a sisterhood of happy nuns", but leaves upon hearing the approach of others, and Juliet stabs herself. The final scene is short in Garrick's version. The explanation of everything is briefly carried out. Montague and Capulet become reconciled, and the Prince closes in six of Garrick's lines:

> Let Romeo's man, and let the boy attend us:
> We'll hence, and further scan this sad disaster.
> Well may you mourn, my lords (now wise too late)
> These tragic issues of your mortal hate:
> From private feuds, what dire misfortunes flow,
> Whate'er the cause, the sure effect is WOE.

Garrick continued to play the part of Romeo with great success for ten years. It is easier for a youth of ability to impersonate age than for an older man to give a convincing representation of such a youth as Romeo. Garrick wisely relinquished the character to younger members of his company after 1760. Three times, however, during the month of April, 1761, he acted in the play, but in the role of Mercutio.[27] I have found no comment on his playing of this part.[28] It was as Romeo that he was remembered.

The play became well established in the repertory of Drury Lane and was performed each year until 1773, very often as a command performance, or as an actor's benefit, aside from its place in the regular program. Garrick used it again and again as a proving ground for young Shakespearian actors. He taught Ross, Fleetwood,[29] Holland, Cautherly, Reddish, and Diamond the part of Romeo when they were beginning their careers. And he instructed Miss Houghton, Miss Pritchard, Miss Bride, Mrs. Barry, Miss Younge, and Miss Morland in the part of Juliet, when they were beginners.

Despite the change of principle in Garrick's handling of the text, and despite his additions to the play, Romeo and Juliet are more indebted to him than to any other man in the eighteenth century, for bringing them back from the characters of Marius Junior and Lavinia to a lasting life, love, and death of their own. Whether he or Barry played Romeo, or whether Mrs. Cibber, Miss Bellamy, or Miss Pritchard played Juliet, or whether he or Woodward played Mercutio, Garrick was responsible for them all, and changed though it was, his was by far and away the best text of Shakespeare's play which carried on the stage from 1680 until 1846.

New York University

[27] April 6, 13, 20.

[28] All three were novel benefit performances for his friends and fellow actors: Charles Holland, the Lawrence Kennedys, and Charles Blakes.

[29] A son of the former manager of Drury Lane, who played Romeo at first with more gusto than skill, as noted by Cross in his diary for 28 Sept. and 13 Oct. 1758 (Folger Shakespeare Library): "Mr. Fleetwood in ye fight with Paris in ye last act having a sword by his side instead of a foil, run Mr. Austin [Paris] into the Belly. He lay some time but at last call'd to be taken off—a surgeon was sent for—no harm, a small wound & he is recover'd."

Dramatic Structure and Criticism:
Plot in *Hamlet*

FREDSON BOWERS

F we are to base aesthetic criticism of the drama on any kind of evidence that may seem tangible, we must start with the plot. The chief fault of most searchers for tangible evidence is their treatment of a play as if it were a transcript of real life, a view that Stoll and his followers have effectively exploded. Characters in a play do not have secret lives off-stage that are subject to guesswork as if actions, thoughts, and emotions not portrayed, or even mentioned, in the play can nevertheless be reconstructed. Speculation cannot piece together a full continuum of detail that will weld what we see and hear on-stage to what we do not see and hear off-stage.

Aristotle defined plot as follows: "the Plot is the imitation of the action: for by plot I here mean the arrangement of the incidents" (*Poetics*, VI. 6), and he remarks shortly (VI. 9), "the most important of all is the structure of the incidents"; and again, "the incidents and the plot are the end of tragedy, and the end is the chief thing of all" (VI. 10). Butcher (p. 347) paraphrases in this manner: "It is the plot . . . which gives to the play its inner meaning and reality as the soul does to the body. To the plot we look in order to learn what the play means; here lies its essence, its true significance. Lastly, the plot is 'the end of a tragedy' as well as the beginning. Through the plot the intention of the play is realised."

Modern critics have tended to overlook the uses of plot analysis in the service of aesthetic criticism, a form that should be aimed at the determination and evaluation of the meaning of a work of art, insofar as this end is possible within the framework of an artistic production. "Meaning" is a slippery term, of course. At one end of the scale we have authorial conscious intention deliberately worked out in a play; at the other, we have unconscious meaning penetrating and shaping any great work of art well beyond an author's precise conceptions. Let us leave the unconscious to other critics and concern ourselves, more humbly, with what must be the starting-point for accurate criticism, of whatever kind: an attempt to utilize the evidence of plot to determine at least some elements of an author's conscious intention. In doing so we shall be escaping the older-fashioned method of seeking meaning through character analysis in the Bradley manner, for Aristotle places character in a tragedy as secondary to plot. We shall also be escaping the presentday analysis of Shakespeare's imagery as the key to his true meaning. Aristotle again disagrees, and assigns to diction a place behind plot and character. Certainly, the complaint is true that criticism of a play as a poem involves an analytical method suitable for lyric but not necessarily appropriate for dramatic poetry on the stage.

Since *Hamlet* has been more than ordinarily subject to critical speculation, we may take this difficult example and see what the analysis of plot in one or two respects can show about problems that lie at the heart of the play.

In every developed play there is one incident, or action, on which the main plot turns. The plot may be said to turn on this episode because, when the whole play is viewed in retrospect, the audience can see that the end (whether for good or for ill) was the direct result of a chain of causality linked to this one episode which, in effect, directed the action into a particular path that determined the outcome of the plot. Aristotle seized on this incident as the determinant whether a plot would be, as he phrased it, single or complex, according to the means by which "the change of fortune" took place (IX. 2). That a tragedy must have an incident in which a change took place that determined the conclusion, however, he never doubted.

The modern term for this incident is the climax, or crisis. In popular thinking, climax is confused with catastrophe or denouement, and is thought to be the high point of the action in the sense that it is the most exciting incident, usually that episode at the end when the decisive conflict takes place that settles the fates of the characters. The true climax is, indeed, an incident in which the fate of the protagonist is irrevocably decided; but the popular identification of the climax as the untying of the knot obscures the important objection that the tragedy (if we may talk only of this form) would scarcely be inevitable if at the last moment its course might be altered. The nature of this catastrophe or outcome has been decided long before in the true climax, the key scene of the play which causes the action to turn against the tragic protagonist. After this point, the details by which his unhappy end will be brought about may be subject to variation, but not the outcome itself.

If we are to attempt to discover what significance the action of a tragedy possesses, we must first determine what is the true turning-point of the action, for that incident will give us the clue to the essential tragic meaning of the play. In truth, if the tragedy itself has any significance, its climactic incident that determines the ultimate fate of the chief character must be the key to unlock this meaning: a climax cannot itself be without meaning in a truly meaningful play.

In the usual tragedy the action in the early stages favors the protagonist; in the last stage of the catastrophe, the action goes contrary to his interests, and usually the chain of events leads to his defeat or death. The incident responsible for the alteration of the course of the action will be the climax. It can be discovered in two ways. First, the turn of the action against the protagonist must be traced to this point and to this point alone. Second, if the tragic action is to have a significance, a significant decision by the hero must be contained in this episode, a decision that is in some way mistaken or unfortunate, and usually one that will justify the tragic fate that as a result overtakes him. When these two criteria join, the critic has isolated the climax.

In the action of *Hamlet* three scenes are commonly suggested: the play-within-a-play, the prayer scene, and the closet scene.

The play-within-a-play, it is asserted, is crucial because only after the test is Hamlet positive that Claudius is the murderer of his father and that the revenge can proceed with justice. We must admit that if Hamlet throughout the antecedent action had been tormented by doubts of the Ghost, and if as a result of the mousetrap his mind was so clarified that he engaged himself to a course of revengeful action that succeeded, and, at the end, he survived, then the play-within-a-play would certainly be the climax in a very different drama called *Hamlet*. In such a plot the incident that changes paralyzing uncertainty and delay to certainty and action, and thus leads to the successful conclusion, must be the turning-point.

But if we take *Hamlet* as it is, we may ask, first, was Hamlet's doubt of the Ghost the major reason for his failure to revenge between the time of the Ghost's revelation and the acting of *The Murder of Gonzago?* If so, Shakespeare has neglected to inform us. The hard truth is that no concrete reason for delay in this interval is ever given us by narrative or by action up to the moment, the night before the play-within-a-play, that Hamlet decides to test whether the Ghost be demon or spirit and in the process to secure "grounds more relative" than the mere word of an apparition. If doubt of the Ghost has been a deterrent to action, we do not know it. A climax is very odd indeed that clarifies the hero's mind on a problem that the audience has not known existed until two scenes before.[1]

Secondly, we may enquire what is the significant issue of this scene, what the fateful decision that thereupon makes the tragic catastrophe inevitable. Might not the identical scene serve as the climax for a denouement in which Hamlet succeeds in a well-planned revenge and ascends the throne of Denmark?

There is, however, another argument in favor of the mousetrap scene as crisis that might be advanced: the play-within-a-play warns Claudius that Hamlet knows his secret and thus turns the King from an ostensible benefactor to Hamlet's mortal enemy. It is perfectly clear that Claudius' first action after his exposure is to alter the innocent commission for the English voyage to a command to execute Hamlet on arrival. The catastrophe, moreover, is directly brought about by another plot of Claudius against Hamlet's life that succeeds where the initial one had failed. Thus it is true, in one sense, that the plot line alters after the play-within-a-play, and that the change in Claudius' attitude to Hamlet that brings about the catastrophe can be traced back directly to the mousetrap scene.

Is this, then, the turning-point, the incident in the plot in which the action veers from prosperity to defeat as a consequence? The answer would be yes were Claudius the protagonist. Yet the enmity of Claudius, as an antagonist, need not be successful, even though it is admittedly aroused in this scene. Moreover, the second test for the climax will not work. If the play-within-a-play is the turning-point, then a fateful decision by Hamlet must be involved that arises in some sort from character. A subtle critic might argue that Hamlet made a fatal blunder in staging *The Murder of Gonzago,* since the clarification of his mind was achieved, ironically, only at the expense of warning his foe that the murderer of Old Hamlet was known and that a revenger was in being.

---

[1] I am taking the soliloquy that ends II. ii substantially at its face value and thus not concerning myself with the view that this doubt of the Ghost is a sudden rationalizing of Hamlet's congenital inability to act.

Hence the gain was ironically accompanied by inevitable loss, and Hamlet sealed his doom by alerting his victim to the danger of his position.

Such an argument might suit melodrama but not Shakespearian tragedy, for it omits not only the role of character in the decision but also the ethical issue. What Elder Olson calls a morally determinate action (closely related to the requirements of Aristotle's tragic law) would be inoperative.[2] I do not wish to argue that all tragic heroes must conform to the Aristotelian formula, no matter how psychologically sound it may be. But the linking of a fateful decision to some principle of action is essential if a tragedy is to be a meaningful criticism of life. If Hamlet is damned if he does, and damned if he doesn't—which is the crux of the ironic argument just sketched—then no decision can be right or wrong, and therefore no significance can inhere to whatever choice is made. This dilemma might suit a naturalistic or existentialist drama, or a Theater of the Absurd, but it would not suit Shakespeare and the Elizabethans.

Let us revert for a moment to the meaning of the phrase "a morally determinate action" as a requirement for tragic drama. The heart of the matter is that a decision that triggers the climax cannot be one dictated by chance or accident, for such a choice has no personal significance, whatever its philosophic import may be in respect to the human condition for those to whom the world and human life possess no significant pattern. Even in such a semi-tragedy as *Romeo and Juliet* in which the ending seems removed from any rigorous application of the doctrine of tragic flaw, the climax in Romeo's decision to fight with Tybalt involves a personal choice that carries moral responsibility and is therefore morally determinate.[3]

Thus a morally determinate action means not only that the character is aware of the issue and nevertheless makes a choice that is inherently fatal, but also that the audience is aware of the significance of the choice on a plane higher than simple expediency and can approve or disapprove accordingly. That is, if the hero is to suffer death as a result of his choice, the audience must acknowledge the justice of the outcome. This recognition can be achieved only if the audience sees the violation of some important moral principle in the

[2] See Olson, *Tragedy and the Theory of Drama* (Detroit: Wayne State University Press, 1961), pp. 37-41. Actually, Olson's statement is, "Plot is a system of actions of a determinate moral quality", and he regards the phrase as a generalization of Aristotle's *spoudaios*. I am, perhaps, applying the sense more narrowly than he would approve.

[3] I refer to attempts to equate a tragic flaw with Romeo and Juliet's precipitate falling in love and immediate marriage. If every elopement were to be condemned by death—a view that is the logical extension—we should need to alter our beliefs about romantic love. Although Aristotle's doctrine of the tragic flaw does not explain very much of the tragic situation, nevertheless Shakespeare does succeed in portraying life in this play according to some sort of significant pattern. The theme of the "star-crossed lovers"—that is, Fate—seems to be the answer. If so, the tragic plot concerns two lovers caught up in an action that draws its rationale from the logic of externally motivated events and less from character flowering into (and ultimately responsible for) the consequences of the action. In these circumstances Shakespeare is in serious danger of arousing, as Aristotle remarks, the audience's resentment at a lack of justice. He avoids this danger, it would seem, by finding his climax in a morally determinate action, even though it is so strongly shaped by external events as to constitute less than a real tragic flaw. Moreover, the emphasis on Fate as a positive force lends a dignity and a pattern to the action that might not otherwise be felt as significant. Finally, Shakespeare chooses to emphasize the pity of the cathartic reaction rather than the fear, perhaps, although fear is not entirely absent. However, the fear is not created by the identification of the audience with the lovers—the feeling, "There but for the grace of God go I". Instead, the fear is generated by the identification of the audience with parental blindness: "But for the grace of God I might behave like this to my children".

choice and agrees that the decisive action had significance and was not entered upon by accident, or blindly selected without a recognition of the issues involved. This is only to re-state the Aristotelian doctrine of the tragic flaw in a man who is neither a devil nor an angel, and the cathartic effect that results from contemplating his fall.

Under these circumstances it is proper to inquire whether Hamlet's choice to prove Claudius' guilt at the expense of alerting his opponent to the mortal danger in which he stood was a morally determinate action—anything that could qualify as an action springing from a tragic flaw. The answer can be only a strong denial. Hamlet's choice in setting the mousetrap may be existentially tragic, but it is not tragic in any sense known to Shakespeare or his contemporaries. No ethical issue is raised by the choice, only one of expediency. The play-within-a-play cannot be the climax to a meaningful tragedy.

However, it is argued that the information received in this scene gives Hamlet the readiness to kill Claudius, as he thinks, in the closet scene. This may well be, depending upon the seriousness with which one takes the final soliloquy in II. ii, with its statement of need to test the Ghost's revelations. The play-within-a-play followed by the prayer scene, it is true, offers a rising sequence of strain; but this is only to say that the decision to kill made in the closet scene was more important than the motivation, such as it was, offered by the success of the mousetrap in respect to that decision. Indeed, that the closet scene follows the play-within-a-play is largely adventitious, and the sequence is deliberately emphasized as not an effect of a cause.

Instead, Shakespeare has very carefully arranged the cause-and-effect linkage of the incidents to show that the interview with Gertrude and the concealment of Polonius were planned before the play-within-a-play, and that Hamlet went to his mother's apartment not because of the success of the mousetrap but as the result of a plan laid much earlier. Indeed, it is an irony that the scheme for Gertrude to worm the secret of his melancholy from her son is no longer necessary after the play-within-a-play, for Claudius has learned the secret but is not in a position to countermand the orders for the original plan to go into effect. Polonius and Gertrude, the audience knows, are engaged to a plan that has no longer any rationale. If, in the plot, there is no necessary connection between the play-within-a-play and the closet scene (indeed, quite the reverse), then the argument fails that the closet-scene killing of Polonius is only the working-out of the climax decision made as a result of Claudius' self-betrayal at the play. The climax, thus, is still to seek.

The prayer scene is also a candidate, and superficially there is something to be said for it. Certainly, if Hamlet had not spared the King here, Claudius would not have lived to fight another day and to lay the plot that finally caused Hamlet's death in the catastrophe. Yet analysis shows that all evidence in favor of the prayer scene is superficial. In relation to the plot line, no definite action from Claudius directly depends upon his being spared. It is only his determination to conceal his initial crime at all costs that leads him to the specific practice against Hamlet's life that causes the catastrophe. For example, Claudius alters the commission for the English embassy to order Hamlet's execution, as the first result of the play-within-a-play revelation. But this counter-action proves abortive. Hamlet escapes the danger, and thus the altered commission has nothing to do with the terms of the catastrophe. Another, and later, intrigue causes Hamlet's death.

Correspondingly, the failure to dispose of Claudius in the prayer scene merely enables him to continue with the same plan for the English voyage that is later to prove useless. At this point no action has been taken that will necessarily prove to have a tragic outcome. There is no reason why Hamlet cannot still outwit Claudius and take his revenge in safety. That Claudius could not rise from the grave to kill Hamlet in the catastrophe if he had been slain at his prayers is obvious enough, but the action of a dramatic plot requires more of a chain of cause and effect between specific incidents, one leading to another, than this very general connection. No specific action derives from Claudius as a direct result of his having been spared, unwittingly, in the prayer scene, but only a continuation of an action decided upon after the play-within-a-play. Whatever the significance of the prayer scene, therefore, it cannot be defended in terms of the dramatic plot as the turning-point of the action in which the advantage, previously in Hamlet's favor, shifts to Claudius' side.

Indeed, to revert for a moment, it would be a poor matching of wits if the revelation of Hamlet's revengeful purpose were actually the turning-point. If Hamlet is so weak that he must kill an unsuspecting victim instead of an opponent on guard, he would have been a puny tragic hero. We must agree that Claudius' recognition of his own danger does not mark the crisis of the drama, for the baring of his secret only makes the two men equally matched in their knowledge of each other. Shakespeare emphasizes this point by showing us Claudius' first retaliatory action after the mousetrap as a failure. The crucial incident that decides the issue between them is yet to come.

Within these terms the prayer scene cannot be that incident, for no new line of the plot leads from it that has not already had its origin in the play-within-a-play, to which the prayer scene is only an appendage. This is to speak technically. In terms of the plot, it is the joining of Laertes to Claudius that directly leads to Hamlet's death. What the action of the play would have been like if Laertes had not had the occasion to revenge his father's death, we cannot tell. In itself, this point is enough to remove the prayer scene from consideration as the climax.

But other and even more important considerations appear: the ethical implications of the climax that are part and parcel of the Aristotelian doctrine of the tragic flaw as it appears in English Renaissance drama.[4] If Hamlet's sparing of Claudius at prayer is to be a tragic error of such magnitude that the audience will accept his death in the catastrophe as an act of justice, we must take it that he should have killed Claudius at this moment. If so, the audience must believe that Hamlet's decision to spare him was not only ill-advised but even culpable despite his belief that Claudius was then in a state of grace. It is difficult to see how such a bloodthirsty and morally obtuse theory could be defended on the grounds of heroic action. If a tragic flaw in a sympathetic character is to be pin-pointed as his refusal to kill a defenseless man at prayer,

---

[4] The English Renaissance drama had a strong impulse to intensify the Aristotelian tragic flaw by associating it with the Christian doctrine of personal responsibility for actions, a concept that stems from a belief in the significance of free will, and hence one that sometimes was far removed from the Greek spirit.

then the English dramatic hero was modelled on the tradition of the Renaissance Italian villain, a patently absurd proposition. Hamlet's refusal to slaughter Claudius when he is presumably at peace with his Maker is a morally determinate action, right enough, but it does not result from an inner weakness, a character flaw.[5] If it were a fault requiring death in the denouement, Christian doctrine would have no influence on an audience's moral judgment. Let us move on.

The direct means by which Claudius kills Hamlet is the poisoned rapier in the hand of Laertes. This is the only counteraction we see except for the abortive attempt to have Hamlet executed in England. If Laertes had not joined with Claudius against Hamlet, we have no means of knowing how the play's catastrophe would have been brought about and whether its action would have been for or against Hamlet. But Laertes, a noble young gentleman, could not have been suborned like Rosencrantz and Guildenstern to join Claudius' party. The one cause that leads him to seek Hamlet's death is the murder of Polonius. Since it is the revenge of Laertes that tips the scales against Hamlet and directly brings about the catastrophe, whatever scene it is that shows the origin of his revenge on Hamlet will meet one part of the plot requirements for the climax. This scene is, of course, the interview with Hamlet's mother in the course of which Polonius is slain by mistake for the King. If, as I have suggested, Claudius and Hamlet are two evenly matched opponents, the turning-point of the plot must be this mistake of Hamlet that causes Laertes to intervene and to ally himself with Claudius against Hamlet's life. By a chain of cause and effect, the events of the catastrophe are firmly bound to the closet scene.

The closet scene must next pass the second test, that of being a morally determinate action resulting from a tragic flaw. I suggest that this ethical climax does indeed coincide with the climax of the action. Greek tragedy might have made of this scene a study of simple fatal error, something like the hotheaded bad luck by which Oedipus slew his father; and in this manner it might have drawn a moral of the ways in which supernal fate interferes, with a force too strong for mortals to triumph over. But the Elizabethan is not the Greek drama, and the English tragic writers would necessarily have agreed with Milton's God, Who pronounces, "What I will is Fate". The general framework of Elizabethan tragic ethics, which depend upon the Christian doctrine of free will and personal responsibility, demands that the slaying of Polonius be more than an unlucky accident.

We now come to a view of the closet scene that may be briefly summarized, since it has been considered elsewhere in some detail.[6] Shakespeare's *Hamlet*

---

[5] The point, actually, is not whether Hamlet would have been culpable if he had known the truth about Claudius' lack of repentance but not culpable if he acted on the assumption that Claudius was in a state of grace. Critics are in general agreement that Hamlet's bloodthirsty reasons are a rationalization of (or a recompense for) his unwillingness to kill at this moment. If the drawing back from the commission of a murder when the opportunity is first offered is a weakness in character that will enable catharsis to operate in the consequences, then an argument for the climactic nature of this scene can be made. But, it should be noted, not in a civilized Christian society, whatever would have been the reaction of Hrothgar's subjects. One simply cannot argue that an Elizabethan, or a modern, audience would take the refusal to commit a cold-blooded murder as a moral weakness rather than a moral strength.

[6] Bowers, "Hamlet as Minister and Scourge", *PMLA*, LXX (1955), 740-749; "Hamlet's Fifth Soliloquy", *Essays on Shakespeare and Elizabethan Drama in Honor of Hardin Craig*, ed. Richard Hosley (Columbia: University of Missouri Press, 1962), pp. 213-222.

is not a play glorifying pagan ethics; it cannot help being addressed to an audience that takes the Christian point of view for granted. Blood-revenge is a
pagan, or at least an anti-Christian, duty, since it requires a man to place his
will above that of God and to violate the commandment, "Thou shalt not kill".
The premeditated murder sought by a revenger of blood endangered his immortal soul. Elizabethan law joined with Christian doctrine to exclude private
blood-revenge as a way of justice. When public justice was not practicable, men
must rely on the biblical promise, "Vengeance is mine; I will repay, saith the
Lord". Generally interpreted, this punishment for crime might be delayed until
the after-life; but, obviously, a more concrete manifestation was desirable, and
thus the Elizabethans were inclined to see God's justice dealing hand in the
downfall or death of all evil-doers. Sometimes God might work through natural
forces, as a storm; sometimes through brute creation. But often He used human agents as ministers of His justice. In doing so, however, He reserved those
actions that repaid a crime by a crime for men called scourges who by their
fixed rejection of divine grace had damned themselves irremediably in this life.
Justice that required no crime for its administration was performed by good
men, called ministers.

When we apply this ethos to *Hamlet,* we see the absurdity of taking it that
God would release the Ghost from Purgatory to corrupt his son by urging
Hamlet to a murder that would condemn his immortal soul to hell fire. In fact,
the Ghost never suggests to Hamlet that Claudius should be killed, even though
that is Hamlet's assumption. As we may see from a very important object lesson,
Cyril Tourneur's play *The Atheist's Tragedy* put the Christian revenger into
God's hands, confident that Providence would offer the means, ultimately, for
a revenge that would not be criminal.

Thus it may be argued that it was a real error for Hamlet to attempt his
private revenge in the closet scene since this action ran contrary to his position
as a minister of Heaven, for whom public justice would be arranged at Heaven's
own pleasure. The tragic error consists in the fact that Hamlet's emotional drive
is too strong, or compulsive, to permit him to wait upon what appears to be
Heaven's quite exorbitant delay.[7] After the mounting pressure of his success in
the play-within-a-play and then the frustration of the prayer scene, the opportunity offered for an ostensible madman to slice up a rat proves more than he
can resist. Hamlet rejects the biblical command against private blood-revenge,
and instantly finds his error when he discovers he has slain an innocent man.
This decision to cast off Heavenly guidance may fairly be called a morally determinate action suitable for tragic dignity, and the inability to endure the
cumulative strain of inaction may fairly be called the tragic flaw. Without
question we have here the true climax.

It rests briefly to assess the value of this analysis for a critical view of the
play, even while we keep in mind that this has been only one episode under
scrutiny and that there are others that need similar analysis before any total
criticism can be attempted.

Tourneur's *Atheist's Tragedy* must be cited once more, with its protagonist
who is in the same dilemma as Hamlet but who successfully overcomes the

---

[7] This is also the reason for the tragic decision made by Hieronimo in Kyd's *Spanish Tragedy*.
See Bowers, "A Note on *The Spanish Tragedy*", MLN, LIII (1938), 590-591.

temptation to anticipate Heaven, and who therefore survives when Heavenly vengeance strikes down his antagonist at the very moment of his anticipated triumph. The lesson to be drawn is—paradoxically—that the tragic fact is not Hamlet's inaction, except for its effect on his cumulative impatience. One cannot emphasize too strongly that the critical identification of the climax reveals this truth: the catastrophe occurs not as a direct consequence of Hamlet's delay but instead as a direct consequence of his rash and overhasty action. This is what the plot tells us. There is no other choice.

The long history of discussion about Hamlet's delay, as if its complex causes were the central fact of the drama, and indeed as if the tragedy were the outcome of this delay, is quite unsupported by the evidence of the plot. The only episode of delay that is shown us in the action (and Aristotle admits as part of the plot only what is shown in action) is the sparing of Claudius at prayer. If under the peculiar circumstances of this scene any audience believes that Hamlet was so culpable in neglecting the opportunity that his catastrophic death is a just return for an egregious error of delay, then there is no ethical relation between art and life, and we have reverted to savagery. The plot tells us that it was Hamlet's ill-advised action, not his inaction, that led by consequence to his death-in-victory.

The critical analysis of Hamlet's delay, therefore, as if it were an error, a weakness, is itself wrong-headed. By its climax the plot tells us that it was the breaking of the inaction that was the fatal error, indeed the tragic flaw that justified his final death and made it acceptable, in Aristotelian as well as in Christian terms, to the audience of his own and of our day, for Hamlet must expiate the murder he has committed. The elevation of psychological delay as the central theme of *Hamlet*, and its main interest, is the result of placing character above plot as the chief end of tragedy, an error that Aristotle warned against.[8] The fault lies in analyzing character in isolation, or in relation only to individual incident, not in relation to the great chain of cause-and-effect incidents forming the coherent plot in Aristotelian terms. In this case much critical theory about Hamlet's character runs contrary to the plain lesson of the action as it links incident to form the plot. "For Tragedy is an imitation, not of men, but of an action and of life, and life consists in action, and its end is a mode of action, not a quality" (*Poetics,* VI. 9).

If we could learn nothing else from relating dramatic structure to critical theory, this alone would be a valuable lesson. Indeed, most analyses of Hamlet's character are based on his frustrated and therefore untrustworthy self-recrimination, or else on speculation about motives that presuppose off-stage incidents not shown to us or even referred to. Here we need Stoll's useful reminder that characters in art do not lead full and independent lives, both on and off-stage, of which we see in the presented episodes only the part of a whole. Quite literally, we see the whole of any dramatic character's life in the action and speech of a play. Nothing is left to silence, or to speculation to fill in. It is a

[8] I shall suggest, in another essay, that, indeed, character is superior to plot in Renaissance tragedy, but with the idea that plot serves character and flowers ultimately in character and in personal decision or responsibility, a Christian doctrine that Aristotle could not be expected to consider. The critics to whom I refer have treated character in comparative isolation and not as the flowering of plot, which must mean that character is organized and given significance by plot.

fallacy to attempt to build critical theories on our reconstruction from the non-existence of a wraith.

But something more can be gained towards our understanding of *Hamlet* the play and Hamlet the man. I select only two of a number of points. The first must rest on simple statement, for discussion would be burdensome if not superfluous. The turning point of the play exhibits an action disobedient to divine command about a general rule of life, "Thou shalt not kill", and also, more specifically, an action that is contrary to a justice that must not involve crime if Hamlet is to remain a Heaven-selected minister. If this is so, Hamlet's earlier neutrality of action in respect to the revenge must be taken as showing obedience to God and therefore admirable. Certainly this is the way Tourneur's *Atheist's Tragedy* views a similar, though more didactic, hero. Thus it is strength, not weakness, that lies behind the delay, and it is a lack of fortitude that causes Hamlet to crack and to make his fatal blunder in the closet scene. In view of this clear lesson of the plot once an analysis is made of its parts, how ridiculous is Olivier's sepulchral introduction to his film, "This is the tragedy of a man who could not make up his mind". And how off the mark are all critics who take Hamlet's initial delay as a sign of confusion and of weakness rather than of strength.

Second, the significance of the catastrophe of a tragedy cannot differ from the significance of its climax. The way of the denouement must seem to the audience to be the just consequence of the tragic error of the climax, or else, as Aristotle observed, the catharsis of pity and fear will not operate. Once again, statement must take the place of lengthy analysis. Let me suggest, therefore, that the end of Hamlet is a true death-in-victory.[9] Only by the assumption that Hamlet in some measure retrieves his error of the climax while paying the price of his life can the audience accept the justice of the final holocaust and undergo the catharsis that is essential. It is necessary, thus, to ask how Hamlet retrieves his climactic error. Is it only that he got the wrong man the first time, but succeeded in knocking off the right one at the end? This would be a trivial view indeed. The irony of the closet scene is that as a penalty for disobedience he kills the wrong man. He commits what turns out to be a useless murder, and must expiate this crime with his life.

A parallel can be drawn, I think, between *Hamlet* and Milton's *Samson Agonistes*. Samson fails in a charge given him by divine agency and is therefore alienated from God; but later, as a result of an insight previously denied him, he recovers his sense of original mission and carries out his charge. But his disobedience, although it has not, in fact, altered God's purpose for him, has changed the circumstances under which this purpose is achieved. Instead of a triumph that he will survive, his last victory over the Philistines requires his death in expiation for the consequences of his crime. God gives him the promised victory, but it is a death-in-victory. Nonetheless, we rejoice as does Samson's father when finally he sees in it the immutability of divine purpose and the justice of the ways of God to man.

[9] Bowers, "The Death of Hamlet", *Studies in the English Renaissance Drama in Memory of Karl Julius Holzknecht,* ed. J. W. Bennett, O. Cargill, V. Hall, Jr. (New York: New York University Press, 1959), pp. 28-42; see also "The Moment of Final Suspense in *Hamlet*: We Defy Augury", forthcoming in the Brown University Shakespeare Anniversary volume.

In large part this formula applies to Hamlet. His disobedience in the closet scene when he seeks a private blood-revenge contrary to divine law seems to remove him as God's minister to enact justice. He recognizes that he is being punished by the murder of the wrong man, Polonius:

> ... but heaven hath pleas'd it so,
> To punish me with this, and this with me,
> That I must be their scourge and minister.

The recognition of his error is, in effect, his repentance, and it draws on signs of Heaven's reassertion of his original mission. We must not overlook Hamlet's own attribution of divine ordination to his wakefulness on shipboard, the discovery of the commissions, the circumstance that he could reseal them without discovery, and, finally, his rescue by the pirate ship.

When he returns, and Horatio warns him that the time is short, Hamlet serenely replies that the interim will be his. This confidence in the successful outcome of his duty is backed by no known plan, and critics have never satisfied themselves why Hamlet should be so confident here. I suggest that he is confident because, like Samson, he feels himself once more reconciled to divine Providence. This time he will not repeat his tragic error but will wait for the proper opportunity to be given him, as indeed it later is given, both for him and for Samson. In this light, his denial of the omen of the pain about his heart that so alarms Horatio, and his refusal to follow Horatio's prudent advice to decline the fencing match, are as clearcut a hint of Hamlet's reconciliation as Shakespeare could give the audience.

> ... we defy augury; there's a special providence in the fall of a sparrow.
> If it be now, 'tis not to come; if it be not to come, it will be now; if it be
> not now, yet it will come: the readiness is all.

No more comprehensive words could be contrived to show Hamlet's faith that he is in God's hand.

As a consequence we can accept the justice of the catastrophe, content with Hamlet's death, because like Samson to whom God returned (although He had never departed), Hamlet dies in a victory that is the age-old demonstration of God's unchanging purposes as well as the symbol of a personal reconciliation and acceptance. This is a true Christian catharsis, superior to any possible for the Greeks, and it is important that we should not overlook its significance.

If, as has been suggested, an audience will accept the death of a tragic hero if it feels that in some manner his tragic experiences have given him a personal clarification and ennoblement, then the insight that comes to Hamlet, especially just before the fencing match, and his rectification in the same terms of his original error, constitute that ennoblement. Shakespeare is so concerned with this matter that he gives Hamlet the opportunity to flee when the omen strikes him. But when Hamlet rejects the omen and refuses to put his own will above that of divine purpose, even though it means his death, he wins through to final victory. Hamlet had erred in this manner once before, when he thought he detected the King behind the arras and had taken justice into his own hands in an action that could not be divinely appointed. Now, at the end of the tragedy, he knows his previous error and he wills himself not to repeat it. This last action before the fencing match I take to be an important episode in the plot, one that serves to link the climax in significance to the catastrophe and to remove the final scene from the imputation of accident. Hence a reading of the plot may serve once again to let us see something of Shakespeare's larger purposes in this play.

If these suggestions I have made are correct, then we may see how salutary is a return to the analysis and comprehension of the significance of dramatic structure, which is to say, plot, as a service to accurate criticism. It is important, in my view, not to discuss any incident in vacuum but only as a part of the whole and only as it contributes to the effect of the whole, which must be clearly seen before the parts can be tackled. It is important, in my view, to analyze dramatic characters only after the plot and its intent are thoroughly comprehended, for these characters—as Aristotle remarks—have no life except in the action of the plot.

Finally, when dealing with great literature we must see that dramatic structure and the weight, or significance, of a play—what Galsworthy calls its "spire of meaning"—are mutually interdependent. One must check one's analysis of plot and its technical details by correlation with the ultimate significance of the action. In reverse, the structural parts of the plot cannot be distinguished clearly unless the significance, or meaning, of the play relates to them.

This double method offers a critical course that rests on what we may properly call evidence, not mere opinion or assertion; and we can trust its results, for the heart of a play lies in its action.

University of Virginia

Kittredge on Hamlet

KENNETH MYRICK

EORGE Lyman Kittredge (1860-1941) was for most of his long career generally regarded as this country's most distinguished Shakespeare scholar and teacher. Legends grew up about him. Among the Harvard undergraduates of a half-century ago, rumor had it that if all existing copies of Shakespeare were destroyed, nothing would be permanently lost, for Professor Kittredge would reproduce every play and poem verbatim. One could not over-far believe that. Erudition alone, of course, never made a great critic or teacher. Kittredge delighted in any vivid manifestation of human nature whether he found it in the Old Norse sagas, *Beowulf*, Chaucer, the Greek poets, or at first hand among the old-time New Englanders on Cape Cod. As he wrote of his master Francis James Child, he had "an infectious enthusiasm and a power of lucid and fruitful exposition that made him one of the greatest of teachers".[1] He had also the humor, the imagination, and the sanity of judgment which mark the great critic.

His publications on Shakespeare are surprisingly few. They include the *Complete Works* (1936), a volume representing the textual studies of more than forty years; the richly annotated editions of sixteen plays; and *Shakspere: An Address,* in which he describes his critical method and brings together many of his most illuminating and provocative interpretations of major characters. His complete text has become a standard reference work. His glosses on moot passages are cited by critics of every school of thought. But his most significant comments, which give his insights into action and character, seem not to have received the same attention. It is a very great loss that he never put his major findings into critical studies comparable to his masterly *Chaucer and his Poetry.*

None of his former students could supply this omission, especially one who like myself was never close to him personally. The purpose of this article is to discuss and evaluate his critical method and his interpretation of *Hamlet,* particularly in his annotated edition of the play.[1a]

HIS CRITICAL METHOD

In contrast to Bradley's Hegelian approach, Kittredge's united the empiricism of a scientist with the sympathetic insight of a poet. Like the scientist, he

---

[1] Quoted by Clyde Kenneth Hyder, *George Lyman Kittredge: Teacher and Scholar* (U. of Kansas Press, 1962), p. 80; from Kittredge's "Professor Child", *Atlantic Monthly,* LXXVIII (1896), 737.

[1a] Elsewhere I am discussing the question why Hamlet spares the King at prayer, together with several related matters, and therefore shall omit them here. My chief concern is with Kittredge's interpretation of the dramatic conflict and of seven characters.

formulated his method with the greatest care and exactitude. In his tercentenary *Address* he raises the problem of the relativity of critical judgments: "As with our fellow-creatures in real life, so is it with our fellow-creatures in Shakspere. There neither is nor can be be any exclusive or orthodox interpretation. . . . There will be as many Hamlets or Macbeths or Othellos as there are readers or spectators."[2] But he adds "one corrective and restraining proviso":

> Somewhere there exists, and must be discoverable, the solid fact—and that fact is Shakespere's Hamlet or Macbeth or Othello. And this actual being is not to be confused, in your apprehension or in mine, with any of the figures that we have constructed, each for himself, by the instinctive reaction of our several personalities under the stimulus of the poet's art. Each of us has a prescriptive right to his own Hamlet; but none of us has a charter to impose it either upon his neighbor or upon himself as the poet's intent. (P. 13)

Believing that the "primal duty" of the interpretive critic is to "expound what Shakspere meant" (p. 16), Kittredge worked out a few simple and explicit guiding principles, which he, like Aristotle, derived from a keen study of the actual practice of the dramatists. With Shakespeare we must obviously "comprehend his media of expression: which were, first, dramatic; and second, Elizabethan. And the second medium, the Elizabethan, includes two elements, the times and the language" (pp. 23f.).

His lifelong study of Shakespeare's media provided the scientific foundation for his interpretation of the plays. His keen "feeling for the finer shades of Elizabethan English"[3] often enabled him to discover shadings of character which most of us would miss. A striking example, as we shall see, is Ophelia. His understanding of the dramatic medium and of the Elizabethan customs and beliefs largely accounts for his interpretation of the action, the relation of character to character, and the causes of Hamlet's delay.

As for the dramatic medium,

> in his exposition Shakspere always follows the established Elizabethan method, which was, to make every significant point as clear as daylight, and to omit nothing that the writer regarded as of importance. However much the *dramatis personae* mystify each other, the audience is never to be perplexed: it is invariably in the secret.[4] . . .
>
> This method of exposition carries a momentous corollary . . .:—Nothing that is omitted is of any significance.[5]

The depths and subtleties in Shakespeare's art, of which only the few will be aware, can supplement but not contradict the broad effects: there must "be no possibility of confusion in the barrenest-witted groundling" (p. 20). This principle, of course, is not peculiarly Elizabethan. It applies equally to any truly popular drama. Witness George Bartley's famous remark to Planché.[6] Only

---

[2] *Shakspere: An Address*, delivered on April 23, 1916 (Harvard Univ. Press, 1916), p. 12.
[3] Hyder, p. 181.
[4] *An Address*, pp. 19f.
[5] P. 22.
[6] See Planché, *Recollections and Reflections* (London, 1872), II, 208. Quoted in A. C. Sprague, *Shakespeare and the Audience* (Harvard Univ. Press, 1935), p. 5.

when the spectators understand plot and characters in much the same way, can they be united in a powerful common emotion in the supreme moments of the play.

"The audience is . . . invariably in the secret." This idea could revolutionize Shakespeare criticism. Is Hamlet's madness real or feigned? We can know it is always feigned, because he tells us he will put on madness as a disguise; because after a very short interval we hear of his "mad" behavior toward Ophelia and find the king has called in Rosencrantz and Guildenstern to watch over him; because Hamlet tells his mother

> That I essentially am not in madness,
> But mad in craft;

because he always talks sanely with Horatio; and because Horatio invariably regards him as sane.

Does Hamlet really love Ophelia? Of course. We learn the truth from her own lips, afterwards from his letters, and at the end from his words and actions at her grave. Why he treats her as he does is a question we must ask. But whatever answer we give must be consistent with the plain fact that he loves her throughout the play. Why he acts mad is for us a puzzling problem, but we can never solve it by turning plain expository statements upside down in order to find Shakespeare's meaning.

KING AND PRINCE—THE INITIAL CONFLICT

Though methodology was indispensable for Kittredge, it was his native gift of sympathetic imagination that enabled him to gain his deep insights into character. A case in point is one of his major contributions to Shakespeare criticism, his interpretation of Claudius. The style of the King's first speech has often been considered evidence of hypocrisy. One critic finds in the "unctuous . . . rhythms" "the tone and accent of Milton's Belial",[7] forgetting perhaps that

> neither do the Spirits damn'd
> Lose all their virtue.[8]

Kittredge, with all his sensitivity to the Elizabethan idiom, finds no suggestion of hypocrisy in the King's speech. It is his first official speech from the throne, and must be formal to suit a very formal occasion. Hamlet's own speeches to his mother in this scene have a similar formality.

Claudius is "affable as well as kingly",[9] and is not yet a confirmed criminal. "His conscience, like Macbeth's, torments him constantly."[10] The good will that he expresses toward Hamlet in the court scene is in Kittredge's judgement not insincere; for "he loves the Queen passionately, and she is devoted to her son.

---

[7] L. C. Knights, *An Approach to Hamlet* (1960), pp. 41f.
[8] *Paradise Lost*, ed. M. Y. Hughes (1935), II, 482f.
[9] *Hamlet*, ed. Kittredge (Boston, 1939), n. on I. ii. 42ff., p. 141.
[10] N. on III. i. 49-54, p. 207.

. . . He hopes to live at peace with Hamlet and to atone for past wrongs by kindness in the days to come. That this cannot be, is a part of the tragedy. It is the King's nemesis that the good he intends turns to evil in his hands."[11] That he is "passionately remorseful" is proved in the prayer scene in which he "unlocks his soul". His soliloquy—"one of the supreme passages in all Shakespeare"[12]—reveals him as so relentlessly honest intellectually that he reasons himself "into assurance of his own damnation."[13]

He has immense ability. A man of eloquence, charm,[14] and force, efficient in handling the business of state, he is "graciously familiar when familiarity is in place", a good fellow in his drinking bouts, but "always and everywhere a model of royal dignity".[15] When Laertes breaks into the palace at the head of an armed mob, Claudius subdues him "with a glance, and a calm word. . . . The thing is magnificent."[16] Even in the final catastrophe, when he sees his wife drink the poisoned cup, "Claudius is panic-proof".[17] Thus, although he has "sinned hideously under the influence of temptation",[18] he has from the beginning to the end some share of our dramatic sympathy. "We have a man before us—a very great man, though an enormous malefactor."[19]

For most of us the impression the King makes is more ambiguous than Kittredge has indicated. Claudius seems to gloss over the scandalous haste and the incestuous character of his marriage. His graciousness to Polonius and Laertes expresses genuine good will, but seems also to suggest an unkingly flattery. He has gained the loyal support of the Court. But when we contrast him with the majestic figure of his brother's ghost, we feel the difference between a politician or diplomat and a soldier-king. Yet there can be no doubt that Claudius is essentially the man described by Kittredge—a great and very complex man—gifted with charm, force, and high intelligence, who is caught in the consequences of his own acts.

In his Introduction to the play, Kittredge has drawn a full-length picture of the King. It is a pity that he has not done the same for the Prince, even though from his many and varied comments one can discover an extraordinarily vigorous and magnetic hero. He is a very young man, not over twenty. "The grave-digger's evidence" is a "flat contradiction of the testimony of Laertes and Ophelia (both of whom describe Hamlet as a very young man), of the King, and of Hamlet himself."[20] A marvelously gifted youth, he is the "courtier, scholar, soldier", "the first gentleman of Denmark"[20a], a man of courtesy and good will, of great courage, shrewdness, and energy, endowed with a mind that works like lightning, and an impetuous temperament that chafes at frustration. Kittredge sees in him no evidence of psychological disease, whether it be the

[11] N. on I. ii. 108-117, p. 144.
[12] Introduction to *Hamlet*, p. xix.
[13] *An Address*, p. 37.
[14] Cf. I. v. 43, "witchcraft of his wit".
[15] Introduction, pp. xviii-xix.
[16] *An Address*, p. 42.
[17] N. on V. ii. 319, p 296.
[18] N. on III. i. 49-54, p. 207.
[19] *An Address*, p. 43.
[20] Introduction, p. xvii. See I. iii. 5-16 (and notes); III. i. 167, 168; II. ii. 12; II. v. 101. [Kittredge's footnote.]
[20a] N. on III. i. 158-162, p. 214.

melancholia described by Bradley, or the sadism or the unhealthy attitudes toward sex which are described by others. Hamlet has the normal faults of a young man, of which impatience and a tendency to quick, hot anger seem the most important. Yet Kittredge never refers to either as a tragic flaw.

His delayed revenge, as we shall see, is due to two chief causes: the extraordinary genius of the King, and the total unreliability of all uncorroborated spectral evidence.

Why is Hamlet so antagonistic to the King in the Court scene? First, because only Hamlet is clear-sighted about the hasty, incestuous marriage. For many months after Sir Philip Sidney's funeral, it was considered a gross breach of decorum for anyone to appear at the English Court except in mourning garments.[21] One month after the elder Hamlet's funeral it was considered a breach of decorum for even his son to appear at the Danish Court except in gay garments. Sidney was a famous knight. Hamlet's father was a king who had had a great reign. Yet within less than two months after his death, his widow had married his brother. The old King's dog "would have mourned longer".[22] In the entire court, as Bertram Joseph observes, Hamlet is "the only person to react normally to an abnormal situation."[23]

He has no definite suspicion of murder. On hearing Horatio's account of the Ghost, he "doubts some foul play", i.e., he "suspects that something is wrong",[24] but the Ghost's revelation of crime is a tremendous shock to him, and his "O my prophetic soul" means only, "my soul, by its abhorrence of my uncle, foreshadowed this revelation".[25] In Richard II there is, I think, a striking parallel in the deep depression of Queen Anne, just before hearing of Bolingbroke's rebellion, which comes to her also as a great shock.[26]

Thus Hamlet's initial hostility to his uncle is based on right reason and a sound instinct: on reason because the marriage is an insult to his father's memory and violates Church Law; on instinct, because he abhorred his father's murderer before any thought of murder had crossed his mind. There is no trace of abnormality in the first soliloquy. In the love and honor the Prince gives his father, the Elizabethans would see the profoundly right attitude of a worthy son.[27] He does not feel that his flesh is "sullied".[28] He is gloomy and feels he would like to die if suicide were not against God's law, but such "reflections are not purposes".[29]

A further reason for the Prince's gloom, I think, is his enforced idleness.

---

[21] "For so general was the Lamentation, that it was accounted a Sin for any Gentleman of Quality, for many Months after, to appear at Court or City, in any light or gaudy Apparel." "Life of Sidney", The Works of Sir Philip Sidney (London, 1724-25), 3 vols., I, 17-18.

[22] Cf. I. ii. 150f.

[23] Conscience and the King (London, 1953), p. 54.

[24] N. on I. ii. 256, p. 151.

[25] N. on I. v. 40, p. 168.

[26] Richard II, II. ii. 1-65.

[27] For a different interpretation, cf. Clifford Leech, Shakespeare's Tragedies and Other Studies (New York: O. U. P., 1950), p. 85: "It is not surprising that [Shakespeare] saw the germ of possible madness in Hamlet's veneration for his father and persistent dwelling on his mother's sexuality." Cf. also John Vyvyan, The Shakespearean Ethic (New York: Barnes and Noble, [n.d.]), p. 34. "The fact that Hamlet had already begun to romanticize his father and to hate his uncle reveals to us his most vulnerable point."

[28] N. on I. ii. 129, p. 146.

[29] N. on III. i. 56-88, p. 208.

Laertes can travel to Paris, Fortinbras can go to war, but Hamlet cannot return
to the university. Like so many gifted men who adorned the Renaissance courts,
Hamlet finds enforced idleness bitterly frustrating. By his mourning garments
he can silently rebuke the King and Court, but that is all. "Break my heart, for
I must hold my peace."

Thus the unexpected entrance of Horatio, with Bernardo and Marcellus,
brings a happy change. To the soldiers he is most courteous, and to Horatio
he is an open-hearted fellow student. When Horatio tells of the Ghost, he responds with a series of quick, searching questions, thinks he finds a contradiction at one point but sees his error, and ends with an instant decision to act.
Here is not the least hint of a feeble will or of a procrastinating character. He
dismisses his companions with beautiful courtesy. "He will not allow Horatio
and the rest to call themselves his servants and offer him their duty. Let them
rather regard him as their friend and offer him their love."[30]

In Shakespeare's greatest figures, Kittredge sees often a union of opposite
qualities. Macbeth begins as a man of honorable ambition, of "valour and
loyalty, . . . of a scrupulous conscience and a humane and kindly temper".[31]
Claudius has many kingly virtues. Yet each commits regicide. Hamlet has
a poet's imagination and almost a philosopher's power of reflection, but in his
first meeting with his friends we see also a shrewd and decisive young man
eager for action. His melancholy has *not* paralyzed his will.

From his first sight of the Ghost "he is fully alive to the possibility that this
may be a demon in his father's shape", and calls on heavenly agents to guard
him. When the Ghost beckons, he follows it without hesitation, though the
danger is so great that his friends "actually lay hands on the Prince".[32] When
alone with the Ghost, however, he heeds Horatio's warning, halts, and refuses
to go further. Here surely is that union of boldness and prudence which in
Aristotle's ethics constitutes the truest courage.

Hamlet's emotional let-down after his scene alone with the Ghost is commonly cited as proof of his instability. But compare his response to the spectre
with Horatio's in the opening scene. There, at its initial appearance, Horatio
is at first too stunned to speak. At its next appearance he is calmer, but when it
starts "like a guilty thing", he calls to Marcellus to stop it with his partisan,
though "it is as the air, invulnerable".[33] Horatio and the two brave soldiers lose
their self-possession entirely for a few moments.

When Hamlet first sees the Ghost, he addresses it instantly. His self-possession never fails until he has heard all the hideous disclosure. The bravest
Elizabethan would fear a spectre which he knew might be a demon. Brutus,
one of the calmest of Shakespeare's men, feels his blood run cold and his hair
stand on end during his dialogue with Caesar's Ghost. Twelve lines are spoken
during that episode, ninety-one during Hamlet's ordeal, besides forty-eight while
his father's Ghost was silent in the preceding scene. As Hamlet listens to the
Ghost, almost every item of the revelation is more horrifying than the preceding: the dark references to purgatorial flames, the climactic words "revenge"

[30] N. on I. ii. 254, p. 151.
[31] *Macbeth*, ed. Kittredge (Boston *etc.*, 1939), Introduction, p. xiii.
[32] N. on I. iv. 39 ff., p. 164. The second quoted phrase was used by Kittredge in the classroom.
[33] I. i. 42-44, 54 ff., 139-148.

and "murder", the details of his uncle's treacherous crime, his mother's adultery, the agonizing uncertainty whether she had a hand in the murder. Does any other man in Shakespeare endure a more nerve-racking experience? Inevitably he is excited and exhausted when his friends re-enter.

> In what follows he speaks flippantly of the Ghost and its errand. This does not mean that he wishes to conceal the seriousness of the whole matter from his friends. . . . Nor is this light tone a symptom of madness. It is merely revulsion of feeling after an emotional crisis. The fearful strain to which Hamlet has been subjected demands relief, and in such cases the relief may come either in tears or in laughter and reckless jesting. When he recovers his self-possession, he speaks soberly and coherently (ll. 165ff.).[34]

TWO PROBLEMS

At the end of this scene most readers are puzzled by two questions: Why did Hamlet feign madness? Why did he delay his revenge?

As to the first I must observe that I have never heard or thought of an explanation that seems to me fully satisfactory. In Kittredge's view, Hamlet's motive was "obvious. We speak unguardedly in the presence of children and madmen, for we take it for granted that they will not listen or will not understand; and so the King or the Queen . . . may say something that will afford the evidence needed to confirm the testimony of the Ghost."[35] This seems at first a very plausible explanation. But never do we find Hamlet listening to either the King or the Queen in the way suggested, nor is the idea ever mentioned by anyone else. Here Kittredge seems clearly in error.

Dover Wilson's view that he "assumes madness because he cannot help it" —as a mask to "conceal his nervous breakdown"—[36] is no answer if we deny the breakdown. Hamlet, however, does seem to me clearly to recognize that the interview with the Ghost has left him temporarily so exhausted that all who knew him would note the change and try to discover the cause. It is absolutely imperative to keep them ignorant of the Ghost and its message. It seems likely, therefore, that Hamlet assumes madness because he thinks he can avoid answering awkward questions more easily if he is believed to be mad than if he is considered wholly responsible. There appears to be some confirmation of this interpretation in the fact that his words to Horatio and Marcellus link the antic disposition with the injunction to keep the interview with the Ghost an absolute secret.[37]

Obviously, the feigned madness is a legacy from the old Hamlet play. Shakespeare must have seen in it opportunities for such "good theater" that he could not leave it out. Perhaps he failed to state Hamlet's motive because the audience cared so much less about that than about the fascinating dramatic situations which it produced. Perhaps Stoll was right: "Why Hamlet feigns madness . . . no one will ever know."[38]

In any case, if Hamlet is always sane, we have some 350 lines of delightful

[34] N. on I. v. 116, p. 171. Cf. n. on III. iv. 214, p. 247.
[35] Introduction, p. xiii.
[36] *What Happens in Hamlet* (Cambridge U. P., 1956), p. 92.
[37] Cf. I. v. 153, 159, 169-181.
[38] E. E. Stoll, *Shakespeare Studies* (New York, 1960), p. 98.

high comedy (in Act II, scene ii), beginning where Polonius starts to expostu-
late on brevity. Just before and just after the play-within-the-play, the Prince,
by feigning madness, can again reduce the tension for himself and for us by
poking harmless fun at the Lord Chamberlain.[39]

As for the delayed revenge, we may observe that it troubles the reader
much more than the spectator. In the theater the interval of six or eight weeks
between the first and the second acts can pass almost unnoticed. From the beginning of Act II until Hamlet's departure for England is less than two days,
and from his speedy return to Denmark until the end is less than three.

Hamlet's revenge is delayed for two reasons. The first is the genius and the
great power of his opponent. When Hamlet acts mad, Claudius sends for Rosencrantz and Guildenstern to spy on him. When he overhears Hamlet's talk with
Ophelia, he senses danger and orders Hamlet to England. Immediately after
the play (Kittredge says[40]) he makes out the sealed mandate for his nephew's
execution. When that plot fails he instantly contrives another. Thus *Hamlet* "is
not the tragedy of a weak-willed procrastinator. . . . It is a duel to the death
between well-matched antagonists."[41]

The second and even more important reason for the delayed vengeance is
the ambiguity of all spectral evidence. Kittredge seems to have been a lifelong
student of ghost lore and witchcraft. His most erudite book is *Witchcraft in
Old and New England*,[42] and long before I studied *Hamlet* in his class in 1916
he was driving into his students' heads the criminal folly of acting on a ghost's
word until it is proved beyond the least doubt to be true.

Hamlet believes that he has seen his father's Ghost and that it spoke the
truth. But he soon realizes that he does not actually know. What he does know
is that any ghost *may* be a demon, sent to lure an unwary mortal into a crime
that will damn his soul. "Shakespeare has done his best to enforce the imperative
scruple as to the apparition",[43] Kittredge writes, and as proof he cites no less
than eight passages in the first three acts.[44]

Unlike Wilson and others in recent decades, Kittredge did not stress the
difference between the traditional and Catholic view of demonology, and the
new and Protestant view. I surmise that he thought the difference of little importance for Shakespeare. Though Puritan ministers preached that every ghost
was either an hallucination or a demon, yet the very fact that they urged the
point so often suggests that even their own people were not easy to convince.
The Protestant who attended the theater was seldom an ardent Puritan, and
must have found it easy to accept the traditional view that Shakespeare assumes
in *Hamlet*.

A very perceptive scholar has argued that by the end of Act I both Hamlet
and the audience know the Ghost to be honest:

---

[39] See pp. 228-229 below.

[40] N. on III. iii. 3, p. 234. This I think is an error. The King's agony of remorse would seem
very hollow if we thought he had just ordered a second murder. He says nothing of that, and
"nothing that is omitted is of any significance". He must have given the order after despairing of
God's pardon, probably in his sudden dismay at Polonius' death.

[41] *An Address*, pp. 39 f.

[42] Harvard Univ. Press, 1929.

[43] Introduction to *Hamlet*, p. xi.

[44] I. i. 46 ff., and 109; I. ii. 244-246; I. iv. 40 ff. and 69 ff.; II. ii. 626-633; III. ii. 80-92, 297-301.

Remember thee!
Ay, thou poor Ghost, while memory holds a seat
In this distracted globe. . . .

"If Shakespeare did not want this passionate speech to carry instant and complete conviction, he should never have written it in such terms."[45]

The strength of Hamlet's conviction, however, only emphasizes his dilemma. If he does not kill his uncle he may be allowing his father's murderer to go scot-free and the kingdom to suffer under a criminal usurper. If he kills him, and if the Ghost is a demon, Hamlet himself becomes guilty of the worst form of murder, regicide; he will go down in Danish history as an infamous traitor, and his soul will be damned.

Nevertheless, Hamlet by the end of Act II has devised a stratagem both brilliant and daring, and by the middle of Act III he has forced the indispensable evidence from the King himself. Between this stunning victory and Hamlet's final vengeance, his formidable opponent affords him only one brief opportunity. By a supreme dramatic irony "this is the one moment when it is impossible for anyone but an assassin to strike".[46] A few minutes later he kills Polonius in mistake for his foe, and is placed under surveillance until he leaves for England. After his quick return, the only moment when he encounters Claudius before the end is at the funeral of Ophelia. No sane critic has considered this an opportune moment to kill his country's ruler.

When we realize that Hamlet's madness is always feigned and that he has an imperative obligation to prove the Ghost's story before killing his king, most of the evidence for any procrastination simply melts away. I will glance, however, at Kittredge's striking comments on five famous passages that are commonly interpreted to Hamlet's discredit. Four passages are soliloquies.

The phrase "O cursed spite", "in Elizabeth usage, was equivalent to the modern, 'What an infernal nuisance!'—though more dignified than our idiom. Hamlet is resolved to avenge his father, but he is too civilized to welcome the duty that the savage code of his nation and time imposes."[47]

In his soliloquy, "O, what a rogue and peasant slave am I!" he "rages against himself for stupid inactivity—not for hesitation or weakness of will. . . . Thus he relieves his excitement by railing until, at the end of the soliloquy, he grows calm and expresses in the plainest language what the matter really is: *he needs evidence.* . . . 'The play's the thing.' "[48]

In his most famous soliloquy, Hamlet is not, as is so often supposed, "dallying with the purpose of suicide. . . . He has formed his plan to make the King betray himself, . . . and is eager to try the crucial experiment. Meanwhile . . . inaction brings depression of spirits, and the thought recurs to him that death would be a relief. All men have such thoughts at such moments. . . . But reflections are not purposes."[49]

When Hamlet finds the King at prayer, he "cannot butcher a defenceless man", particularly "when our very souls have been shaken by the terrific mental

[45] H. D. F. Kitto, *Form and Meaning in Drama* (London and New York, 1960), p. 287.
[46] *Introduction,* p. xiv.
[47] N. on I. v. 189, p. 173.
[48] N. on II. ii. 598 ff., pp. 203 f.
[49] N. on III. i. 56-88, p. 208.

and spiritual struggle through which Claudius has just passed." [50] The "diabolical sentiments" uttered by Hamlet are not his. They simply "accord with an old-established convention with regard to adequate revenge" (p. xv).

On the final soliloquy Kittredge's published notes are very sparing. In class he emphasized that the concluding couplet, declaring Hamlet's readiness to act, creates suspense, and that when next we hear of him he has acted decisively, to the great alarm of the King.

HAMLET WITH OTHER PEOPLE

For many thoughtful students, Hamlet's apparent "grossness and cruelty" are a most "disturbing element in the play".[51] Thus Professor Leech speaks of Hamlet's "bawdy and brutal talk" (p. 10). Fifty years earlier, Bradley spoke of "the disgusting and insulting grossness of his language to [Ophelia] in the play-scene. . . . It is such language as you will find addressed to a woman by no other hero of Shakespeare's."[52] Similar though less vigorous complaints have been made about Hamlet's behavior to Polonius and the Queen.

If there is any explanation that will exonerate Hamlet of these charges it must be one that would be "as clear as daylight" to the Elizabethan audience. A simple and obvious explanation, therefore, is more likely to be true than a fine-spun theory. To Kittredge the explanation is obvious. Hamlet is feigning insanity. His normal manners are beautifully courteous. "Such talk . . . is quite at variance with his character as a gentleman and a scholar." [52a] The audience knows that such talk and his other bad manners are merely part of his pretended madness. Among the dramatis personae, *"nobody takes offence at his rudeness, for all accept it as a symptom of insanity".*[53] The result in Act II, Scene ii, as I have remarked, is high comedy—a much-needed change of pace after the extreme tension of the ghost scenes.

a. Hamlet and Polonius

This brings us to Hamlet's relations with Polonius. The breadth of Kittredge's imaginative sympathy is wonderfully illustrated in his treatment of both Ophelia and her father. In his view, Polonius, though not tragic and sometimes comic, is a figure of real dignity. As Dr. Johnson indicates, he is a man who has been wise. For many years he was a shrewd, far-sighted man of affairs, and he is still a "benevolent diplomatist and devoted father", loving his son and daughter "with the pathetic tenderness of an old and failing man". They on their part "return his affection as it deserves".[54] The King and Queen are fond of him and indulgent of his foibles, "slightly bored though they may sometimes be by his occasional prosing".[55] The Queen's famous words to him, "More

[50] *Introduction,* p. xiv.

[51] Leech, *"Studies in Hamlet", Shakespeare Survey 9* (1956), p. 11.

[52] *Shakespearean Tragedy* (1922), p. 103.

[52a] N. on III. ii. 110, p. 221.

[53] N. on II. ii. 223, p. 186. (The italics are mine.) Cf. nn. on II. ii. 174, p. 185; and III. ii. 158, p. 223; l. 261, p. 228.

[54] "He knows that his mind was once strong, and knows not that it is become weak. . . . While he depends upon his memory, and can draw from his repository of knowledge, he utters weighty sentences, and gives useful counsel". *The Plays of Shakespeare,* ed. Samuel Johnson, [2nd ed.] (London, 1765), VIII, 183.

[55] N. on I. ii. 47-49, p. 141.

matter, with less art", are friendly, not impatient, in tone.[56] Though there is at
least one "clear instance of [his] falling into dotage",[57] his famous advice to his
son is "sound and sensible" and the great truth with which he ends does not
contradict his worldly precepts, but "includes and ennobles them all".[58]
Kittredge is silent about Polonius' failure to understand Ophelia, his cynical
suspicions of Hamlet's intentions, and the hugeness of the vanity which lies
at the root of all his errors and makes him a ridiculous figure more often, I
think, than Kittredge has indicated. Yet he has shown the old courtier to be a
much more complex, more likeable, and more significant figure than he is
commonly thought to be—like most real people in being sometimes absurd and
blind, sometimes wise, and often kind.

His confidence in his own sagacity makes him fair sport for Hamlet's wit,
as we see in his first meeting with the supposedly mad prince. When to
Polonius' earnest question, "Do you know me, my lord?" Hamlet replies with
equal gravity, "Excellent well. You are a fishmonger", the effect is pure comedy.
"Fishmonger" here has no occult sense, in spite of the ingenious efforts of
Coleridge, Dover Wilson, and others, to find one. For the Prince "to call the
elegantly dressed, dignified, and over-refined courtier . . . a fish-seller was the
very maddest thing that he could say. The audience, too, would be infinitely
amused by the . . . effect . . . on Polonius himself. He receives it, however,
with an indulgent smile."[59]

Hamlet's relations with the old man provide bits of comic relief on two
other occasions. One is when Polonius speaks of acting the part of Caesar in his
student days, and when he explains carefully that he was killed by Brutus, a
remark that shows how far gone he must think the scholarly prince really is.
Another is when he brings word that the Queen desires to speak to her son, and
Hamlet gets him to declare that the non-existent cloud which he sees in the
shape of a hump-backed camel is "backed like a weasel" and also very like a
whale.[59a] This bit of comic relief has overtones of tragic irony when we think of
their next meeting.

b. Hamlet and Ophelia

There is no character in *Hamlet* whom Kittredge treats with more sympathetic insight than Ophelia. In this respect he resembles Dr. Johnson and
Bradley, rather than a large number of contemporary students, some of whom
regard her as a heartless jilt, others as a hussy, and many as a colorless weakling.
Her gentle nature, quiet manner, and filial obedience would be counted heavily
in her favor in Shakespeare's time if not in ours. Kittredge emphasizes with
special force that there is in her no "lack of spirit". In her first scene she "is full
of the joy of living". "Quietly amused at the wise airs of her brother, . . . she
receives [his] sermon demurely; and then, when he is least expecting a retort, she
bids him take a leaf out of his own book. The effect is diverting: Laertes suddenly remembers that he is in a hurry." When her father, too, warns her

[56] N. on II. ii. 95, p. 182.
[57] N. on II. ii. 153-155, p. 184.
[58] Nn. on I. iii. 58 ff., p. 155; ll. 78-80, p. 157.
[59] N. on II. ii. 174, p. 185.
[59a] Nn. on III. ii. 108, 393ff. Kittredge sees no comedy in the second passage.

against Hamlet, she "speaks with gentle dignity and defends herself, with spirit, though with perfect respect".[60]

In this scene she has not admitted her love to Hamlet, and I think perhaps not to herself.[61] She seems to have discovered the intensity of her passion only after her hopes for a happy outcome have been all but destroyed. Hamlet, as we have seen, loves her passionately throughout the play. When he visits her in her private sitting room, "his study of Ophelia's face is but the long look in which he says farewell to his hopes". "As for taking her into his confidence, . . . he cannot think for a moment of making her his accomplice in a deed of blood."[62]

In the nunnery scene they are tragically unable to understand one another, because neither can be frank. Here Ophelia shows the gentle strength that we found in the first scene with her father. When Hamlet says abruptly, "I did love you once", and then a moment later, "I loved you not", her replies are "gentle and spirited". At the end of the scene we discover what we already have guessed, the depth of her love and grief. Hamlet, Kittredge thinks, "talks as insanely as he knows how" after his first two short speeches, no doubt suspecting "that somebody is listening". At the play-within-the-play, the same relationship continues. Only a few hours after she has revealed her desperate loneliness, she can watch the play with apparent enjoyment, listen to Hamlet's bawdry without prudishness, rebuke him gently, forgive it as a sign of madness, and try to soothe him "by remarking quietly" on the dumb show.[63] Like Viola, in a play written within a few years of *Hamlet,* Ophelia can sit "smiling at grief".

Kittredge shows us what very few others have seen in our century—a young woman whom a man so richly endowed as the Prince can love and deeply respect. Like Horatio, she lacks Hamlet's imagination and the wonderful variety of his gifts. Yet she resembles him in possessing a mind of her own, a quick wit, courtesy, dignity, a strong sense of duty, and a religious earnestness. Though no philosopher, she readily sees the difference between her brother's sermonizing and the prince's reflective and original mind. She is no great talker, but is a perceptive listener. Young as she is, she has understood Hamlet better than has anyone else except perhaps Horatio, for she describes his best qualities more truly than does anyone else (III. i. 159ff.). Their marriage could have been a very happy one.

This gentle, high-minded, spirited lady whom Kittredge has discerned invites neither contempt nor sentimenetal pity, but compassion and deep respect. It is easy to understand Hamlet's extreme grief at her death.

c. Hamlet and the Queen

Gertrude is far more than the easy-going, unthinking, sensual creature that she is often taken to be. She can defy a wild mob:

> How cheerfully on the false trail they cry!
> O, this is counter, you false Danish dogs!
>
> (IV. v. 109f.)

[60] Nn. on I. iii. 10, p. 152; ll. 45-52, p. 154; l. 110, p. 158.
[61] Cf. I. iii. 104.
[62] Nn. on II. ii. 96, p. 178; III. i. 95, p. 211.
[63] Nn. on III. i. 117, 121, pp. 211 f.; l. 95, p. 211; III. ii. 147, 148, 158, p. 223.

From the hunting metaphor, Kittredge caught a glimpse of a sportswoman who loves to follow the hounds when they are hot on the scent.[63a] Here is a woman of energy, courage, and royal will. These qualities come out sharply in Hamlet's scene with his mother after the play.

She is beaten in the battle of wills, but not quickly or easily. Beginning with a sharp challenge to her son, she continues to be imperious until she hears what seems to her a madman's threat of death. Hamlet, blazing with indignation, is determined to discover what part, if any, she had in his father's murder. He can do so only by a shock treatment, which frightens her and leads to the fatal stabbing of Polonius. Discovering her innocence of murder, he denounces her for adultery until the Ghost enters and induces in him a more compassionate mood. Before the scene ends, he is troubled by his harsh treatment of her.[64] Kittredge is silent on the significant point made by Bradley, that after the Ghost's departure Hamlet's "chief desire . . . is to save her soul".[65] On the other hand, he has an illuminating comment on the last lines of the scene, in which many have found evidence of hysteria or brutal callousness: "Hamlet's levity of tone is, as on previous occasions, due to excitement and revulsion of feeling."[66]

Through the last two acts the Queen is "torn asunder by her love for her husband and her love for her son". The King, in turn, finds "he must destroy the son without alienating the mother. And so he becomes his own Nemesis. . . . Two lines condense the tragedy of Claudius and Gertrude:

> Gertrude, do not drink!
> It is the poisoned cup—it is too late."[67]

Kittredge has no comment on Gertrude's reply to her husband's last command:

> I will, my lord; I pray you pardon me.
>
> (V. ii. 302)

One detects here the charming and respectful independence of a strong-minded woman, and moments later a touch of tragic greatness as she summons her last strength to warn Hamlet of the poisoned wine.

d. Horatio

Horatio is a general favorite with students of Shakespeare. Everyone has noted his loyalty, his scholarly skepticism, his clear judgment and steady poise. Kittredge brought out revealing smaller touches. There is Horatio's way of saying "Yes". Hamlet asks concerning the Ghost, "His beard was grizzled— no?" and his friend replies, "A sable silver'd"; which is the exact meaning of *grizzled* but carries a sharper image. Waiting for the Ghost, Hamlet remarks, "It is very cold", and Horatio answers, "It is a nipping and an eager air."[68] One who uses imagery like this has keen senses and the power to condense much meaning into a phrase.

[63a] *An Address*, p. 50.

[64] Nn. on III. iv. 152-155, p. 244, and l. 178, p. 246.

[65] Bradley, p. 138.

[66] N. on l. 214, p. 247. Kittredge adds cross-references to I. v. 116 ff., 150 ff.; and III. ii. 282 ff. Cf. also his notes on the first passage, p. 171, and on III. ii. 286-289, p. 229.

[67] *An Address*, pp. 37, 38.

[68] I. ii. 240, 242; I. iv. 1 f.

Still more characteristic is the quality of his humor. Frequently it is the humor of understatement. "What, is Horatio there?" "A piece of him." It is also kind and wonderfully quick. When the sailors bring him letters from Hamlet, their spokesman greets him with "God bless you, sir." "Horatio's reply ['Let him bless thee too'] accords with custom. . . . But there is a touch of Horatio's mild humor, for the sailor (who doubtless looks like the pirate that he is) may well need God's blessing." [69] We have a similar touch after the ordeal of Hamlet's interview with the Ghost:

> *Ham.* There's ne'er a villain dwelling in all Denmark
>   But he's an arrant knave.
> *Hor.* There needs no ghost, my lord, come from the grave
>   To tell us this. (I. v. 123-126)

It is only a flicker of humor from a serious man in a moment of crisis. But it has just the quality that can steady Hamlet after his ordeal. His friend sees into his state of mind, and responds to his need.

On a few occasions Horatio shows his friendship by frankly warning his friend of mistakes or probable disappointment, as when he tries to dissuade Hamlet from following the Ghost, or to quiet him during the quarrel in the graveyard; or when he predicts that he will lose the fencing match.[70]

Failure to recognize Horatio's language of understatement and his readiness to point out Hamlet's mistakes when necessary has led sometimes to a serious misreading of key speeches. Some critics have supposed that after the play-within-the-play, his four brief replies to Hamlet—totalling sixteen words—imply that he does not agree that the King has revealed his guilt. But Horatio is not the man to be silent if his friend is making a colossal error. Others have thought his dry observation, "So Guildenstern and Rosencrantz go to it", implies disapproval of Hamlet's sending them to execution. I see rather a touch of his ironical humor. Kittredge thinks "he feels some satisfaction in the poetical justice that has overtaken the King's agents. But Hamlet . . . feels that he must justify himself to his friend, as he has already justified himself to his own conscience."[71]

A strange misapprehension of some critics is that Shakespeare presents Horatio as the temperate man in contrast to the prince's intemperance. But Horatio's own self-control is by no means flawless, as we saw in the opening scene of the play.[72] At the end, when Hamlet is dying, his friend impulsively seizes the poisoned cup, forgetting that his duty is not to die with the Prince, but to live and clear his wounded name. The strongest of Shakespeare's men are never absolute Stoics. Even Brutus, silently mourning over Portia's terrible death, cannot keep his self-control in his disagreement with Cassius.[73] Characters endowed with passion and imagination are not necessarily weaker than quieter types, and in the theater they are immensely more interesting. Witness the contrast between the quiet Celia and the more excitable Rosalind, or between the stolid Captain Gower and the wonderful Welsh Captain Fluellen.

The poet did not create Horatio to set off Hamlet's supposed weaknesses,

---

[69] I. i. 19; and n. on IV. vi. 7, 8, p. 266.
[70] I. iv. 64-85; V. i. 288; V. ii. 219.
[71] N. on V. ii. 57-62, pp. 285 f.
[72] See p. 224 above.
[73] *Julius Caesar* IV. iii. 37-82, 143 f.

but to show that he has the steady support of a virtuous and clear-minded friend. A man whom Horatio approves, no sensible spectator can disapprove.

e. Laertes

The real foil to Hamlet, as Kittredge observes,[74] is Laertes. When we see him first, with Ophelia, we share her not unkind amusement at his wise airs. His father's abundant advice perhaps suggests that he may need a lot of it. An affectionate son and brother, he becomes the typical hot-headed, unreflecting avenger. If he knew all the facts, he could find no adequate cause to attack either the King or the Prince. But he rushes headlong into action against first one and then the other. In the final scene, the "monstrous hypocrisy" of his reply to Hamlet's apology "shows the blind ruthlessness of the doctrine of revenge, and stands in marked contrast to Hamlet's caution and conscience in his own case".[75]

The contrast is sharpened if we recall any of Polonius' advice to his son. When Laertes listens to buzzers who "infect his ear", gathers a howling mob, and forces entrance into the royal palace, he is hardly giving his

> thoughts no tongue
> Nor any unproportioned thought his act.

He has not tried his friends (as Hamlet tested Rosencrantz and Guildenstern at once). He does not beware of entrance to a quarrel. And when to avenge his father he joins the King's treacherous plot, and even suggests the use of poison, he has forgotten that father's most solemn injunction: "To thine own self be true". In the failure of this foolish, warm-hearted boy there is both pathos and ghastly irony.

The Prince, who never heard Polonius' maxims, unconsciously follows nearly all of them. He keeps his thoughts to himself, tries his friends, grapples one to his soul, bewares of entrance to a quarrel even with a man he hates. Ironically, his significant failures are when he carries an unproportioned thought into action, as in slaying Polonius and in striding forward in a towering passion to face Laertes at the grave of Ophelia.

Thus Polonius' famous maxims are an organic part of the tragic pattern, a fact that strongly supports Kittredge's favorable interpretation of them.

KITTREDGE'S ACHIEVEMENT

Among the interpretations of a great masterpiece, none can be orthodox, but they may vary enormously in their significance. In his interpretation of *Hamlet,* Kittredge leaves out many subjects that interest his successors—such as the themes, the patterns of imagery, the religious implications. Neither in his class lectures nor in his writings can I recall any mention of the tragic flaw. I would defend this omission, for although the idea is wonderfully suggestive as Bradley treats it, too often it hardens into a binding dogma; but it is strange that, except by implication, Kittredge says so little about the nature of tragedy. His explanations of Hamlet's feigning madness and of his sparing the King at prayer seem to me mistaken. In Claudius I sense a blacker evil, in Polonius a

---

[74] *An Address,* pp. 38 f.
[75] N. on V. ii. 261-263, p. 294.

deeper vanity, in Hamlet during the prayer scene a more guilty arrogance than Kittredge has shown. In the latter part of the play he has not observed what seems to me a fundamental change for the worse in Claudius, and for the better in Hamlet, Laertes, and the Queen.

Among the merits of his interpretation are that it presents both a fearlessly accurate and a noble interpretation of the human scene with all its evil, and that it makes for an extraordinarily powerful acting play.

Kittredge grew to fame in what has been called America's "Age of Confidence", and was fifty-four years old when that period ended in 1914. Thus he escaped the disillusionment and the preoccupation with the abnormal and the morbid which have often marked the outlook of many gifted younger critics. If he had a bias it was toward the healthy and the normal. He could say with Dr. Johnson that Shakespeare's "scenes are occupied only by men, who act and speak as the reader thinks that he should himself have spoken and acted on the same occasion".[76] The greatness of his interpretations of Shakespeare and of Chaucer is due to his sharing the sanity and nobility of their outlook.

In *Hamlet*, the best men have faults, the worst have marked virtues. In nearly all we can see ourselves. There are Claudius, with his immense ability, his charm, his remorse, his futile effort to cleanse his soul; Gertrude with her sensuality, her good nature, her devotion to her husband and her son, and at times her regal spirit; Polonius with his kindliness, his vanity, and sometimes his wise words if not his wise actions; Laertes, the hot-headed, foolish boy who in his grief for his father and his sister blunders into mortal sin and exchanges forgiveness at the end with the man he now sees as "noble Hamlet"; Horatio, the Prince's wise, frank, quietly humorous, devoted friend, one of Shakespeare's men of gold; and Ophelia, the gentle, devoted, perceptive girl, endowed with a quick wit and a happy spirit, who deservedly wins a prince's love, and is crushed by forces beyond her control.

There is Hamlet himself, a very young man with a high temper, who can threaten his best friends when his fate cries out, rage against the King as he spares his life, storm at the Queen and bring her to repentance, slay Polonius in mistake for his enemy; but who is free of the crippled will, the sadism, the sex nausea of which he is often accused; a soldier, a thinker, a poet who sees into everyone else and knows the national vices as well as the virtues of the subjects he may sometime govern; a man of charm, of bitter scornfulness, of magnanimity; the most complex, the most humanly credible, perhaps the most noble of Shakespeare's tragic heroes.

With characters so vivid and so representative of our human nature in its weakness and greatness, and with the bitter conflict between two giant antagonists who destroy each other at the end, the tragedy could be today, as it was in Shakespeare's time, an extraordinarily powerful play for a general audience.

Nearly half a century has passed since I sat in Professor Kittredge's classroom and heard his lectures on *Hamlet*. I still believe there has never been a saner or more illuminating interpretation of the play.

Tufts University

---

[76] "Preface to Shakespeare Criticism", *Criticism: The Major Texts,* ed. W. J. Bate (New York, 1952), p. 209.

Hamlet's Mother

BALDWIN MAXWELL

N an article entitled "The Character of Hamlet's Mother" (*Shakespeare Quarterly*, VIII (1957), 201-206), Miss Carolyn Heilbrun expressed strong disagreement with what had been the generally accepted estimate of Queen Gertrude. Seemingly unaware of the essay by Professor Draper[1], the Queen's most ardent defender, Miss Heilbrun wrote that "critics, with no exception that I have been able to find, have accepted Hamlet's word 'frailty' as applying to [Gertrude's] whole personality, and have seen in her . . . a character of which weakness and lack of depth and rigorous intelligence are the entire explanation" (p. 201). She, as had Professor Draper, rejected almost *in toto* the views of such critics as A. C. Bradley, Miss Agnes Mackenzie, H. Granville-Barker,[2] and others who had declared the Queen "weak", "neutral", or "little more than a puppet".

Professor Draper, who thought Gertrude innocent of adultery prior to King Hamlet's death, not only denied her weakness but excused her hasty and incestuous marriage as politically necessary because of a national crisis, "a marriage more of convenience than of love" (p. 121). To him the Queen appeared "dignified, gracious, and resourceful", one who "as a wife, as a mother, as a queen . . . seems to approximate, if not the Elizabethan ideal, at least the Elizabethan norm". She is, he insisted, "no slave to lust" (pp. 123, 126). It is only on this last point that Miss Heilbrun and Professor Draper markedly disagreed. Although persuaded that Gertrude was innocent of adultery prior to the elder Hamlet's death, Miss Heilbrun argued that her marriage to Claudius was brought about not by a need to settle a national crisis, not by the witchcraft of Claudius' wit, but by lust alone, "the need of sexual passion" in her widowhood. Apart from this passion, the Queen is, Miss Heilbrun believed, a "strong-

---

[1] John W. Draper, "Queen Gertrude", *The Hamlet of Shakespeare's Audience* (Durham: Duke University Press, 1938), pp. 109-126. The essay first appeared in *Revue Anglo-Américaine* for 1934.

[2] To Bradley "The Queen was not a bad-hearted woman. . . . But she had a soft animal nature, and was very dull and very shallow. She loved to be happy. . . . The belief at the bottom of her heart was that the world is a place constructed simply that people may be happy in it in a good-humoured sensual fashion" (*Shakespearean Tragedy*, London: Macmillan, 1929, p. 167).

Miss Mackenzie follows Bradley but is more severe. To her Gertrude is "simply . . . stupid, coarse, ["cheap"] and shallow". "She has", continued Miss Mackenzie, "the qualities of a pleasant animal—docility, kindliness, affection for her offspring, a courage in defence of her mate. She would have made a very lovable cat or dog" (*The Women in Shakespeare's Plays*, New York: Doubleday, Page & Co., 1924, pp. 202, 224).

Granville-Barker was more kind. He saw Gertrude as "a woman who does not mature, who clings to her youth and all that belongs to it. . . . She is drawn for us with unemphatic strokes, and she has but a passive part in the play's action. She moves throughout in Claudius' shadow; he holds her as he had won her, by the witchcraft of his wit" (*Prefaces to Shakespeare*, 3rd Series, London: Sidgwick & Jackson, 1937, p. 284).

minded, intelligent, succinct, and . . . sensible woman", who is, except for her description of Ophelia's death, "concise and pithy in speech, with a talent for seeing the essence of every situation presented before her eyes" (pp. 202-203).

This view of the Queen's character is at such variance with that previously current that one may wish to reexamine her appearances in the play, scene by scene, for light upon the impression Shakespeare sought to create. Little time is needed to do so, for however important the part of the Queen in *the story* of Hamlet, her role in *the play* is definitely subordinate. She appears in ten of the play's twenty scenes, but in those ten scenes she speaks fewer lines than does Ophelia, who appears in only five; and, unlike Ophelia, the Queen is never the central or dominant figure on the stage. She speaks but one brief aside and never the concluding line of a scene. To be sure, a gifted actress may, by clever stage business and a gracious manner, provide for the role an illusion of importance; but this importance is not supported by the lines she speaks and presumably was not purposed by Shakespeare.

Practically all recent critics have agreed that Gertrude was not only innocent of complicity in the murder of her first husband but wholly unaware of it. That she was, however, guilty of an "o'erhasty [second] marriage", she herself testifies. Nor is it permissible to see that marriage as other than incestuous. The one sin of which the Queen has been accused but of which her guilt may be debatable is that she had been Claudius' mistress while the elder Hamlet was alive.

When in I. ii, the Queen appears on stage for the first time, the audience has heard nothing whatsoever about her. It is prejudiced neither in her favor nor against her. She doubtless enters on the arm of King Claudius, who directs his ingratiating smile towards her during part of the remarkable speech with which the scene opens and from which we learn that he, having shortly before lost a brother, has recently taken to wife his brother's widow. Incest, to be sure—a horrible sin in the eyes of both church and state. But with such consummate skill has the King's speech been phrased that all on the crowded stage—or at least all but one—show neither shock nor disapproval. As a result the audience may naturally assume that the general satisfaction should outweigh the displeasure of one individual, and, in the absence of other details, accept the unusual marriage—at least for the time being—as an act which may well be shown to be both wise and—under the circumstances—permissible.

After the King has explained the present situation and expressed "For all, our thanks", the Queen, apart perhaps from a smile, offers no word of thanks for herself. She remains silent as the King instructs the departing ambassadors and questions Laertes and Polonius on the former's desire to return to France. Gertrude is the last to speak. Upon Hamlet's bitter punning reply to the King,

> Not so, my lord. I am too much in the sun,

the Queen makes her first speech—six lines, one of the three longest she speaks in the entire play. She urges Hamlet to "look like a friend on Denmark", to cease mourning for his father since

> Thou know'st 'tis common. All that lives must die,
> Passing through nature to eternity.

That she misunderstands Hamlet's reply to her cliché, "Ay madam, it is common", is shown by her then asking

> If it be,
> Why seems it so particular with thee?—

indicative not only that she has herself ceased to mourn her late husband's death but as well that she completely fails to understand her son. After Hamlet's answer, the King, his composure recovered, quickly speaks thirty-one lines, ending with the wish that Hamlet remain at Elsinore. This wish the Queen now seconds in her third and last speech of the scene:

> Let not thy mother lose her prayers, Hamlet.
> I pray thee stay with us, go not to Wittenberg.

Nine lines later all exeunt save Hamlet.

Such is the Queen's part on her first appearance. She speaks slightly over nine lines in her three speeches—nine lines to the King's ninety-four. Her speeches are short but hardly seem more "concise and pithy" than speech in dramatic verse normally is. Nor do they, composed as they are of a cliché, a misunderstanding, and an echo, encourage the view that she is a "resourceful", "strong-minded" woman, "with a talent for seeing the essence of every situation presented before her eyes". Perhaps, too, her obedient rising at the King's "Madam, come", suggests her domination by him. Such a suggestion is supported by her leaving the stage in three later scenes upon similar words from the King ("Come, Gertrude", IV.i; "Let's follow, Gertrude", IV.vii; "Sweet Gertrude, leave us", III.i) and by her only once speaking as she makes her exit.

Such is our introduction to Queen Gertrude. So much do we know about her when Hamlet later in the scene, in his first soliloquy, expresses his disgust that his mother

> A little month, or ere those shoes were old
> With which she followed my poor father's body
> Like Niobe, all tears, why she, even she—
> O God, a beast that wants discourse of reason
> Would have mourned longer—married with mine uncle,
> My father's brother. . . .
> O, most wicked speed, to post
> With such dexterity to incestuous sheets!

That unusual marriage, upon which we had earlier in the scene passed no verdict, we now begin to question. But Hamlet is only one; the court as a whole had seemed neither to disapprove of the marriage nor to condemn its haste. Yet Hamlet's view, as we are soon to learn, is not peculiar to him, does not spring from thwarted ambition or from an excess of filial affection for his mother. Before we again see Queen Gertrude we are to hear another witness, one eminently qualified to judge her. Three scenes later the Ghost of the dead king is to inform Hamlet that his uncle,

> . . . that incestuous, that adulterate beast,
> With witchcraft of his wit, with traitorous gifts—
> O wicked wit and gifts, that have the power

> So to seduce!—won to his shameful lust
> The will of my most seeming-virtuous queen. . . .
> But virtue, as it never will be moved,
> Though lewdness court it in the shape of heaven,
> So lust, though to a radiant angel linked,
> Will sate itself in a celestial bed
> And prey on garbage.

Surely we are not now likely to attribute Gertrude's quietness during her earlier appearance either to remorse for her o'erhasty marriage or to an awareness that her former husband was to her present as "Hyperion to a satyr".

But, one may ask, is the Ghost a wholly disinterested witness? Are we to accept everything he relates? Does he really know whereof he speaks? To the accuracy of his knowledge of the present and the future, I must return later, but I think it can hardly be contested that we are to assume that he has, from his vantage point beyond the grave, learned specifically all that concerned his murder. He was asleep when the poison was poured into his ear, and the dumb-show of the play-within-the-play—though that at best is only Hamlet's interpretation of what the Ghost had revealed—does not show him as awakening before he died. Yet, be it noted, the Ghost reveals not only the identity of the murderer and the instant effect which the poison had upon him but, even more remarkable, the very poison used—the "juice of cursed hebona". Further, the King's reaction to the play-within-the-play confirms the Ghost's account of the murder in every detail. Must we not assume, therefore, that every other revelation of the past which the Ghost gives is equally accurate: that Claudius,

> With witchcraft of his wit, with traitorous gifts
> . . . won to his shameful lust
> The will of [the] most seeming-virtuous queen.

Miss Heilbrun, who thinks Gertrude had not been Claudius' mistress, denies that Claudius had won her by the witchcraft of his wit. The real reason Gertrude had entered upon her hasty second marriage, Miss Heilbrun claimed, was given by the Ghost later in the same speech:

> But virtue, as it never will be moved,
> Though lewdness court it in the shape of heaven,
> So lust, though to a radiant angel linked,
> Will sate itself in a celestial bed
> And prey on garbage.

But if we accept as true one part of the Ghost's speech, must we not accept the other also? And do not the last three lines quoted above suggest a violation of the marriage vows? That they were intended to do so is evidenced by the Ghost's having protested in the same speech, in lines immediately preceding, that his

> . . . love was of that dignity
> That it went hand in hand even with the vow
> I made to her in marriage;

and that Hamlet understood the Ghost's words as indicating Gertrude's adultery is shown by his charging her in the Closet Scene with

> Such an act
> That blurs the grace and blush of modesty,
> ... makes marriage vows
> As false as dicers' oaths.

So much, then, do we learn of Gertrude in Act I. On these lines must be based the original impression Shakespeare wished to give us. It is interesting and, I suspect, significant that a very large part of what we have so far learned of Gertrude and Claudius represents modification or elaboration by Shakespeare of what is found in Belleforest's account. There, of course, Gertrude is neither weak nor neutral. Although she is not said to have participated in planning the murder of her husband, she was an accomplice after the murder, for she did not deny her lover's claim that it was in defence of her that he had slain his brother. Where, asked Belleforest, would one find "a more wicked and bold woman?" Such a question would never be asked by one writing of the Gertrude of the play. Her character Shakespeare has decidedly softened, even though in the play she appears guilty on every count cited by Belleforest except that of giving support to a false account of her husband's slaying. Shakespeare has softened her character not only by making her ignorant of the murder of her husband but by elaborating, in a way most effective upon the stage, that artful craft of Claudius as reported in Belleforest's account. There the murderer "covered his boldnesse and wicked practise with so great subtiltie and policie, and under the vaile of meere simplicitie . . . that his sinne found excuse among the common people, and of the nobilitie was esteemed for justice". Claudius' persuasive cunning is further suggested by Belleforest's observing that Gertrude, "as soone as she once gave eare to [her husband's brother], forgot both the ranke she helde . . . and the dutie of an honest wife".[3] To portray this smooth persuasiveness and subtle craft the dramatist introduced a brilliant dramatic touch for which there is no suggestion in Belleforest—the ingratiating smiling which leads Hamlet to declare Claudius a "smiling damned villain", and to cry out:

> My tables—meet it is I set it down
> That one may smile, and smile, and be a villain.
> At least I am sure it may be so in Denmark.

So much for Act I. The Queen next appears in II. ii. Rosencrantz and Guildenstern have been summoned to spy upon Hamlet, and Gertrude's first two speeches merely echo in fewer words the welcome given them by the King. With one exception her five remaining speeches in this scene are of one line or less, most of them designed to break and give a semblance of dialogue to Polonius' artful narration. The one exception is a speech of two lines in reply to the King's reporting to her that Polonius claims to have found

> The head and source of all your son's distemper.

The Queen replies:

> I doubt it is no other but the main,
> His father's death, and our o'erhasty marriage.

---

[3] Quoted from Furness, *Hamlet* (Variorum ed.), II, 93-94.

This speech, which some critics (mistakenly, I think) have seen as evidence that the Queen's conscience is already troubled, Miss Heilbrun pronounced "concise, remarkably to the point, and not a little courageous" (p. 203). One could the more readily agree with her had Gertrude omitted the word "o'erhasty". When the King first announced his marriage to his brother's widow, he passed quickly on to important affairs of state, but since then we have heard the incestuous nature of that marriage emphasized by both Hamlet and the Ghost. Are we to assume from her mentioning only the hastiness of their marriage—a censurable indiscretion perhaps but no mortal sin—that Gertrude failed to realize that her marriage to Claudius, no matter when performed, must bear the graver stain of incest? As she is at the time alone with the King, I think we must so assume. She hardly reveals here "a talent for seeing the essence of every situation presented before her eyes". But how can she have been so blind to the true nature of her marriage? The only explanation would seem to be that she is blinded by the traitorous gifts of Claudius, by the witchcraft of his wit. She thinks as he directs, acts as he wishes.

The next scene in which the Queen appears is III. ii—the play scene. Here she is on stage for 187 lines and speaks a total of two and one half lines. When to her first speech, "Come hither, my dear Hamlet, sit by me", Hamlet replies that he prefers to sit by Ophelia, the Queen is silent until 127 lines later, when, to emphasize the purport of such lines as "None wed the second but who killed the first", Hamlet asks, "Madam, how like you this play?" She answers simply, "The lady doth protest too much, methinks"—a speech which need not suggest stupidity, for she, unlike us, has not heard the ghost and knows not what is in Hamlet's mind; but unless we are to think of her as an artful villainess indeed, the simplicity of her reply is enough to urge her complete innocence of any participation in the murder. She now follows the play intently, saying nothing more until, when the frightened King rises, she anxiously enquires "How fares my lord?" In this scene then, aside from the first clear indication that Gertrude has been no accomplice in the murder, we see in her just what we see in her in other scenes—her love for her son, her devoted concern for Claudius, and her remarkable quietness, with long periods of silence.

It is when she next appears, in III. iv—the so-called Closet Scene—that the Queen has her biggest part. The scene opens with Polonius' hiding himself behind the arras that he may overhear the interview between mother and son—an interview in which the Queen has promised to "be round with him" in the hope of discovering the cause of Hamlet's strange behavior. The scheme had been conceived by Polonius and suggested to Claudius in II. ii, when Gertrude was not on stage. We do not witness the King's persuading the Queen to assist in this eavesdropping upon her son, but that she had received specific instructions on how the interview should be conducted is brought out in her conversation with Polonius before Hamlet enters:

> *Polonius:* 'A will come straight. Look you lay home to him.
> Tell him his pranks have been too broad to bear with,
> And that your grace hath screened and stood between
> Much heat and him. I'll silence me even here.
> Pray you be round with him. . . .
> *Queen:* I'll warrant you; fear me not.

The Queen had consented to these "lawful espials", as she had consented earlier when Ophelia had been used as a decoy, probably both because she is hopeful that such a scheme may indeed unearth the secret of Hamlet's strange behavior and because the stronger Claudius is able always to dominate her will and persuade her to serve his purpose. That this second explanation is sound is, I believe, shown by a departure which Shakespeare here makes from the account of the Closet Scene as related by Belleforest. In Belleforest the King and his councillor, without taking the Queen into their confidence, arrange for the councillor to secrete himself where he may overhear mother and son; the Queen not only has no part in planning the interview, but does not suspect the presence of the eavesdropper until he is discovered by the crafty and suspicious Hamlet's beating his arms upon the hangings. By this change in the Queen's part from that of an unwitting participant to that of an active accomplice Shakespeare seems to emphasize the extent to which Claudius dominates her and uses her as his tool.

The Queen begins the closet interview with bluster and some confidence. She has apparently been well briefed as to what she shall say. But when Hamlet proves recalcitrant, when in an ugly mood he assumes the offensive and by so doing throws her out of the part she has been coached to play, she is for a brief moment bold and stubborn. "What have I done?" she cries:

> What have I done, that thou dar'st wag thy tongue
> In noise so rude against me?

But as Hamlet becomes more specific in his charges, Gertrude has neither the strength nor the inclination to bluster it further. She appears, indeed, stricken in conscience:

> O Hamlet, speak no more,
> Thou turn'st mine eyes into my very soul,
> And there I see such black and grainèd spots
> As will not leave their tinct.

And again,

> O Hamlet, thou hast cleft my heart in twain.

Although in this scene the Queen has more speeches and more lines than she has in any other scene, she is throughout overshadowed by Hamlet. In the same number of speeches he speaks four times as many lines as does she. Of her twenty-four speeches, thirteen—more than half—are one line or less, and four others are less than two lines.

Some of her speeches invite comment. Miss Mackenzie has noted that Gertrude sees her penitence not as the consequence of her own actions but rather as a result of Hamlet's harsh words to her:

> O Hamlet, thou hast cleft my heart in twain.

Second, it is important to note that the question which she, contrite, puzzled, and helpless, addresses to Hamlet as he prepares to leave, "What shall I do?", illustrates the lack of initiative and independence which mark her throughout. Too weak to determine any procedure for herself, she must rely upon others for guidance in every action.

More puzzling is the Queen's last speech in the scene—a reply to Hamlet's

> I must to England, you know that?
> *Ger.* Alack,
> I had forgot. 'Tis so concluded on.

No one has ever questioned Gertrude's devotion to her son, although in urging him earlier to "stay with us, go not to Wittenberg", she may have spoken the instructions of Claudius as well as her motherly affection. It is impossible that by "I had forgot" she could have meant other than that the many unhappy events of the evening had crowded out of her mind the realization that Hamlet was to be sent to England. But the King's decision that he be sent away she had apparently accepted without protest as one accustomed to accepting without question what others decide for her.

In Belleforest's account the Queen, although she never appears after the Closet Scene, is definitely and actively an ally of her son, working in his absence to facilitate his revenge. In Shakespeare, although she protests to Hamlet:

> Be thou assured, if words be made of breath,
> And breath of life, I have no life to breathe
> What thou hast said to me,

and although she keeps her promise, the Queen utters not one word in condemnation of the crimes of Claudius which Hamlet has revealed to her, and indeed in the very next scene greets him as "mine own lord". Never is there an indication in the later scenes that her attitude toward Claudius or her relations with him have been altered by what Hamlet has told her. True it is that immediately following the Closet Scene she apparently lies to the King in an effort to protect her son. Although Hamlet has confessed to her that he is "not in madness, But mad in craft", she assures the King that Hamlet is

> Mad as the sea and wind when both contend
> Which is the mightier. In his lawless fit,
> Behind the arras hearing something stir,
> Whips out his rapier, cries 'A rat, a rat!'
> And in this brainish apprehension kills
> The unseen good old man.

And she reports that Hamlet has gone

> To draw apart the body he hath killed;
> O'er whom his very madness, like some ore
> Among a mineral of metals base,
> Shows itself pure. 'A weeps for what is done.

One need have little hesitation in concluding that Gertrude is here lying in an effort to render Hamlet's act less responsible and therefore more pardonable. The Queen has not seen Hamlet since the audience witnessed their parting, and Hamlet was surely not weeping then. But though the Queen lies to help her son, it is important to add in any assay of her character that it was not upon her own initiative that she does so. Here no more than earlier is she acting independently. Incapable of herself determining any course of action, she is merely following the course which Hamlet had suggested to her. To her helpless "What shall I do?" Hamlet had replied:

Not this, by no means, that I bid you do:
Let the bloat King . . .
Make you to ravel all this matter out,
That I essentially am not in madness,
But mad in craft. 'Twere good you let him know,
For who that's but a queen, fair, sober, wise,
Would from a paddock, from a bat, a gib,
Such dear concernings hide? Who would do so?
No, in despite of sense and secrecy,
Unpeg the basket on the house's top,
Let the birds fly, and like the famous ape,
To try conclusions, in the basket creep
And break your own neck down.

Such is Hamlet's sarcastic direction in answer to the Queen's uncertain "What shall I do?" She must decide upon some course immediately, for the King is impatiently awaiting a report of the interview. Accordingly she follows Hamlet's direction; she lies to keep his secret, perhaps because maternal love demands that she protect him, but also because, accustomed to having others make all important decisions for her, she is incapable of substituting for Hamlet's direction any procedure of her own.

In Belleforest, as has been said, the Queen never appears after the account of the interview in her closet. Although we learn later that she had kept her promise to assist her son in his revenge upon her second husband by fashioning, during her son's absence in England, the means of his revenge, we are told nothing of her later life—how she conducted herself in her relations with the King or how she died. In Shakespeare's play, however, she figures in five later scenes—exactly half of the total number in which she appears. Her part in these scenes, having no basis in the older accounts, must have been added either by Shakespeare or by the author of an earlier lost play. The first of these scenes is that just mentioned—that in which she reports to the King. In only one of them, IV. v, her next appearance, does she reveal any remorse or any sense of guilt; and before the end of that scene her sense of guilt seems completely erased by a determination to follow the easier way, to accept the *status quo,* to continue a way of life she had found pleasant.

IV. v opens with her refusal to admit the mad Ophelia to her presence— a refusal due perhaps to a characteristic desire to escape any distressing situation, or perhaps to her already being burdened with grief and remorse. When Ophelia enters, Gertrude is sympathetic but quite inarticulate. Her three speeches to Ophelia are—in full:

    1. How now, Ophelia?
    2. Alas, sweet lady, what imports this song?
    3. Nay, but Ophelia—

Then, upon the King's welcome entry, with "Alas, look here, my lord", the Queen turns the unpleasant situation over to him and retires into silence until after Ophelia has departed. Her unwillingness to see Ophelia and her inability to express any words of comfort or sympathy may, as I have said, be due in part to her being, at the moment, too heavily oppressed by her own griefs and her own sense of guilt. As Ophelia enters, Gertrude offers in an aside the only admission of guilt she makes after the Closet Scene:

> To my sick soul (as sin's true nature is)
> Each toy seems prologue to some great amiss.
> So full of artless jealousy is guilt,
> It spills itself in fearing to be spilt.

Before the end of the scene, however, the Queen is to cry out upon Laertes' mob threatening the King:

> How cheerfully on the false trail they cry!
> O, this is counter, you false Danish dogs!

and, in order to save Claudius, is first to seize Laertes' arm and then to assure him that it was not Claudius who had caused the death of his father. Having, perhaps unconsciously, directed Laertes' hatred towards Hamlet, she offers no fuller explanation and is silent for the remaining ninety lines of the scene. Her extended silence here is certainly not indicative of remorse for her earlier acts; it has been characteristic of her throughout the play. In this scene she reveals perhaps, as she reveals nowhere else in the play, the sensual side of her love for Claudius. Before the scene is half over her sense of guilt has been crowded out of her mind. She shows no repentance. Unlike the Queen in Belleforest or the Queen in the pirated first quarto, she has not aligned herself on the side of her son. Now that he has gone, she finds it easier simply to continue the life she had led before he had made his dreadful revelation. Had Hamlet remained in Denmark, had he been at hand to remind her of her weakness and to answer whenever necessary her question "What shall I do?" it is possible that her sense of guilt might have persisted, that she might even have repented and changed her way of life. But without initiative and independence, she can in Hamlet's absence only drift with the current.

Only twice, then, does Gertrude reveal the least remorse—in the latter part of the Closet Scene and in the single aside as she awaits the entrance of the mad Ophelia. From that time on, as earlier in the play, her actions and speeches evince no prick of conscience although the Ghost, in his instructions to Hamlet in I. v, had implied that she was to suffer the consequence of her sins. ". . . Howsomever thou pursues this act", the Ghost had told his son,

> Taint not thy mind, nor let thy soul contrive
> Against thy mother aught. Leave her to heaven
> And to those thorns that in her bosom lodge
> To prick and sting her. . . .

The Ghost is, as I have noted, most accurately informed of the past. That ghosts were often well informed of the future is indicated by Horatio's beseeching the Ghost to speak

> If thou art privy to thy country's fate,
> Which happily foreknowing may avoid.

But that ghosts might be ignorant of the future and even uncomprehending of the present is shown in *The Spanish Tragedy* by the repeated questioning by the Ghost of Andrea as he watches the play unfold. The Ghost of King Hamlet clearly expects his son to sweep to a swift revenge; he does not understand the delay; nor surely did he expect such complete catastrophe to engulf the entire royal family. In spite of his exact knowledge of the past, therefore, it would appear that the Ghost's knowledge of the immediate present and of the future was far too limited to warrant our acceptance as testimony of Gertrude's remorse his mention of

> ... those thorns that in her bosom lodge
> To prick and sting her....

Indeed, if one may, without confusing life and art, delve into the past of characters in a drama, it may be said that King Hamlet had ever but slenderly known his wife. Created in an heroic mould, he understood not the mortal frailties which might lead his "most seeming-virtuous queen"

> to decline
> Upon a wretch whose natural gifts were poor
> To those of [his].

Just as he had, before learning of her transgressions, been deceived by his wife's seeming-virtue, so, after learning of them, he expected her to be tortured by the stings of conscience. He was apparently twice deceived.

But to continue tracing the Queen's part in the play. She appears, of course, in all of the last three scenes. She enters late in IV. vii, after the King and Laertes have completed their plans for bringing about Hamlet's death, and in her longest speech in the play announces Ophelia's drowning. Her purpose here, however, is that of a messenger; her speech throws little light on her character—and certainly reveals no awareness of her own responsibility for the young girl's death.

In V. i, the scene in the graveyard, the Queen first mentions in a single speech her thwarted hope that Ophelia might have been Hamlet's bride, and then, as Hamlet and Laertes struggle in the grave, she, in her remaining speeches, follows the lead of Claudius:

> *King:* Pluck them asunder.
> *Queen:* Hamlet, Hamlet!
> *King:* O, he is mad, Laertes.
> *Queen:* For love of God, forbear him.

Then:

> This is mere madness;
> And thus a while the fit will work on him.
> Anon as patient as the female dove ...
> His silence will sit drooping.

The Queen, of course, does not know of the treachery plotted by Claudius and Laertes. She must by these speeches have sought to end the struggle in the grave and to lessen Laertes' resentment at Hamlet's behavior, but it is noticeable —and I think characteristic—that in each of her speeches she echoes or enlarges upon ideas just expressed by Claudius.

In V. ii, the concluding scene of the play, the Queen for the first time, I believe, acts with initiative and speaks for herself. Just before the court enters to watch the fencing match, an unnamed lord brings a message to Hamlet: "The Queen desires you to use some gentle entertainment to Laertes before you fall to play". As the effect of this message would be to lessen any suspicions of foul play, to encourage Hamlet's acceptance of the match as a "brother's wager frankly play[ed]", one is tempted to suggest that the Queen's message may have originated with the King, that here as earlier the Queen is being used to further the plan of another. (It will be remembered that immediately after the play-within-the-play Polonius brought Hamlet word that "the Queen would speak with you, and presently" (III.ii. 359), but, as previously noted, the idea of the interview was not the Queen's. It had originated with Polonius, and the King, to whom he suggested it (III.i. 182ff.), had off-stage persuaded the Queen to cooperate.) However, in the absence of any statement to the contrary, I presume we must accept the message as the lord delivers it, as the Queen's own suggestion. And in some respects it is a thoroughly characteristic suggestion, revealing as it does her recurring hope that in spite of all that had gone before, she and others, without being required to pay the price of penitence, may go on enjoying the present by simply refusing to remember the past.

During the closing scene the Queen is silent for the first sixty-one lines she is on stage. She then within a space of twenty-four lines has four speeches, totaling six pentameter lines. She refers to Hamlet's scantness of breath and offers her napkin to mop his brow. Then, for the first time in the play escaping the dominance of Claudius, she acts independently and counter to his expressed wish—and her crossing him means her death.

> *Queen:* . . . The queen carouses to thy fortune, Hamlet.
> *King:* Gertrude, do not drink.
> *Queen:* I will, my lord; I pray you pardon me.

And so she drinks from the poisoned cup. I can see no justification whatsoever for the view of a critic who sought to defend the Queen's character by suggesting that she, suspecting the wine to be poisoned, drank it to protect Hamlet and to atone for the wrongs and sins of her past. Others, like the author of the *New Exegesis of Shakespeare* (1859), have remarked that her death was "as exquisitely negative as possible—that is, by poison, from *her own hand,* in a VINOUS BEVERIDGE [sic], and THROUGH MISTAKE."[4] But however negative her death, it was, ironically, the result of her one act of independence. And her final speech, in answer to the King's hasty explanation, "She sounds to see them bleed":

> No, no, the drink, the drink! O my dear Hamlet!
> The drink, the drink! I am poisoned—

Here for the first time the Queen seems to understand the essence of the situation. Only in this last speech does she recognize or admit to herself the villainy of her second husband. Only here—long after her counterpart in Belleforest had done so—does she take her position beside her son and against the King.

University of Iowa

[4] *New Exegesis of Shakespeare; interpretation of his principal characters and plays on the principle of races* (Edinburgh: A. & C. Black, 1859, p. 66).

On Ophelia's Madness

CARROLL CAMDEN

HE character of Ophelia seems to have been puzzling to many critics who have written about the play. As a minor personage of the tragedy, she has not received the careful analysis accorded Hamlet, Gertrude, or Claudius, or even Laertes, Horatio, or Polonius. Her role in the play is not clear to critical writers who have attempted to answer the many questions which arise about Ophelia's relations with her father and with Hamlet —questions which must be answered if her madness is to be explained. Is her madness occasioned by her father's death? by her rejected love for Hamlet? or by both, in varying degrees?

The romantic critics apparently felt that the less said about Ophelia the better. "What shall be said of her? for eloquence is mute before her!" asks Mrs. Jameson. Hazlitt considers that she "is a character almost too exquisitely touching to be dwelt upon", and calls her a "flower too soon faded". Strachey writes, "There is more to be felt than to be said in the study of Ophelia's character just because she is a creation of such perfectly feminine proportions and beauty". And Bradley believes that in her fate we have "an element, not of deep tragedy, but of pathetic beauty, which makes the analysis of her character seem almost a desecration".[1]

Ophelia has received better treatment than this, of course, and she deserves better. She is not just the "poor wispy Ophelia" which Katherine Mansfield would make her, but a tenderhearted, delicate-minded young girl, well reared in proper obedience to her father, and experiencing what is apparently her first introduction to the bittersweet delights of love. And yet her tragedy seems to me to have been misinterpreted by a long array of critics, who have emphasized that her madness is due chiefly to the death of her father. According to John Draper, Ophelia's madness "comes about . . . because that father, whom she loved so dearly, came to a sudden and shocking end". L. L. Schücking, after remarking that "Grief at her father's sudden and unexplained death has unbalanced her mind", argues that any modern spectator who thinks that her madness is due to the broken relations with Hamlet is confuted by Shakespeare's making Claudius "expressly state that her madness is due to Polonius' death". Rebecca West goes so far as to say, "No line in the play suggests that she felt either passion or affection for Hamlet". In the last century, Roderick Benedix writes of Polonius' death as serving a dramatic purpose, "inasmuch as it is the cause of Ophelia's madness", but at the same time he perceives that

[1] Anna Brownell Jameson, *Shakespeare's Heroines* (London, 1858), p. 257; William Hazlitt, *The Characters of Shakespeare's Plays* (London, 1817), p. 111; Edward Strachey, *Shakespeare's Hamlet* (London, 1848), p. 84; A. C. Bradley, *Shakespearean Tragedy* (London, 1951), p. 160.

"No girl becomes insane because her father dies, least of all Ophelia. . . ." Even Laurence Babb, although he notes the resemblance between the madness of Ophelia and that of the Jailer's daughter in *The Two Noble Kinsmen,* and though he believes that the "lovesick maidens of the early Stuart drama" were influenced by Ophelia, can write that it is not unrequited love which is chiefly responsible for Ophelia's condition but rather "grief for her father's death". Despite these pronouncements, as well as that of G. L. Kittredge that "it is the mysterious tragedy of her father's death that has driven her mad", I believe it can be shown that the overriding cause of Ophelia's madness is clearly spelled out in the play; it is more "the pangs of despiz'd love" which cause her tragic fate than the death of Polonius.[2]

The first we see of Ophelia is when she receives some parting advice from her brother, as Laertes prepares to go abroad. He thinks of himself as a worldly-wise young man explaining the chief pitfall which a green girl is likely to encounter in the life at court. He warns her that Hamlet is merely playing with her affections and that she must not consider his attentions as more than "a violet in the youth of primy nature . . . the perfume and suppliance of a minute". And he continues by saying that as the body becomes of age, the mind and soul which service the temple of the body also grow and cause youth to be attracted toward the opposite sex. Laertes cautions her to realize that her own feelings are somewhat in this category, since "the chariest maid is prodigal enough" when opportunity is afforded her, and "youth to itself rebels". Of course Laertes' advice is shallow; he seemingly judges Hamlet to be a man like himself. And Ophelia is perceptively aware of his shallowness as she reminds him in sisterly fashion to heed his own warnings; then Laertes suddenly remembers that he is in a hurry to depart. But through this speech Laertes may well have aroused what he sought to allay, by focusing Ophelia's thoughts on the subject of love, already kindled by her own inchoate desires.

Polonius contributes to Ophelia's absorption in matters of love as he indicates how the senses of youth are easily inflamed. She must not take the heat of Hamlet's desire as true love. Polonius then delivers the blow which has blighted the lives of many girls as he tells his daughter that she must break off with Hamlet and never again talk with him.

A further shock to Ophelia, one full of dramatic irony, occurs offstage when Hamlet bursts into her boudoir. Having been warned by her brother and her father of the sexual frailties of youth, she finds some support for their remarks in the actions of Hamlet in her closet. She fears that Hamlet is mad for love, and if so he is mad for the love that she has been forbidden to give him— she is the cause of Hamlet's madness. We need not pause to consider the real significance of Hamlet's actions here. It suffices that Hamlet's behavior gives her every reason to believe her father right in his diagnosis of the cause of Hamlet's madness. It is a species of irony that the proscription given by Polonius

---

[2] Katherine Mansfield: *Hamlet,* ed. John Hampden (London, 1937), p. 182; John Draper, *The Hamlet of Shakespeare's Audience* (Durham, 1938), p. 61; L. L. Schücking, *The Meaning of Hamlet* (Oxford, 1937), p. 153; Rebecca West, *The Nature of Will* (New Haven, 1957), pp. 21-22; Roderick Benedix, *Die Shakespearomanie* (Stuttgart, 1873; in New Variorum *Hamlet,* II, appendix); Laurence Babb, "Love Melancholy in the Elizabethan and Early Stuart Drama", *Bulletin of the History of Medicine,* XIII (1943), p. 129; G. L. Kittredge, *Sixteen Plays of Shakespeare* (Boston, 1946), p. 1086.

seems to bring about Hamlet's pretended madness but actually contributes to Ophelia's real madness. When Ophelia reports Hamlet's conduct, Polonius sees that Hamlet suffers from "the very ecstasy of love", but never suspects that in following his orders Ophelia is about to succumb to the same ecstasy, "whose violent property fordoes itself and leads the will to desperate undertakings". Polonius is quick to tell his daughter that when she "did repel his letters and denied his access" to her she caused Hamlet to run mad; but since he is a self-absorbed busybody who regards his daughter as a tool, he gives no thought to the effect that all this will have on Ophelia. Indeed, a further irony lies in the actual words of Polonius as he gives to the King and Queen his prognosis of the disease in Hamlet:

> I prescripts gave her
> That she should lock herself from his resort,
> Admit no messengers, receive no tokens.
> Which done, she took the fruits of my advice;
> And he, repulsed—a short tale to make—
> Fell into a sadness, then into a fast,
> Thence to a watch, thence into a weakness,
> Thence to a lightness, and, by this declension,
> Into the madness wherein now he raves,
> And we all mourn for.   (II. ii, 142-151)

The defective effect of Ophelia's madness to come has the same cause; Polonius' prescripts have their effect on Ophelia too. Throughout the play, indeed, the appearance of Hamlet's pretended madness is contrasted with the reality of Ophelia's madness.

The next shock to the tender sensibilities of Ophelia is the get-thee-to-a-nunnery scene. She now believes that she herself is the immediate source of Hamlet's madness. She believes, too, that Hamlet loves her; and her actions, if not her words, indicate that she has more than warm feelings for him, as witness the patience with which she listens to Hamlet during his mad speech. Yet when she meets him to return his tokens of love, he tells her, "I did love you once. . . . You should not have believed me. . . . I loved you not." She must wonder whether her father and brother were not right after all. To complete the disillusionment, Hamlet uses offensive language to her, language that no sensitive girl could endure with equanimity. He asks her if she is chaste, and insults her further with comment on her affected walk and speech, her use of cosmetics, her "wantonness". Though the language is general enough in its reflections on womankind, and though it is used for the benefit of the hidden Claudius and Polonius, yet the tone is ill-mannered and is an affront which Ophelia would feel deeply.

Commentators also wonder whether or not Hamlet really loved Ophelia. But the point here is that whether he did or not, Ophelia thought he did. In his letter to her he wrote: "That I love thee best, O most best, believe it. . . . Thine evermore". When in the scene just examined Hamlet says, "I did love you once", Ophelia replies, "Indeed, my lord, you made me believe so". And when Hamlet retires from the scene, Ophelia speaks of herself as being "of ladies most deject and wretched". That she returned the love is clearly indicated as she lets the audience know in a soliloquy what is running through her mind, characterizing herself as one "that sucked the honey of his music vows". Vows and words of love are music only in the ears of those who return the feelings of love.

In the play scene, the relations between Hamlet and Ophelia remain much the same as in the scene just discussed. Hamlet continues to use bawdy language; Ophelia modestly declines the obscene implications of his question, "Shall I lie in your lap?" and seems not to understand some of the conversation. But when the Prologue enters and Hamlet puns on the word "show", she tells him he is naughty. Several lines further, Ophelia comments on the sharpness of his repartee, only to receive the reply, "It would cost you a groaning to take off my edge". Although Hamlet's language may have been calculated to convince Claudius that he is mad for love, it certainly was the sort to disturb even more the delicate balance of the susceptible girl who saw herself to blame.

Ophelia's mind is further agitated in the same scene. When Hamlet asks whether the actor is speaking a true prologue or giving a "posy" for a ring, she agreeably replies that it certainly is brief, only to hear Hamlet's "As woman's love". His remark is usually glossed as being his comment on the conduct of his mother, and this interpretation may well be correct. But Ophelia must think that Hamlet is speaking of her own conduct toward him.

When we next hear of Ophelia, it is to learn of her madness. The Gentleman prepares us for her entrance by describing her actions for the Queen. According to him Ophelia talks much of her father and says there are deceptions in the world. She should know, since she has practised some herself in lying to Hamlet concerning her father's whereabouts, and she has had others practised on her by Hamlet. Her first words upon entering are, "Where is the beauteous majesty of Denmark?" Surely she is not talking of her father here, since the words fit neither what we know of Polonius nor what a girl would say of a father who fails to understand her. Nor is there any reason why Gertrude should be the subject of her question. Rather it is to Hamlet that her words apply, whom she has already characterized as

> The glass of fashion and the mould of form,
> The observed of all observers, quite, quite down!
> And I, of ladies most deject and wretched,
> That suck'd the honey of his music vows,
> Now see that noble and most sovereign reason,
> Like sweet bells jangled, out of tune and harsh;
> That unmatch'd form and feature of blown youth
> Blasted with ecstasy.   (III. i. 161-168)

Hamlet, then, is the "beauteous majesty"; it is upon Hamlet that her mind in its madness dwells. And the first of the song-snatches she sings is about "true love".

> How should I your true love know
>   From another one?
> By his cockle hat and staff,
>   And his sandal shoon.

Surely no one contends that Polonius is her true love. And when the Queen inquires the import of the song, Ophelia asks her to listen to the next lines:

> He is dead and gone, lady,
>   He is dead and gone;
> At his head a grass-green turf,
>   At his heels a stone.

The Queen starts to say something, but again Ophelia asks her to listen:

> White was his shroud as the mountain snow,—
>   Larded with sweet flowers;
> Which to the grave did go
>   With true-love showers.   (IV. v. 23-39)

The first four lines are apparently part of a traditional verse. The other lines have no connection with this Walsingham poem as printed in the *Garland of Good Will* or the version in the Bodleian manuscript. It is possible, however, that the three quatrains were part of a single poem. Whether they were or not is unimportant; what is important is that both the first and third quatrains tell of true love and would naturally be linked in Ophelia's mind with Hamlet. Perhaps, then, in her mind it is Hamlet who is "dead and gone" since he is dead and gone for her. The point is that Polonius makes an unlikely candidate to appear among verses on true love.

The King has already made his entrance; he now greets Ophelia: "How do you, pretty lady?" She responds to the greeting in the conventional fashion, scarcely noticing him. Then she speaks a line referring to a moral tale designed to teach children to be kind and generous to the poor, and follows it with the words: "Lord, we know what we are, but know not what we may be. God be at your table." The King thinks her ramblings to be "conceit upon her father". That can hardly be. The moral tale has no apparent application; and knowing what we are but not what we may become wonderfully expresses both Ophelia's former concern over Hamlet's condition and her own distressing state.

Of course we should probably make little or nothing of Ophelia's non sequiturs in this scene. To derive intelligent meaning from them would be to group ourselves with others who remark her ramblings and "botch the words up to fit their own thoughts". Yet in apparent reply to the King's words Ophelia rejects his interpretation and recites sixteen lines of immodest verse on sexual love, the effect of which underlines strongly the chief cause of her madness: "Pray you, let's have no words of this; but when they ask you what it means, say you this":

> To-morrow is Saint Valentine's day,
>   All in the morning betime,
> And I a maid at your window,
>   To be your Valentine.
> Then up he rose, and donn'd his clothes,
>   And dupp'd the chamber-door;
> Let in the maid, that out a maid
>   Never departed more. . . .
> By Gis and by Saint Charity,
>   Alack, and fie for shame!
> Young men will do't, if they come to't;
>   By cock, they are to blame.

> Quoth she, before you tumbled me,
>   You promised me to wed.
> So would I ha' done, by yonder sun,
>   An thou hadst not come to my bed.   (IV. v. 48-66)

These coarse and uninhibited lines are the sort which might unconsciously and naturally float to the top of Ophelia's muddled mind if her thoughts had been dwelling on Hamlet's love and on possible marriage to him. As by certain dreams "may we conjecture of *the sinnes of the heart:* because what we conceiue or practice in the day will be corruptly dreamed of in the night",[8] so when one mentally disturbed speaks "things in doubt, that carry but half sense", we may rightly judge the sources of her perturbations to lie in her secret desires.

Ophelia now indeed speaks of her father, saying that she cannot help weeping "to think they should lay him i' the cold ground". After she makes her exit, the King repeats his first diagnosis, saying, "this is the poison of deep grief; it springs all from her father's death". But of course Claudius has his own axe to grind since he wishes to stir Laertes up to ridding him of Hamlet. We can allow the statement that Ophelia's words and actions spring from deep grief, but not all from the death of Polonius.

When Ophelia re-enters later in the scene, her brother is on stage; as he sees her madness he speaks of her in extravagant terms of sorrow, concluding somewhat enigmatically that human nature is delicate in matters of love, and when it is so "it sends some previous instance of itself after the thing it loves". Immediately following the words of Laertes, Ophelia sings more snatches of songs. The first indeed sounds as though her father is in her mind. Yet if so, the last line of the quatrain as it is printed in F_1 is curious: "Fare you well, my dove!" Are these not rather the words Ophelia might use to Hamlet? Her next little song ("You must sing a-down a-down, An you call him a-down-a") might suit anyone: Laertes or Claudius, as well as Polonius or Hamlet. Ophelia comments: "O, how the wheel becomes it! It is the false steward, that stole his master's daughter." We can only conjecture the antecedent of *it;* but the story of the false steward does have something to do with love, and nothing to do with a dead father. The language of flowers follows, though there are no violets since "they withered all when my father died". But the next snatch ("For bonny sweet Robin is all my joy") again is from a song of love. The last song must refer to Polonius, since in it occur the lines, "No, no, he is dead" and "His beard was as white as snow".

The remaining act of Ophelia's pitiful tragedy takes place off stage, and we learn of it from the beautifully poetic account of the Queen. According to Gertrude, to put it prosaically, Ophelia crowned herself with a garland of oddly assorted flowers and weeds, climbed a willow tree, and fell into a stream when the branch on which she sat broke. She floated for a while, continuing to sing "snatches of old tunes", then sank to "muddy death". Note that even at her watery end, the "envious sliver" which let her fall is that of a willow, a tree linked in Shakespeare and elsewhere in Elizabethan literature with unrequited love.

Of course it seems quite reasonable that Ophelia would have some degree of affection for her father. And obviously, too, his death was a traumatic ex-

---

[8] Thomas Casper, *The Mystery of Witch-craft* (London, 1617), p. 146.

perience for her. Yet I believe that Katherine Mansfield is quite perceptive in her brief analysis of the relationship between father and daughter. Concerning Polonius she says, "Who can believe that a solitary violet withered when that silly old Pomposity died? And who can believe that Ophelia really loved him, and wasn't thankful to think how peaceful breakfast would be without his preaching."[4] The death of Polonius, then, may well have been only the last in a series of shocks to her basically weak personality. First the love that Hamlet had declared for her, then the warning of her brother and her father, her father's orders not to receive Hamlet or talk with him or accept messages or gifts from him, Hamlet's visiting her closet and indicating that she herself is responsible for his madness, the return of Hamlet's tokens and his unseemly language to her in the nunnery scene, his refusal of her, his gross proposal to her (though perhaps spoken facetiously or to confuse Claudius) and his indecent speech at the play scene, together with the constant references made in her presence throughout the tragedy to such matters as "a fashion and a toy in blood", "blazes", "mad for love", "desperate undertakings", "are you honest?" "I loved you not", "believe none of us", "make your wantonness your ignorance", "country matters", "lie between a maid's legs", "be not you ashamed to show", "brief . . . as woman's love"—these are the overt causes of Ophelia's madness. Though every kind of suggestion has been made to interpret practically every line in the play, we can be thankful that no one has suggested an Electra complex in Ophelia; she was not in love with Polonius. Thomas Hanmer, early in the eighteenth century, clearly stated the principle: "It is not often that young women run mad for the loss of their fathers".[5] Young people can usually regard the death of a parent with some degree of equanimity, but the death of their own prospects is quite another matter.

The parallel of Ophelia's madness and that of the Jailer's daughter in *The Two Noble Kinsmen* is very apt; and it strengthens the belief that Ophelia is "distract" from unrequited love. Early in the play the Jailer's daughter, feeling her madness coming on, says: "Let not my sense unsettle, Lest I should drown or stab or hang myself". Later in the play she rushes into the water ("sought the flood") but is saved by her Wooer. Further, she sings snatches of many songs, as does Ophelia. One of the songs has the refrain "Hey, nonny, nonny, nonny". She forgets one song but remembers that its refrain is "Down a, down a". She says she knows the song "Bonny Robin", and sings "Willow, willow, willow", the song of unrequited love also sung by Desdemona.[6] Like Ophelia, too, she frequently talks in a bawdy fashion and asks the Wooer, thinking him to be Palamon, to go to bed with her.[7] Interestingly also, although it is specifically stated that she is mad for love, she too talks of her father's death and says that when he dies she will gather flowers for his burial; but "then she sang nothing but 'Willow, willow'", and instead of a coronet of

---

[4] Mansfield, p. 182.

[5] Thomas Hanmer, *Some Remarks on the Tragedy of Hamlet* (London, 1736), p. 46.

[6] *Othello* IV. iii. 26-57. See *Much Ado* II. i. 124-126, "I offered him my company to a willow-tree, either to make him a Garland, as being forsaken, or to bind him up a rod. . . ."; *Merchant of Venice* V. i. 9-10; *Twelfth Night* I. v. 287-288.

[7] It is interesting that this occurrence is duplicated in *Der Bestrafte Brudermord*—a play in which all agree that Ophelia is mad for love—where Ophelia mistakes Phantasmo for her sweetheart and suggests that they go to bed together.

weeds she makes rings of the rushes and speaks to them such pretty posies of love as "Thus our true love's tied" and "This you may lose, not me". Later she remarks, "We maids that have our livers perish'd, crack'd to pieces with love, we shall come there and do nothing all day long but pick flowers with Proserpine. Then will I make Palamon a Nosegay." She speaks of hell and says that "if one be mad, or hang or drown themselves, thither they go. . . ." When the Doctor is asked to diagnose her sickness, he states that she is suffering from love melancholy, which he believes can be cured only if the Wooer, as Palamon, makes love with her.

The Elizabethans, further, would have been prepared to accept Ophelia as a girl suffering from the effects of love, erotic melancholy *(erotomania)*, or a fit of the mother. They knew that "the passive condition of woman kind is subject vnto more diseases and of other sortes and natures then men are".[8] They recognized that "the diverse and violent perturbations which afflict the mind of the Passionate Lover, are the causes of greater mischiefes, then any other passion of the mind whatsoever". "Love is the ground and Principall cause of all our Affections, and the Abstract of all the Passions and perturbations of the minde. . . ." Furthermore, Doctor James Ferrand continues, erotic melancholy is particularly common in women; they are "farre more subject to this passion, and more cruelly tormented with it, then men are". And he notes that "daily experience affords us Examples great store of Women, that are ready to run Mad for Love. . . ."[9] André du Laurens and John Bishop continue in the same vein, the latter emphasizing the suicidal tendencies of those suffering from erotic melancholy; he states that he believes this disease "to be of all other most painful: seeing that so many [women] do willingly runne into euerlasting paines of hell fire, by cruelly murthering them selues, that they may thereby escape and rid them from the broyling brendes of *Cupide*. . . ."[10]

Ophelia exhibits many of the classical symptoms of *passio hysterica* brought on by *erotomania*.[11] She is mad, cries "hem" to clear her throat because of a feeling of choking or suffocation, beats her heart to relieve the sensation of oppression around it, weeps, prattles constantly, sings snatches of old songs, is distracted and has a depraved imagination, and ends her life by drowning. It is possible that the drowning may not have been deliberate, but at least Ophelia made no attempt to save herself. Though the priest says she is allowed her virgin rites, yet the rites are "maimed" because "her death was doubtful". Dr. Jorden warns that many good physicians are deceived by the symptoms of the disease (such as "*suffocation* in the throate, . . . convulsions, hickcockes, laugh-

---

[8] In discussing the medical aspects of Ophelia's malady, the books I have used are: Edward Jorden, *A Briefe Discourse of a Disease Called the Suffocation of the Mother* (London, 1603); James Ferrand, *Erotomania, or A Treatise Discoursing of the Essence, Cause, Symptomes, Prognosticks, and Cure of Love. Or Erotique Melancholy* (Oxford, 1640; 1st French ed., Paris, 1623); Robert Burton, *The Anatomy of Melancholy* (New York, 1941); André du Laurens, *Of the Preservation of the Sight* (London, 1599); Tomaso Garzoni, *The Hospital of Incurable Fooles* (London, 1600); Pierre Boaistuau, *Theatrum Mundi* (London, 1581); John Bishop, *Beautiful Blossomes* (London, 1577); Nicolas Coeffeteau, *A Table of Humane Passions* (London, 1621). These first references are to Jorden (sig. B 1) and Ferrand (p. 9).

[9] Ferrand, pp. 7, 9-10, 214-215; see Coeffeteau, pp. 170-171; Jorden, sig. G2^v; and Garzoni, p. 151.

[10] Du Laurens, pp. 117-118; Bishop, fol. 52^v.

[11] Ferrand, pp. 11, 94-96.

ing, singing, weeping, crying, &c.") believing them "to proceede from some metaphysicall power, when in deede . . . they are meerely naturall".[12]

Similarly, Dr. Ferrand speaks of the person suffering from *erotomania*: "For you shall see him now very jocund and laughing and presently within a moment he falls a weeping, and is extreame sad: then by and by againe he entertaines himselfe with some pleasant merry conceipts or other. . . . These Perturbations proceed from the Diversity of those objects they fancy to themselves. . . . To this we may adde their excessive talking, ..." Finally, in treating the subject of young girls ready for marriage, Dr. Ferrand gives this warning: "For the cure of which Disease [Hippocrates] prescribes speedy Marriages otherwise it is to be feared, that through Madnesse and Impatience, they will make away themselves, either by drowning or hanging; falsely perswading themselves, that by these Remedies, . . . being very sure ones, and as they conceive, the best they can finde; they shall set a period to their miseries."[13] Whatever the exact nature of Ophelia's malady of love, whether it is pure *erotomania* or *passio hysterica* brought on by lovesickness, the symptoms which she exhibits are so clearly portrayed and most of them so easily recognized that the Elizabethan audience, we have reason to suppose, would at least see Ophelia as a girl suffering physically and mentally the pangs of rejected love.[14]

Rice University

[12] Jorden, sig. B2, E1. See Ferrand, pp. 94-97.

[13] Ferrand, pp. 97, 107-110.

[14] It is rather interesting to note, though perhaps of no significance, that in the discussion of the remedies of love Burton quotes the line, "Young men will do it when they come to it", but without reference to *Hamlet* (p. 736).

THEATRE.

Mr. MASON.

The Manager has much pleasure in announcing an engagement for **FOUR NIGHTS** with this distinguished and talented Tragedian, who will make his first appearance before the St. Louis audience on

THIS EVENING,
Friday, July 31st, 1835,

In Shakspeare's celebrated Tragedy of

HAMLET,
Prince of Denmark!

HAMLET,	Mr. MASON,
LAERTES,	SPENCER,
King,	Johnson,
Polonius,	Kelly,
Ghost,	Ludlow,
Horatio,	M. Field,
Rosencrantz,	Thompson,
Guildenstern,	Barclay,
Bernardo,	Morris,
Marcellus,	Egerton,
Francisco,	Wolfe,
Priest,	La Rue,
Grave Digger,	Watson.
QUEEN,	Mrs. LUDLOW,
OPHELIA,	Miss ST'ANNARD,
(Her first appearance in this city.)	
Actress,	Mrs Johnson.

The entertainments of the evening will conclude with a laughable Farce, (in one act,) called

INTRIGUE
Or, Married Yesterday!

Tom,	Mr. Watson,
Varnish,	Johnson,
Rambleton,	Spencer,
Ellen,	Mrs. Watson.

☞ *Curtain rises* precisely at half past 8 o'clock.

☞ In preparation, a beautiful Petit Drama, called

NAPOLEON:
Or, The Emperor and Soldier!

NAPOLEON, - - - - - Mr. MASON

The Manager has the pleasure of announcing the arrival of

Mrs. HAMBLIN,

Who will appear on Saturday in a favorite Comedy.

In preparation, the celebrated Operas of the

DEVIL'S BRIDGE
AND
BROTHER & SISTER.

PRICES OF ADMISSION—Box and Pit, One Dollar; Gallery, Fifty cents.

Tickets and Seats can be secured by applying at the Office of the Theatre, from 10 till 12—from 2 till 4—and from 6 till the end of the performance. Tickets good only for the night for which they are purchased.

Smoking prohibited in the Theatre. The utmost order and decorum will be expected. Officers are provided for the purpose of attending to the same.

Playbill for the performance of *Hamlet* on 31 July 1835 in St. Louis. 5″ x 15¾″. Reproduced by permission of The Folger Shakespeare Library.

Troilus in Shapes of Infinite Desire

WILLARD FARNHAM

HEN Shakespeare wrote *Troilus and Cressida* his imagination was full of cross-currents. In twentieth-century critical opinion about the play there are currents even more at odds. Their forces seem bent upon canceling each other out. In a way it can be understood why a reviewer of the 1960 Stratford-upon-Avon production of *Troilus and Cressida* could find that what its author provides is "merely a collection of beautiful speeches" and that a good producer of the piece must provide on the stage "the shape which Shakespeare himself missed".[1]

In this essay I confine myself to one poetic concern of Shakespeare's imagination within the play, a concern which creates shapes of infinite desire for the forming of Troilus. It works strongly and surely, despite cross-currents, to make two figures of Troilus in one. It serves to give Troilus the lover and Troilus the warrior a recognizable distinctness at the same time that it gives them a bond of substance. What one sees in the result must have bearing upon one's finding of shape in the play as a whole.

There will be an advantage in looking first at Troilus the lover. When Shakespeare makes Troilus tell Cressida that in love "the will is infinite and the execution confin'd", and that "the desire is boundless and the act a slave to limit" (III. ii. 88-90), we see concentric circles of application.[2] One is the circle of those "pretty encounters" to which Pandarus is immediately to lead the lovers and which Troilus has not long before envisioned in no ordinary way. He has thought of these encounters as about to take place in Elysian fields where he "may wallow in the lily beds / Propos'd for the deserver". In this circle there is a fleshly core of limitless desire, and it is the sexual act that we must take to be the slave to limit.

Beyond this is a circle where the desirous courtly lover becomes all fire and air as he pictures impossible deeds that will prove his merit to his beloved. Troilus, becoming forgetful of his lily beds, takes us into this farther realm by speaking of bounds set to those "undertakings" of love in which "we vow to weep seas, live in fire, eat rocks, tame tigers—thinking it harder for our mistress to devise imposition enough than for us to undergo any difficulty imposed".

And beyond that is still another circle where, again to draw upon words of Troilus, desire even challenges mutability and strives to convert love into a "fair faith" by which beloved as well as lover will keep

---

[1] Harold Hobson, *The Sunday Times,* July 31, 1960.
[2] Shakespeare quotations are from the text of G. L. Kittredge.

> constancy in plight and youth,
> Outliving beauties outward, with a mind
> That doth renew swifter than blood decays. (III. ii. 168-170)

Here at last is "a winnowed purity in love". But even as he attains to thought of it Troilus says in ominous sadness:

> But, alas,
> I am as true as truth's simplicity
> And simpler than the infancy of truth. (III. ii. 175-177)

What we find here is poetry of that special flight of the human spirit toward the limitless which our postclassical western world has made much of and has embodied, often dramatically, in some deeply meaningful culture-icons. Of such figures the Tamburlaine and the Faustus of Marlowe are good, if unsubtle, Elizabethan examples. Different from them though he is in many ways, the Troilus of Shakespeare in one way stands with them. His vision of infinite will or boundless desire matched with human action fated to suffer indignity by confinement or slavery is of their kind. It serves well as a reminder of the hold that the concept of infinity has had upon our western Christian world, whether in religion, in astronomy and mathematics, or in thought and feeling generally. Troilus is created within the frame of Renaissance infinitization of man's quest on earth. We find in the Marlovian Tamburlaine a hero who can link a restless "climbing after knowledge infinite", for which Nature teaches us all to have "aspiring minds", with his own climbing after "an earthly crown", that "ripest fruit of all". We find in the Shakespearian Troilus a hero who can aspire in love toward something not in any Marlovian hero's ken. The Renaissance urge to infinitize man's earthly quest is of course very different from what Erwin Panofsky calls a tendency the mystic has "to infinitize the ego because he believes in the self-extinction of the human soul in God".[3] With some simplicity this Renaissance urge can present the celestial cosmos as measureless. With less simplicity it can in painting from the beginning of the fourteenth century onward make use of perspective, which, as Panofsky says, is an interpretation of space that gives visual expression to the concept of the infinite by making the perspective vanishing point the projection of the point in which parallels intersect (pp. 16-17).

As a figure of infinite desire in love Troilus makes out that he is simple. He stands for the truth that is the keeping of faith and says:

> I with great truth catch mere simplicity.   (IV. iv. 106)

But of course he is not by any means all simple. The complexity that appears in the poetry given to Troilus when we put together such words of his as "great truth", "true as truth's simplicity", "mere simplicity", and "simpler than the infancy of truth" defies final statement. It goes beyond irony that is undoubtedly there to something that transforms irony by working opposites toward oneness.

We should look back to Troilus' "imaginary relish" of lily beds in Elysium. To beds of asphodel (the asphodel being literally enough a kind of lily) Pandarus as Charon is to carry the deserver of what by all classic connotations is to be

---

[3] *Gothic Architecture and Scholasticism* (New York, 1957), p. 15.

noble bliss. But there Troilus is to "wallow". What this word "wallow" brings with it achieves nothing short of a declaration of war upon the imagery in which it is set. Its dominant connotations are unavoidably those of animal action, often under befouling conditions, and we are bound to feel at a loss about them so long as we try to keep Troilus the lover an uncomplicated creation. A Troilus simpler than truth's infancy who with orthodox poetic elevation is in the full cry of aspiration toward love's Elysium is not to be allowed suddenly and casually to image its enjoyment as a wallowing. We cannot make him ironist enough for that. Nor does it help to make him nothing more than a base sensualist who is suddenly revealed in his true nature by such imaging. The expression of something else in him is far too important poetically to be discarded. The idealistic Troilus does exist—dramatically because poetically— but he does not exist to speak that word "wallow". The Troilus who actually speaks the word also exists, just as surely. But he could not have being without the other. The fullness of truth is that Troilus is indeed to wallow, though at the same time he will take his idealism to bed with him and though in fact he can never lose it. The unsimple Troilus says bluntly to the simple that such is to be. Such is what can happen to man in a world where the aspiration of love is called upon often enough to undergo what the flesh devises as its contribution to the range of love's experience. The unsimple Troilus can be a mocking Troilus but he is a very knowing one, who is certainly not without earnestness.

In the soliloquy that follows we find the unsimple Troilus taking inspiration from the simple for a transformation of sensual wallowing into a sensual flight toward the infinite. This is mockery so much in earnest that it tends to join with earnestness mocked. The flight rises from an anticipation by the simple Troilus that would once more give his coming possession of Cressida a classic-poetic elevation. The "sweet" expectation "enchants" his sense as he wonders what effect the tasting of "Love's thrice-repured nectar" will have upon him. At that point the flight takes form. The unsimple Troilus seizes from his simple other self this contemplation of delectable sweetness and whirls it into a presentiment of a sweetness so extreme that it will take a form monstrous and terrible:

> Death, I fear me;
> Sounding destruction; or some joy too fine,
> Too subtile-potent, tun'd too sharp in sweetness
> For the capacity of my ruder powers.
> I fear it much; and I do fear besides
> That I shall lose distinction in my joys,
> As doth a battle when they charge on heaps
> The enemy flying.   (III. ii. 23-30)

These images draw love's sensation toward a point where separateness within being can no longer exist—where, as we might say, parallel lines at last come together in infinity. For man's "ruder powers", which make his love a slave to limit, this is a refinement beyond bearing. Yet it starts in homely senses of the flesh like the one that belongs to "the wat'ry palate". What Shakespeare does here and elsewhere to make the Troilus of infinite desire in love reach

toward the abolition of distinctions reminds one of lines in which John Donne
has it that

> separation
> Falls not on such things as are infinite,
> Nor things which are but one, can disunite.

Donne comes to the wording of these lines by way of the image of married
love in which

> one glorious flame
> Meeting Another, growes the same,

and in which the two flames

> To an unseparable union growe.[4]

We have considered some basic imagery of infinite desire for Troilus as
lover. We have now to look at some of such imagery for Troilus as warrior.
With surety of touch Shakespeare unites in Troilus a lover's vision with a warrior's, through a poetry of infinity at the center of the character creation, and
yet gives differences to these visions that go deep.

Basic imagery for Troilus the warrior comparable to that just considered
for Troilus the lover is found in the Trojan debate on whether the war should
be ended by the giving up of Helen to the Greeks. Here Troilus becomes a
figure of honor, whatever he is earlier in the play when, out of his absorption in
love, he speaks of the war as fought by "fools on both sides". His contribution to
the debate is a full poetic statement of a concept of honor developed from
imagery of the infinite. Contrast is quickly apparent between this figure and
the Troilus figure of love. This figure shows nothing of a tendency we have just
found in Troilus the lover to play two parts, one simple and one unsimple. It
reveals only a simple Troilus of the most utter consistency.

Priam starts the debate by asking Hector whether Helen should be surrendered, and Hector by his reply sets Troilus on his course. Hector concludes
that Helen is "not ours nor worth to us" and asks:

> What merit's in that reason which denies
> The yielding of her up?   (II. ii. 24-25)

Troilus rises at once beyond finite considerations and beyond reason:

> Fie, fie, my brother!
> Weigh you the worth and honour of a king
> So great as our dread father in a scale
> Of common ounces? Will you with counters sum
> The past-proportion of his infinite?
> And buckle in a waist most fathomless
> With spans and inches so diminutive
> As fears and reasons? Fie, for godly shame!

Thus he comes to a vision of boundlessness for the will of honor to match his
vision of boundlessness for the will of love. It is to be noted, both here and

---

[4] "An Epithalamion, Or, mariage Song on the Lady Elizabeth and Count Palatine being married on St. Valentines day", *The Poems of John Donne*, ed. H. J. C. Grierson (Oxford, 1912), I,
128-129.

later on, that Troilus in what he says of honor never declares or assumes that the act is a slave to limit whereas the will is infinite. With love it must be thus. With honor, on the other hand, there is freedom of execution for the spirit that has infinite desire. In the debate Troilus sets out confidently to carry all before him. And he does carry all before him, so much so that he wins Hector over to his side and shapes Trojan policy in accordance with his conviction, after receiving some help from Paris that is not too free from involvement of personal interest.

But it is not only that there is no tension now between infinite will and finite act. Infinity itself for Troilus is now but simple measurelessness. There is nothing like a drawing of separatenesses toward conjunction in infinity, such as we have seen in the case of love. There is only a scheme of things where when honor does not guide there is base finite calculation according to "fears" and according to a justification of fears by "reason" but where when honor does guide there is infinite surety and a plain path to travel. The plain path is one of truth. In the way of honor, just as in the way of love, truth is for Troilus an archaic matter out of the feudal and chivalric age. It is loyalty, fidelity, constancy, steadfastness. It means keeping one's word to the death when one has solemnly promised adherence to a person or a cause. It means a reality that lies in the word one has given and not in the changing array of "facts" in one's surrounding world, which may appear, but according to Troilus can do no more than deceitfully appear, to make the given word of no validity.

It seems to be natural for some critics to condemn Troilus the warrior as though he were speaking only out of our own time and speaking most meaningfully to those in our own time who are antipathetic to the professional fighting man. It is revealing enough to put this Troilus now and then in modern dress, since some part of him looks forward to our age out of an earlier age. But he is not merely a modern "militarist" any more than Troilus the medieval and Renaissance courtly lover is merely a modern sensualist having trouble with a mistress who is susceptible to other men. His upholding of honor can today perhaps too easily be made to count against him rather than for him. Though on this score Hector can be thought "more culpable", Troilus can be joined with him in culpability for a "love of honour" that is an "obsession" and a "personal indulgence".[5] A love of honor looked upon as a personal indulgence would seem to be a love of fame. We owe it to Shakespeare to remember that love of honor in his hands can very plainly be love of a virtue for itself as well as love of fame for the practice of that virtue.[6] Troilus and Hector are not without a Renaissance love of honor as public esteem but they show also a love of honor as something more, which can be condemned as personal indulgence only at the risk of making all personal integrity into personal indulgence.[7] The

---

[5] The words quoted are Alice Walker's in her edition of *Troilus and Cressida* (Cambridge, 1957), pp. xiii, xxviii.

[6] See, for example, Curtis Brown Watson, *Shakespeare and the Renaissance Concept of Honor* (Princeton, New Jersey, 1960), pp. 206 ff.

[7] Recent opinion which works against such condemnation is to be found in: William R. Bowden, "The Human Shakespeare and Troilus and Cressida," *Shakespeare Quarterly*, VIII (1957), 167-177; Richard C. Harrier, "Troilus Divided", *Studies in the English Renaissance Drama*, ed. Josephine W. Bennett, Oscar Cargill, and Vernon Hall, Jr. (1959), pp. 142-156; David Kaula, "Will and Reason in *Troilus and Cressida*", *Shakespeare Quarterly*, XII (1961), 271-283.

ruling idea of honor is most certainly not an idea of fame in these lines of Troilus'

> Manhood and honour
> Should have hare hearts, would they but fat their thoughts
> With this cramm'd reason.   (II. ii. 47-49)

Infinite will does make Troilus absolute for honor, at whatever cost not only to his own life but likewise to other lives. The extremes to which he goes in this way make it all the more notable that when he talks of honor he never plays the detached choric part to comment ironically upon himself. He never expresses a mock-rueful realization that in his puruit of honor he with his "great truth" catches "mere simplicity". Of his being true in love he says to Cressida when she questions him about it:

> Who? I? Alas, it is my vice, my fault!   (IV. iv. 104)

But when honor is his theme he never takes such liberty with his faith in the virtue of truth as to look at truth in two ways and make it a vice as well as a virtue. In the crucial Trojan debate his argument is that Priam's honor is the honor of Troy because Priam as king *is* Troy and is ultimately responsible for sending out the Trojan expedition that captured Helen. But there was a Trojan council before the departure of the expedition and this participated in the decision to send it. It gave "full consent". So all Troy made the choice solemnly. By such an election promises are made that in honor are unbreakable and effects are produced on human life and on human values that in honor are irreversible. Such an election is like marriage. In honor one does not divorce one's wife although the "will" come to "distaste what it elected". (In other words, odd as it may sound to anyone who thinks of the speaker as having an "affair" with Cressida, there is honor in faithful marriage of which faithful courtly love knows the peculiar virtue.) At this point in the debate Cassandra comes in to cry of destruction fated for Troy unless it lets Helen go. Of course she moves Troilus not at all. No fear of destruction, even fear of inevitable destruction, should "deject the courage" of honorable Trojan minds.

When Hector makes his sudden about-face to take a stand on the side of Troilus and Paris because, as he declares, the "joint and several dignities" of the Trojans are after all a decisive consideration, it would seem that we are called upon not to condemn Hector for first seeing truth and then being false to it but rather to understand that he sees, and that we ourselves should see, validity in two truths, one out of a modernity of tough-minded reason (a late Renaissance modernity, if we like) and one out of a chivalric past. The idea of the first truth he develops himself. The idea of the second he allows Troilus to develop. It is well in accord with other unsimple things in *Troilus and Cressida* that he insists his own contribution to the debate has been offered "in way of truth" even as he turns to embrace the truth urged by Troilus. The warring truths of honor and reason undergo being brought together in Hector's recognition of both and become one complex truth of honesty (*honestas*) where integrity knows not only a loyalty to persons and causes that have been given pledges but also a loyalty to more general principles that can be clarified by intellect. The fact that Hector can choose but one of these loyalties as a guide to action thus becomes an expression of human limitation in putting truth into practice.

One of the most memorable of the unsimple things in the play is found near the end in Troilus' vision of a Cressida who is and is not Cressida. When we come upon this we know that we are once more observing the Troilus for whom infinity is not mere measurelessness. It is the Troilus who has to deal with truth in the way of love, not in the way of honor. He is finding that when love is drawn out by man to the farthest extent of his understanding it can produce opposites which become baffling oxymorons. But it is not the ruefully ironic or mocking Troilus that we now see. It is one filled with the agony of discovery that his foreboding about attainment with Cressida of "winnowed purity in love" was all too well founded. The oxymoron of Cressida's being "secretly open" with Diomed, which is presented to him as he stands hidden with Ulysses, makes him perceive a more essential oxymoron of lying truth:

> But if I tell how these two did coact,
> Shall I not lie in publishing a truth? (V. ii. 118-119)

Troilus here is trying to conquer both time and disunity. In thought, by process of reason, he constructs an infinity which is a realm of timelessness as well as of oneness. In this realm of infinite truth Cressida cannot change from true to false any more than she can suffer division into Troilus' Cressida and Diomed's. But his reason wavers in the construction as it attempts to hold together as a single reality the Cressida infinitely desired by himself and the Cressida finitely won by Diomed. It is thus that he comes to exclaim:

> Bifold authority! where reason can revolt
> Without perdition, and loss assume all reason
> Without revolt: this is, and is not, Cressid! (V. ii. 144-146)

After coming to full realization of his powerlessness before a falsity in Cressida already accomplished he does not hesitate. When he tears up her letter and throws it to the wind he surrenders her and her untrue love completely to the eddying medium of time as to their proper element:

> Go, wind, to wind! there turn and change together. (V. iii. 110)

Thus in his pursuit of love Troilus as a figure of infinite desire suffers defeat. Aspiring toward truth in love he undergoes, with greater pain than he has ever foreboded, a slavery to limit. He finds as he explores love that it has doublenesses. In the finite world even the truest of infinite desire cannot make these doublenesses yield to what he calls "rule in unity itself". The least subtle of them comes from the fact that for love to be at all there must be two beings who remain separate no matter how far they go toward oneness.

Yet in his pursuit of honor Troilus as a figure of infinite desire does not suffer defeat at all. One who is inclined to make *Troilus and Cressida* into an unqualified tragedy may be given pause by a consideration of its last scene. This ending of the drama belongs to Troilus the warrior. In a sense it is no ending at all because it implies so much still to come, and its very inconclusiveness, its failure to bound the action, gives it all the more surely to a Troilus unconquered. The infinite aspiration of Troilus in honor, which

Shakespeare has created as a poetic counterpart of his aspiration in love and which is just as much a shaper of his action, is here all that remains of moving force in Troilus. It is not weakened by working alone in him. It makes him "dare all imminence that gods and men / Address their dangers in" as he looks off into the distance, in which there is to be honor sustained unfailingly in spite of what he recognizes as the "sure destructions" of Troy and himself.

This is the Troilus who sees infinity as mere measurelessness. He is a man who in his kind of infinite desire is able to prevail. Troilus the lover loses himself on his search for the winnowed purity of faith-keeping and one may even say that in a sense he dies if one wishes to have for him a tragedy in Elizabethan terms. But Troilus the warrior finds what the other misses. He comes to know by trial that the grasp of man the individual upon faith-keeping can be sure, however unsure the grasp upon it may be of the paired man and woman in love.

There is irony in the way this Troilus prevails and in the fact that it is he and not the other Troilus who prevails. In the light of reason the irony draws power from all that is said in the play about reason and anti-reason, for his prevailing is seen to be by anti-reason. The irony also draws power from a dramatic pattern within the play that Shakespeare found place for in other plays. In *Hamlet* there is irony in the fact that Hamlet himself, who is the greater spirit, is overthrown where Fortinbras, the plain man of war, prevails. About *Timon of Athens* one can say the same thing with Timon substituted for Hamlet and Alcibiades for Fortinbras. What we find in *Troilus and Cressida* is not, as in these plays, a hero who falls tragically while another man who is a lesser spirit rises to a place of leadership that the hero could not achieve. Yet we find the same irony essentially. In *Troilus and Cressida* the hero is both the greater figure and the lesser, all within himself. Troilus the lover, the greater Troilus because greater in human reach, falls tragically. Troilus the warrior (in accord with tradition in the line of Dares) rises to lead Troy in outfacing the "discomfort" of Hector's death. This Troilus who prevails is an estimable man within the framework of honor, as we are meant not to forget. But while the other Troilus speaks of having "mere simplicity" and is by no means so simple as he would be thought, this Troilus is simple in all truth.

University of California (Berkeley)

"Perplex'd in the Extreme":
The Role of Thought in *Othello*

PAUL A. JORGENSEN

IN *Julius Caesar* and *Hamlet* Shakespeare had discovered the great dramatic and intellectual value of a thinking man as hero.[1] The meditative hero gave him opportunity to deal with tragic stories more articulately than had ever been possible before on the English stage, with the doubtful exception of *Doctor Faustus*. Suffering and spiritual realization could be voiced by the hero and not by a chorus or by a relatively minor character like Friar Laurence in *Romeo and Juliet*.

It is therefore puzzling, after his successful and doubtless satisfying experiments in *Julius Caesar* and *Hamlet,* that Shakespeare should turn next in his creation of tragedy to a protagonist like Othello, whom critics agree in seeing as a strong, impressive, but not thoughtful man. For Othello can express only lyrically the agony of his plight. He is not intellectually equipped to enlarge by his own sense of tragedy upon man's plight in general; it is even questionable whether he ever fully understands what has happened to him as an individual.

This limitation of the play cannot successfully be disputed; and perhaps for this reason *Othello* is commonly regarded as the slightest of Shakespeare's four great tragedies. I would, however, call attention in this essay to the overlooked fact that Shakespeare does not suddenly in *Othello* abandon his newly found interest in the role of thought in great tragedy. He merely alters the quality and function of thought in the play. I am led to this view by my interest in Shakespeare's use of key words as leitmotifs. My previous experience has been that Shakespeare conceives of the meaning of his play not by leading images only but also by one or two words repeated and played upon significantly.[2]

What impresses me about *Othello* is that in a supposedly unintellectual play the significant word that is most frequently used (even more frequently than *honest*) is *think* or *thought*. In one form or another *think* occurs eighty-four times in the play. Furthermore, it is heavily emphasized in the temptation scene. A similar, but contrasting word, *know,* is used twenty-five times through the first scene of the third act, mainly by Othello. Thereafter, it is used hardly at all, being supplanted in the mouths of both Othello and Iago by the word *think*. In fact, the intellectual progress of Othello in the play may be seen as a painful advance from knowing to a distorted form of thinking, then back again to a hardened kind of knowing. And we shall further see that the kind

---

[1] The intellectual content of these plays is best discussed by Virgil K. Whitaker in *Shakespeare's Use of Learning* (San Marino, California, 1953), Chapters X and XI.

[2] My conclusions are given in *Redeeming Shakespeare's Words* (Berkeley and Los Angeles, 1962).

of thought occurring in the play is painful, sinister, bloody, or obscene. Typical expressions are "impatient thoughts" (I. iii. 243), "foul thoughts" (II. i. 265), "villainous thoughts" (II. i. 266), "thoughts unnatural" (III. iii. 233), "bloody thoughts" (III. iii. 457), "ill thinking" (III. iv. 29), and "leaden thoughts" (III. iv. 177).[3] Cassio's thoughts are presumably so unpleasant, even before his disgrace, that he has to drown them in drink (II. iii. 288). There is furthermore a kind of thematic symbolism in the handkerchief, which was woven by a "charmer" who "could almost read / The thoughts of people" (III. iv. 56), and who thus presumably transfers with the handkerchief the faculty which Othello so eagerly seeks in the temptation scene.

Shakespeare does not usually give thematic emphasis to a word that was not already popularly emphasized in the poetry or prose of the time. And to appreciate his dramatic exploitation of *think* in *Othello*, we need to look briefly at the vogue already established for the word before the composition of the play. Like the word *nothing,* it was a word which lent itself to manipulations so clever that they seem at times to be merely intended to delight by puzzling. Much of the repetition of the word in verse is mere verbal cleverness. Nevertheless, the formula generally is that it is painful to think about thinking. In *The Arbor of Amorous Devices* (1597), under the title "A Poeme", occurs a good example of both the repetition and the usual formula:

> . . . I got me to my bed,
> Thinking to rest my heavie heart: but then
> There came strange thoughts into my troubled hed,
> Which made me thinke upon my thoughts agen:
>   And thus in thinking on my thoughts did sleep.
>   And dreamed that another did her keepe.[4]

There is a further possible significance in the poem in that the "strange thoughts" seem to be jealous ones. More like a mere jingle is a stanza from Breton's "Say That I Should Say I Love Ye", in *England's Helicon*:

> Think I think that Love should know ye,
>   will you thinke, 'tis but a thinking?
> But if Love the thought do show ye,
>   will ye lose your eyes with winking?[5]

Though pointless, however, it reflects cerebration of the kind which we shall see is credited to Iago, and which is stressed in the Ancient's line: "I think you think I love you" (II. iii. 315).

Prose likewise, though not so frequently, exploits artfully the intricate semantics of *think,* but it is usually done with a serious purpose. The following passage from William Perkins' *A Discourse of Conscience* (Cambridge, 1596) solemnly explains two "actions of the understanding", the second of which makes thinking a compound process (pp. 6-7):

---

[3] Shakespeare citations throughout are to *The Complete Plays and Poems of William Shakespeare,* ed. William Allan Neilson and Charles Jarvis Hill (Boston, 1942).

[4] Stanza 2. Ed. Hyder Edward Rollins (Cambridge, Massachusetts, 1936), p. 12.

[5] Reprinted from the edition of 1600 (London, 1925), p. 194. See also Sidney's Sidera, no. VIII ("Rebell Sence"), in *The Complete Poems of Sir Philip Sidney,* ed. A. B. Grosart (Fuller Worthies Library, London, 1873), I, 177; also *The Phoenix Nest,* ed. Hyder Edward Rollins (Cambridge, Massachusetts, 1931), p. 58.

For there must be two actions of the understanding, the one is simple, which barely conceiveth or thinketh this or that: the other is a reflecting or doubling of the former, whereby a man conceives and thinkes with himselfe what he thinks. . . . The minde thinks a thought, now conscience goes beyond the minde, and knowes what the minde thinks

Indeed, most of the verse and prose exploiting *think* prior to *Othello* will be found to serve the purpose of "reflecting or doubling of the former". But before turning to Shakespeare's early use of *think*, we should look at an apparently unique kind of early usage. This is to be found in a four-stanza poem by Sir Thomas Wyatt. All four stanzas develop the central idea; but the nature of this idea, and the repetition which cleverly secures it, may be seen in the following excerpt:

> Deme as ye list uppon goode cause
>   I maye and thinke of this or that,
> But what or whye my self best knowes,
>   Wherebye I thinck and fere not;
> But thereunto I maye well think
>   The doubtefull sentence of this clause:
> I wolde yt ware not as I think,
>   I wolde I thought yt ware not.
> Ffor if I thought yt ware not soo,
>   Though yt ware so yt greved me not;
> Unto my thought yt ware as tho
>   I harkened tho I here not.
> At that I see I cannot wynk,
>   Nor from mye thought soo let it goo:
> I wolde yt ware not as I think,
>   I wolde I thought yt ware not.
> Lo how my thought might make me free
>   Of that perchance yt nedeth nott.[6]

Herein, as indicated principally by the refrain, the point is that it would be better if the cause for suspicion (or jealousy) did not exist, but that it would still be an improvement if the poet did not think it. By controlling his thought, the poet might make himself free. This happens to be—and I can find it no place else, not even in the early Shakespeare—the basis for much of the "psychology" of the temptation scene.

Shakespeare's iterative use of the word *think* before *Othello* is mainly a clever one, without much point except that of tantalizing the mind "past thought". The sonnets exemplify the mindless animation with which *thought* is used:

> If the dull substance of my flesh were thought,
> Injurious distance should not stop my way;
>   . . . .
> For nimble thought can jump both sea and land
> As soon as think the place where he would be.

[6] Poem 166, in *Collected Poems of Sir Thomas Wyatt*, ed. Kenneth Muir (London, 1949), pp. 153-154.

> But, ah! thought kills me that I am not thought,
> To leap large lengths of miles when thou art gone. . . .
>   (Sonnet 44)

Similarly in *Much Ado about Nothing*, Margaret (with no dramatic or intellectual purpose) gives a vapidly bright commentary on thought:

> I am not such a fool to think what I list, nor I list not to think what I can,
> nor indeed I cannot think, if I would think my heart out of thinking.[7]
>   (III. iv. 82)

Almost all of Shakespeare's iterative uses of *think* occur before *Othello*. With *Othello,* he continues to use the word iteratively, but also makes the idea of the word central to the play.

With the related word *know,* which is prominent in the first half of *Othello,* there is less of a tradition which would alert audiences to a rhetorical exploitation, and there was no strong semantic convention. Shakespeare does not play upon the word at all. But that it was a lively and tricky word may be seen from the following poem from *The Phoenix Nest* (ed. cit., p. 92):

> I know it not, I knew it not,
>   But all too late I rew it,
> I rew not that I knew it not,
>   But that I ever knew it.

These lines are not unlike the idea that is ultimately forced upon Othello.

It is, at any rate, with the word *know* that we must begin our examination of thought in *Othello,* for here, most effectively, knowing precedes thinking. In an article which uses entirely different data and methods from the present one, Terence Hawkes has usefully pointed out that Othello is torn between two kinds of reason, demarcated by Aquinas, the lower and the higher. The lower is a "ratiocinative" kind, exemplified by Iago, and the higher is the sort exemplified (rather strangely, it seems to me) by Desdemona. What concerns us here is the higher type of reason. According to Hawkes, "no ratiocination is involved in it, and no discursive thought-process is required; all knowledge is infused in a moment, in an intuitive flash, and as a result a literally inspired vision of the Godhead and the life of the spirit is achieved".[8] Without fully subscribing to a theological interpretation of the play—an area which has recently been profitably mined—we can still recognize, from vocabulary if from no other source, that Othello's native state of thought, that which has secured for him "the tranquil mind", is that of intuitive knowing rather than thinking. On the other hand, it does not seem to be—nor does Desdemona's seem to be—a kind of knowing that can withstand for too long the agile antics of a "thinking" Iago; nor, more important, is it the kind of trustworty knowledge that can avert mental chaos when one is exposed to new evidence about self and others.

Whatever degree of perception is implied in the word, *know* is used by Othello repeatedly before the temptation scene, and almost entirely to the ex-

---

[7] See also *The Merchant of Venice* I. i. 36; *Richard II*, II. ii. 29.

[8] "Iago's Use of Reason", *Studies in Philology*, LVIII (1961), 162. A similar dichotomy had been earlier pointed out by Robert Heilman in distinguishing between "wit" and "witchcraft". See his *Magic in the Web* (Lexington, Kentucky, 1956), particularly Chapter VII.

clusion of *think*. A typical speech is the following, significantly one in which he confidently affirms his role in life:

> 'Tis yet to *know*,—
> Which when I *know* that boasting is an honor,
> I shall promulgate—I fetch my life and being
> From men of royal siege, and my demerits
> May speak unbonneted to as proud a fortune
> As this that I have reach'd; for *know*, Iago. . . .
> (I. ii. 19)

Similarly, when he is first provoked in the play, he declares:

> Were it my cue to fight, I should have *known* it
> Without a prompter.[9]
> (I. ii. 83)

There is irony in the utterance, for Othello *will* need a prompter to achieve, by thinking, a new kind of knowing. There is further irony, in a richly ironic play, in the fact that Othello—though seldom using the word *think* before it is forced on him by Iago—regards himself as highly competent in mind. In expressing his scornful rejection of the idea that love may make him dote, he affirms the belief in the value of his intellect:

> No, when light-wing'd toys
> Of feather'd Cupid seel with wanton dullness
> My speculative and offic'd instruments
> That my disports corrupt and taint my business,
> Let housewives make a skillet of my helm. . . .
> (I. iii. 269)

This is, as has often been noted, the utterance befitting a man "not easily jealous". On the other hand, it is not the utterance of an agile, or even flexible, thinker. It is that of a mind that is adequate so long as it does not have to shift from its orientation, from what it "knows". It is also significant that besides his addiction to *know*, Othello's vocabulary for his own mental activity suggests emotional rather than intellectual apprehension. One short speech in the first scene of Act II contains the following expressions: "fear" and "wonder" (185), "soul's joy" (186), "this content" (198), and "too much of joy" (199).

In contrast, Iago is from the first depicted—or rather self-depicted—as the thinking man. "By Janus, I think so" (I. ii. 33)—his first use of the word should indicate his cerebration and should be spoken by the actor in a connotative way; for a modern audience will not otherwise be aware until the temptation scene of the fact that here is a man who thinks rather than accepts. And even after the temptation scene the modern audience may not be aware that Iago is playing a favorite Elizabethan sport in dallying with the word. There are clues all along to suggest to the modern actor that he is to represent a man who lives by thought. "Probal to thinking" (II. iii. 343) is Iago's touchstone. And there are

---

[9] Also on the second occasion when he is seriously provoked, his reaction is one of knowing about it:

> Give me to *know*
> How this foul rout began. . . .
> (II. iii. 209)

lines almost as clear as stage directions. Thus, when he is speaking cleverly in
dispraise of women, he describes the intense concentration he undergoes:

> I am about it; but indeed my invention
> Comes from my pate as birdlime does from frieze;
> It plucks out brains and all.
>
>   (II. i. 126)

And during the temptation scene Othello provides a graphic clue for the actor
playing Iago:

> And when I told thee he was of my counsel
> In my whole course of wooing, thou criedst, "Indeed!"
> And didst contract and purse thy brow together,
> As if thou then hadst shut up in thy brain
> Some horrible conceit. If thou dost love me,
> Show me thy thought.
>
>   (III. iii. 111)

Though Iago is the "thinking man" to everyone else in the play, and especially so to Othello ("O, thou art wise; 'tis certain". "This honest creature
doubtless / Sees and knows more, much more, than he unfolds".), the audience
is permitted to see the incredible muddle of his thought. In his soliloquies, Iago
indicates that he does indeed set much store by thought, for the word *think*
dominates them. But *think* (or a similar word like "apprehend") is usually employed not in the sense of logical cerebration, but in the sense of imperfect
knowledge, suspicion. In his first soliloquy this is particularly apparent:

> I hate the Moor;
> And it is *thought* abroad that 'twixt my sheets
> He has done my office. I know not if 't be true;
> But I, for mere suspicion in that kind,
> Will do as if for surety.
>
>   (I. iii. 392)

The same kind of irresponsible thinking, with emphasis upon suspicion rather
than logical thought, is visible in his second soliloquy. Note that even *believe*
is used (quite differently from the way Othello would use it or the similar word
know) in a putative sense. *Believe, apt and of great credit, think,* and *suspect*
are of one piece in Iago's mind:

> That Cassio loves her, I do well *believe* 't;
> That she loves him, 'tis *apt and of great credit;*
> The Moor, howbeit that I endure him not,
> Is of a constant, loving, noble nature,
> And I dare *think* he'll prove to Desdemona
> A most dear husband. . . .
>   I do *suspect* the lusty Moor
> Hath leap'd into my seat, the thought whereof
> Doth, like a poisonous mineral, gnaw my inwards. . . .
>
>   (II. i. 295)

He ends the soliloquy with a sentence that betrays the puzzled, almost insanely vague quality of his vicious thoughts:

> 'Tis here, but yet confus'd;
> Knavery's plain face is never seen till us'd.

This sudden illumination of the psychopathically incoherent and unreasonable that is Iago's real mentality is in shockingly dramatic contrast with the smooth discourses that his friends have to judge him by. These seemingly deliberate discussions on subjects like reason, good name, patience, and love are so patently Renaissance textbook material that it is a wonder that critics have not treated his mentality as contemptuously as they have that of Polonius. Yet Bradley, Kittredge, and many others consider him to be a man of great, but misplaced, ability.[10] However, we must also remember that his friends consider him wise, and that they do not have—as do we—access to his soliloquies.

They do have, however, access to one quality that is psychopathic in the second soliloquy: his appalling prurience. The mere "thought" that the Moor has leaped into his seat is enough to gnaw his inwards like a poisonous mineral. And his thoughts seem to turn constantly towards the more voyeuristic aspects of sex. It should be noticed that his prurience gives to his language and his thought the one quality linking him with Macbeth: he pictures sex as vividly and as painfully as Macbeth pictures the bloodiness of murder or the innocence of Duncan. Elsewhere, Iago's imagery is relatively plain. But he *sees* sex— sees the sheets, the lipping, the "topping". And he tells his friends his psychopathically obscene thoughts:

> Didst thou not see her paddle with the palm of his hand? Didst not mark that? . . . Lechery, by this hand; an index and obscure prologue to the history of lust and foul thoughts. They met so near with their lips that their breaths embrac'd together. Villainous thoughts, Roderigo! When these mutualities so marshal the way, hard at hand comes the master and main exercise, th' incorporate conclusion.
>
> (II. i. 259)

The incredible conclusion seems possible: that Iago is speaking truth in one of his last (and most generally overlooked) utterances:

> I told him what I *thought,* and told no more
> Than what he found himself was apt and true.
>
> (V. ii. 176)

His thought is truly diseased. He comes close in this respect to being, as Marvin Rosenberg has recently contended, a real person, a proud man suffering from ulcers because he must be respectful to his betters. The result, according to Rosenberg, is a violent neurosis.[11]

---

[10] G. L. Kittredge is impressed by his "utterance of great truths". See his *Shakespeare* (Cambridge, Massachusetts, 1930), pp. 45-46. But cf. Leo Kirschbaum, "The Modern Othello", *ELH,* II (1944), 284. Bradley is particularly troublesome in his description of Iago's mind, because along with his tribute to the villain's intellect is to be found, in another section of the book, his statement that Iago's mind is circumscribed because it is incapable of seeing love. See his *Shakespearean Tragedy* (New York, 1949), p. 36.

[11] Rosenberg's theatrical diagnosis of Iago is impressively better than his medical, though both are stimulating. See his *The Masks of Othello* (Berkeley and Los Angeles, 1961), p. 177.

We can grant that he is mentally aberrant and therefore as "honest" as a neurotic can be. But perhaps a Renaissance rather than a psychoanalytic view of Iago's "foul thoughts" is in order. His mind, in its native vileness, would I think have been understood in the Renaissance as a particularly ugly and transparent example of man's depravity since the Fall. In a sermon preached in 1606, under the caption "The illnesse of mans naturall cogitations", William Perkins elaborates upon the Biblical statement, "for the frame and thoughts of mans heart is evill continually". Perkins comments:

> Where by *thoughtes* or *Imaginations* can nothing else bee meant, but that which is devised and plotted in the thoughtes of mans heart: as Salomon speaking of an *heart which God hateth,* saith *it is framing or thinking thoughtes of wickednes.* Prov. 6.8. . . . *Is evill,* that is, it imagineth, and thinketh that which is against the lawe of God: *From his childhood;* that is, so soone as he beginneth to thinke, to reason or conceive of any thing, so soone doth hee imagine & conceive that which is evill.[12]

Iago, as well as the part of Othello that responds to Iagoism, would have been more credible to the Renaissance than he is to us. Theology was less an intellectual curiosity than psychoanalysis is today.

We come now to the temptation scene, where we see brilliantly but confusedly exploited Iago's reputation as a painful and "realistic" thinker. The word *think* is used thirty-one times in this scene, accounting for more than a third of its appearances in the play. It is in this scene also that Othello begins for the first time to become aware of the word. No reader—certainly no actor—can be unaware of the importance of the word in this scene. John Lawlor, however, would seemingly close the subject by his recent statement that the iteration of the word "has been commented on often enough".[13] Irritatingly, he cites not a single example of this superfluous commentary. I have been reading on this subject for years, and have gone through all major editions and critics, and yet I find no evidence that it is ever given more than casual mention; usually it is not referred to at all. The only fairly extended reference (an interrupted one) is by Harley Granville-Barker, who as a man of the theater is brilliantly alert to the word.[14] He does not, however, consider the role of thought in the play as a whole, nor is he aware that *think* had a Renaissance literary and theological tradition. What he does is direct the modern actor to a few of the intonations needed. He would accept, I hope, my proposal that Iago prospers in this scene because he is the "thinking man". But one good example does not prove that the high incidence of the word *think* "has been commented upon often enough". Certainly some mention of it should get into editions of the play.[15]

Besides the background that I have so far supplied, I should like to suggest another work, perhaps even a source, that may have prompted Shakespeare to use the word so richly in the temptation scene and elsewhere. This is Thomas Preston's *Cambises,* a play which Shakespeare obviously knew quite well.

---

[12] *A Treatise of Mans Imaginations. Shewing His naturall evill thoughts: His want of good thoughts: The way to reform them* (Cambridge, 1607), pp. 18-21.

[13] *The Tragic Sense in Shakespeare* (London, 1960), p. 93.

[14] *Prefaces to Shakespeare, Fourth Series* (London, 1945), pp. 41-44.

[15] It is not even mentioned in the two latest major editions: the Arden and the Cambridge.

There is a "temptation scene" in this play, staged as in *Othello* by the Vice of the piece, Ambidexter. He informs King Cambises, with a technique that would seem subtle if we were not acquainted with *Othello,* that the King's brother Smirdis has ambitious designs on his life and crown. A lord comments upon the accusation: "I cannot think it in my hart that he would report so." The King demands the unequivocal truth from Ambidexter: "How saist thou? speake the truth: was it so or no?" Ambidexter replies: "I think so, if it please your Grace, but I cannot tell", to which the King answers, "Thou plaist with both hands, now I perceive well!" but he does take measures for his brother's murder.[16] "I think so . . . , but I cannot tell" may well be the immediate suggestion for Shakespeare's temptation scene; certainly it is the shortest formula for what occurs in the scene, if for *tell* we read *know*.

To discuss every use of *think* and *know* in this very large scene would be a tedious difficulty. Let us therefore look only at some of the more crucial instances. At the very beginning Iago establishes the prevailing contrast between *know* and *think*. In reply to Othello's "What dost thou say?" he furtively retreats behind Othello's favorite verb—here disturbingly inadequate:

> Nothing, my lord: or if—I *know* not what.
> *Oth.* Was not that Cassio parted from my wife?
> *Iago.* Cassio, my lord! No, sure, I cannot *think* it.

Thereby he swings the discourse from knowing to thinking. A few lines further on Iago answers another demand for information by the unsatisfying "My lord, for aught I *know*", and Othello is easily prompted to play into his hands with "What dost thou *think*?" Iago is able to act with some conviction and some sincerity in his role. *Think* is for him, if my earlier remarks are just, both a complex and an obscene word. He recoils with proper horror: "*Think,* my lord!" and in his reply behaves as though "there were some monster in his thought / Too hideous to be seen". Actually, of course, there well may be, though I do not rule out the likelihood that he is improvising as well as reacting, particularly in his repeated refusal to show Othello his thought.

There is, interestingly, a skilful progression, or rather a slowly developed reversal, in Iago's professed attitude toward whether Othello should be allowed to discover his thought. His earliest attitude is (besides his horror at revealing an obscenity) that

> It were not for your quiet nor your good,
> Nor for my manhood, honesty, and wisdom,
> To let you know my thoughts.

The attitude here is akin to that of Wyatt's poem: it is best not to think it. But in the next act, once Othello is set on bloody thoughts, he has shifted his ground and assures Othello that it is best to know (really to think) the worst. He instructs the Moor in what seems to be a creed of realistic thinking:

> Think every bearded fellow that's but yok'd
> May draw with you. There's millions now alive
> That nightly lie in those improper beds
> Which they dare swear peculiar; your case is better.

16 *Cambises,* in *Specimens of the Pre-Shakespearean Drama,* ed. John Matthews Manly (Boston, 1897), II, 189.

> O, 'tis the spite of hell, the fiend's arch-mock,
> To lip a wanton in a secure couch,
> And to suppose her chaste! No, let me know;
> And knowing what I am, I know what she shall be.
>   (IV. i. 67)

Partly the reversal in attitude is unintentional. From his soliloquies we can observe the same erratic thinking. Iago, himself excruciatingly afflicted with jealousy, may very well have come naturally around to this attitude as he almost lives Othello's experience. A total skepticism may have given him what little peace of mind he enjoys. He personally has found that it is better to think the worst.

But he may have come around to his new point of view partly by trying to follow what is happening within Othello, with whom he is now closely engaged in thought. Othello during this scene has been launched on an agonizing, though brief, career of thinking. Watching the eager, helpful, thought-racked face of his most intimate friend, he tries to reckon with a world in which all is doubtful rather than known. This conflict between what he now thinks and what he has hitherto known provides much of the tension and poetry of this great scene. He cannot sustain indecision, or thought, for long.

> By the world,
> I *think* my wife be honest and *think* she is not.
> I *think* that thou art honest and *think* thou art not.

He demands proof, or a return to his habit of knowing. As a result he leaps at the flimsiest evidence that Iago offers him (the dream) and resolves: "I'll tear her to pieces." He cries out for "blood, blood, blood". Iago warns him, "your mind perhaps may change". But Othello, who is by now through with thinking, pronounces the great Pontic Sea speech, in which he declares that his

> bloody thoughts, with violent pace,
> Shall ne'er look back, ne'er ebb to humble love,
> Till that a capable and wide revenge
> Swallow them up.

Iago, himself almost a participant in what is happening within Othello, kneels with him and swears not only vengeance but in effect an end to indecision, to thought. It is partially because the rack of thinking has so emotionally broken Othello during this scene that he cannot later on listen to Emilia or Desdemona with any thoughtful attention.

The foregoing is of course simply an indication of the range and, above all, the meaningfulness of Shakespeare's use of a complex word in a play whose thought is far more complex than is usually acknowledged. We have necessarily left many details untouched. How, for example, is Othello's use of *think* to be taken in the following exchange:

> *Iago.*   For Michael Cassio,
> I dare be sworn I *think* that he is honest.
> *Oth.* I *think* so too.

According to my theory, Iago's use of the word is heavily, reluctantly stressed. But does Othello simply pronounce the word with the assurance of *know*?

Or has he by this point come to reflect Iago's mentality when he "thinks"? I am inclined to feel that Othello, too, stresses the word, implying that he only thinks so, but does not know. Thus it is an invitation to Iago to clarify his "thinkings". Certainly there must be great hesitation in Othello's use of the word in the following passage:

> No, not much mov'd.
> I do not *think* but Desdemona's honest.
> *Iago*. Long live she so! and long live you to *think* so!

In both instances, I assume that Othello has become sufficiently aware of thinking to permit him the attitude of thought, though not much of the actual process.

Incomplete as this survey necessarily is, we have at least enough evidence to appreciate the remarkable advance which Shakespeare made upon earlier Renaissance poetry dealing with *think*. His achievement here is similar to that in *Much Ado About Nothing*. In the earlier play Shakespeare capitalized upon the many merely verbal elaborations of the word *nothing,* but he also went beyond the verbal to a full dramatic orchestration of the theme of nothing. In *Othello,* I am likewise convinced, he shows that he knew the poetic tradition which made much ado about *think;* otherwise he would not have used the word so often and with such cunning ambiguities. But beyond this, he takes the idea as well as the word and makes of thinking a central preoccupation in the play, just as to a more limited extent he does with knowing.

To return to our original idea, however, it is obvious that the quality of thought in the play is either grossly distorted or superficial. For his thinking man, Shakespeare chose a character who has a reputation for thought, but this is as ill founded as is his reputation for honesty. And the burden of real thought is put upon a man who is unaccustomed to it and cannot long endure the ordeal. As a tragedy, *Othello* must like other great tragedies be judged partially by the intellectual character of the hero. If he cannot benefit by thought, he is likely to be no wiser at the end than at the beginning. And I am inclined to agree with T. S. Eliot that Othello's great speech at the end is not a new wisdom, but a "cheering up" of himself—really a regression to the imperfect "knowing" that marked his speeches early in the play.

It is interesting to note that for his next tragedy, *King Lear,* Shakespeare chose another hero for whom thought is not congenial (his first emphatic word is "Know") and who is at an age when recognition is almost impossible. Lear resists thinking with all the obduracy of Othello. But the amazing thing is that he does learn to think, and perhaps in his thinking expresses more profound truths than even Hamlet. Shakespeare did not, after *Hamlet,* tire of the role of thought in his tragedies. He merely tired of the intellectual hero for whom thought came too easily to be greatly dramatic.

University of California (Los Angeles)

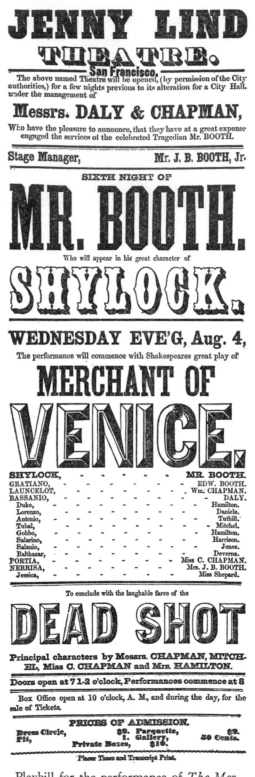

JENNY LIND
THEATRE.
San Francisco,

The above named Theatre will be opened, (by permission of the City authorities,) for a few nights previous to its alteration for a City Hall. under the management of

Messrs. DALY & CHAPMAN,

Who have the pleasure to announce, that they have at a great expense engaged the services of the celebrated Tragedian Mr. BOOTH.

Stage Manager,   Mr. J. B. BOOTH, Jr.

SIXTH NIGHT OF

MR. BOOTH.

Who will appear in his great character of

SHYLOCK,

WEDNESDAY EVE'G, Aug. 4,

The performance will commence with Shakespeares great play of

MERCHANT OF
VENICE.

SHYLOCK,	- - - - -	MR. BOOTH.
GRATIANO,	- - - - - - - -	EDW. BOOTH.
LAUNCELOT,	- - - - - - - -	Wm. CHAPMAN.
BASSANIO,	- - - - - - -	DALY.
Duke,	- - - - - - -	Hamilton.
Lorenzo,	- - - - - - -	Daniels.
Antonio,	- - - - - - -	Tuthill.
Tubal,	- - - - - - -	Mitchel.
Gobbo,	- - - - - - -	Hamilton.
Salarino,	- - - - - - -	Harrison.
Salanio,	- - - - - - -	Jones.
Balthazar,	- - - - - - -	Deverna.
PORTIA,	- - - - - - -	Miss C. CHAPMAN.
NERRISA,	- - - - - - -	Mrs. J. B. BOOTH.
Jessica,	- - - - - - -	Miss Shepard.

To conclude with the laughable farce of the

DEAD SHOT

Principal characters by Messrs. CHAPMAN, MITCH-ELL, Miss C. CHAPMAN and Mrs. HAMILTON.

Doors open at 7 1-2 o'clock, Performances commence at 8

Box Office open at 10 o'clock, A. M., and during the day, for the sale of Tickets.

PRICES OF ADMISSION.

Dress Circle,	$2.	Parquette,	$2.
Pit,	1.	Gallery,	50 Cents.
	Private Boxes,	$10.	

Placer Times and Transcript Print.

Playbill for the performance of *The Merchant of Venice* on 4 August 1852 in San Francisco. 6½″ x 16⅜″. Reproduced by permission of the Harvard Theatre Collection.

Charity in *King Lear*

SEARS JAYNE

N Christopher Morley's novel, *The Haunted Bookshop*,[1] the proprietor of the shop, confessing that he has never read *King Lear*, gives as his reason, "If I were ever very ill, I would only need to say to myself, 'You can't die yet, you haven't read *Lear*.'" The judgment implied in this remark is, of course, that of a man who *has* read the play, and is perfectly sound in its suggestion that *King Lear* belongs among the extremities of human experience. It is a play of the most shattering impact. Violent in language and even more violent in action, it staggers the sensibilities with a relentless torrent of quarrels, curses, stabbings, and a blinding. It is as though Shapespeare had herded his characters into a special corrall[2] and set out to flay them alive. Lashing and raking them, he writes with a reckless fury rarely seen in his other plays.

What is the object of Shakespeare's rage in *King Lear?* The play has several important themes, including the dangers of political disorder,[3] the infirmities of old age,[4] conflicting conceptions of nature,[5] and others.[6] But the theme with the highest emotional temperature is the theme of charity in human relations: the desperate need which human beings have for each other, and their paradoxical inability to satisfy that need. The presence of this theme in the play has often been noticed,[7] but rarely, I think, with sufficient emphasis. In this essay I should

---

[1] (New York, 1918), p. 182.

[2] Especially in Act III, where the good characters on the heath appear in scenes ii, iv, and vi, and the evil characters in the castle appear in scenes iii, v, and vii.

[3] E.g., Edwin Muir, "The Politics of *King Lear*", *Essays on Literature and Society* (London, 1949), pp. 31-48.

[4] As in Lily Bess Campbell, *Shakespeare's Tragic Heroes: Slaves of Passion* (Cambridge, 1930), pp. 175-207.

[5] See J. F. Danby, *Shakespeare's Doctrine of Nature* (London, 1949).

[6] The fullest recent bibliography of the criticism on *King Lear* is that in Helmut Bonheim, *The King Lear Perplex* (San Francisco, 1960), pp. 179-189. (A similar work, published in 1962 by G. B. Harrison and R. F. McDowell, has a skimpier bibliography.) Vol. 13 of *Shakespeare Survey*, though devoted to this play, does not include a review of *Lear* criticism, as might have been expected from the pattern of the earlier volume (7) devoted to *Hamlet*. Among the numerous articles and essays on the play which have appeared since the Bonheim bibliography, one should notice especially the series in *Critical Quarterly*, II (1960), 171-176 and 325-339, and III (1961), 67-75. Bonheim does not mention the book-length studies of the play by Salvatori Rosati, *Il Giro della Ruota* (Florence, 1958) and Russell Fraser, *Shakespeare's Poetics* (London, 1963); or the essays in the following books: Harold Wilson, *On the Design of Shakespearean Tragedy* (Toronto, 1957); L. C. Knights, *Some Shakespearean Themes* (London, 1960); John Lawlor, *The Tragic Sense in Shakespeare* (London, 1960); Olav Lokse, *Outrageous Fortune* (Oslo, 1960); Irving Ribner, *Patterns in Shakespearean Tragedy* (London, 1960); William Rosen, *Shakespeare and the Craft of Tragedy* (Cambridge, Mass., 1960); and John Holloway, *The Story of the Night* (London, 1961).

[7] A number of essays on *King Lear* have dealt with some aspect of this problem. Those most relevant are: J. Stampfer, "The Catharsis of *King Lear*", *Shakespeare Survey 13* (1960), pp. 1-10;

like to point out just three things about it: how crucial it is in the first scene of the play, how fundamental it is to the parallelism of the plots, and how powerful it is in determining the pessimistic tone of the play

I

What matters most in the first scene of the play is not the dissolution of the kingdom, but what happens to Lear himself, and this is that he is alienated from the person he most loves, and whose love he most needs, because he is unable at the critical moment himself to give the kind of love which he needs. The play begins with this alienation from Cordelia and ends with his reconciliation to her. This is the central incident, the main fable, the vehicular metaphor of the play.

The fault in the quarrel is partly Cordelia's. Had she been more mature, more experienced, she might have understood the dependence of human beings upon each other in general, and in particular the increased need for love which comes with old age. She might also have learned, incidentally, that one often has to do from motives of love things which one doesn't admire in others, and that different motives often produce the same results. Had she been older she might have understood that the situation called for a statement of love, not a statement of truth. But she is not older; truth seems more important to her than love, and she simply cannot say what she should say.

Still, the fault is mainly Lear's. He is old enough to have known better. It is usual to identify his fault with rashness. His own daughters say of him, "he hath ever but slenderly known himself" and "the best and soundest of his time hath been but rash" (I.i. 293-296). It is true that he lacks that serene wisdom and sense of control which we so much admire in some older people, but his basic fault is lack of love. If Lear had loved sufficiently, his feelings would have guided him through the crisis. He would have realized the motives behind Cordelia's awkward disruption of his ritual. He would have sympathized with them, forgiven them. But lacking love, perhaps because he is too old, he gives way to the demands of self, and with that violence which characterizes the actions of people who are stung by a consciousness of their own guilt, he disinherits Cordelia and erects a foolish and impossible arrangement in place of the reasonable one which he had previously prepared. So daughter is alienated from father, man from woman, youth from age, ruler from ruled. Needing Cordelia in a thousand ways, Lear relentlessly cuts himself off from her by an act which he could have helped, but could not help. What matters most in the incident of Lear's alienation from his favorite daughter is his ironic inability to give love, even at the moment when he most needs and seeks it.

I have suggested that Cordelia could not love properly because she was too young, and that Lear could not because he was too old. But unripeness is not the only obstacle to love. The other characters all have different excuses, but

L. C. Knights, *Some Shakespearean Themes*, pp. 84-119; G. C. Williams, "Shakespeare's Basic Plot Situation", *SQ*, II (1951), 313-317; Paul Siegel, "Adversity and the Miracle of Love in *King Lear*", *SQ*, VI (1955), 325-336; and J. A. Barish and Marshall Waingrow, "Service in *King Lear*", *SQ*, IX (1958), 347-355. The article by Terry Hawkes entitled "Love in *King Lear*", *RES*, X (1959), 178-181, is merely a linguistic note on the early meaning of the word *love* as "set a value on". E. A. Block, "*King Lear*: A Study in Balanced and Shifting Sympathies", *SQ*, X (1959), 499-512, deals mainly with Shakespeare's modification of his sources.

they, too, fail the test of love. Like Lear they are all quick to complain of the heartlessness of others, "Is there any cause in nature that makes these hard hearts?" (III. vi. 78-9); and like Lear, when the demand is put to them personally, they reply, "No, do thy worst, blind Cupid, I'll not love" (IV. vi. 139).

II

The obvious parallel to Lear, of course, is Gloucester, and I shall come to him shortly, but there is another and less obvious parallel in Kent. I should like to review his career in some detail.

In the opening scene of the play Kent finds himself in the uncomfortable position of having to choose between Love and Truth. Like most idealists, he decides that he must defend what he takes to be the truth of Cordelia's position, as opposed to the hypocrisy of that of her sisters, and so he momentarily puts aside his love for Lear and springs to the defense of Cordelia. He is promptly exiled for his pains.

After his momentary lapse, Kent realizes at once that he cannot live apart from Lear, and his devotion drives him to risk entering Lear's service in disguise. He embarks on a life of hope that some day a moment of reconciliation will take place to heal the cruel separation. But he has learned nothing from his experience of being banished. He proceeds to repeat his earlier bluntness, this time with Oswald, and this time he is put in the stocks for his pains. Lear has him released from the stocks, but has no conception of the kind of release Kent really wants, release from alienation. Lear shows more sensitivity to Kent's position as his new servant than he had shown to Kent in court, and yet this new servant *is* Kent; this ironic complex of sensitivity and insensitivity, awareness and unawareness, is more than a matter of appearance and reality; it is, as Lear himself says it is, failing to know because of failure to feel.

When finally Cordelia restores Lear to sanity, and Kent's long-hoped-for moment of reconciliation arrives, he does not achieve it after all, for *his* first opportunity turns out to be also Cordelia's first opportunity, and Kent is ironically forced by his very love for Lear to remain silent, because this moment belongs properly to Cordelia. Kent has a second opportunity a few moments later, when Lear comes in with the dead Cordelia in his arms. Lear lays her down and tries to find some spark of life in her, first by holding a mirror to her lips, and then irrationally trying a less sensitive method, a feather. As Lear mistakes his nervous shaking of the feather for the breathing of Cordelia, Kent throws himself to his master's side, and Edgar explains to Lear who Kent is. But to Lear, this interruption of his effort to revive Cordelia is like murder, and he snarls,

> A plague upon you, murderers, traitors all!
> I might have sav'd her; now she's gone forever!
> (V. iii. 269-270)

But a dislodged log of memory floats up toward the surface of Lear's mind, and he asks Kent a few lines later, "Who are you?" Then, "Are you not Kent?" Kent's life ambition seems about to be realized, but is dashed immediately when Lear's memory sinks back and he says to Kent with cruel, unknowing courtesy, "You are welcome hither" (V. iii. 289). When Lear dies, a few moments later,

Kent realizes that the whole dogged purpose of his own life, to effect a reconciliation with his master, has failed, and that he, too, has "a journey to go".

If Kent fails to solve the problem of relating himself to the rest of humanity
because of a tactless lack of charity, Gloucester fails because he is insensitive.
When Edgar, later in the play, heartlessly reminds his own brother of his
illegitimacy,

> The dark and vicious place where thee he got
> Cost him his eyes
>   (V. iii. 172-173)

we are hearing a son's echo of his father's own insensitivity:

> there was good sport at his making, . . .
>   (I. i. 23-24)

Because of Gloucester's blindness and Gloucester's own recognition of its
metaphorical significance ("I stumbled when I saw" [IV. i. 19]) it is usual to
think of Gloucester's defect as an intellectual one, a failure to understand, but
he has failed not so much intellectually as emotionally. He himself makes this
clear when he says "I see it [the world] feelingly" (IV. vi. 150) and calls down
Heaven's vengeance on all such men as himself:

> Heavens, deal so still!
> Let the superfluous and lust-dieted man,
> That slaves your ordinance, that *will not see*
> Because he does not feel, feel your power quickly; . . .
>   (IV. i. 66-69; italics mine)

Because of his early insensitivity, Gloucester is totally unaware of the starvation
for love which gnaws at Edmund, and so is unaware of Edmund's hatred of
Edgar; innumerable critics have observed that this unawareness of Gloucester's
is one of the serious improbabilities of the play, but surely one has only to look
around to see that unawareness like Gloucester's is pitifully commonplace in
human affairs.

The whole of Gloucester's career may be seen as a gradual and painful in-
doctrination in sensitivity and charity, partly under the loving tutelage of
Edgar, partly under the brutal tutelage of experience. Gloucester's final joy
when he learns Edgar's identity stems not so much from realizing that he is
loved, as from feeling that he can now exhibit his own love for Edgar and so
genuinely atone for his earlier non-love. But he is cut off by death from doing
this; he has no opportunity to demonstrate such a love for Edgar. Gloucester
learns that he is loved, but only when it is too late. Gloucester's career, like
Kent's, is not so much the story of a redemption or of learning a lesson as it
is the story of a man's hopeless effort to maintain an attitude of charity toward
the rest of mankind. I shall not go through Gloucester's career in detail, but
shall instead turn directly to the parallel and more important example of Lear
himself.

After his division of the kingdom Lear goes first to live with Goneril, but
his sense of guilt in having mistreated his youngest daughter makes him
waspish and hateful to his eldest. He strikes one of Goneril's servants for "chid-
ing of" the fool, and soon Goneril complains:

> himself upbraids us
>
> On every trifle.
> I will not speak with him; ... say I am sick; ...
>> (I. iii. 7-9)

When he returns from hunting, Lear peremptorily orders his meal: "Dinner, ho! dinner" (I. iv. 45), curses Oswald: "you whoreson dog! you slave! you cur!" (I. iv. 85-86), and calls Goneril "Degenerate bastard" (I. iv. 262). Within a few lines Lear is pronouncing a terrible curse on his own daughter:

> Hear, Nature, hear! dear Goddess, hear!
> Suspend thy purpose, if thou didst intend
> To make this creature fruitful! ...
> Turn all her mother's pains and benefits
> To laughter and contempt, that she may feel
> How sharper than a serpent's tooth it is
> To have a thankless child!
>> (I. iv. 284-298)

The new shame of having hurt Goneril as well as Cordelia makes it even more difficult for him to be agreeable when he goes to live with Regan. He makes an effort at first:

> *Lear:* No, Regan, thou shalt never have my curse:
> Thy tender-hefted nature shall not give
> Thee o'er to harshness: her eyes are fierce, thine
> Do comfort and not burn. ...
>> thou better know'st
> The offices of nature, bond of childhood,
> Effects of courtesy, dues of gratitude; ...
>> (II. iv. 172-181)

But within a few lines he is again raging:

> Who put my man i' th' stocks?
>> (II. iv. 184)

Regan, on her part, is totally unable to "reason" the need for love which lies behind her father's desire to keep a retinue of one hundred knights, and this issue soon explodes.

Ultimately Lear has to give up his retinue as well as his family, and become an unaccommodated man, a man whose desires and needs are no longer supplied by other people. In the storm on the heath, which externalizes Lear's feeling of having the entire universe against him, Lear finally sees the depth of cleavage between the individual self and the rest of humanity. During the early stages of the whirlwind of self-revelation, he tries to ride the blast, using the normal human device of blaming humanity:

> Blow, winds, and crack your cheeks! rage! blow! ...
> Crack Nature's moulds, all germens spill at once
> That makes ingrateful man!
>> (III. ii. 1-9)

He also tries the expedient of self-pity, but he sees that that will not do, and he makes a visible turn from concern for self to concern for others:

> *Lear:*   O Regan, Goneril!
> Your old kind father, whose frank heart gave all,—
> O! that way madness lies; let me shun that;
> No more of that.
> *Kent:*   Good my lord, enter here.
> *Lear:*   Prithee, go in thyself; seek thine own ease:
> This tempest will not give me leave to ponder
> On things would hurt me more. But I'll go in.
> In, boy; go first. You houseless poverty,
> Nay, get thee in. I'll pray, and then I'll sleep.
> Poor naked wretches, whereso'er you are
> That bide the pelting of this pitiless storm
> How shall your houseless heads and unfed sides
> Your loop'd and window'd raggedness, defend you
> From seasons such as these? O I have ta'en
> Too little care of this. Take physic, Pomp;
> Expose thyself to feel what wretches feel,
> That thou mayst shake the superflux to them,
> And show the Heavens more just. (III. iv. 19-36)

For the first time Lear feels physical need and so becomes sensitive to the same needs in others. Lear's discovery of concern for "poor naked wretches" brings him to the brink of madness. The sudden appearance of Tom o' Bedlam pushes him over the brink by violently particularizing and emotionalizing his concern. From this point to the end of the play Lear's mind flaps wildly back and forth between his old concern for himself and his new concern for others. This alternation is in fact the principle behind Lear's "mad speeches".

When Lear sees Gloucester's sunken and bloody eye-sockets, his self-motive speaks, first:

> I remember thine eyes well enough. Dost thou squiny at me?
> No, do thy worst, blind Cupid; I'll not love.
>   (IV. vi. 138-139)

A few lines later Lear's love-motive returns:

> Thou rascal beadle, hold thy bloody hand!
> Why dost thou lash that whore? Strip thine own back; ...
>   (IV. vi. 162-163)

A few lines more, and the self-motive is reasserting itself:

> It were a delicate stratagem to shoe
> A troop of horse with felt; I'll put 't in proof,
> And when I have stol'n upon these son-in-laws,
> Then kill, kill, kill, kill, kill, kill.
>   (IV. vi. 186-189)

From his distracted alternation between compassion and hatred Lear's wracked mind is temporarily rescued by the combined ministrations of Cordelia and the doctor, who between them bring accommodation for both soul and body. Under their care his tortured mind is restored to a few moments of sanity; in sanity the tired Lear is nothing but an old man; all the old pride is gone, only the need for love remains, and it is a humble need. Here is the sane Lear as he awakes from his madness and kneels before Cordelia:

> *Lear:*   Pray do not mock me:
> I am a very foolish fond old man,
> Fourscore and upward, not an hour more nor less;
> And, to deal plainly,
> I fear I am not in my perfect mind.
> Methinks I should know you and know this man;
> Yet I am doubtful: for I am mainly ignorant
> What place this is, and all the skill I have
> Remembers not these garments; nor I know not
> Where I did lodge last night. Do not laugh at me;
> For, as I am a man, I think this lady
> To be my child Cordelia. . . .
>   You must bear with me.
> Pray you now, forget and forgive: I am old and foolish.
>   (IV. vii. 52-84)

A few hours later, when Edmund has captured Lear and Cordelia, and has sent them off to prison, Lear is still sane, and he welcomes the opportunity to go to a place where life can be all love and no struggle.

> *Lear:*   Come, let's away to prison;
> We two alone will sing like birds i' th' cage:
> When thou dost ask me blessing, I'll kneel down,
> And ask of thee forgiveness: so we'll live,
> And pray, and sing, and tell old tales, and laugh
> At gilded butterflies, and hear poor rogues
> Talk of court news; and we'll talk with them too,
> Who loses and who wins; who's in, who's out;
> And take upon's the mystery of things,
> As if we were God's spies: and we'll wear out,
> In a wall'd prison, packs and sects of great ones
> That ebb and flow by th' moon.
>   (V. iii. 8-19)

But a life of love, a life with all the protections and accommodations and none of the struggle, is a life away from man. The world of men is a world in which men think only of themselves, as we see moments later, when Kent comes looking for Lear, and Albany exclaims that he has forgotten all about the King, "Great thing of us forgot!" A few moment later Lear carries in the dead Cordelia. In Lear's returned madness in the final scene he resumes the old alternation between self and other; this time it takes the form of alternating between a fatherly concern for Cordelia and an old man's pride in his own prowess:

> A plague upon you, murderers, traitors all!
> I might have sav'd her; Now she's gone for ever!
> Cordelia, Cordelia! stay a little. Ha!

What is't thou say'st? Her voice was ever soft,
Gentle and low, an excellent thing in woman.
I kill'd the slave that was a-hanging thee ...
                              Did I not fellow?
I have seen the day, with my good biting falchion
I would have made them skip: I am old now,
And these same crosses spoil me.
                              (V. iii. 269-278)

Lear's mad alternation between self and other is still pulsating in his very last speech, as he pays alternate attention to (a) Cordelia's need for breath and (b) his own:

(a) Why should a dog, a horse, a rat, have life,
And thou no breath at all? Thou'll come no more,
Never, never, never, never, never!
(b) Pray you, undo this button: thank you, Sir.
(a) Do you see this? Look on her, look, her lips,
Look there, look there!
                              (V. iii. 307-311)

Like Kent, Gloucester, and Lear, Edmund, too, is stretched on the rack of charity and uncharity. In Edmund's case the excuse is not age but bastardy.[8] We need not review his case in detail to see that he, too, is best understood as a creature starved for love ("Yet Edmund was belov'd", he boasts [V. iii. 239]) but incapable of giving love. Thus we may say that the key to the parallelism of all four of the major lines of action in the play is the theme of charity.

III

The third and perhaps most important influence of the charity theme upon *King Lear* is its influence on Shakespeare's objectivity in the play. Shakespeare's normal practice, regardless of genre, is to set up two poles of a value problem and let the reader generate his own imaginative spark across the gap. In *King Lear*, however, Shakespeare's own voltage is too high, and on the theme of charity his own lightning flashes out, throwing the whole play into an essentially pessimistic light.

The question of whether *King Lear* is optimistic or pessimistic has long been a major issue among critics of the play. Most critics regard the play as optimistic, and they emphasize the fact that both Lear and Gloucester achieve something positive in the course of the play, either a moral regeneration, or an intellectual enlightenment[9] of some kind. But it does not seem to me that

---

[8] The career of Edmund rather than that of Oswald constitutes the important obverse of Kent's career. Edmund's situation is normally seen in terms of his illegitimacy. See especially Danby, *Shakespeare's Doctrine of Nature*, pp. 31-43, 57-101; Johnston Parr, "Edmund's Birth under Ursa Major" and "The 'Late Eclipses' in King Lear", in *Tamburlaine's Malady and Other Essays* (Tuscaloosa, 1953); and R. C. Bald, " 'Thou, Nature, Art my Goddess': Edmund and Renaissance Free Thought", *Joseph Quincy Adams Memorial Studies* (Washington, D. C., 1948), 337-349.

[9] See, for example, Winifred Nowottny, "Lear's Questions," *Shakespeare Survey 10* (1957), pp. 90-97. Another example of this kind of interpretation is R. B. Heilman, *This Great Stage* (Baton Rouge, 1948). By contrast, W. R. Keast, in "Imagery and Meaning in the Interpretation of *King Lear, MP,* XLVII (1950), 45-64, asserts that Lear's problem is mainly moral, not intellectual.

anyone really achieves anything very significant in the play. Every single charac-
ter fails in his effort to re-establish a bond with society. Lear dies deluded,
Cordelia dies, having failed to undo the damage which she has done. Gloucester
recovers Edgar only to die; Kent goes off to die of disappointment; Oswald,
Goneril, Regan, Cornwall, and Edmund all die unreconciled to man. Only
Albany and Edgar are left, surviving for a life without love.

It is true that both Lear and Gloucester may be said to have learned something about man's need for love and about man's inability to provide love,
but they both learn it too late. What Lear *needs* is the opportunity to love by
way of atonement for his earlier non-love. But like Gloucester, he is cruelly not
given this opportunity; Lear is cut off from it not by his own death but by
Cordelia's. We should notice that Cordelia's dying *before* Lear is Shakespeare's
own idea; in all the sources she dies *after* Lear. Like Gloucester, Lear experiences
the joy of thinking that he has the opportunity at last to love; but after a
lifetime of non-loving, that joy proves fatal to Lear, as it had to Gloucester.
The great difference between Gloucester and Lear is that Gloucester's opportunity to love Edgar is a real one, whereas Lear's opportunity to love Cordelia
is only an illusion. In Gloucester's lovelessness Shakespeare had left a spark
of hope; in Lear's the absolute bottom of the world is scraped; it is empty all
the way down. Man must have love, but is not allowed to give it.

In ordinary experience everyone can think of cases in which love does succeed in making tolerable the torture of man's inhumanity. It often happens
that parental or filial devotion, or more often, marital devotion, can reach into
the jaws of despair and pluck the lost soul out. But there is no such relief in
King Lear; there is no compensating love anywhere in the world of this play.
Shakespeare has ruthlessly suppressed it. Everyone in the play is isolated in
some special way from everyone else. Lear has no wife; not even to serve that
function which Bacon conceded to old men's wives: that of nursing; moreover
Shakespeare has deprived him of even the little sympathy which he commanded
in the source play, where his bad judgment is explained by the fact that he is
grieving over the loss of his "late deceast Queen". Gloucester has no wife. Kent
has no family. Neither Cordelia nor Edmund at the critical moment has a mate.
Behind Goneril's and Regan's hate lies the fact that Lear does not love them.
Edmund feels alien in the whole world because of his illegitimacy. Gloucester
is first isolated by his insensitivity, and then by his blindness. Cordelia is isolated
by her disinheritance, Lear by his deliberate withdrawal from the throne. Edgar
is driven into isolation by his fear of his father and brother, and assumes a
position outside society as a mad beggar. Kent is banished the realm and dares
not be himself. The Fool is isolated by his profession as well as by his natural
intellectual superiority. Goneril and Regan are isolated, even from each other,
by their rival sexual passions.

There are many instances in the play, of course, in which human beings in
need try to help each other, but these efforts characteristically fail, so that even
the most ordinary rituals of "refreshment of the bond"[10] among human beings,

---

Duthie, in his Cambridge edition of 1960 (p. xx), says that Lear undergoes a "spiritual" regeneration.

[10] This phrase is a modification of one used by Stampfer in the article cited above (note 7); it
deserves to be quoted in context:

such as dining together, talking together, holding of hands, writing letters, and sending messages all are commonly frustrated. I shall cite only a few examples. Notice how the men on the heath try vainly to comfort each other; Lear, for example, tries awkwardly to comfort the Fool:

> Come on, my boy. How dost, my boy? Art cold?
> I am cold myself. . . . I have one part in my heart
> That's sorry yet for thee.
>
> (III. ii. 68-73)

Notice that the servant who tries to save Gloucester's second eye is slain by Regan, and that the nameless Old Man, who generously promises to bring "the best 'parel that [he has]" to clothe Poor Tom, never succeeds. When Goneril and Regan meet in Act II, Regan takes her sister by the hand, but this gesture of affection ironically outrages their father, who complains, "O Regan, will you take her by the hand?" (II. iv. 196), and is ironic to us in a different way because one of the two sisters will later poison the other. Similarly, when Lear wishes to hurt Regan most, he kneels to her in mock submission, saying,

> Do you but hark how this becomes the house:
> "Dear daughter, I confess that I am old;
> Age is unnecessary. . . ."
>
> (II. iv. 154-156)

Thus the act of genuflexion itself is turned from a gesture of respect to a gesture of hate.

It is almost as if Shakespeare had drawn up a catalogue of all the forms which man's inhumanity to man can take. Fathers quarrel with children, husbands with wives, sisters with sisters and brothers with brothers, brother-in-law with brother-in-law, and nation with nation. A father disinherits one child, curses another, and swears revenge on another. Another father commits his child to illegitimacy. A man is exiled from his own country and then put in stocks before the public gaze. One brother kills another, one sister poisons another, and one man puts out the eyes of another. Rudeness, discourtesy, lying, suspicion, hypocrisy, deception, and insensitivity of all kinds are rife throughout the play.

The characters themselves comment upon it. So Gloucester says:

> Love cools, friendship falls off, brothers divide: in cities, mutinies; in countries, discord; in palaces, treason; and the bond crack'd 'twixt son and father. This villain of mine comes under the prediction; there's son against

---

All men, in all societies, make, as it were, a covenant with society in their earliest infancy. By this covenant, the dawning human consciousness accepts society's deepest ordinances, beliefs, and moral standards in exchange for a promise of whatever rewards and blessings society offers. . . . But given the contingency of human life, that covenant is constantly broken by corruption within and without. A man's life and that of his family are at all times hostages of his limited wisdom, his tainted morality, the waywardness of chance, and the decay of institutions. Indeed, social ritual, whether religious in character, like confession or periodic fasting, or secular, like the ceremonial convening of a legislature, is an attempt to strengthen the bond of a covenant inevitably weakened by the attrition of evil and the brute passage of time. These are all, in a sense, acts of penance, that is, acts whose deepest intent is to purge us of guilt and the fear of being abandoned, to refresh our bond with one another and with our private and collective destiny.

father: the King falls from bias of nature; there's father against child. We have seen the best of our time: machinations, hollowness, treachery, and all ruinous disorders follow us disquietly to our graves.

(I. ii. 110-120)

And Edmund echoes his father in these sentiments:

I promise you the effects he writes of succeed unhappily; as of unnaturalness between the child and the parent; death, dearth, dissolutions of ancient amities; divisions in state; menaces and maledictions against King and nobles; needless diffidences, banishment of friends, dissipation of cohorts, nuptial breaches, and I know not what.

(I. ii. 150-156)

Albany, too, observes that

Humanity must perforce prey on itself
Like monsters of the deep.

(IV. ii. 49-50)

Thus with a slashing knife *King Lear* exposes the human cancer in all its livid and noisome horror. Man cannot live without love but cannot himself give it.

Finally, Shakespeare makes sure that there is no one else to give it, by keeping the play harshly pagan. The jungle of *King Lear* is a purely human jungle, without benefit of clergy, or deity, or of any other religious solace. It is a world in which unaccommodated man has no one to turn to[11] but unaccommodating man, a world in which no one is any more "kind and comfortable" (I. iv. 314-315) than Lear finds Regan to be.

The ultimate measure of the horror of Lear's world is of course his own reaction to it. It is true that Lear is not an ordinary man; he is a poet, a man who (with the help of the Fool in the first part of the play) walks among men like one of God's spies, understanding and feeling too much. Still, he is not represented as a monster or freak of nature. He is a man; and the world he sees and deplores is the human world.

At first he sees his relation to Cordelia in narrow terms, blaming her "ingratitude", but he soon begins to see that his daughters' lack of love is more than merely the reflection of his own nature (which all parents see in their children); it is in fact rather a manifestation of a universal human condition of lovelessness. It is not Goneril alone (or Cordelia) "that will sliver and disbranch / From her material sap" (IV. ii. 34-35), but every human being. It is man in general who is trapped in the paradox of requiring love but being unable to give it. Nor is there anyone else to give it. As soon as Lear understands this, he goes mad, paying the penalty of understanding too much.

In stressing the importance of the paradox of charity in *King Lear,* I do not mean to oversimplify the play or to ignore the many other themes which are woven through its marvelously complex fabric. I simply want to point out how

---

[11] For Christian interpretations of the play, see especially O. J. Campbell, "The Salvation of Lear", *ELH*, XV (1948), 93-109; and Irving Ribner, "'The Gods are Just'. A Reading of *King Lear*", *Tulane Drama Review*, II (1958), 34-54. Ribner stresses the morality-play aspects of *King Lear*.

much of the deepest emotion of the play is carried by this theme, how this theme illuminates individual parts of the play, such as Lear's mad speeches, how it clarifies the parallelism of the plots, especially in the case of Kent, and finally, how it explains the central issue in that amazing first scene, showing in what special sense the play is about King Lear, as the title shows. If I am right about this subject of the play, about the violence of Shakespeare's treatment of it, and about the pessimism of the play as a whole, perhaps Morley's timid shopkeeper is right in preferring to put off *King Lear* to the end.

Queens College, Flushing

The Structure of *Antony and Cleopatra*

THOMAS B. STROUP

OR a long time it was almost a commonplace of criticism to say, as F. S. Boas said, that *Antony and Cleopatra* "has a grave share of defects to which Romantic Drama has been liable from the first". Shakespeare seems to have felt an "obligation to introduce every incident, . . . mentioned by Plutarch, and the result is a loss of dramatic unity and perspective". Furthermore, "no single event stands out boldly as the pivot on which the catastrophe turns".[1] Consciously or not, Boas is here reaching far back to Dryden's brilliant statement in his *Grounds for Criticism in Tragedy:* "Therefore, as in perspective, so in Tragedy, there must be a point of sight in which all the lines terminate; otherwise the eye wanders, and the work is false." As recently as 1939 Mark Van Doren remarked that the play had nothing Aristotle would have called a plot.[2] The substance of these remarks can be multiplied indefinitely.

But within the last two or three decades the grounds for criticism have shifted, or new grounds have been discovered, on which to base a more sympathetic, if less authoritarian, judgment of this play. Perhaps the key to this shift is to be found in Granville-Barker's perceptive statement that Shakespeare was planning "more spaciously than those that have need to plan", as he examines the play with reference to its fast-moving production on the Elizabethan stage.[3] Others (I cite here only representative examples) have more lately found evidence of this conscious and careful planning, some of it even supporting the poet's awareness of the "rules". Professor Hereward T. Price, calling for a more careful study of the relation of the scene to the entire structure of the Elizabethan play, shows how three "mirror scenes" create character and dramatic image in *Antony and Cleopatra*.[4] Professor Paul J. Aldus shows how Shakespeare by extensive use of "analogical probability" binds together and foreshadows events in the play.[5] Professor Sylvan Barnet shows that "recognition" and "reversal" take place in the characters of Enobarbus, Antony, and Cleopatra.[6] The late Harold S. Wilson briefly indicated that the construction of the play, though "expansive and comprehensive—in keeping with the theme—rather than

---

[1] See *Antony and Cleopatra*. Variorum Edition, ed. H. H. Furness (Philadelphia, 1907), p. 487. Much the same appears in all the summaries in the Variorum: Schlegel, Hartley Coleridge, and W. H. Hudson object to the number and variety of scenes and incidents.

[2] *Shakespeare* (New York, 1939), p. 273.

[3] *Prefaces to Shakespeare.* Second Series (London, 1939), p. 129.

[4] " 'Mirror-Scenes' in Shakespeare", *Joseph Quincy Adams Memorial Studies* (Washington, 1948), pp. 101-113. As Professor Price points out, W. Creizenach had suggested the importance of these scenes as far back as his *Geschichte des neuren Dramen* (Halle, 1909), IV, 303-304.

[5] "Analogical Probability in Shakespeare's Plays", *SQ*, VI (1955), 397-414.

[6] "Recognition and Reversal in *Antony and Cleopatra*", *SQ*, VIII (1957), 331-334.

economically concentrated", is nevertheless "most carefully articulated".[7] And Professor Paul N. Siegel points out some of the foreshadowings of Cleopatra's death.[8] Now all of these—and many scattered defenses elsewhere—indicate a conscious and subtle artist binding into one design a drama of grand proportions, not a hasty adapter, though brilliant, of a sketchy biography written by a moralizing Greek. The new apologists defend it as a play to be represented; they do not excuse it as a story unfortunately written in dramatic form. It is beyond my purpose here to enter a full defence, but I may be able to suggest another approach to the artist's purpose which may in turn add a little to our understanding and improve our appraisal of it as a well-planned work.

Our chief concern is with unity in its broad sense. The play's numerous and scattered scenes, its many characters, its lack of pivotal event, the so-called double catastrophe—these and other defects, though perhaps of slight consequence in a piece to be read, we are told, destroy its effectiveness *as a play* to be represented. These provide great poetry, characters whose infinite variety fascinates us, and exciting single scenes, but no well-wrought play. The audience are not brought breathless to the final tableau. But were the audience for whom this play was written, we may ask, really much concerned with the cumulation of tension, the snowball build-up? Might not they have found other forces, other unifying elements, quite as satisfying? And might not these less obvious means give a dramatic richness and variety not so frequently found in the more direct and economically concentrated sequence of events of the more "regular" plays? Likewise, may not we, laying aside our aesthetic absolutes, even in our later times find the same? Perhaps the "Gothic play", as this has so often been called, can furnish a sort of satisfaction even to us who have for so long looked through the proscenium arch to where Dryden's perspective lines converge.

Antony and Cleopatra belongs to Polonius' "tragical-historical" kind; and though this kind may employ a Senecan device, style, or character here and there, it takes its shape chiefly from the later morality play, its direct ancestor, as has been repeatedly shown.[9] And the later morality depended upon the earlier for its form, and that upon the mystery plays and the psychomachia. The stage for these earlier forms was not confined, nor was the action. There was scarcely world enough or time for them. For their action they literally required the earth and all that surrounded it. Indeed, I think it not without significance that the stage of the *Castle of Perseverance* was quite round. Though restricted perforce to the stage of this world for his deeds, just beyond and surrounding Mankind were the heavens, whence he might ultimately, if he accepted God's grace and asked his mercy, be sung to his rest. He was never allowed to forget for long this connection with the infinite. His actions were consciously related to the whole; his stage was the cosmos. Likewise, in the later and hybrid moralities the cosmic frame of reference was not ignored. Greene's *A Looking Glass for London and England* (1594), for example, shows Jonah unable to escape God's command, and, at his preaching, the people of Nineveh, even one called "Usurer", repent

---

[7] *On the Design of Shakespearean Tragedy* (University of Toronto Press, 1957), pp. 178-182.

[8] "Foreshadowings of Cleopatra's Death", *N. & Q.*, CCIII (Sept., 1958), 386-387.

[9] For the most recent examples, see David M. Bevington, *From Mankind to Marlowe: Growth and Structure in the Popular Drama of Tudor England* (Harvard University Press, 1962) and Bernard Spivack, *Shakespeare and the Allegory of Evil: The History of a Metaphor in Relation to His Major Villains* (Columbia University Press, 1958).

and are saved; and the whole action is a lesson for London. Local habitations and names may be used, but they do not lose their universal significance. These plays were given "presenters", furthermore, or later "prologues", or "Inductions", which directly related them to the universal—devices for tying up the action on the stage to the cosmic pageant. These are comparable to, if not directly descended from, the other framework devices of Medieval literature, such as the introductory first canto of the *Divine Comedy* or the plan for the *Decameron* or the Prologue to the *Canterbury Tales* or the numerous dream-visions or *speculi*. They are a means to enable the spectator to see the particular in relation to the universal. The design attempted suggests the design of Medieval and much Renaissance painting, in which the interior must not be without its surrounding earthly exterior and both must be seen together with the heavens bending over them and hell often yawning below. The world indeed was a stage and this life a play. Hence what was represented on a stage must take its proper shape from the world's vast unity. The metaphor of the Chain of Being was an effective way of expressing this unity. It is out of such background that the tragical-historical play emerges. And if one recognizes its forebears, one may find in *Antony and Cleopatra* a kind of unity within its "Gothic" diversity not noted hitherto—and a delight in its grand design.

The evidence for such design is plentiful. Shakespeare either uses outright or else refers to the commonplace that "the world is a stage" at least fourteen times in the plays and once in the sonnets.[10] In *Antony and Cleopatra* his indirect reference to the idea is notable, for it is complicated with another: "man is a little world", a microcosm. Cleopatra tells Dolabella her dream of the dead Antony:

> *Cleo.* His face was as the heavens, and therein stuck
> A sun and moon, which kept their course, and lighted
> The little O, the earth.
>
> *Dol.*   Most sovereign creature,—
>
> *Cleo.* His legs bestrid the ocean, and his rear'd arm
> Crested the world: his voice was propertied
> As all the tuned spheres, and that to friends:
> But when he meant to quail, and shake the orb,
> He was a rattling thunder. For his bounty,
> There was no winter in't: an autumn 'twas
> That grew the more by reaping: his delights
> Were dolphin-like, they show'd his back above
> The element they lived in: in his livery

[10] The best known of these are in *The Merchant of Venice* I. i. 77-79, where Antonio says, "I hold the world but as the world, Gratiano—/ A stage, where every man must play a part, / And mine a sad one": and in *As You Like It* II. vii. 137-143, where Jaques says memorably, "All the world's a stage, / And all the men and women merely players." Others are in *Henry IV*, Part II, I. i. 153-160, and IV. v. 196-199; *Winter's Tale* V. i. 55-61; *Henry VI*, Part II, I. ii. 63-67; *Macbeth* II. iv. 4-7 and V. v. 23-28; *King Lear* IV. vi. 186-187; *Henry V*, Prologue, 1-4; *Richard II*, V. v. 31-40; *Coriolanus* V. iii. 182-185; *The Tempest* IV. i. 146-156; and *Sonnet* XV, 1-4. This trope goes back as far as Democritus, was used by the Church Fathers, the neo-Platonists and Christian humanists to explain the presence of evil in the world, and became a widely used commonplace among the English poets. My study of this concept as a shaping force in English drama is well on toward completion.

Walk'd crowns and crownets: realms and islands were
As plates dropp'd from his pocket.   (V. ii. 79-92)[11]

The Antony of the Queen's dream (and we are such stuff as dreams are made
on) is the Antony of the theater, and her words suggest the quality of acting
required of him; for this Colossus, lighting up the earth and speaking the music
of the spheres as well as rattling thunder, has done so within the very hour and
within this very Globe Theatre, this "little O". The microcosm, Antony the
actor, has played out his part in the microcosm of the theater, one little world of
make-believe set within another, and that within the great macrocosm of
reality. The Elizabethan audience then saw characters and action within the
Globe in proper relation to the whole.

That this was true is emphasized by the use of the word *world* in the play
some thirty-two or -three times to indicate just this vast design and action. The
first speech of the play refers to Antony as "The triple pillar of the world", and
Antony shortly thereafter says Cleopatra must "find out new heaven, new earth"
if she would set limit to his love for her. Toward the end when Caesar is told of
Antony's death, he speaks in cosmic terms of the breaking of the order of nature;
"The round world / Should have shook lions into civil streets,/ And citizens
to their dens. The death of Antony / Is not a single doom, in the name lay / A
moiety of the world" (V. i. 15-19). He later speaks regretfully of his and
Antony's not being able to "stall together, / In the whole world". They belong to
the whole.

Likewise, the character of Cleopatra suggests the same thing, for she is
always the actress playing upon the stage of the world, self-conscious of every
deed and of how her public will react to it. Not only does she think of Antony
in theatrical terms as she speaks her apotheosizing dream of him, but Enobarbus'
famous description of her in her barge on the Cydnus is a stage set: she conquered Antony with her pageant. And if this her first meeting with Antony
was a staged affair, the preparation for her last was equally so; only in it he is
the conqueror, not she: "Give me my robe, put on my crown, I have / Immortal
longings in me . . . methinks I hear / Antony call. I see him rouse himself /
To praise my noble act" (V. ii. 279-284). And Charmian, seeing her dead mistress' crown askew: "Your crown's awry, / I'll mend it, and then play" (V. ii.
317-318). Or long before, when Antony came to tell her he must return to
Rome, she put on an act, calling upon him to "play one scene / Of excellent
dissembling, and let it look / Like perfect honour" (I. iii. 78-79). We have
known from the beginning in Antony's words that everything becomes her—
"to chide, to laugh, / To weep"—and that the two of them will wander at
night in the streets, apparently incognito, "and note / The qualities of people".
One might multiply such illustrations.

Adapted from the earlier drama, the world stage, upon which this fascinating
couple arrives, reveals the pageant of human life, the story of Humanum Genus
now individualized into many persons, each one of whom has his proper place
in the order and degrees of society. At the center of the human pageant is a
protagonist and his closest associates whose actions touch still others less near

---

[11] References are to be the New Arden Edition of *Antony and Cleopatra*, ed. by W. R. Ridley
(London, 1960).

the center; and those actions touch still others, so that the psychomachia of the central figure (or figures) ultimately reaches out to those on the periphery. And surrounding the whole are the spiritual powers, sometimes personified and instigating or watching the action, sometimes indicated only as abstract but ever-present forces. The sparrow's fall is still God's business. It is as if the action were carried out through a series of concentric circles or spheres, waves made from a pebble dropped into a pool rippling outward to the infinite. Is it not possible, as Dryden suggested in *An Essay of Dramatic Poesy,* that the Ptolemaic system furnished a pattern? However that may be, the grand pageantry of the whole play is realized by means of the individual pageantry of the single scene.

And brief examination of the scenes of *Antony and Cleopatra* should be sufficient to show forth its pageantry. For the play is rich in it. As Granville-Barker argues, if we see it as a series of fast-moving, contrasting scenes, we are better able to realize what the author was trying to do. Moreover, at least fifty-two entrances and exits of the play are formalized. That is, they are processional, with soldiers marching on and off in formation, or diplomats with attendants, or rulers with entourage, or the court with "Train", or others making ceremonious entry and exit, all observing protocol. Within the very first scene the stage direction calls for *"Flourish.* Enter ANTONY, CLEOPATRA, *her Ladies, the Train, with Eunuchs fanning her."* The court leaves the stage doubtless in the same formal fashion, Demetrius and Philo staying behind to close up the scene. And the last entrance of the play is similar in its formality and ceremonious quality: *"Enter* CAESAR *and all his Train, marching."* Thus the final exit with the bodies of Cleopatra and her ladies carried out in state requires "High order, in this great solemnity". One of the finest of these is Ventidius' entry at the opening of Act III, *"as it were in triumph . . . the dead body of* PACORUS *borne before him."* The triumphal procession is ironically combined here with the funeral procession, both types often appearing on the Elizabethan stage, and the whole scene stands in brilliant contrast to the reeling world preceding it on board Pompey's galley. More is here than meets the eye.

So with the ceremonials and rituals, closely associated with the formal entries and exits. At least ten or a dozen of these may be picked out in the play. Such is Caesar's taking leave of Antony and Octavia as they depart for Athens (III. ii); such the contrasting leave-taking of Antony and Octavia, as she returns to Caesar (III. iv); such the oath taken by the Triumvirs and Pompey to patch up the world (II. vi), in which Pompey makes a very formal oration; such the ceremonial changing of the guard before the palace (IV. iii); such the arming of Antony by Cleopatra before the battle (IV. iv); such Enobarbus' prayer before his death (IV. ix. 12-23); such Dercetas' delivery of Antony's sword to Caesar (V. i); such Cleopatra's reception of Caesar, kneeling in her false humility (V. ii. 111-116); and such the ritual of her suicide (V. ii. 279-312). Here are enough to indicate the ceremonial richness.

Such pageantry and ceremonial are not to be confused with what Aristotle calls the least important part of tragedy, spectacle; for he seems to regard spectacle as the whole public performance of the play, involving the producer and costumer, and not necessary to the securing of tragic effect. The Elizabethan processions and ceremonials, however, were, if not necessary, at least effective in

securing such effects. The audience were moved by the grandeur of the procession, by the solemnity of the oaths upon which the fate of empire turned, by the
depth of feeling of the prayer, and by the nobility of the suicide ceremony. Consciously or not, they were no less moved by the ironic and contrasting values such
devices provide. If they took thought, they realized that these formalities served
to make all the action one, since they recognized that all the action was indeed a
part of the pageant of the ages.

And this pageant involved the whole of society. The crumbling of the triple
pillar of the world affected the whole. The cast of characters must include not
only the Triumvirs and the Queen, but the counsellors of state, such as Agrippa
and Enobarbus, and the various courtiers and ladies, the military including the
common soldiers as well as the generals, the priesthood in the person of the
Soothsayer, the countrymen, merchant, and working class in the person of the
Clown with the asps, and the servants including the messengers. All of these
are affected by the character and deeds of the main figures, Antony, Cleopatra,
and Caesar: sometimes very directly, as when Cleopatra beats the messenger or
as when Antony has Caesar's envoy whipped; sometimes very indirectly, as when
the dotage of Antony restricts the conquests of his general in far-off Syria. It
is not for the pleasure of the groundlings merely that the Soothsayer or the
Clown are brought into the play (or into any other play of the period, for that
matter); they move the plot along, and they represent certain groups to fill out
the social spectrum, the manifold personifications of Mankind. For as Roger
Ascham maintains in *The Schoolmaster,* "The whole doctrine of Comedies and
Tragedies is a perfite *imitation,* or faire livelie painted picture of the life of
everie degree of man." In *Julius Caesar* and in *Coriolanus* where the Tribunes
of the people and the Citizens have designated parts perhaps the "life of everie
degree" is better represented, but enough are here to serve very well.

This concept, moreover, does not require the dramatist to account for all
characters in the end. It is with the principals he is concerned; and here as in
the life of any man, many a friend and associate is in time lost sight of, if not
forgotten entirely. What becomes of Ventidius we do not know, and we know
only vaguely what happens to Lepidus and to Pompey, to Agrippa and to
Menas, to Canidius and to Octavia. Miss Una Ellis-Fermor observes in her
posthumous essay "The Nature of Plot in Drama" that "in the plays of Shakespeare's maturity, we perceive a third dimension, akin to the depth given by
perspective to a painting; in dimensions and tone alike the characters retreat
successively from the foreground towards a background where they reach a
virtual vanishing point."[12] And she uses *Antony and Cleopatra* as a particular
example of this phenomenon, as well as another closely associated with it, the
extension of the action in space. She notes that in this play "the grandeur of the
chief characters, the multiplicity of figures and events witness to the vastness of
its design and the cosmic imagery leads the imagination on to a universe beyond,
into which the immediate world of the play seems limitlessly extended" (p. 71).
Both persons and events recede—and, I may add, time and space grow vague
in the distances.

Not only are all conditions and degrees of men represented, but their actions
range outward from their personal center to a universal circumference. To be

[12] *Essays and Studies* (1960), p. 70.

more particular, one may notice, as Victor Hugo did long ago, that at the center of the plot is basically a simple domestic tragedy: a spendthrift, infatuated by a courtesan, to mend his fortune marries a woman he does not love and with her fortune returns to the courtesan. But his wife gets help from her brother, who attacks the spendthrift and defeats him; the courtesan commits suicide.[13] But outside this personal tragedy is the tragedy of the state. The liaison between Antony and Cleopatra is broken off by the urgent call to duty: Antony is no private man; he is a pillar of the world. The personal and private affairs of public men cannot remain personal and private. The threat of Pompey and civil war pulls Antony away from Egypt. What is more, these affairs of state are embroiled abroad and become international, as in the campaign in Syria. Outside these are still others, though less well defined, the affairs of the stars. The Soothsayer, perhaps the Clown even who fetches immortality for three, represents these affairs; and though the spiritual forces are not so clearly operative as in the moralities or in Marlowe or in Shakespeare elsewhere (as in *Hamlet* or *Lear* or *Macbeth*), they are always present to the minds of the principals. The Queen answers Antony's call from beyond. Thus the actions of a man, especially a public man, affect all men; and the play is consciously designed to illustrate the point. Here is a unity based on the unity of the universe.

At the very center, of course, is the microcosm, the soul of a man. It is really out of Antony's character-struggle, his psychomachia, that the tragedy develops. Had he been like Octavius Caesar, he would have had no struggle. But the emphasis is not so much upon *hamartia* here as upon the equally divided qualities of soul: "His taints and honours / Wag'd equal with him." Certainly the soul-warfare of the morality play is indicated. The Soothsayer explains as much to Antony. When asked whose fortunes shall rise higher, he says,

> Caesar's.
> Therefore, O Antony, stay not by his side:
> Thy demon, that's thy spirit which keeps thee, is
> Noble, courageous, high, unmatchable,
> Where Caesar's is not. But near him, thy angel
> Becomes afeard; as being o'erpower'd, therefore
> Make space enough between you.   (II. iii. 16-22)

We can trace the conflict through, beginning long before the Soothsayer's words. Chafing in his dotage already, Antony is stricken by conscience with the death of Fulvia, and her he wished gone he now wishes returned. So duty for a time wins out, and the General assumes his responsibilities of state, going so far as to cement the bargain as well with himself as with Caesar by marrying Octavia. But Enobarbus knew the man better than the man knew himself. The invention of this character of Enobarbus was indeed necessary unless Shakespeare was to change the objective, outgoing, generous Triumvir into a subjective, reflective, self-analytical Antony; for Enobarbus is for a time at least a sort of alter ego for Antony. It is oftenest through his eyes we see the fascinating Egyptian actress. It is he as an echo almost from Antony's unconscious who tells Maecenas that Antony will "Never" stay away from the Queen, and it is he who says later, "He [Antony] will to his Egyptian dish again." (It is note-

---

[13] See *Anthony and Cleopatra*, Variorum ed., p. 496.

worthy that Antony's six soliloquies are brief, five of them exactly ten lines long and the other one twelve; their subject, with one slight exception, is Antony's momentary condition.) Enobarbus was right: the flesh was too strong for Antony, and back to her he went. Against his better judgment (against the advice of Enobarbus) he allowed her a command at Actium, and against his better judgment (and Enobarbus' advice) he fought at sea. Actium lost, Enobarbus gives her the counsel of despair: "Think, and die." Representing what should be Antony's reason, he says that Antony has allowed his will to become lord of his reason; and when in desperation Antony challenges Caesar to single combat, he comments that Caesar has now overcome Antony's judgment. Soon thereafter, as if to illustrate his point in person, he deserts to Caesar. But judgment and reason are not enough utterly to destroy: they may be overcome by magnanimity—the greatest of virtues, if not the sum of them. If Antony's judgment and reason (in the person of Enobarbus) desert him, he may overcome this desertion by his essential nobility, his great-mindedness, his ability to forgive. In remorse Enobarbus takes his own life. And so does Antony. But it is deception, not exactly wilful choice, not loss of judgment alone, which brings on his suicide; and deception and hypocrisy are the wiles of Satan most difficult for even the Christian hero to detect. (Witness Red Cross or Eve.) Antony's act may on this account be something extenuate, if not forgivable. Though he failed in government and then in war, he was yet in the end far more than a "strumpet's fool". Those words were Roman. In the end Maecenas finds his character a mirror into which Caesar must look, and in the end she to whom he had so often gone now comes to him—and as wife. In her going she defeats both Enobarbus and Caesar, and in the end both would seem pleased at their defeat. Antony thus conquers at Alexandria in somewhat the same sense that Julius Caesar may be said to have conquered at Philippi.

Kept to the fore, his psychomachia helps to shape the drama. At the opening he is found deep in sin; like Mankind in the *Castle of Perseverance* he repents and reforms; like Mankind through his uncontrolled will he slides back, and recognizing his failures and his Queen's deceit, he despairs; but unlike Mankind, being deceived by the Queen, he tries suicide, then welcomes his punishment, and concludes his life by asking that his nobility and magnanimity be remembered. In spite of all, he made a good end. Though his salvation may be left to the gods, their pattern of testing him is clear enough.

Other patterns are, I believe, equally clear. By them unity and variety are achieved within a vast complexity. If one may adapt the circular movement oneself and return to the pageantry of the world stage, one may the better indicate such another pattern. As Granville-Barker has so appropriately emphasized (p. 127), the text of *Antony and Cleopatra* (our only source is the Folio) has neither act nor scene divisions; and whatever Shakespeare's intentions in other plays, in this one he intended their omission. Event follows hard upon event, one often contrasting with the one preceding it; the action is continuous, fast, and sometimes kaleidoscopic; and each so-called scene has an effective relation with the next, which makes a pause between the two not only unnecessary but dramatically weakening. I would add that such pause likewise destroys the unity of effect by breaking the onward movement of events and their vast sweep toward a concentrated close. As every reader has discovered, the action takes place all over the Roman world—in and near Alexandria, in Rome, Messina,

Misenum, Syria, Athens, and at Actium. Besides these places, we hear vividly of the great scene on the Cydnus, and within the various places mentioned are a variety of scenes: tableaux, processions, a banquet (or formal drinking scene), scenes before palaces, palace interiors of various kinds, a scene laid on shipboard, and the puzzling monument scenes. But as every reader may not have observed, the geography of the play narrows as the action moves forward. After Actium it is restricted to Alexandria and environs. Thus as the fortunes of the protagonists become more circumscribed, so does the area of their action, until it is confined to the monument. What was once as wide as the world has now been concentrated in a point, has come literally to its period.

This did not come about merely because Plutarch's story goes this way: it does not exactly. Rather, as one may see from the first, it was by Shakespeare's design. Some of his design, especially foreshadowings and anticipations, have been indicated by Professors Price, Aldus, and Siegel cited above. I believe I have some further suggestions. Though he gives no detail, Professor Aldus says the opening scene has significance for the whole play in that it establishes probability. It does more, I think. It serves as tableau, prologue, and miniature play, an indication both of the action to follow and of the kind of protagonists. Like the Medieval devices, it furnishes a framework for the whole. From the Roman point of view of Philo, we shall see the triple pillar of the world transformed into a strumpet's fool, and not merely in this scene but in the whole action. Antony, receiving a messenger, refuses to hear him, neglecting his statesman's duties under Cleopatra's tauntings, and plans to go out with her alone into the night. Here is the play in little, to be illustrated or acted out in full later on. The chorus, Demetrius and Philo, serve to open and close the scene, moreover, much as if they were pulling back the curtains before a picture, letting us look at it for a while, and then drawing them to. We look at a little *tableau vivant* of the whole play. And this first tableau suggests the last; for if we will forget scene divisions and remember only episodes, we will remember that the final episode is a tableau, though not *vivant:* the Queen seated in state with her ladies about her, and Caesar to close the picture and speak the epilogue. As was anticipated by Demetrius' question in the first scene, Octavius Caesar might be expected to have the last word: "Is Caesar with Antonius prized so slight?"

This opening event, moreover, is not separate from the one immediately following. In the last two lines of the scene Demetrius hopes for "better deeds tomorrow". Whether or not the next scene does follow on the next day, better deeds do follow in it: Antony resolves to leave Cleopatra and Alexandria. The two scenes are carefully linked.[14] But this is less important than other linkings. If the first scene of the play suggests the last episode, the second suggests the episode next to the last, Cleopatra's death. From Warburton onward, annota-

---

14 So are numerous others: for example, the last lines of the very next scene, in which Antony's words about the courser's hair in Rome breeding much that is alive and yet not filled with serpent's poison anticipate, not only affairs in Rome where he is going, but unwittingly and ironically Cleopatra's death; or the leave-taking in the next scene following, in which unwittingly and ironically he indicates that Cleopatra will be with him in his venture into Rome and affairs of state. It is her presence in his mind that makes the venture disastrous. Such also is the episode of Dercetas and Antony's sword: he take it up in IV. xiv. 112-113, suggesting the possibility of a meeting with Caesar; he reappears with it in V. i. 5, to make a dramatic announcement of the death of Antony in a ceremony of surrender. Other scenes, though not so directly linked, are so logically placed as to be properly expected by the audience, such as I. iv, in which we are introduced to Caesar and affairs in Rome; or II. i, in which we find out how matters stand with

tors have suggested, very cautiously for the most part, some of these anticipations, such as Charmian's mention of "figs", the ultimate accomplishment of the prophecies of the Soothsayer (I wonder sometimes what critics think soothsayers are for, that they find, as here, so little in them beyond their bringing fun for the groundlings), and Enobarbus' witty speech about Cleopatra's habit of dying. But there are others. The episode of the Soothsayer (I. ii) and that of Cleopatra's actual death (V. ii. 225-318) involve some of the same witty characters, and the Soothsayer in the one balances the Clown in the other. More to the point, the Clown is the very means for carrying out the Soothsayer's prophecies. The same wit, especially the same ironic *double entendre,* prevails in the words of the two. Fulvia's death as announced a little later in I. ii, suggests Cleopatra's own death in that the one took from Antony a woman he did not want, though he admired her virtue, and the other took from Caesar a woman he did not want, though he admired her courage. Her witty remark about Antony that "A Roman thought has struck him" turns upon her later, for just such a thought did later rob her of him. And Enobarbus' sarcasm about her dying (I. ii. 134 ff.), "I do think there is mettle in death, which commits some loving act upon her, she has such a celerity in dying", is obviously designed for the alert playgoer to remember as he sees her apply the asp that will suck the nurse asleep.

Not the least important of these conscious linkings or anticipations are the three "mirror-scenes" noted by Professor Price and the anticipation of Pompey's loss, Antony's defeat at sea, and Caesar's triumph in the final scene of Act II pointed out by Professor Aldus. But more evidence seems unnecessary to indicate Shakespeare's careful planning, and more evidence seems unnecessary to show that the poet actually thought of his stage as a little world upon which he might place the action of his play, with all its pageantry, its soul-tested protagonists at its center, whose deeds range outward to affect all ranks and conditions of men and to be themselves conditioned by, if not subject to, the powers beyond. As Professor Price has said, "All his [Shakespeare's] persons are shown in relation to the society to which they belong, and they and the society are shown in relation to the immense forces that shape our lives" (p. 111). Perhaps there is a unity and design in his plays, especially in *Antony and Cleopatra,* of a somewhat different order from that we have so long looked for. And yet perhaps it is not so different from Dryden's perspective as one might think. If we look through the words of Demetrius' and Philo's proscenium to their tableau, perhaps we may see the ultimate convergence of lines in the final scene.

University of Kentucky

Pompey, about whom we have heard. Incidentally this scene, since it completes the basic exposition of the play, should be the final scene of Act I, not the first of Act II. Besides, it balances perfectly the great final scene of Act II, a fact which suggests a third type of relationship among scenes. Other such balancing scenes are II. i, with I. iv, the introduction of opposed forces; or II. vi, the agreement of the Triumvirs with Pompey, with II. ii; or the two scenes of the messenger reporting to Cleopatra from Rome, II. v, with III. iii. One may find out a further sort of logical order and connection if one regards the first six so-called scenes as exposition; the next six as a patching up of alliances, reformation and amendment of both character and state; the next 24, from III. iii, to IV. xiv, ending with Antony's attempted suicide, as the decay of man and empire; and the last four as recognition and recovery, a sort of apotheosis. The pattern suggests, but will not follow closely, the Greek pattern of protasis, epitasis, catastasis, and catastrophe.

Cleopatra's Scene with Seleucus: Plutarch, Daniel, and Shakespeare

BRENTS STIRLING

NTONY is dead. Cleopatra, now a captive, has learned from Dolabella that Caesar will take her to Rome in triumph. To escape this indignity, which she has forseen without Dolabella's help, she has tried to end her life and, recklessly, has sent word to Caesar that she still intends to die. Caesar, of course, must intervene. At their meeting in V. ii he promises to treat her well if she will not "lay on [him] a cruelty by taking Antony's course". But if she follows Antony in death, he will order death for her children. At this she appears to submit: ". . . we, / Your scutcheons and your signs of conquest, shall / Hang in what place you please." With a terseness matching Caesar's—"Here, my good lord"—she offers a written account of her "money, plate, and jewels", calling on Seleucus, her treasurer, to vouch for its honesty. In the familiar passage that follows, Seleucus lets Caesar know that she has concealed "enough to purchase what [she has] made known", Here Cleopatra responds with the last of her royal tantrums, "catching" at Seleucus as he retreats to save his eyes from her nails, compounding the sound and fury of her "wounding shame" with tears and marvelous excuses: she merely failed to list some "lady trifles" and a "nobler token" reserved for Livia and Octavia "to induce their mediation". Capping this is her interpretation of the strident episode as a tragic "fall". "Be it known that we, the greatest, are misthought / For things that others do; and when we fall / We answer others' merits [Seleucus' demerits] in our name." She is "therefore to be pitied". The pitiable fall of greatness, with the dubious "flaw" palmed off on a civil servant, is Shakespeare's addition to Plutarch, a mischievous play on tragic convention that comes just before Cleopatra's true tragedy is enacted. The interlude ends as Octavius in a benevolent exit declines the treasure and assures Cleopatra that she is free. Immediately she shows contempt for his deceit and puts her fatal plan "to the haste". The great death scene follows.

It is hard to tell how we might judge this episode if there were no external clue to its meaning. If Shakespeare's source were unknown, how many of us would sense a trick in Cleopatra's mercenary scheme and her shrill outburst when Seleucus exposes it? Who would find her striking a worldly pose that lulls Caesar's fear of her suicide, and thus makes it possible? Were this explanation from Plutarch lacking, surely someone would have improvised it to dispel Shakespeare's ambiguity, but most of us would have found the idea gratuitous.

There is irony here, for a gratuitous note is hardly absent in standard commentary. From the outset many critics have either misread Plutarch, or enlarged his meaning, in a way that doubles the burden Shakespeare's lines must carry. The Variorum editor (1907) tells us that "Adolf Stahr, the learned German historian of Cleopatra" so construed the episode "as to convert our humiliation into approval". In Furness' terms, Stahr showed from Plutarch that Cleopatra's "low, unqueenly dishonesty" and "opprobrious epithets" were merely pretended, that her scene with Seleucus *was pre-arranged between the two*" [my emphasis] in order to deceive Caesar. Moreover, "if Caesar was deceived by it, the guile becomes finer by its having deceived even Plutarch" (Variorum edition, pp. xiii-xiv).

The statement last quoted apparently means that Plutarch revealed collusion between Seleucus and Cleopatra without being aware of it—a very odd idea and an oblique way of saying that the collusion is not in Plutarch. Had Furness granted this in plain language, the history of interpretation might have been different. Repeatedly we have been told that Shakespeare's Cleopatra and Seleucus plan, even rehearse, their scene as a joint deception of Caesar,[1] and the notion must owe its currency to an impression that the source contains or implies it. Although MacCallum (1910) read Plutarch correctly,[2] the misconception still prospers in editions, in journals, in the class room, and "in the air".[3] And it is not a harmless error, for when read into *Antony and Cleopatra* it strongly affects the final quality of the tragedy.

Plutarch mentions no understanding between the two characters. According to his account, at Cleopatra's offer of the inventory "by chance there stood Seleucus by, one of her Treasurers, who to seem a good servant, came straight to Caesar to disprove Cleopatra. . . ."[4] Unless the phrases "by chance" and "to seem" are ironical, a reading not even suggested by the context, Cleopatra's ruse is hers alone and is an impulse of the moment. She makes no plans for it with Seleucus. Nor does she actually prearrange it herself; there is no clear hint that she falsifies her accounts expecting that Seleucus will rise to the bait. It is not even plain that the accounting is false, for a possible inference from Plutarch's story is that Seleucus could be lying. We learn only that when accused of concealment Cleopatra exploits anger and shame, and thus "finely deceiveth" Caesar, who assumes that her admitted avarice implies her desire to live.

These Plutarchan uncertainties are carried into Shakespeare's scene. A reading of V. ii. 124-196 leaves no clear impression that Cleopatra offers her "brief" to Caesar believing that Seleucus will try to expose her. Nor does the text tell us whether the accounting is really fraudulent or whether Seleucus fraudulently discredits it; actors could render the lines to suggest either possibility. Nothing is immediately clear save that when Cleopatra blushes at Seleucus' accusation (line 149), Caesar compliments her on the "wisdom" shown in concealing her wealth, and that she responds with garish violence and wonderfully efferves-

---

[1] For example, Dover Wilson in the New Cambridge edition (1950), pp. xxxiv-xxxvi, and Ridley in the new Arden edition (1954), pp. xlv-xlvii. Willard Farnham sees an intentional ambiguity in Shakespeare but recognizes as one alternative that Cleopatra has "arranged with Seleucus for the exposure" (*Shakespeare's Tragic Frontier* (1950), p. 199).

[2] *Shakespeare's Roman Plays*, pp. 426-437.

[3] Very recent examples are Donald J. McGinn, in *Essays in Literary History* (Rutgers University Press, 1960), pp. 71-72; Raymond Jenkins, *MLQ*, XXIII (1962), 88-89 (a review); and Richard Harrier, *SQ*, XIII (1962), 64. In these cases the traditional view appears casually or incidentally; I cite them only to show its currency.

[4] See *Shakespeare's Plutarch*, ed. Tucker Brooke, II, 130-131.

cent excuses. Duly impressed, Shakespeare's Caesar restores Cleopatra's goods, withheld and otherwise, ends her captivity ("Make not your thoughts your prisons"), and invites her to make her own terms. He then exits as "master" and "lord", a role immediately undercut by Cleopatra's "He words me, girls, he words me, that I should not / Be noble to myself."

As the scene unfolds in *Antony and Cleopatra,* ordinary spectators or readers (unless they happen to know Plutarch) will not sense Cleopatra's duping of Caesar until the encounter ends. The more alert might catch it earlier from her contrived and disarming pleas which exploit Caesar's patronizing approval. But from the text alone, we cannot intuit her strategy before this point. And even if we find it there we are sure to entertain a competing possibility—that Cleopatra is actually turning away from a dead Antony toward the living world of compromise. That she merely pretends to do so is not probable until after Caesar exits. Such is the episode as Shakespeare wrote it or, at least, as the Folio preserves it.

Since in Shakespeare the tricking of Caesar cannot be judged a trick until after it is over, there should be no surprise at the difficulty of staging it as an act prearranged by Cleopatra and Seleucus. To understand it thus, spectators must either have read and misunderstood Plutarch (in the Stahr-Furness tradition), or they must respond to something actors add to the text. The first alternative hardly inspires confidence, but there is no lack of optimism about the second. Here is a recent prescription: "I think the vital point is the way in which the actress playing Cleopatra delivers the words 'Speak the truth, Seleucus.' They are his cue. After that both he and Cleopatra, by slight exaggeration, he of his fears and she of her tantrums and her humiliation, indicate that they are playing a game."[5] But how does one exaggerate a Cleopatran tantrum, and if it could be done what impression would the performance make? The audience has enjoyed Cleopatra before as she railed at another servant when he merely told the truth—as she ordered him "whipped with wire, and stewed in brine" to smart in "ling'ring pickle" (II. v. 65-66). The actress who has presented this, and has drawn a knife besides, is now asked in the Seleucus scene to exaggerate slightly a role already stretched to the limit. If she thus attempts the impossible, and if Seleucus somehow exaggerates the dread any servant will have of an enraged Cleopatra, it will appear that "they are playing a game".

If Shakespeare changed Plutarch's story by adding a noble conspiracy between Cleopatra and Seleucus, he could scarcely have relied on such tactics to convey it. But there is another possibility. We all know that Shakespeare departs from Plutarch as Cleopatra herself calls for Seleucus and announces him to Caesar as one who will certify her honesty. The simplest explanation of this change is that it makes Seleucus' response more dramatic as a breach of trust. Nevertheless, Cleopatra's call for her servant might be Shakespeare's way of introducing cooperation between the two. Is it possible that the whole matter hinges on a missing stage direction? (In this part of the play—witness the two monument scenes—such directions are often inadequate or lacking at key points.) Imagine V. ii. 136-148 performed thus: Cleopatra asks for Seleucus and, as Caesar is naturally preoccupied with the inventory, she and Seleucus whisper together, exchanging ironic looks. Then with a meaningful "Speak the truth",

[5] Ridley, in the new Arden edition (1954), p. xlvi.

she launches him into his role. Could this hypothetical posturing make it clear that the rest of their scene is "put on"? Unfortunately, or fortunately, no. The device would undo itself by suggesting nothing more than Seleucus' agreement to "do something" for Cleopatra. And when he treacherously fails to do it, i.e. when he refuses to vouch for the "brief", an audience will think it has the simple message. From that point Cleopatra and her servant will hardly be understood as partners in any sense.

Nothing can be done with the collusion theory save abandon it as a cluttering of the text; for even as one of those pleasant surmises that begin, "Shakespeare may well have intended . . .", it is wide of the mark. There is no suggestion from Plutarch that Seleucus and Cleopatra prearrange their clash which fools Caesar. Nor is there a sign that Shakespeare "improved" on his source by adding an impromptu conspiracy; his lines are silent on the subject and there is nothing to show that they could have been supplemented by stage business.

Yet it remains possible that Cleopatra acts on her own. Does this become clear? In other words, does Shakespeare tell the story as Plutarch actually set it down? Despite ambiguities already noted, the source is plain enough, for just after Cleopatra "explains" her concealed wealth as a provision for Octavia and Livia, we read that "Caesar was glad to hear her say so, persuading himself thereby that she had yet a desire to save her life". In addition, a strong hint of motive appears earlier: "Then she suddenly altered her speech, and prayed him to pardon her, as though she were afraid to die, and desirous to live."[6] This line actually introduces Cleopatra's offer of the accounting. Plutarch thus explains her motive as he describes her behavior. But Shakespeare, as we have seen, keeps his audience guessing; not until after the set-to with Seleucus is over does he reveal that Cleopatra has played for time—that she has already planned her death carefully and is able at last to act. Until the delayed revelation occurs, an impression remains that she rages at Seleucus and tries to appease Caesar because she has compromised, has been caught in the act, and seeks to compromise still further.

Two critics say openly that the scene must remain a puzzle. Willard Farnham finds that Shakespeare "is very careful not to let us know" whether Cleopatra has thought she might "remain in the dull world" and "thus perhaps have use for some of her treasure", or whether "having arranged with Seleucus for the exposure" she has tried to "mask a full-formed intention to die by giving the appearance of wanting to live".[7] Although Farnham accepts as one alternative the Cleopatra-Seleucus collusion so commonly misascribed to Plutarch, his respect for Shakespeare's text allows no simple equation of dramatic intention with source materials. Still, he leaves us wondering why Shakespeare was so "very careful" to remain unclear. Unless it is merely perverse, careful ambiguity is ambiguity with a purpose. Does it have a purpose in the Seleucus scene?

If this question proves hard to answer we begin to entertain MacCallum's quite different view: that Shakespeare failed to give "adequate guidance" to his audience, a lapse calling for "a very severe criticism of his art".[8] MacCallum's

---

[6] Brooke, p. 130.

[7] *Shakespeare's Tragic Frontier*, p. 199.

[8] *Shakespeare's Roman Plays*, p. 433. MacCallum's complaint that Shakespeare fails to give adequate guidance surely applies to his own interpretation: that the "nobler token" Cleopatra

premise granted, his conclusion follows. Here would be no minor lapse, no slight crux that resilient readers or spectators can ignore while pedants have their day. If it has no ultimate meaning the Seleucus incident is a semi-farcical intrusion—no less an intrusion for being well done—placed directly between Cleopatra's defiance of her captors and her awesome ritual that shackles accident and bolts up change. The problem is not one of Cleopatra's decorum; we need not worry, with Furness and others, about an "unqueenly" queen who may lack solemnity. But we must be concerned over possible incoherence in the concluding action. No tragedy can sustain this without serious loss.

A scene will appear incoherent if we expect it to do what it was never meant to do. Have we been wrong in expecting the Seleucus scene to duplicate its source? Although Shakespeare's text must decide this question, another text, Daniel's *Tragedie of Cleopatra,* is pertinent for two reasons: Daniel did follow Plutarch quite literally and Shakespeare knew Daniel's play.[9] Hence any major difference between the two is likely to be significant. As an example of what Shakespeare strives not to do with Cleopatra, Seleucus, and Caesar, nothing serves better than Daniel's *Tragedie.*

After presenting a Cleopatra who must dissemble in "base content" to hide her "last dissigne" (lines 187-196),[10] Daniel moves in Act II to a colloquy between Caesar and Proculeius. Proculeius tells his master that he had found Cleopatra bent on suicide but that he believes she is now "well pacifide" by his tactful embassage. Caesar remains skeptical. Just before Daniel's Seleucus scene Arius proclaims Caesar's approach:

> But see where *Caesar* comes himselfe, to try
> And worke the mind of our distressed Queene
> To apprehend some falsed hope, whereby
> She might be drawne to have her fortune seene.
> But yet I thinke, Rome will not see that face
> (That queld her champions) blush in base disgrace.
>
> (Lines 593-598)

Thus at Caesar's very entry he is looking for a sign of Cleopatra's desire to live; but if he finds it he will be duped—there will be no Roman triumph. Daniel interprets the Seleucus scene for his audience even before it begins. And he continues this reinforcement of Plutarch with another note absent in Shakespeare: Cleopatra cast from the outset in a deceiver's role that prepares us for her trick with the inventory. First, she blames Antony for her own misdeeds: "What should a woman doe / Opprest with greatnes? . . . was it for me / To contradict my Lord, being bent thereto?" She "but obey'd" (lines 626-636). She then tells Caesar, "What I have beene to Antony, I might have beene to thee". Directly after these transparent efforts to gull Octavius comes her offer of the accounting:

---

speaks of reserving is actually a provision for her own regalia, so that after death she may meet Antony in due pomp and state.

[9] See the account of older findings, with added evidence, by Arthur Norman, *SQ*, IX (1958), 11-18.

[10] Grosart's text (London, 1885). I have consulted Daniel's progressive revisions; they do not materially affect the conclusions reached here.

> And here I do present thee with the note
> Of all the treasure, all the iewels rare
> That Egypt hath in many ages got;
> And looke what *Cleopatra* hath is there.
>   (Lines 675-678)

Unlike Shakespeare, Daniel presents Cleopatra's accounting as the last in a series of impostures; the inventory can be understood as deceptive because it climaxes unmistakable deception. Seleucus treacherously exposes what is by now a bill of goods in both senses; and when Cleopatra explains part of the withheld treasure as a gift meant for Livia and Octavia, Caesar is won over (lines 684-704). He rebukes the smitten Dolabella for being impressed by Cleopatra's grace in adversity and suddenly, fatuously, displays his own misunderstanding.

> And now, sith that she seemes so well content
> To be disposed by us, without more stay
> She with her children shall to Rome be sent,
> Whilst I by *Syria* thither take my way.
>   (Lines 749-752)

There is no doubt of Daniel's intent. In the Seleucus scene he means what Plutarch meant, so much so that his variations merely stress the simple original idea.

Shakespeare is not so obviously tied to his source. W. W. Greg has referred to "obsessed" editors who adapt details from Plutarch "in fussy elaboration of the simplicity of Shakespeare".[11] We could apply Greg's remarks to critical tampering with the Seleucus scene, although we should have to reverse his terms and point to a fussy simplification of Shakespeare's complexity. Doubtless the epigram would compact some truth, but it could be misleading. The present confusion stems not so much from concern over the source as from misinformation about it, along with a failure to read Shakespeare's episode in a context of prior action.

What is this context? In IV.xii a journey to death begins with the two protagonists in an untragic predicament. Antony has raged at the "triple-turn'd whore" who has "sold" him to Octavius, and has ordered Cleopatra out of his sight lest he kill her and "blemish Caesar's triumph". "Let him take thee / And hoist thee up to the shouting plebeians! / Follow his chariot . . . ; most monster-like, be shown . . .; and let / Patient Octavia plough thy visage up / With her prepared nails." Here is Shakespeare's introduction of a theme lacking in Plutarch (although present in Daniel): the horror to Cleopatra of captivity and public shame in Rome. Terrified, she hides in the monument and from that significant place sends word to Antony. Mardian is to say she is dead—that "the last [she] spoke was 'Antony' "; he is to "word it . . . piteously" and, of course, return to let her know how the news is received. The gist of this is from Plutarch but Shakespeare has added Cleopatra's quality of appalling mischief. And all the grandeur of later events will be an outgrowth of her frivolously calculated, timidly audacious trick.

The long closing action of *Antony and Cleopatra* presents a "school of

---

[11] *The Shakespeare First Folio* (1955), pp. 400-401 and note 5.

death" for both protagonists: dying becomes a discipline, a perfecting of motive or attitude, and an art calling for significant gesture. In the fulfillment of life through insight, courage, and dignity, a man or a woman must learn to die well. But there will be wavering or blundering, and a "high Roman fashion" may not grace the event. The theme actually begins in IV. vi with Enobarbus, who after temporizing with honor seeks the right place for atonement—"some ditch wherein to die". He has found truth in Antony's magnanimity, which leads him to find the kind of death that will express his self-discovery and earn him, after all, "a place i' th' story". Now (IV. xiv), Antony finds truth in the example, real only to him, of Cleopatra's "suicide". But he must falter, as she will falter when his death in turn requires hers. Emulation as a ruling motive will make progressive demands. Hearing Mardian's news, Antony sets out to "o'ertake" of a woman", for being less noble than she who by dying has told Caesar, "I am Cleopatra, to weep for pardon; he condemns himself for lacking "the courage conqueror of myself". Yet, for the moment, self-conquest is beyond him. He orders Eros to do the deed and Eros, as his master's eyes are turned away, kills himself. So for Antony there are now two compelling examples: "My queen and Eros / Have by their brave instruction got upon me [gained over me] / A nobleness in record. . . . Come then; and, Eros, / Thy master dies thy scholar." Inwardly, Antony has met the standard, but the scholar of death who has blundered into knowledge of his role must blunder in acting it. After the unsure stroke he gives himself he must say, "I have done my work ill" and beg others to finish what he has begun. At the same time he will learn that one of the deaths he tried to imitate in completing his own tragedy was the pseudo-death in a bad tragicomedy improvised by Cleopatra. And dying, he must wait outside the monument which she is afraid to open lest she be "taken" and dispatched to that awful Roman triumph. Tragedy flourishes in a merely adverse world, but if the protagonist falls in a setting of banality or inconsequence, and if infatuation brings him to the impasse, tragedy may be compromised to the limit. In *Antony and Cleopatra* Shakespeare deliberately tests the tragic mode. To a degree, his source makes the test inevitable, but he accepted Plutarch's conditions when he could have changed them, emphasized them when he could have lessened their effect.

At the end of Act IV Antony's tragedy is equivocal, and only Cleopatra can fulfill it. Led by her counterfeit example, Antony has found mere disaster. Now she will be led by his example, but she must surpass it and become, for both of them, the exemplar of high tragedy. Nothing could require more of a dramatist. Conventionally, he might allow Cleopatra to gain stature through submissive remorse, but it would be grossly out of character. Besides, if she rejects her former self she will imply that Antony followed an unworthy vision. Yet she must change, for otherwise the anticlimax of Act IV will control the play. In effect, she must be transformed while remaining in word and act the Cleopatra Antony knew. Shakespeare seems to intensify this paradox as he resolves it.

Cleopatra's emergence from "double-mindedness" (R. C. Harrier's term) may be well understood,[12] but the art responsible for it is not. I hope to show

---

[12] See Harrier's terse, forthright essay, *SQ*, XIII (1962), 63-65. Disagreement occurs, however, between critics who sentimentalize Cleopatra's emergence and those who find it involved almost to the end with worldly compromise. But there is a position between these extremes. I agree with

that Shakespeare's achievement is largely a structural one, an arrangement of parallel scenes[13] in cumulative order. Each of them presents the old Cleopatra of whim and contradiction who can hold the stage as a new Cleopatra is suddenly revealed. And each time the process is more telling. Preparatory scenes thus set a pattern which is repeated with great effect in the Seleucus episode. As a result the audience, not mystified but in a proper state of wonder and expectation, is ready for Cleopatra's final role.

The rise to tragedy begins at IV. xiv with Cleopatra's awareness of her mischief and her attempt, just a little late, to stop its course. Her messenger Diomedes arrives to tell Antony, already dying, that her "prophesying fear / Of what hath come to pass", her concern how the false news of her death "might work", has led her "to proclaim the truth". In flighty egoism her new honesty equals the lie it countermands. Yet as Antony is carried to the monument (IV. xv) Cleopatra, unaware of his impending death, has turned from shallow anxiety to the mood of tragedy.

> All strange and terrible events are welcome,
> But comforts we despise; our size of sorrow,
> Proportioned to our cause, must be as great
> As that which makes it.

With these lines the emergent Cleopatra is at hand, but their quotation out of context is reductive. They follow directly from a line eloquent of the old Cleopatra, of her less than heroic concern for sanctuary in the monument: "O Charmian, I will never go from hence! . . . No, I will not." Only after this comes her passage welcoming a magnitude of danger and grief. But having declared for grand tragedy she can veer again to the timorous. As she completes her affirmation of "strange and terrible events" with a "size of sorrow" proportioned to their cause, as she accepts the monument for what it must become, she can then refuse to open its gates for Antony who remains outside until he is dragged in mortal pain to an upper entry. "I dare not, dear— / Dear my lord, pardon—I dare not, / Lest I be taken."

What has appeared? First, as the scene begins, a self-protective anxiety; then the mood of tragedy finely stated; then the anxiety again in an equally fine statement—all of this continuous, an expression of one motive, one action, one character. Here is the Queen of Egypt, and we are given a chance—not the first—to understand her. As we approach the Seleucus scene we might try to forget a traditional Cleopatra who is now contriving, timid, or tawdry and then ingenuous, bold, or queenly. Instead, she is at once contriving—ingenuous—

Mr. Harrier that "the illusion of double-mindedness is . . . quite concrete and intended", but cannot agree with his view that "Cleopatra has indeed planned on suicide only if her terms are not met". In the Seleucus scene this inference becomes possible but other possibilities compete strongly with it. See the later discussion. From IV. xiv onward Shakespeare implies from time to time that Cleopatra is hedging, but he never permits us to "settle down" with the impression; at telling intervals it is dramatically repudiated. The effect, as I shall try to show, is one of growing assurance that Cleopatra will not temporize. My purpose, however, is not to rest with a dramatist's intended effect but to show how his structural plan, capped by the Seleucus scene, achieves it.

[13] It will be clear that what I call a "scene" or episode in the scheme is not equivalent to a scene in the standard divisions of Shakespeare's text. It is always, however, a clearly defined "situation". "Episode" could be used throughout, but repetition of the word would become very awkward.

timid—bold—tawdry—queenly. Because she is Shakespeare's creation her opposing qualities cannot be weighed discursively but must be sensed together.

The union of contraries in IV.xv has merely begun. Cleopatra's fear of opening the monument to Antony still has the old motive: within locked gates she is safe from the triumph in Rome, "th' imperious show / Of the full-fortuned Caesar". But she adds a new, prophetic note: in the locked refuge she can die, whether by "knife, drugs, [or] serpents". Thus her fear of capture is briefly transformed as her monument, no longer a place of mere safety, becomes the sanctum which not even Caesar may enter to prevent her honorable death. Again, however, the old note returns. Antony, still excluded, must hear Cleopatra out as she mixes fortitude with petulance: "I am safe. / Your wife Octavia, with her modest eyes / And still conclusion, shall acquire no honour, / Demuring upon me." In the context this is almost beyond comment, yet no more so than the next line: "But come, come, Antony . . . we must draw thee up". After such deft undercutting Cleopatra's lapse would seem irrevocable. But in the same stroke Shakespeare can bring her to another ascent: "Assist, good friends. . . . / Here's sport indeed! How heavy weighs my lord! / . . . Yet come a little—/ Wishers were ever fools—O come, come, come: / And welcome, welcome!" Then, as Antony begs her to seek honor and safety with Caesar, she can respond simply, "They do not go together". At Antony's death the earlier Cleopatra can be heard in her momentary protest, "Hast thou no care of me?" but after that the scene's only note is commitment.

> Patience is sottish, and impatience does
> Become a dog that's mad: then is it sin
> To rush into the secret house of death
> Ere death dare come to us?

And finally:

> what's brave, what's noble,
> Let's do it after the high Roman fashion,
> And make death proud to take us.

Hence in IV.xv a dialectic of resolution and back-sliding, selflessness and vanity—all of it in Cleopatra's provocative style—prepares for a decisive turn that ends the episode. The scene thus becomes a model for two subsequent scenes, including the Seleucus incident.

Toward the end of V.i Cleopatra's messenger tells Caesar that the queen, "confined in all she has, her monument, / Of thy intents desires instruction, / That she preparedly may frame herself / To the way she's forced to." This is beautiful; read in one way it means renewed wavering after the resolution ending IV.xv, but read in another it says to an uncomprehending Caesar, "Tell me what you plan to do, that I may plan against you, and die as I am forced to die." Twenty lines later (V.ii) the ambiguity disappears as Cleopatra repeats her dedication:

> and it is great
> To do that thing that ends all other deeds;
> Which shackles accidents and bolts up change;
> Which sleeps, and never palates more the dung,
> The beggar's nurse and Caesar's.

Since no Roman hears Cleopatra's lines, they lack the protective double meaning of her message to Caesar. But the situation changes as Proculeius enters to announce Octavius' gracious terms. His real purpose, of course, is to see that no irresponsible suicide shall mar Caesar's plans (note V. i. 61 ff.). As the correct Proculeius, for whom Antony had vouched, asks Cleopatra to state her "fair demands", the audience inescapably wonders what she will do. Will she hold to the deed that ends all other deeds or will she temporize? Her answer continues the ambiguity of her earlier message to Octavius which has brought Proculeius bustling to the monument. She has "no use for trusting", but if Caesar "would have a queen his beggar", what less, "to keep decorum", can she demand than a whole kingdom? If Caesar pleases "to give me conquered Egypt for my son, / He gives me so much of mine own as I / Will kneel to him with thanks." Is this negotiation or a superb hint, clear even to Proculeius, that negotiation is impossible? An audience will sense the latter meaning, but instantly will doubt its own insight when Cleopatra ends her quips with a new message for Octavius: "I send him / The greatness he has got. I hourly learn / A doctrine of obedience, and would gladly / Look him i' the face." With this she more than implies submission, but Shakespeare deliberately forestalls the effect. Whatever the lines convey is cancelled by sudden action as soldiers, who have somehow entered the monument, seize Cleopatra. Her obsessive fear of capture is realized, and as Roman hands are laid upon her the scene now presents exactly what IV. xv had presented, and what the Seleucus incident in turn will offer—a climax of decision after uncertainty. Here her decisive act is memorable. Taken prisoner, she attempts death and as Proculeius cries, "O temperance, lady", gives him a third and final message for Caesar. It is entirely in terms of the old Cleopatra dreading a Roman triumph, but, to understate matters, the shallow and timorous note is gone. "Sir, . . . this mortal house I'll ruin, / Do Caesar what he can",

> Know, sir, that I
> Will not wait pinioned at your master's court,
> Nor once be chastised with the sober eye
> Of dull Octavia. Shall they hoist me up
> And show me to the shouting varletry
> Of censuring Rome? Rather a ditch in Egypt
> Be gentle grave unto me! Rather on Nilus' mud
> Lay me stark naked, and let the water-flies
> Blow me into abhorring!

As a shocked Proculeius lingers before returning to his master with this news, he offers Cleopatra a chance to reconsider. Her retort, awesome and direct, is "Say I would die". Yet, after Proculeius leaves she can still ask Dolabella what Caesar "means to do" with her, and the answer, of course, is what she knows it will be. The anticlimax of her question to Dolabella reveals the frightened woman behind Cleopatra's open defiance of Caesar and (if the phrase can be forgiven) what it took out of her. She is earning her way.

Thus Shakespeare brings us to the Seleucus episode with a dramatic preparation quite different from Plutarch's or Daniel's. In two vivid scenes Cleopatra has found resolution only after equivocation, actual or apparent, and in the second one her literal shock from capture and loss of opportunity for suicide has led to an abandoned showing of her hand. In Plutarch and Daniel, Caesar suspects Cleopatra's intentions; here, from Cleopatra herself, he has learned just what they are. So as the two now meet in Shakespeare's scene, she has no secret to keep. The *femme fatale* pose Daniel gives her or the self-abasement Plutarch describes would be pointless.

Since emperor and queen understand each other perfectly their encounter opens with formal courtesy. But Caesar can come to the point. With few preliminaries he tells Cleopatra that "benefit" is hers for the asking but that if she destroys herself he will destroy her children. Unlike Plutarch and Daniel, who simply inform us of this threat, Shakespeare times it for maximum effect: just after she has recklessly sent word to Caesar that, do what he may, she will ruin her mortal house, Cleopatra learns what the consequences of her death will be. Although we critics have seemed unconcerned over a mother in her predicament, dramatists and audiences are likely to take it seriously. How will she respond? At Caesar's "I'll take my leave", her style at least can rise to the occasion: "And may, through all the world; 'tis yours. . . ." Then with laconic dignity she offers her "brief" of money, plate, and jewels. "Here, my good lord." Immediately mindful of Cleopatra's children, an audience will interpret this as surrender, with the brief, the inventory, as a manual rendering to Caesar of the things that are Caesar's. Now, as the crux begins, Shakespeare departs altogether from his source with Cleopatra's insistence that Seleucus verify the accounting. Here we are told that by protesting too much she hints at concealed motives. But how will an audience gather this? If Cleopatra and Caesar have little faith in one another will a verified accounting seem contrived? And when Seleucus exposes her, not as a volunteer (his role in Plutarch) but in response to her trust in his support, will an audience shrewdly guess that he plays into her hand? At this stage of Cleopatra's fall it is expecting the unkindest cut of all and will have little doubt that Seleucus provides it.

I am not assuming an audience with no curiosity, for after all, the strange incident provokes questions. But again, action will not stay for an answer. Spectators are asked not to ponder but to wonder—just as they have done in the preparatory scenes which show Cleopatra on an ambiguous course that ends each time in resolution. "Wait and see" has been the pattern. So here in the Seleucus episode. Plutarch, the historian, could explain Cleopatra's pose while describing it; Daniel the undramatic dramatist, could tell his audience what to expect even before he staged the scene. Shakespeare relies on events to declare their own meaning. At Seleucus' disclosure there must be Cleopatra's unbelieving silence (line 148). It can be impressive, and action can pause while we consider. We may wonder briefly whether Seleucus has told the truth, and if he has, whether it means that Cleopatra has hedged in her resolve to die. Perhaps we may also surmise that the withheld treasure could be a provision for her children made before she learned that her own death would decree theirs. We can wonder for the moment, but in terms of text and stage performance we can not decide. Nor are we meant to, for new action intervenes. Caesar now speaks in a mood of self-congratulation, the first stage of his error: "Nay, blush not, Cleopatra; I approve / Your wisdom in the deed." Perhaps another pause as Cleopatra, with the audience, senses his amusement at being cheated so long as the cheater has revealed something that pleases him. But again there is no lingering, for immediately we have an uproar matching Cleopatra's scene with the messenger who was forced to tell her of Antony's marriage to Octavia. She drives Seleucus back swearing she will catch his eyes "though they had wings". She cries out over the "wounding shame" of an emperor's visit marred by impudence from a household servant. She changes the subject in mid-flight to tell Caesar that part of the concealed treasure was meant for Livia and Octavia "to induce their mediation". (In Plutarch "Caesar fell a-laughing", and the Livia-Octavia lines are his cue for levity if Shakespeare meant to stage it.) Then, absent in both sources, the final Shakespearian touch: Cleopatra still tearing at Seleucus' eyes interprets the fracas *de casibus* style as part of her "fall", an extravagance she continues after Seleucus' frightened exit. "We, the greatest" are blamed "for things that others do". "When we fall" we answer for the faults of others, and "are therefore to be pitied". Just before the Seleucus scene she had held up to Dolabella a fulsome *de casibus* vision of Antony. Now we have this matchless half-comic, half-tragic counterpart of it.[14]

From Shakespeare's text and from action used to supplement it, an audience engrossed in Cleopatra's outburst cannot know that she is improvising it, that it is an "act" meant to convince Caesar of her worldly commitment to life instead of death. Shakespeare did not assume an audience fresh from Plutarch, and he knew that an act put on by Cleopatra would be clear only if she appeared to be acting. Here the ambiguity is complete. But it is successful because inevitable. Who by this time is able to tell whether the mercurial, protean queen is being herself or playing a part? No matter what her response to Seleucus—riotous or dignified, tearful or stoical, mendacious or truthful—she can only be strangely and convincingly the Cleopatra we have known from the beginning. And if we conclude from Plutarch that Shakespeare intends her behavior as a pose, our response must still be ambivalent, for we have an "actress" before us who, beyond a doubt, lives her role. Pose or not, she *means* it when she catches at Seleucus, when she is ashamed at losing face, and when she descants on her "fall".

Has anyone suggested that in Shakespeare this is just what deceives Caesar? Cleopatra's fury and bizarre self-justification dupe him, make him "ass unpolicied", not because she can act a part (as Plutarch and Daniel have it) but because, in a paradoxical sense, she cannot. Any interesting role she assumes will so aptly express her nature that she will remain herself. Small wonder Octavius is taken in, for even the audience cannot tell until later that a deception is in the making. Caesar judges that Cleopatra loves life too well to die. In Shakespeare he is deceived because she does love life well enough to reach for Seleucus' eyes and attempt other absurdities in one last indulgence of combative pride. As we delight in this we forget the shrewd contriver who manipulates Caesar in Plutarch or Daniel, and we can understand on later reflection why Shakespeare is so reticent about her tactical motives.

An audience is wiser than Caesar only because it is more privileged. In each of the preparatory scenes Cleopatra has come through uncertainty, equivocation

---

[14] Elsewhere, I have discussed the elaborate play upon conventional doctrines of tragedy to be found in this part of *Antony and Cleopatra*. See *Unity in Shakespearian Tragedy* (1956), pp. 176-184.

or relapse, to a resolving climax. In the Seleucus scene the audience has encount-ered every element of this set form but the climax, which it can now expect. Caesar's exit provides the moment. Ambiguity ends once more as Cleopatra finds herself, this time conclusively: "He words me . . . he words me, that I should not / Be noble to myself." Caesar's guard now down (lines 179-189), she is ready for the dark. "Hie thee again. / I have spoke already, and it is provided. / Go put it to the haste."

So ends the last, the most critical of the scenes that "test" Cleopatra, and she emerges from it ready for her tragedy. Yet only the latent can emerge; a new Cleopatra in no way repudiates the old one Antony had known. Hence her role lacks an alleged necessity of tragedy—"recognition", hard-won humil-ity, or (according to some critics) even formal repentance. But before we decide that Cleopatra's is a pseudo-tragedy, or at best an anomalous one, we might well question the standard of judgment. Although tragedy may call for a regenerated protagonist, must the change it requires amount to self-rejection? There is a kind of regeneration that simply appears without anxious, voluble regret for the past, and if not altogether humble by some standards, it is one level of grace. Brutus finds it. So, in her own way, does Cleopatra. As her new quality evolves in action capped by the Seleucus episode, Shakespeare keeps her old perversities in constant view. She does not reject them[15] or even leave them behind; she takes them with her, and for that reason her death can be heroic, tragic, without a trace of falsehood or ostentation.

University of Washington

[15] The one suggestion of this is momentary and, in terms of dramatic emphasis, quite incon-clusive. See V. ii. 1-2.

Playbill for the performance of *The Merchant of Venice* in Salt Lake City on 23 July 1864. 11" x 31". Reproduced by permission of the Church of Jesus Christ of Latter-day Saints.

The Shakespeare Association of America

MRS. DONALD F. HYDE

T the same time that the quatercentenary of Shakespeare's birth is being celebrated by the world in general, there is a small anniversary which I think members of The Shakespeare Association of America can take pleasure in commemorating as well, the fortieth anniversary of our journal. Its history is virtually the Association's history for, though not originally intended as the chief function, it was the first project undertaken and has continued as its major one throughout the years.

Our Association was established only after many vicissitudes. The original spark was generated, appropriately enough, in 1864, the 300th anniversary of Shakespeare's birth. This was the time when his statue was placed at the foot of the Mall in Central Park in New York City. During the celebration the hope was often expressed of forming a permanent Shakespeare organization. In 1914, for the 350th anniversary, there was an even larger celebration in New York. Mayor Mitchell appointed a committee of 500 prominent citizens to organize a week of memorable events. Over 800,000 school children, it was reported, took part. A planning committee was formed at this time to consider the possibilities of a permanent association to further the study and interpretation of Shakespeare and "issue bulletins at intervals". In 1916 at the New York Public Library this committee met with scholars and delegates from Shakespeare clubs throughout the country. Shortly after the meeting a national Shakespeare Society was established in Washington, but under the duress of the First World War the organization never became active. In 1921 the attempt was made to move the headquarters to New York City, but this was forbidden by the charter. It was decided, after some differences of opinion had been settled, to dissolve The Shakespeare Society of Washington and to found The Shakespeare Association of America. Articles of incorporation were signed in New York State in November 1923.

Ashley Horace Thorndike, the distinguished Columbia Shakespearian, was chosen as President, and Mrs. James Madison Bass, an important person in the events of transition, as First Vice-President. She was flanked by a large and impressive panel of Vice-Presidents, a pattern which became traditional. Initially, there were thirty-four, including such eminent Shakespearian scholars as Joseph Quincy Adams of Cornell, Tucker Brooke of Yale, Horace Howard Furness, Jr., of Philadelphia, and Brander Mathews of Columbia, and such celebrated Shakespearian actors as John Barrymore, Walter Hampden, Julia Marlowe, and E. H. Sothern. The Chairman of the Publications Committee was Harry Morgan Ayres of Columbia, with committee members Raymond Alden of Stanford, Robert Adger Law of Texas, E. E. Stoll of Minnesota, and Professor Brooke.

By June of 1924 the first issue of *The Shakespeare Association Bulletin* appeared. In the lead article President Thorndike explained the need for a Shakespeare Association in America; its future dream was a memorial, a building containing a library, a theater, and meeting rooms—a Shakespeare Center. He regarded as important corollary projects a journal devoted to Shakespeare and an adequate annual bibliography.

The Publication Committee outlined plans for the future of the journal. It should carry important original articles on Shakespeare and thoughtful reviews of outstanding books. There should be a department devoted to notes and queries, to criticisms of important stage productions, to reports on the activities of Shakespeare clubs throughout the country, and to comments on notable Shakespeare study carried on in schools. There should be space for Association news, financial reports, and notes on the activities of outstanding members; there should also be place for an occasional light touch, a poem or a sketch.

All the various departments did not materialize at once, but all have existed at some time during the journal's history. At certain periods particular sections have received more emphasis than others. There have been omissions and additions, but in principle the concept has remained the same.

In the second year of publication, 1926, Paul Kaufman of American University, who had been a prime mover in The Shakespeare Society of Washington, became Editor. He was devoted to his task and greatly extended the scope of the *Bulletin*. There were now about 900 members receiving the journal, almost a tripling of membership in two years. He was backed by a newly created Advisory Board: Dr. Adams, Hardin Craig of Iowa, Edwin Greenlaw of North Carolina, Myra B. Martin, Secretary of the Association, President William Allen Neilson of Smith, and Professor Thorndike.

He also designated two Contributing Editors: Robert M. Smith of Lehigh and Mrs. Robert Carlton Morris of Toledo, Ohio. Both supplied important new features. Professor Smith's "Notes on Shakespeareana" were articles which appeared in the April, July, and October issues. They were highly readable accounts of important events in the rare book world, a lively place in the late twenties, both in New York and in London. Sustaining member Henry C. Folger, and A. S. W. Rosenbach were often in the news. Activities of Shakespeare clubs throughout the country were well handled by Mrs. Morris in "The Club Forum".

The third feature, which had been envisioned by President Thorndike, an annual Shakespeare bibliography, was made possible in 1926 and for several years thereafter by a grant from the Carnegie Corporation. The Bibliographer was Samuel A. Tannenbaum, a well-known New York doctor, who found time beyond his practice to devote himself to this formidable and valuable task. His bibliography was soon a familiar feature, filling the entire January issue.

By 1929 the Association's dream of having a Shakespeare Center, though still "an unfailing topic of discussion", seemed remote. There were only a hundred dollars in the building fund, and in this year memorials were established elsewhere: the theater in Stratford-upon-Avon and The Furness Library at the University of Pennsylvania. Still, in May of 1930 when Dr. Adams delivered the major address at the Association's annual meeting and dinner, he described in detail the appearance and the operation of its projected Shakespeare Center. The next month Henry Folger died, and within two years The Folger Shakespeare Library was opened in Washington, with Dr. Adams as its Director. With the dream fulfilled by others and the deepening of the depression, The Association surrendered its goal of a Shakespeare Center. The journal from this time on was acknowledged as its major undertaking.

The stature of the *Bulletin* grew with successive issues. Beyond the special features there were sound articles by scholars, a number of reviews, and interesting articles on Shakespeare productions such as "Shakespeare on the Professional Stage" by Carl Carmer, "The Shakespearean Civic Theatre in Chicago" by Brooks Atkinson, and "Shakespeare on the Air" by Edward Peyton Harris. In 1933 the publication seemed to be in a strong position. But the depression took its toll among the members despite the vigorous efforts of Committee Chairman Arthur Heine. The termination of the Carnegie grant for the Bibliography was threatened. The second issue of the year concluded with the tragic announcement, "As we go to press we read of the sudden death of our beloved President, Ashley Thorndike, on the evening of April 17th. We are too grieved and shocked to say more at present."

This was the nadir of the Association. The Board of Directors searched for a successor but no President was chosen for the rest of the year. The July and October numbers were combined as a single issue, and regular memberships were regretfully doubled to assure the publication of the year's Bibliography.

At the annual meeting in 1934 Dr. Rosenbach of Philadelphia and New York was "unanimously and enthusiastically" elected President of the Association. Dr. Rosenbach was, as noted before, a great bookman, through whose offices much of the finest Shakespeare material had come into collections in this country—his own collection was an outstanding one. He was also a Shakespeare scholar. The April 1934 issue described his plans to make the *Bulletin* less general in nature. He hoped it would become one of the most important scholarly magazines in America, "a magazine which all bibliophiles and scholars the world over will not only consult but treasure".

Dr. Tannenbaum, previously the Bibliographer and an increasingly frequent contributor, became Editor of the *Bulletin*. William T. Hastings, of Brown, joined Mrs. Morris and Professor Smith as a Contributing Editor, and wrote a number of excellent articles for the journal over the next years. The new Editor desired a change in policy. In his first issue he announced that he wished "to throw open the pages of the *Bulletin* to essays dealing with any phase of Elizabethan literature", not restricted to Shakespeare alone. He cordially invited articles on Elizabethan and Jacobean subjects from scholars in America and abroad. His own annual bibliographies, he stated, would no longer be limited to Shakespeare but would cover his contemporaries as well. Despite these announcements the scope of the *Bulletin* narrowed. Fewer important essays by prominent scholars were published, fewer serious long reviews. Extremely short reviews by the Editor appeared at intervals, strongly colored by his own opinion. Professor Smith's "Shakespeareana Notes" lapsed as did Mrs. Morris' "Club Forum". The character of the magazine came to reflect most clearly the particular interests of the Editor, which were bibliography, textual problems and readings. His "Editorial Comments" in successive issues dealt less and less with Association news, finally becoming isolated literary notes with an occasional anguished plea for more members to assure the magazine's continuance. Communication with the various realms of Shakespearian activity, envisioned in the original plan, and progressively furthered for a number of years, seemed lost. Wide participation, lightness, and zest were gone. To be sure there were some exceptions—a few strong articles, an occasional poem, a lively communication now and then—and, quite startlingly, in 1938 a playful birthday letter to Shakespeare from Arthur A. Houghton, Jr., a prominent young book collector, who had been one of the many Vice-Presidents for three years.

Understandably, it was difficult for Dr. Tannenbaum, with the demands of his profession, to keep in touch with the academic and theater worlds. Information was asked for in the columns of the *Bulletin,* but it did not come of its own accord. Difficulties of all kinds were multiplied with the onset of the Second World War, and it is surprising that the *Bulletin* continued to be published at all. Dr. Tannenbaum was self-sufficient; he fought his lone battle with tireless devotion, preserving the *Bulletin,* still the only journal of its kind. The Shakespeare Association itself would not have survived the war, if the President, Dr. Rosenbach, had not felt great affection for it and sustained it by his own generosity.

In the gloom of the war, there was one happy event which augured well for the future. James G. McManaway of The Folger Shakespeare Library entered the scene as Treasurer of the Association, succeeding George W. Davison, President of The Central Hanover Bank, who had served as Treasurer since 1931. The story of Dr. McManaway's first official act clearly illustrates both the poverty of the Association at the time and the high regard in which it was held. The Treasurer issued a check to the Tenny Press, payment for the last issue of the *Bulletin,* without knowing there were insufficient funds to cover it. However, the check went through, and Mr. Tenny graciously replied to the Treasurer's abject apology: "It would seem that the Shakespeare Association has a good fairy somewhere in the vicinity of the Central Hanover Bank."

In October 1947 Dr. Tannenbaum, pressed by his professional obligations and in failing health, resigned as Editor of the *Bulletin* and Secretary of the Association. Professor Smith took over both offices *pro tem.*

The new Editor's first issue of the *Bulletin,* January 1948, showed marked changes, including a new cover design and a larger number of pages. This January issue was no longer devoted solely to the annual Bibliography; four articles preceded it. The Editor's section, "Notes and Comments", in the July issue gave, in the old manner, a wide and varied coverage. Included was a salutation to a sister publication, *Shakespeare Survey,* which had been launched in England under the editorship of Professor Allardyce Nicoll. The scholar representing the United States in the panel of world correspondents was Dr. McManaway, who furnished accounts of the treasures and facilities of the Folger Library.

The last issue of the *Bulletin* in 1948 continued the reshaping of the journal with well-apportioned articles and literary notes, and a regular book section of "Quarterly Reviews". In the Editor's "Notes and Comments" was recorded the sad news of the deaths of Tucker Brooke, a long-time friend and advisor to the *Bulletin,* and of Dr. Tannenbaum. A tribute of appreciation to this faithful editor was written by Vice-President John H. H. Lyon.

The year 1949 was a time of sweeping change. Dr. Rosenbach, who had been President of the Association for fifteen years, was firmly resolved to leave office. At the annual meeting Mr. Houghton was elected President and John Fleming Secretary and Treasurer. Professor Smith was elected a Director and Chairman of the Editorial Board, its other members being Giles E. Dawson of the Folger, Virgil B. Heltzel of Northwestern, Mrs. Donald Hyde, and Dr. McManaway. Sidney Thomas of Queen's College, New York, was appointed Bibliographer. The large and passive group of "Honorary Vice-Presidents" (thirty in number) was dissolved and replaced by a more active "Advisory Board", its twenty members selected for their prominence in the fields of Shakespearian scholarship and drama. Dr. McManaway headed the Advisory Board.

Professor Smith, under whose editorship the *Bulletin* had reached a new level of excellence and interest, offered further suggestions for improvement. He felt that the journal should again be limited in its scope to Shakespeare, including the annual Bibliography. Within the rich Shakespearian range, he felt that the approach should be to general rather than particular interests, appealing not only to scholars but, as formerly, to theater people, teachers, libraries, schools, and reading groups. He felt that the journal needed a more significant title and suggested *Shakespeare Quarterly.* In the matter of details he wanted the measurements to be more standard, and the books stitched rather than stapled for ease in handling. He also wished to increase the pages of an issue to eighty, and to have more illustrations.

Most of his suggestions were accepted. Dues of the Association's 476 members could not sustain these changes; they were carried by a subsidy. In January 1950 the first issue of *Shakespeare Quarterly* appeared in its new, handsome, and slightly larger format. Throughout the year articles and reviews were of high caliber. The Bibliography in the April issue was limited to Shakespeare but greatly enlarged within this limit, due in considerable measure to the initiation of a committee of foreign correspondents. Club notes came again from Mrs. Morris. The Editor's section, "Notes and Comments", took a growing interest in brief reports on Shakespeare festivals and productions in various parts of the world. Another addition was the "Contributors Column", which gave short identification of each issue's authors. The journal had greatly improved. Members had doubled by annual meeting time!

In 1951 Dr. McManaway became Editor of the *Quarterly,* changing positions with Professor Smith, who became Chairman of the Advisory Board. Dr. McManaway's first issue seemed large at the time, over eighty pages (one issue in 1960 was over 200 pages!). The review section was notably strong and the section devoted to notes, queries, and communications was given several times its original space. There was an extremely attractive new feature, significant illustrations, most often rarities owned by the Folger. In April 1953 there were handsome and unusual portraits of Elizabeth I in honor of her namesake's coronation; in July a note of thanks was printed from Elizabeth II, who had been sent a copy. The various illustrations, sometimes of manuscripts or printed books, were effectively placed in the issue and explained in the Editor's "Notes and Comments". On a blank page one might find a reproduction of an early printing of a Shakespeare sonnet. The frontispiece illustration and its description became in time a feature in itself. The section, "Current Theatre Notes", began in 1951, a listing of Shakespeare performances the world over, so far as they could be discovered. This became an annual report, and was carried on in turn by Mrs. Hyde, Alice V. Griffin, and Thomas B. Kilfoil.

Innovations continued to be made. The aesthetic and practical changes were well carried out by the new printer, The William Byrd Press in Richmond. In 1952 a new coat of arms was designed for the cover, which now changed color from volume to volume. After January 1954 the issues were named by season rather than by month. An Index for each volume was undertaken, which greatly facilitated the use of back issues. Among the most rewarding additions were annual surveys of Shakespearian scholarship which were carried on for some years, excellent and comprehensive reports by Professors Law, Craig, Price, and Hastings. The reviewing of theater productions was given increased attention with critical articles of some length on Shakespeare productions in London and New York, on festivals at the three Stratfords, and on those at Ashland, Antioch, and San Diego. There were also occasional reports on Shakespeare in such places as Turkey, Japan, and Uruguay. The number of foreign correspondents who contributed to the annual Bibliography grew to twenty-four. These progressively useful lists were compiled, as noted, by Professor Thomas, later by Paul A. Jorgensen of the University of California in Los Angeles, and now by Robert W. Dent of the same university.

In 1956 a new idea was tried. The entire summer issue was given over to G. Blakemore Evans' supplement to the Variorum Edition of *Henry IV, Part 1*. This could also be bought as a separate volume. The project was enthusiastically received.

During the years several distinguished scholars have replaced certain of the original members on the Editorial Board: Harold S. Wilson of Toronto, Virgil K. Whitaker of Stanford, and Richard Hosley of Arizona. In 1959 outstanding Shakespearians from abroad were added to the Advisory Board and their guidance has been most helpful: Allardyce Nicoll of Birmingham, Peter Alexander of Glasgow, Mario Praz of Rome, Rudolf Schroeder of Berlin, D. Nichol Smith of Oxford. Others joined the Board later: F. P. Wilson of Oxford, Levin Ludwig Schücking of Erlangen, Charles Jasper Sisson of London, Harold J. Oliver of New South Wales, J.-B. Fort of the Sorbonne, and R. W. Zandvoort of Groningen.

The editorship of Dr. McManaway continues. He has progressively enlarged the departments and generally strengthened the *Quarterly,* thus increasing the influence of the Association. This now has approximately 1800 members, every state in the Union being represented and more than 60 foreign countries. Though at first almost all the members were individuals, the trend in recent years has been toward institutions, three quarters of the present membership being held by libraries.

As has often been said, The Shakespeare Association *is* the *Quarterly*. All its activities are devoted to the journal's continuance and development. Within the organization there have been a number of changes in officers and directors and, as is always the sad pattern of passing time, the severance of certain strong ties.

Professor Smith died suddenly in January 1952 (his place on the Editorial Board was filled by Harold S. Wilson of the University of Toronto). He was still active in the publication and his loss was deeply felt. If it had not been for his determined efforts in the late forties the *Bulletin* might not have survived nor the *Quarterly* come into being. Professor Hastings was elected to follow him as Chairman of the Advisory Board.

In July of 1952, Dr. Rosenbach died. This was a sharp break with the past, for through the long, dark years of the depression and the Second World War, this loyal President had kept the Association alive.

In 1956 Mr. Houghton, who had been a remarkably fine President, asked that he be relieved of the office because of the pressure of other important projects. His resignation was regretfully accepted. We have not, however, been deprived of his continuing interest. We have benefitted by his good counsel on many occasions and have been greatly aided both by his generous assistance and that of the Houghton Foundation.

The writer has followed him as President. I have depended greatly on Dr. McManaway, an ideal Editor, ideally situated. I have also leaned heavily upon a fine Board of Directors and a strong group of officers, particularly upon John Fleming, without whom I could have done little.

This year an old custom of a dinner is being revived as part of the celebration of Shakespeare's four-hundredth anniversary. Our Vice-President (we now have only one), Frederick B. Adams, Jr., has invited the Association to hold a special dinner at the Morgan Library, a magnificent complement to our chief activity of publishing the *Quarterly*.

The special result of this activity in 1964 is this selection of essays by distinguished American Shakespearians, our tribute to the master playwright and poet.

Somerville, New Jersey

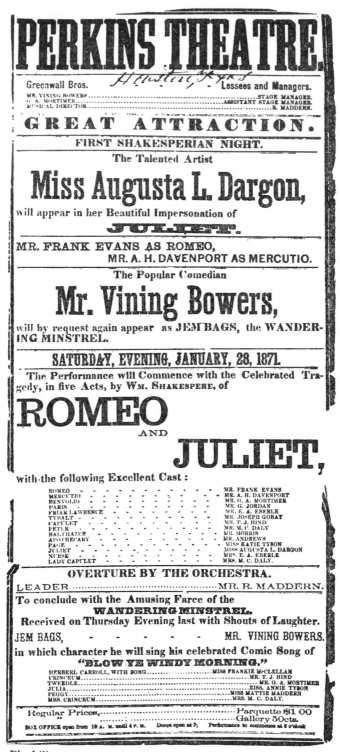

PERKINS THEATRE.

Greenwall Bros. *Houston, Texas* Lessees and Managers.

MR. VINING BOWERS..STAGE MANAGER.
G. A. MORTIMER...ASSISTANT STAGE MANAGER.
MUSICAL DIRECTOR...R. MADDERN.

GREAT ATTRACTION.

FIRST SHAKESPERIAN NIGHT.

The Talented Artist

Miss Augusta L. Dargon,

will appear in her Beautiful Impersonation of

JULIET.

MR. FRANK EVANS AS ROMEO,
MR. A. H. DAVENPORT AS MERCUTIO.

The Popular Comedian

Mr. Vining Bowers,

will by request again appear as JEM BAGS, the WANDER-ING MINSTREL.

SATURDAY, EVENING, JANUARY, 28, 1871.

The Performance will Commence with the Celebrated Tragedy, in five Acts, by WM. SHAKESPERE, of

ROMEO
AND
JULIET,

with the following Excellent Cast :

ROMEO	MR. FRANK EVANS
MERCUTIO	MR. A. H. DAVENPORT
BENVOLIO	MR. G. A. MORTIMER
PARIS	MR. G. JORDAN
FRIAR LAWRENCE	MR. E. A. EBERLE
TYBALT	MR. JOSEPH GOBAY
CAPULET	MR. T. J. HIND
PETER	MR. M. C. DALY
BALTHAZER	MR. MORRIS
APOTHECARY	MR. ANDREWS
PAGE	MISS KATIE TYSON
JULIET	MISS AUGUSTA L. DARGON
NURSE	MRS. E. A. EBERLE
LADY CAPULET	MRS. M. C. DALY.

OVERTURE BY THE ORCHESTRA.

LEADER..MR. R. MADDERN.

To conclude with the Amusing Farce of the
WANDERING MINSTREL.
Received on Thursday Evening last with Shouts of Laughter.

JEM BAGS, - - - - MR. VINING BOWERS.

in which character he will sing his celebrated Comic Song of
"BLOW YE WINDY MORNING."

HERBERL CARROLL, WITH SONG	MISS FRANKIE McCLELLAN
CRINCRUM	MR. T. J. HIND
TWEEDLE	MR. G. A. MORTIMER
JULIA	MISS ANNIE TYSON
PEGGY	MISS MATTIE MADDERN
MRS. CRINCRUM	MRS. M. C. DALY.

Regular Prices,.....................................Parquette $1 00
....Gallery 50cts.

BOX OFFICE open from 10 A. M. until 4 P. M.   Doors open at 7;   Performance to commence at 8 o'clock

---

Playbill at the Perkins Theatre in Houston, Texas, on 28 January 1871 of *Romeo and Juliet*. 7¼″ x 16½″. Reproduced by permission of The Folger Shakespeare Library.

Contributors

President JOHN CRANFORD ADAMS, author of *The Globe Playhouse*, plans to end his executive labors that in twenty years have built Hofstra into a great urban university and to return to Shakespearian scholarship.

Professor FREDSON BOWERS, of the University of Virginia, who was Phi Beta Kappa Visiting Scholar in 1962-63, is now reading proof of *Bibliography and Textual Criticism*, his James Lyell Lectures at Oxford in 1960. His edition of Marlowe is nearing completion, and, by way of variety, he is bringing out in 1964 his texts of Hawthorne's *House of Seven Gables* and *The Blithedale Romance*.

Professor CARROLL CAMDEN, of Rice University, editor of *Studies in English Literature*, has just seen through the press *Restoration and Eighteenth-century Literature*, a *Festschrift* for Prof. Alan McKillop, and *Critical and Historical Essays*, a collection of lectures delivered in celebration of the semicentennial of Rice University.

Honored by two *Festschriften*—Iowa and Stanford jointly in 1941 and Missouri in 1962—editor of "Recent Literature of the Renaissance" in *Studies in Philology* for twenty-five years, editor of Shakespeare's *Works* (1951), and author of many books and articles, Professor HARDIN CRAIG is now at the Huntington Library, completing a book he has wanted for years to write about the controlling ideas in Shakespeare.

Dr. MILTON CRANE, who is Chief of the Division of Research for the British Commonwealth, Northern and Central Europe in the Department of State's Bureau of Central Intelligence, published an anthology called *Fifty Great Poets* (1961) and has another, *Fifty Great American Short Stories*, in the press. His *Shakespeare's Prose* came out in a second edition in 1963, and he is preparing a volume of Caxton's Prologues and Epilogues.

Professor ROBERT W. DENT, who is Vice-Chairman of the Department of English in the University of California at Los Angeles, has been the compiler of the Annual Shakespeare Bibliography since 1959. His book about *John Webster's Borrowing* has been called a model for such studies.

Professor MADELEINE DORAN, of the University of Wisconsin, added to her very substantial contributions to the study of Shakespeare's text by editing *M.N.D.* (Pelican, 1959), her first book since *Endeavours of Art* (1954). A grantee at the Huntington Library in the autumn of 1963 for work on the background of *Dream*, she will continue her reading as a Fellow at the Folger Shakespeare Library in 1964.

Since his retirement at the University of California at Berkeley, Professor WILLARD FARNHAM has been much in demand. He is Visiting Professor at Wisconsin in 1963-64. His *Hamlet* (Pelican) is a favorite, and both *The Medieval Heritage of Elizabethan Tragedy* and *Shakespeare's Tragic Frontier* are in their second edition.

Professor ALFRED HARBAGE, Cabot Professor of English at Harvard, brought out *William Shakespeare: A Reader's Guide* in 1963, but he confesses that being General Editor of the Pelican Shakespeare is his greatest satisfaction.

Professor ROBERT B. HEILMAN is Chairman of the Department of English at the University of Washington. His first volume of Shakespeare criticism, *This Great Stage*, has been republished. His second volume, *Magic in the Web*, won the *Explicator* prize in 1956, and his essay, "Tragedy and Melodrama: Speculations in Generic Form", won the Longview Award in 1960.

Professor RICHARD HOSLEY, of the University of Arizona, is a member of the Editorial Board of *Shakespeare Quarterly*. He edited *Romeo and Juliet* (1954) for the Yale Shakespeare and *Essays on Shakespeare and Elizabethan Drama in Honor of Hardin Craig* (1962) and is publishing a full-length study of Elizabethan playhouses.

Professor EDWARD HUBLER, of Princeton, was a Fulbright Professor at the Universities of Bordeaux, Algiers, and Toulouse in 1950-51. He has followed *The Sense of Shakespeare's Sonnets* (now reissued as a paperback) with *Shakespeare's Songs and Poems* (1959) and *Hamlet* (Signet Classics, 1963).

Dr. MARY C. HYDE (Mrs. Donald F.) has been President of the Shakespeare Association of America since 1956. A past President of the Johnson Society (Lichfield), author of *Playwriting for Elizabethans, 1600-1605* (1949), and a co-editor of *Diaries, Prayers, and Annals* (1959) in the Yale edition of *The Works of Samuel Johnson*.

Professor SEARS JAYNE, of Queens College of the City University of New York, is back in the United States after a year at I Tatti in Florence, where he worked on his book on Platonism in English Renaissance Poetry. Earlier publications include *Marsilio Ficino's Commentary on Plato's Symposium* (1944) and *John Colet and Marsilio Ficino* (1963).

Professor PAUL A. JORGENSEN, of the University of California at Los Angeles, was for five years Bibliographer for *Shakespeare Quarterly*. He is the author of *Shakespeare's Military World* (1956) and *Redeeming Shakespeare's Words* (1962) and the editor of *The Comedy of Errors* (Pelican, 1963).

Professor JULIAN MARKELS, of Ohio State University, is currently engaged in a study of *Antony and Cleopatra*.

Dr. JAMES G. McMANAWAY, Consultant in Literature and Bibliography of The Folger Shakespeare Library and Chairman of the Editorial Board of *Shakespeare Quarterly*, is co-editor of *A Check List of English Plays, 1640-1700* (1945) and *Joseph Quincy Adams Memorial Studies* (1948), and author of *The Authorship of Shakespeare* (1962).

Upon his retirement at the State University of Iowa in 1962, Professor BALDWIN MAXWELL was honored by the publication of *Studies in English Drama*. From 1920 until 1955, he was editor of *Philological Quarterly*; he is the author of *Studies in the Shakespeare Apocrypha* (1956) and editor of *The Winter's Tale* (Pelican, 1956).

Professor KENNETH O. MYRICK has had his mature professional career at Tufts University, where he served as Chairman of the English Department for five years. An interruption occurred in 1945, when he taught at Shrivenham American University in England and Biarritz University in France, temporary institutions set up by the War Department for soldiers whose college education had been interrupted by the war. Author of *Sir Philip Sidney as a Literary Craftsman*, he is bringing to completion a book that deals with Shakespeare and Christian Humanism.

Professor JAMES E. PHILLIPS, who was for five years Chairman of the Department of English at the University of California in Los Angeles, was a Guggenheim Fellow in 1947-48 and a Fulbright Research Fellow in 1954-55. His study of *The State in Shakespeare's Greek and Roman Plays* (1940) is to be followed in 1964 by *Images of a Queen: Mary Stuart in Sixteenth Century Literature*.

Professor CHARLES TYLER PROUTY, of Yale, is General Editor of *The Life and Works of George Peele* and of the Yale Shakespeare. He is also a Director of the Yale Shakespeare Institute and a Trustee of The American Shakespearean Festival Theatre and Academy. Among his publications are editions of Gascoigne's *A Hundreth Sundry Flowres* and Kyd's *Spanish Tragedy*. His Volume III of Peele's *Works* is nearing completion.

Professor IRVING RIBNER, of Tulane University, is the author of *Patterns in Shakespearian Tragedy* (1960) and *Jacobean Tragedy* (1962). His edition of *The Complete Works of Marlowe* has just come from the press.

Professor BRENTS STIRLING, of the University of Washington, has written a number of essays about Shakespeare and also *The Populace in Shakespeare* (1949) and *Unity in Shakespearian Tragedy* (1956).

Professor GEORGE WINCHESTER STONE, JR., has retired after seven years as General Secretary of the Modern Language Association of America and returned to the profession of English literature. A Guggenheim Fellowship in 1963-64 is enabling him to continue work on *The London Stage, 1660-1800*, of which he was the special editor of the three volumes of *Part 4, 1747-1776* (1962).

Dean ERNEST A. STRATHMANN, of Pomona College, who published *Sir Walter Ralegh, A Study in Elizabethan Skepticism* (1951), is using a Guggenheim Fellowship to continue his studies in the Ralegh canon in English, Irish, and American libraries.

Professor THOMAS B. STROUP, of the University of Kentucky, has published a sheaf of articles and reviews dealing with Shakespeare and has edited *The Works of Nathaniel Lee* (with A. C. Cooke, 1954-55), *The Selected Poems of George Daniel of Beswick* (1959), and *Cestus, A Mask* (1961).